Undergraduate Topics in Computer Science

Series Editor

Ian Mackie, University of Sussex, Brighton, France

Advisory Editors

Samson Abramsky ⓘ, Department of Computer Science, University of Oxford, Oxford, UK

Chris Hankin ⓘ, Department of Computing, Imperial College London, London, UK

Mike Hinchey ⓘ, Lero—The Irish Software Research Centre, University of Limerick, Limerick, Ireland

Dexter C. Kozen, Department of Computer Science, Cornell University, Ithaca, USA

Hanne Riis Nielson ⓘ, Department of Applied Mathematics and Computer Science, Technical University of Denmark, Kongens Lyngby, Denmark

Steven S. Skiena, Department of Computer Science, Stony Brook University, Stony Brook, USA

Iain Stewart ⓘ, Department of Computer Science, Durham University, Durham, UK

Joseph Migga Kizza, Engineering and Computer Science, University of Tennessee at Chattanooga, Chattanooga, USA

Roy Crole, School of Computing and Mathematics Sciences, University of Leicester, Leicester, UK

Elizabeth Scott, Department of Computer Science, Royal Holloway University of London, Egham, UK

'Undergraduate Topics in Computer Science' (UTiCS) delivers high-quality instructional content for undergraduates studying in all areas of computing and information science. From core foundational and theoretical material to final-year topics and applications, UTiCS books take a fresh, concise, and modern approach and are ideal for self-study or for a one- or two-semester course. The texts are authored by established experts in their fields, reviewed by an international advisory board, and contain numerous examples and problems, many of which include fully worked solutions.

The UTiCS concept centers on high-quality, ideally and generally quite concise books in softback format. For advanced undergraduate textbooks that are likely to be longer and more expository, Springer continues to offer the highly regarded *Texts in Computer Science* series, to which we refer potential authors.

K. Erciyes

Guide to Distributed Algorithms

Design, Analysis and Implementation Using Python

K. Erciyes
Department of Computer Engineering
Yaşar University
İzmir, Türkiye

ISSN 1863-7310 ISSN 2197-1781 (electronic)
Undergraduate Topics in Computer Science
ISBN 978-3-031-79017-1 ISBN 978-3-031-79018-8 (eBook)
https://doi.org/10.1007/978-3-031-79018-8

© The Editor(s) (if applicable) and The Author(s), under exclusive license to Springer Nature Switzerland AG 2025

This work is subject to copyright. All rights are solely and exclusively licensed by the Publisher, whether the whole or part of the material is concerned, specifically the rights of translation, reprinting, reuse of illustrations, recitation, broadcasting, reproduction on microfilms or in any other physical way, and transmission or information storage and retrieval, electronic adaptation, computer software, or by similar or dissimilar methodology now known or hereafter developed.
The use of general descriptive names, registered names, trademarks, service marks, etc. in this publication does not imply, even in the absence of a specific statement, that such names are exempt from the relevant protective laws and regulations and therefore free for general use.
The publisher, the authors and the editors are safe to assume that the advice and information in this book are believed to be true and accurate at the date of publication. Neither the publisher nor the authors or the editors give a warranty, expressed or implied, with respect to the material contained herein or for any errors or omissions that may have been made. The publisher remains neutral with regard to jurisdictional claims in published maps and institutional affiliations.

This Springer imprint is published by the registered company Springer Nature Switzerland AG
The registered company address is: Gewerbestrasse 11, 6330 Cham, Switzerland

If disposing of this product, please recycle the paper.

To Çiğdem, Ender, Kerem and Cem

Preface

Distributed systems are part of our lives; ranging from airline reservation system to banking, from process control to a modern car. A distributed system consists of a set of computational nodes, connected by a network that communicate, cooperate and compete to finish an overall task. Key to the operation of a distributed system are the distributed algorithms which are executed at the nodes of a distributed system.

This book is about the design, analysis and most importantly, the implementation of distributed algorithms which we describe in full detail at coding level using the Python programming language. We assume that the reader is exposed to the design and analysis of sequential algorithms over which the distributed algorithms may be constructed.

We follow a simple template for many algorithms introduced in the text; we review the sequential algorithm for the problem briefly and then describe the design of the distributed algorithm for the same problem followed by code in Python programming language. The text can be broadly divided into Background, Fundamental Algorithms, Distributed Graph Algorithms and Applications parts. The Background part is mainly about distributed system concepts, analysis of distributed algorithms and coding templates that will be used in proceeding parts. The Fundamental Algorithms part contains the main distributed algorithm problems such as synchronization, mutual exclusion and fault tolerance. The Distributed Graph Algorithms part consists of three chapters with algorithms on trees and traversals, weighted graphs and graph decomposition. The final part contains distributed algorithms for real-life problems in two major areas of application: mobile ad hoc networks and wireless sensor networks.

Python Implementation

Python programming language is selected for the implementation because of its simplicity and for having rich set of libraries that aid to hide low level details such as data manipulations. The *mpi4py* module of Python is used for distributed algorithm implementations which provides interface for the commonly used Message

Passing Interface (MPI) routines. For almost all algorithms, we provide Python code that can be modified and tested for various inputs. All of the Python code can be easily transported to a real distributed environment with the possible modification of *send* and *receive* communication procedures of the actual environment, a simple way to achieve this goal is to use the basic socket communications. In a distributed application that uses Message Passing Interface for network communications, the modifications are trivial. The codes are not optimized and brevity is forsaken for clarity in many cases. In many cases, we implement similar problems using different models such as finite state machines or just plain code to achieve the same result to display different ways of obtaining the same output. The codes are tested rigorously for various sample graphs, however, as it frequently happens with any software, errors are possible and I would be happy to know any bugs.

The intended audience for this book is the senior/graduate students of computer science, electrical and electronic engineering, bioinformatics and any researcher or a person with background in discrete mathematics, basic graph theory and algorithms. There is a Web page for the book to keep errata and other material at: http://akademik.ube.ege.edu.tr/~erciyes/DA/ with updated and possibly improved Python code.

I would like to thank senior/graduate students at Ege University, University of California Davis, California State University San Marcos, Izmir Institute of Science and Technology, Izmir University, Üsküdar University, Maltepe University, Yaşar University in chronological order, who have taken courses related to distributed systems and algorithms, sometimes under slightly different names, for their valuable feedback when parts of the material covered in the book was presented during lectures. In particular, the material including some of the Python examples on distributed graph algorithms were used as teaching aids and project proposals in "Distributed Computing" senior level elective course and "Distributed and Parallel Algorithms" graduate course at Maltepe University and "Mobile and Wireless Networks" senior level elective course at Yaşar University. I would also like to thank Springer senior editor Wayne Wheeler for his continuous help and encouragement throughout the writing of the book.

İzmir, Türkiye   K. Erciyes

Contents

Part I Background

1 Introduction 3
   1.1 Introduction 3
   1.2 Distributed Algorithms 4
   1.3 Challenges 5
   1.4 Outline of the Book 6
       1.4.1 Background 6
       1.4.2 Fundamental Algorithms 6
       1.4.3 Distributed Graph Algorithms 7
       1.4.4 Applications 7

2 Basic Concepts 9
   2.1 Distributed Systems 9
   2.2 Computer Networks 10
   2.3 Architecture 11
   2.4 Message Passing 13
       2.4.1 Blocking or Non-blocking Message Transfer 13
       2.4.2 Ordering of Messages 14
   2.5 Representations and Models 14
       2.5.1 Timing Diagrams 15
       2.5.2 Basic Finite State Machines 15
       2.5.3 Hierarchical Finite State Machines 17
   2.6 Analysis of Distributed Algorithms 17
       2.6.1 Correctness Proofs 18
       2.6.2 Complexity 21
   2.7 Chapter Notes 21
   References 23

3 Implementation Models Using Python and *mpi4py* 25
   3.1 Introduction 25
   3.2 Message Passing Interface for Python: *mpi4py* 26
       3.2.1 Calculation of π 27

		3.2.2	Stop-and-Wait Automatic Repeat Request Protocol	28
	3.3	Execution Modes		31
		3.3.1	SSI with Determined Rounds	34
		3.3.2	SSI with Determined Rounds Using a Finite State Machine	37
		3.3.3	Synchronous Execution with Undetermined Round Number	41
		3.3.4	Asynchronous Operation	45
	3.4	Chapter Notes		47
	References			49

Part II Fundamental Algorithms

4	**Time Synchronization**			53
	4.1	Introduction		53
	4.2	Physical Clocks		54
		4.2.1	Clock Synchronization with a Central Server	54
		4.2.2	Cristian's Algorithm	55
		4.2.3	Berkeley Algorithm	56
		4.2.4	Network Time Protocol	58
	4.3	Logical Clocks		60
	4.4	Vector Clocks		63
	4.5	Matrix Clocks		65
	4.6	Chapter Notes		67
	References			68

5	**Distributed Mutual Exclusion**			71
	5.1	Introduction		71
	5.2	System Model		72
		5.2.1	Requirements	72
		5.2.2	Performance Metrics	72
		5.2.3	Algorithm Classes	73
	5.3	Permission-Based Algorithms		74
		5.3.1	Central Server Algorithm	74
		5.3.2	Lamport's Algorithm	76
		5.3.3	Ricart-Agrawala Algorithm	77
	5.4	Token-Based Algorithms		81
		5.4.1	Suzuki-Kasami Algorithm	81
		5.4.2	Raymond's Token-Based Algorithm	85
	5.5	Quorum-Based Algorithms		90
	5.6	Chapter Notes		93
	References			94

Contents

6 Global State Analysis 95
  6.1 Introduction 95
  6.2 System Model 96
  6.3 Distributed Snapshot Algorithms 98
    6.3.1 Chandy-Lamport Algorithm 98
    6.3.2 Lai-Yang Algorithm 99
  6.4 Termination Detection 100
    6.4.1 Termination on a Ring 100
    6.4.2 Termination Using a Spanning Tree 102
    6.4.3 Huang's Weight Throwing Algorithm 105
  6.5 Deadlock Detection 108
    6.5.1 Wait-for-Graph 108
    6.5.2 Handling Deadlocks 109
    6.5.3 Distributed Deadlock Detection Algorithms 110
    6.5.4 Chandy-Misra-Haas Algorithm 111
  6.6 Chapter Notes 113
  References 114

7 Coordination 117
  7.1 Introduction 117
  7.2 Leader Election 118
    7.2.1 The Bully Algorithm 118
    7.2.2 LeLann Algorithm 123
    7.2.3 Chang-Roberts Algorithm 126
    7.2.4 Hirschberg-Sinclair Algorithm 129
    7.2.5 Leader Election in a Graph 129
    7.2.6 Leader Election in a Tree 132
  7.3 Synchronizers 134
    7.3.1 The α Synchronizer 134
    7.3.2 The β Synchronizer 135
    7.3.3 The γ Synchronizer 135
  7.4 Chapter Notes 136
  References 138

8 Fault Tolerance 139
  8.1 Introduction 139
  8.2 Faults 140
  8.3 Failure Models 141
  8.4 Fault Tolerance Methods 142
  8.5 Failure Masking by Redundancy 142
  8.6 Replication 143
    8.6.1 Active Replication 143
    8.6.2 Passive Replication 144
  8.7 Process Groups 144
    8.7.1 Group Communication 145
    8.7.2 Single Source FIFO Delivery 148

		8.7.3	Causal Delivery	151
		8.7.4	Total Order Multicast	154
	8.8	Consensus		158
		8.8.1	Consensus with Crash Failures	159
		8.8.2	Byzantine Agreement	159
	8.9	Chapter Notes		161
	References			162

Part III Distributed Graph Algorithms

9 Trees and Traversals 165
   9.1   Introduction 165
   9.2   Spanning Tree Construction 166
         9.2.1   Broadcast over a Spanning Tree 169
         9.2.2   Broadcast Without Acknowledgement 169
         9.2.3   Broadcast with Acknowledgement 170
         9.2.4   Convergecast over a Spanning Tree 172
   9.3   Distributed Breadth-First-Search 174
         9.3.1   Asynchronous Distributed BFS 174
         9.3.2   Synchronous Distributed BFS 178
   9.4   Distributed Depth-First-Search 185
   9.5   Chapter Notes 187
   References 189

10 Weighted Graphs 191
   10.1   Introduction 191
   10.2   Minimum Spanning Trees 192
         10.2.1   A Synchronous Distributed Algorithm 193
         10.2.2   Gallager-Humblet-Spira Algorithm 201
   10.3   Routing 204
         10.3.1   Bellman-Ford Algorithm 205
         10.3.2   Chandy-Misra Algorithm 209
   10.4   Matching 209
         10.4.1   Unweighted Matching 209
         10.4.2   Weighted Matching 211
   10.5   Chapter Notes 215
   References 217

11 Graph Decomposition 219
   11.1   Vertex Coloring 219
   11.2   Vertex Cover 223
         11.2.1   Sequential Algorithm Simulation 224
         11.2.2   The Rank-Based Distributed Algorithm 228
   11.3   Maximal Independent Sets 232
         11.3.1   A Distributed MIS Algorithm Simulating
                  Sequential Operation 233

		11.3.2 Highest Rank First MIS Algorithm	236
		11.3.3 Lowest Degree First MIS Algorithm	237
	11.4	Dominating Sets	240
	11.5	Chapter Notes	241
	References		243

Part IV Applications

12 Mobile Ad hoc Networks ... 247
- 12.1 Introduction ... 247
- 12.2 Models ... 248
  - 12.2.1 Communication Models ... 248
  - 12.2.2 Mobility Models ... 248
- 12.3 Topology Control ... 249
  - 12.3.1 k-Nearest Neighbor Graph ... 250
  - 12.3.2 Gabriel Graphs ... 251
  - 12.3.3 Relative Neighborhood Graphs ... 254
  - 12.3.4 Yao Graphs ... 255
- 12.4 Clustering ... 256
  - 12.4.1 Lowest ID Algorithm ... 256
  - 12.4.2 Lowest ID Algorithm Version 2 ... 261
  - 12.4.3 Highest Degree First Algorithm ... 262
- 12.5 Ad hoc Routing ... 265
  - 12.5.1 Proactive Routing Protocols ... 265
  - 12.5.2 Reactive Routing Protocols ... 265
  - 12.5.3 A Connected Dominating Set Based Algorithm ... 266
- 12.6 Chapter Notes ... 270
- References ... 271

13 Wireless Sensor Networks ... 273
- 13.1 Introduction ... 273
- 13.2 Architecture ... 274
- 13.3 Clustering ... 275
  - 13.3.1 Low-Energy Adaptive Clustering Hierarchy (LEACH) Protocol ... 276
  - 13.3.2 Threshold Sensitive Energy Efficient Sensor Network (TEEN) Protocol ... 276
  - 13.3.3 Spanning Tree-Based Clustering ... 277
- 13.4 Data Aggregation ... 280
- 13.5 Localization ... 283
  - 13.5.1 Estimating the Distance ... 284
  - 13.5.2 Trilateration ... 285
- 13.6 Routing ... 286
  - 13.6.1 Challenges ... 287
  - 13.6.2 Data Centric Protocols ... 287

		13.6.3	Location-Based Protocols	288
13.7	Time Synchronization			289
		13.7.1	Sender-Receiver Synchronization	289
		13.7.2	Receiver-Receiver Synchronization	291
13.8	Chapter Notes			292
References				293

Index 295

Part I
Background

Introduction

1

Abstract

A distributed system consists of a set of computing nodes connected by a computer network to perform a common task. We review basic concepts related to distributed algorithms running in distributed systems in this chapter and provide brief description of the contents of the book which consists of Background, Fundamental Algorithms, Distributed Graph Algorithms and Applications parts.

1.1 Introduction

Distributed systems are part of our lives, they range from an airline reservation system to a nuclear plant to a wireless sensor network configured for intelligent farming. Technically, a distributed system is a set of computers connected by a communication network using operating system facilities and network interface routines to perform some common task as illustrated in Fig. 1.1. These nodes of a distributed system perform communication, cooperation and sometimes competition to finish a given task. The nodes typically communicate only with their neighbors to acquire a global view of the system. There are certain advantages in building distributed systems: first of all, hardware and software resources can be shared in a network of processes, thus, we do not need installation of resources at each computer. A distributed database system is one such example with many users accessing it over a network. Fault tolerance is another facility provided by a distributed system: failures may be detected by correct functioning nodes and recovery procedures may be invoked. Yet, some applications such as banking system, airline reservation system and distributed control system are naturally distributed and the correct operation of such systems depends on building a reliable, fault tolerant distributed system. Some common types of distributed systems can be stated as below.

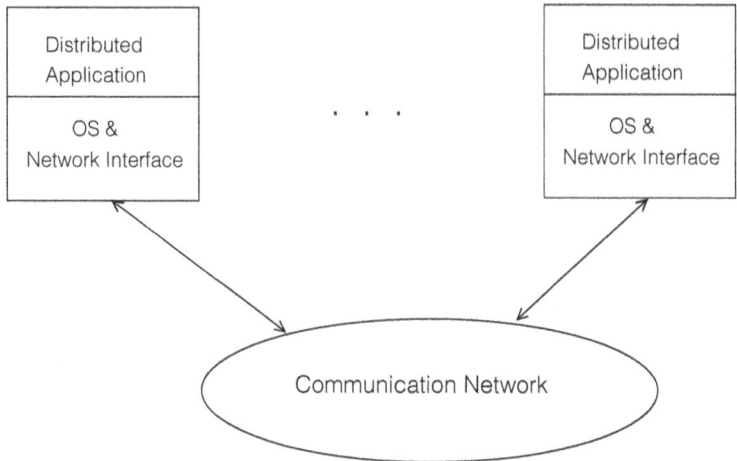

Fig. 1.1 Distributed system structure

- Distributed Control Systems: A factory floor is commonly installed as a distributed real-time system with many processes controlled and synchronized typically over a production line. A modern car is another example of a distributed control system with many embedded computational nodes synchronizing and communicating over a real-time network.
- Mobile Ad hoc Networks: These networks have dynamically moving nodes such as the nodes of a rescue operation team. The system must adapt to dynamic topology changes in such networks.
- Wireless Sensor Networks: This type of network consists of small sensing nodes with capabilities to detect temperature, motion, vibration etc. Data values obtained by the nodes are commonly sent to a central node for control and finer analysis.
- The Web: The Web system provides access to hyper documents over the Internet is a large distributed system with servers running at the nodes.

Key to the correct and effective operation of a distributed system of any kind is the correct and effective design and implementation of distributed algorithms that run on the nodes of a distributed system.

1.2 Distributed Algorithms

A distributed algorithm runs at the nodes of a distributed system typically using the same code with different data. The type of data to run the algorithm commonly depends on the node properties such as the identifier of the node and the number and identifiers of its neighbors. A graph is commonly used to model a distributed system with nodes of the graph representing the computational nodes and edges as the communication links between the nodes.

Many well-known problems such as finding the minimum spanning tree of a weighted graph turns out to be significantly more complicated than the sequential one when a distributed version is sought. A major problem when running a distributed algorithm is the determination of the priority of the node that will have more privilege than its neighbors or various other nodes in the network. In this so-called *symmetry breaking* problem, we can make use of the following methods to select the node with the highest priority among its neighbors.

- *Rank of a node*: Each node of a distributed system is assumed to have a unique identifier called its *rank*. This value may be used to break symmetry among nodes such as the highest rank or the lowest rank node among its neighbors to have priority to decide on some operation to be performed.
- *Randomization*: In this case, each node simply draws a random number and the node with the highest/lowest number wins and decides on the operation to be performed.
- *A physical property of a node*: The degree of a node is the most common parameter to be used when a distinct property of nodes is to be considered. There are other possible parameters such as number of two-hop neighbors, number of neighbors that are not neighbors to each other etc.

1.3 Challenges

There are various challenges in the design and implementation of distributed algorithms. We can classify these problems into the following groups:

- *Message Passing and Ordering of Events*: A sequence of messages sent from a source node to all other nodes in a distributed system must be received in the same sequence by all of the nodes. The ordering of messages is not guaranteed in an asynchronous environment, yet we need to ensure ordering of events based on orderly message receptions.
- *Fault Tolerance*: A distributed system is prone to various type of faults such as link failures, node crashes, software crashes and deadlocks. Yet provision of fault tolerance is an important advantage of a distributed system since a failing hardware or software component may be replaced. Providing fault tolerance in a faulty environment is one of the challenges in distributed system and algorithm design.
- *Termination Detection*: The nodes of a distributed system may finish execution in an arbitrary order. Determining that all nodes in the system have finished execution needs to be done so that system may proceed to another state.
- *Deadlock Detection*: The nodes of a distributed system may deadlock as in a single computational node, waiting for resources held by other processes which will not

release them as they are waiting for other resources. This situation needs to be detected so that recovery procedures to break the deadlock are initiated.
- *NP-Hard Problems*: A number of distributed system problems, mostly the distributed graph problems, are NP-Hard with no known polynomial time solutions. We commonly adhere to heuristics which are common sense rules that are shown to work for a wide range of inputs to provide sub-optimal solutions to these problems.

1.4 Outline of the Book

We have four parts in the book: Background, Fundamental Algorithms, Distributed Graph Algorithms and Applications.

1.4.1 Background

The background part is aimed at first introducing the structure of the text in this chapter. We then review the related concepts and terminology in Chap. 2. The last chapter in this part is on Python programming language and the message passing interface for Python ($mpi4py$) only as much as we will need in the design and implementation of distributed algorithms and the implementation models. These models can be broadly classified as below:

- Asynchronous Single Initiator (ASI) Algorithm: We have a single node that starts the algorithm and the messages may arrive at any time.
- Synchronous Single Initiator (SSI) Algorithm: A single node starts the algorithm which proceeds in rounds. A process performs some operation at each round after exchanging messages with its neighbors.

We will be implementing most of the distributed algorithms using these models by developing working templates in Python in the remaining of the book.

1.4.2 Fundamental Algorithms

This part forms the core part of the book with fundamental distributed algorithms. The first chapter, Chap. 4, is on time synchronization in a distributed system. We review physical clock synchronization, logical clocks, vector clocks and matrix clocks with Python implementations in this chapter. Chapter 5 is about distributed mutual exclusion algorithms to be executed by the processes of a distributed system when they want to perform an operation mutually exclusive of each other. We may need to know the current state of a distributed system by taking a global snapshot of the system as we review in Chap. 6 on global cuts and snapshots. Termination detection and deadlock detection algorithms are also reviewed in this chapter. A leader that decides on behalf of its members is needed in various distributed applications and a leader election algorithm is executed to elect a leader when the current leader fails to operate. Election algorithms form the basis of Chap. 7 together with synchronizers which are software modules that provide synchrony over an asynchronous network.

Chapter 8 is about fault tolerance in a distributed system, we look at ways of achieving redundancy for fault tolerance in this chapter. Processes of a distributed system may be grouped to provide redundancy using replication. Group communication procedures to provide ordered delivery of messages to group members are described in this chapter with routines to recover when some nodes of a distributed system act incorrectly.

1.4.3 Distributed Graph Algorithms

A distributed graph algorithm (DGA) is conceptually different than a general distributed algorithm in which direct communication between any pair of nodes is assumed. That is, the underlying network in a general distributed algorithm is a clique in graph theory terms. A DGA runs at the nodes of a network represented by a general graph where a node can communicate directly only with its neighbors. These algorithms are sometimes called *local algorithms* specifying this local communication property. This part in the text is devoted to DGAs which are divided into Trees and Traversals (Chap. 9), Weighted Graphs (Chap. 10) and Graph Decomposition (Chap. 11) chapters. Our focus in Chap. 9 is on building arbitrary distributed spanning trees in a graph and broadcast and convergecast communications over a constructed spanning tree. We then review asynchronous and synchronous distributed breadth-first-search and synchronous distributed depth-first-search algorithms in a graph with implementations using Python and *mpi4py*.

The second chapter of this part is on weighted graphs which have weights on their edges representing some cost function such as cost of delivery of a message through a link in a computer network. Construction of a minimum spanning tree, routing problem which deals with sending messages over the shortest paths in a network and weighted matching problem are reviewed with implementations.

The last chapter in this part is on graph decomposition algorithms aiming to obtain a subgraph of a graph with a specific property. We review the vertex coloring, vertex cover, maximal independent set, dominating set and matching problems in a distributed setting with implementations.

1.4.4 Applications

Distributed system applications are numerous; in this part, our focus is on two major applications as Mobile Ad hoc Networks (MANETs) and Wireless Sensor Networks (WSNs). We review basic topology algorithms and routing in MANETs in the first chapter with focus on distributed algorithms for this purpose. The second chapter in this part is about WSNs with focus on time synchronization, routing and clustering algorithms.

Basic Concepts 2

Abstract

This chapter is a dense review of basic concepts related to distributed algorithms. We review computer networks with focus on network layers as a distributed algorithm uses network communications to send/receive messages with a peer node. We then describe basic message passing operations in a distributed system. The execution modes of a distributed algorithm may vary, it can be synchronous or asynchronous, a single initiator or a multiple initiators as described. A distributed algorithm may be represented and modelled by various visual aids such as space-time diagrams or finite state machines as we review. Lastly, a distributed algorithm should be analysed to assess its performance and its correctness should be proven as we describe.

2.1 Distributed Systems

A distributed system consists of autonomous computers commonly called *nodes*, connected by a computer network, each with capability to work on its own. Nodes in such a system communicate and cooperate to finish a common task by exchanging messages only. Nodes of a distributed system fail independently, all nodes work concurrently and there is no global clock to synchronize activities. A local area network, a database management system, a mobile ad hoc network and a wireless sensor network are examples of distributed systems.

Typically, a distributed system consists of heterogeneous components with possibly different hardware, operating system and middleware, which is a layer of software between the application and the operating system. A distributed system should be scalable, that is, it should be capable to handle increasing workload without losing significant performance. A linear degradation of performance with linear increase of load is commonly acceptable where the increased load is manifested by added users and nodes to the distributed system.

Faults such as hardware, software and network in a distributed system do happen as in any computer system. A distributed system should be able to handle faults, in other words, it should be fault tolerant which is commonly achieved by redundancy and recovery mechanisms. Replication of the hardware and software components is the main method of redundancy with the aim of selecting a non-faulty replica when the active process crashes. Communication between the nodes in a distributed system is achieved by employing network protocols over a computer network.

2.2 Computer Networks

A distributed application communicates with other distributed applications over a computer network. We assume that the network is reliable and provides guaranteed delivery of messages. Figure 2.1 displays the layers in the Internet. A layered design of communication provides abstraction at each layer where a layer depends on the functions provided at a lower layer and provides services to an upper layer. This way, complicated communication process may be handled more efficiently and reliably. The functions of these layers can be summarized from bottom to top as below:

- *Physical Layer*: This is the lowest layer of the ISO OSI model and is responsible for the transmission of raw data bits and synchronization with external devices. It performs signal to bits and bits to signals conversions. Specifically, it performs bit synchronization using a clock; bit rate control by defining the number of bits sent/received per second. Moreover, the Physical Layer is aware of the topology of the connections to other devices whether star network, a fully connected network or another type of network is employed. It also defines the mode of communica-

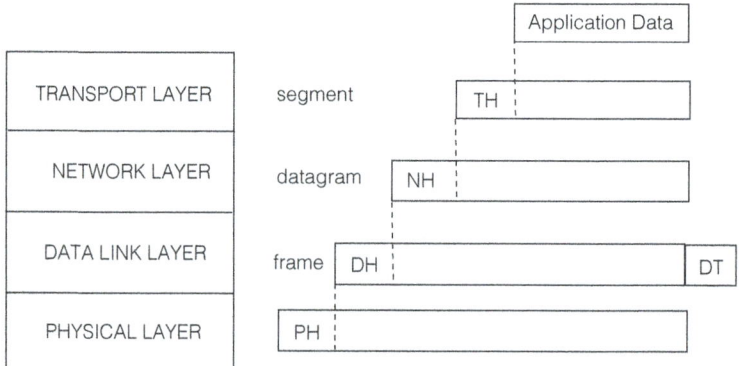

Fig. 2.1 Internet layers

tion which could be simplex, half-duplex or full-duplex. Simplex communication means one way communication over a dedicated communication link is employed. Half-duplex mode allows communication in both direction but only in one direction at any time. The full-duplex operation provides communication in both directions simultaneously.
- *Data Link Layer*: Data link layer provides an error free delivery of messages between a host computer and its first connection to the network. It consists of two sublayers:

  - Logical Link Control (LLC).
  - The Medium Access Control (MAC).
    Packet of the network layer is divided into *frames* in LLC sublayer and physical addresses are processed at MAC sublayer. The main functions performed at this layer are framing, flow control, error control and access control when the communication channel is shared between multiple devices.

- *Network Layer*: This layer provides connection between a host and its peer and it is the lowest layer supplying end-to-end communication procedures. The main protocol at this layer is the Internet Protocol (IP) using IP addresses of the hosts. The main function of this layer is the efficient routing of messages using shortest paths between the nodes in the network. A routing protocol such as Link State or Distance Vector protocol is used for this purpose.
- *Transport Layer*: This layer provides the main interface to the application. It divides the received data from the application into *segments* and maintains flow and error control of transfer of segments over the network for each application. It is aware of each application such as e-mail, file transfer protocol (FTP) thus needs to perform multiplexing and demultiplexing of application messages. The basic interface data structure between the application and this layer is the *socket* which is a structure identified by the IP address and a port number of the communicating hosts.

2.3 Architecture

In a broad sense, a distributed system may have a *client-server* or *peer-to-peer* (P2P) architecture. A client sends a request message to a server and the server responds to this message in the client-server model. A typical client-server application is the submission of a query by a client to a server search engine. Servers may have hierarchical structure in this model such that a server may act as a client to another server. There is at least one server and a number of clients in this type of network as shown in Fig. 2.2 with six clients and one server. Since data and software are commonly stored in the server, it is convenient to upgrade these entities in this model,

Fig. 2.2 A client-server network

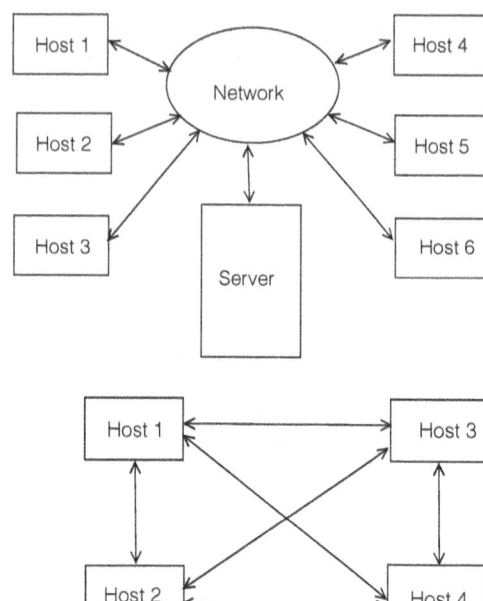

Fig. 2.3 A peer-to-peer network

however, a central server is a single point of failure disruption of which may cause the whole system stopping functioning. Moreover, the central server is a bottleneck for network communications as message traffic would be dense around this computer.

Each node of a P2P network acts as a server or client, working independently, enabling sharing of large data and providing load balancing. A node in such a network may communicate directly with its peers sharing information and resources as depicted in Fig. 2.3.

A typical distributed system is conveniently modeled as a P2P system where nodes may work asynchronously behaving like server or client to their peer nodes. A special node may be assigned to be the root of a distributed system to control and synchronize the operations of other nodes in the synchronous mode of operation.

A distributed system node interacts with the middleware and libraries, the local operating system and the network protocol stack. A middleware consists of modules that may be used by various distributed applications. As we will review in Chap. 4, time synchronization is needed in distributed applications for correctly recording occurrences and sequence of events at the nodes of a distributed system. Time synchronization module is one such middleware to be used by all nodes of a distributed application.

An operating system has two basic roles in a computer system: management of computational resources such as the processor, memory, input/output and software modules efficiently, and provide a convenient interface to the user/application. The tasks of an operating system in a distributed environment is enlarged as to give an overall vision of a single operating system to the application and perform the classical

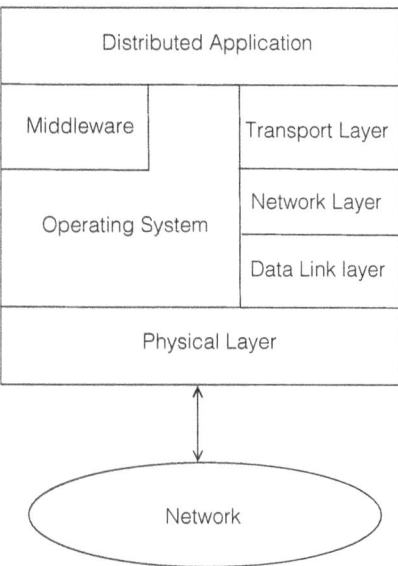

Fig. 2.4 Architecture of a distributed system node

operating system tasks over a computer network. Such an operating system that provides the view of a single operating system is called a *distributed operating system*. The main interface to the network for the distributed application is the Transport Layer. The relationships between these modules is depicted in Fig. 2.4.

2.4 Message Passing

Messages are the fundamental means of communication between the processes of a distributed system. We will assume that a distributed system has a set of n processes $P = \{p_1, ..., p_n\}$ each with a state s_i where the set $S = \{s_1, ..., s_n\}$ denotes the global state of the system. A process p_i is connected to another process p_j using a point-to-point connection called a *channel* which is used for message transfer between p_i and p_j. We will frequently use a graph to represent the processes and their connecting channels of a distributed system. A graph $G = (V, E)$ has a set V of vertices that represent the processes and a set E of edges showing the channels between the processes. A channel may be *reliable* meaning there are no loss of messages in that channel, or *unreliable* otherwise.

2.4.1 Blocking or Non-blocking Message Transfer

The sender of a message may be blocked waiting for an acknowledgement message from the receiver in the blocking *send* system call. The blocking *receive* blocks the

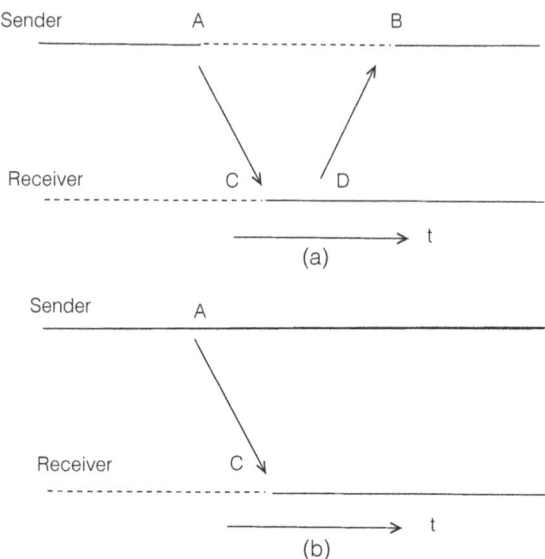

Fig. 2.5 A sample timing diagram

caller until a message is received. A blocking *send* is rarely used in a distributed system since communication network provides guaranteed delivery in most cases. However, using blocking *receive* is sensible as the further actions of a receiver commonly relies on the contents of the message received.

Figure 2.5a displays a blocking *send* and a blocking *receive* where the blocking states are shown in dashed lines between points A and B in the sender, and until point C in the receiver. The sender is not blocked but the receiver is blocked waiting for a message in (b).

2.4.2 Ordering of Messages

A first-in first-out (FIFO) channel delivers the messages sent by process p_i to p_j in the order sent by p_i. A non-FIFO channel may not deliver the messages in the order sent, however, adding sequence numbers to messages and deferring the delivery of the message $m(k)$ to the application at p_j until message $m(k-1)$ arrives imposes synchronous operation over a non-FIFO channel. We will assume all channels used for a distributed algorithm we will study are reliable and FIFO channels. Moreover, we will assume there is a finite propagation delay associated with each message.

2.5 Representations and Models

Various representations and models exist for the analysis of distributed algorithms. A timing diagram represents the execution of a distributed algorithm at the nodes

Fig. 2.6 A sample timing diagram

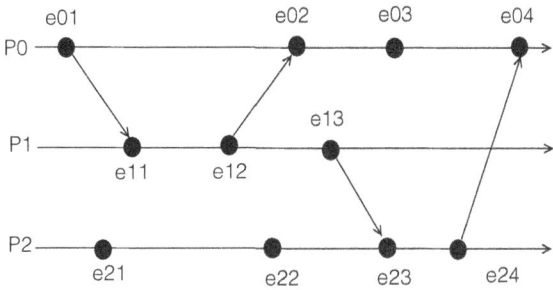

of a distributed system over a time line whereas a finite state machine describes the states and transitions between the states of a distributed algorithm.

2.5.1 Timing Diagrams

A timing diagram is a convenient aid to realize the execution of distributed algorithms running at the nodes of a distributed system. The time of a process is represented by a horizontal line and the events are shown by dots along the time line. An event can be local, a send event or a receive event in general. A timing diagram of a distributed system with 3 processes P_0, P_1 and P_2 is shown in Fig. 2.6 where events e_{03}, e_{21} and e_{22} are local events and all other events are send and receive events.

2.5.2 Basic Finite State Machines

A finite state machine (FSM) can be conveniently used to model a distributed algorithm when the behaviour of the algorithm requires significant computations and message transfers which may be difficult to implement using the basic conditional checks. A finite state machine (FSM) is a tuple as below:

- S: A set of states
- S_0: An initial state
- I: A set of inputs
- O: A set of outputs
- $f : S \times I \to S \times O$

An FSM may be used to open a lock that receives a certain bit pattern. Let us consider a simple lock that needs a '101' to open. The states and transitions between the states of this FSM are depicted in Fig. 2.7 where the final state '101' results in the opening of the lock. Any wrong input at any state results in returning to the state that reflects the correct sequence opened up to that state. The FSM table for this system is depicted in Table 2.1 with states as rows, inputs as columns and actions as table entries.

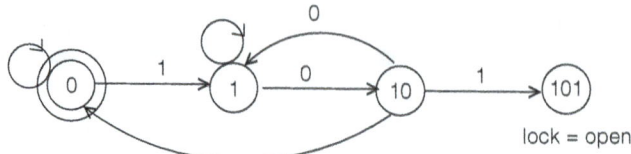

Fig. 2.7 Lock FSM states

Table 2.1 Lock FSM state table

	0	1
0 (init)	–	$act01$
1 (1)	$act10$	$act11$
2 (10)	$act20$	–
3 (101)	–	–

An FSM table of this FSM is provided with the procedures we will call *actions* to be invoked as entries. Each $action_{ij}$ corresponds to a procedure to be called when input j is received at state i with rows representing states and columns the inputs.

This FSM may be coded in Python programming language based on the state table with action addresses stored as entries to a *numpy* array is shown in Listing 2.1. Note that the main program simply waits for an input a and calls the action at row *state* and column a of the fsm table. A trial of 10 entries is allowed and a correct sequence out of 6 entries results in an open lock as shown by the output in Listing 2.2.

Listing 2.1 Lock FSM

```
import numpy as np

lock = 0
state = 0

def act00(): pass
def act01():
    global state
    state = 1
def act10():
    global state
    state = 2
def act11(): pass
def act20():
    global state
    state = 0
def act21():
    global state, lock
    state = 3
    lock = 1

fsm = np.array([[act00,act01],
                [act10,act11],
                [act20,act21]])
count = 1
```

```
26  while count <= 10:
27      a = int(input())
28      fsm[state][a]()
29      if lock == 1:
30          print("Opened, lock: {}, state: {}".format(lock,state))
31          break
32      count = count + 1
```

Listing 2.2 Output of Pi Calculation
```
1
0
0
1
0
1
Opened, lock: 1, state: 3
```

2.5.3 Hierarchical Finite State Machines

When the number of states n of an FSM is large, we may have up to n^2 transitions which may result in a complicated FSM diagram and an FSM table. Besides, whenever we need to add a new state to or remove a state from the FSM, we need to re-evaluate all needed transitions. These observations mean the system is not scalable and easy to maintain when the number of states is large.

Hierarchical finite state machines (HFSMs), or statecharts as widely known [2], are used to solve these problems by grouping states with the two finite state machine types:

- *Substate*: Each state belongs to a parent state
- *Superstate*: A child state is started when a parent state is started and exited when the parent state is exited.

A transition to a substate is first handled in the substate it arrives and any transitions that are not handled are passed to the superstate. A substate inherits all of the properties of the superstate and may have additional properties in a manner similar to the object oriented paradigm. Thus, a substate needs only define its difference from the superstate providing *reuse* of inherited behaviours. A HFSM is depicted in Fig. 2.8 with B as the superstate and B_0 and B_1 as substates, and input events a, b and outputs x and y.

2.6 Analysis of Distributed Algorithms

As in the case of sequential algorithms, a distributed algorithm must be correct and efficient. Efficiency of a distributed algorithm needs to consider message complexity

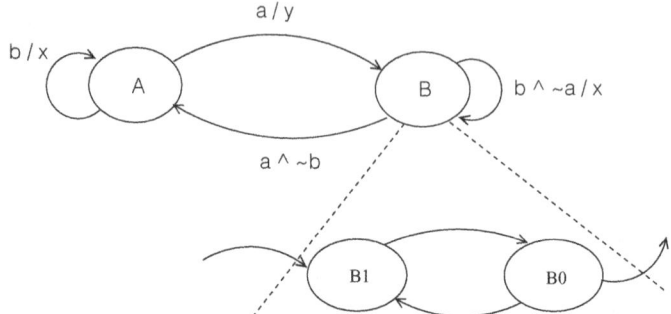

Fig. 2.8 A hierarchical FSM

in addition to time complexity. Moreover, we need to consider termination condition for a distributed algorithm. We will see in Chap. 6 that making sure that distributed algorithms at various nodes of a distributed system terminate is not a trivial problem.

2.6.1 Correctness Proofs

Showing the correctness of a distributed algorithm involves using some mathematical tools. The main methods of theorem proofs are the following:

- *Direct Method*: Given a proposition p, we attempt to prove the proposition q, shown as $p \rightarrow q$ using axioms, previously proved statements, lemmas and theorems.

Example 2.1 If a and b are two odd integers, then $a + b$ is even.

Proof We can write $a = 2k + 1$ and $b = 2l + 1$ for some integers k and l since these are odd integers. Then,

$$a + b = 2k + 1 + 2l + 1$$
$$= 2k + 2l + 2$$
$$= 2(k + l + 1)$$

which means $a + b$ is even. □

- *Contrapositive*: The theorem $p \rightarrow q$ is equivalent to $\neg q \rightarrow \neg p$ called its contrapositive, and sometimes it is more practical to prove a theorem using its contrapositive.

2.6 Analysis of Distributed Algorithms

Example 2.2 For any integer $a > 0$, if a^2 is even, then a is even.

Proof Here, p is "a^2 is even" and q is "a is even". Then, "$\neg q = a$ is odd". Thus, we can write $a = 2k + 1$ for some integer k. Squaring yields:

$$\begin{aligned} a^2 &= (2k+1)^2 \\ &= 4k^2 + 4k + 1 \\ &= 2(k^2 + 2k) + 1 \\ &= 2m + 1 \quad \text{with} \quad m = k^2 + 2k \end{aligned}$$

which is an odd number, thus, we have shown that $\neg p$ is true when $\neg q$ is true. $\square$

- *Contradiction*: Assuming the premises p is correct and the conclusion q is incorrect, we attempt to find a fallacy in this method. Formally, if $(p \wedge \neg q)$ is false, then $\neg(p \wedge \neg q)$ is true which means $(\neg p \vee q)$ is true. Since we assumed p is true, we can conclude q is true.

Example 2.3 Prove that $p =$ "$3n + 5$ is even" $\rightarrow q =$ "n is odd".

Proof We will assume $p \wedge \neg q$ is true and try to find a contradiction.

$$\begin{aligned} n &= 2k \\ 3n + 5 &= 3(2k) + 5 \\ &= 6k + 5 \\ &= 2(3k + 2) + 1 \\ &= 2m + 1 \quad \text{with} \quad m = 3k + 2 \end{aligned}$$

which is an odd number which contradicts the assumption that p is even. $\square$

Note that although the structure seems similar to the contrapositive proof, we have not explicitly tried to prove $\neg p$, we could have encountered any fallacy such as $1 = 0$ using this method.

All of these proof methods may be used to prove distributed algorithms, however, the induction method of proof described in the next section is more commonly used to show the correctness of these algorithms.

2.6.1.1 Induction

The induction proof method is a powerful tool commonly used to prove theorems. It consists of a basis step and the inductive step shown below:

- Basis step: $P(1)$ is proven.
- Inductive step: $P(k) \rightarrow P(k+1)$ is proven for all positive integers k.

Example 2.4 Prove that the sum of first n odd integers is n^2.

Proof The basis step $\sum_1^1 = 1^2 = 1$ is true. For the inductive step, let an odd integer be represented by $2k - 1$ for any integer k. Note that we have used $2k + 1$ in the previous examples to represent an odd integer; both are valid.

$$\begin{aligned} P(k+1) &= P(k) + 2(k+1) - 1 \\ &= k^2 + 2(k+1) - 1 \\ &= k^2 + 2k + 1 \\ &= (k+1)^2 \end{aligned}$$

which is what we would get if $(k+1)$ is substituted in the initial statement. □

2.6.1.2 Loop Invariants

A *loop invariant* is a statement about a loop in an algorithm. It is true before the first iteration of the loop and if it is true before an iteration, then it remains true before the next iteration. The following are to be provided with a loop invariant [1]:

- *Initialization*: The loop invariant must be true before the first iteration of the loop.
- *Maintenance*: If the loop invariant is true for the kth iteration, it should be true for the $(k+1)$th iteration.
- *Termination*: The invariant should result in true value when the loop finishes.

We can see that this structure is similar to induction method. Selection of a loop invariant is mostly performed using common sense.

Example 2.5 Let us consider the following algorithm which finds the maximum element of an integer array.

In this example, we define the loop variable max as the maximum element of the first ith elements of the array at ith iteration of the for loop. The maintenance of the loop invariance is realized since max is *true* before each execution of the loop and remains *true* after each iteration. Based on the above condition, it is *true* when the loop terminates.

Algorithm 2.1 *Max*

1: $a[n] \leftarrow \{3, 1, 5, 7, -2, 9, 4\}$
2: $max \leftarrow -\infty$
3: **for** $i=0$ to 6 **do**
4:    **if** $A[i] > max$ **then**
5:       $A[i] \leftarrow max$
6:    **end if**
7: **end for**

2.6.2 Complexity

The complexity of a distributed algorithm may be expressed mainly as time complexity and message complexity. Time complexity of a sequential algorithm is well defined, however, time complexity of a distributed algorithm requires careful considerations. First of all, each process of a distributed system may finish at arbitrary times. The time complexity of a distributed algorithm is the the time of the last event at any process.

Message complexity is the total number of messages transferred between the nodes until the algorithm terminates. There are four messages transferred in the diagram of Fig. 2.6 which is the message complexity in this system assuming the algorithm has terminated after event e_{04}. Let us consider a distributed system with n nodes connected over a spanning tree. The root of this tree broadcasts a message m simply by sending m to its children and every node other than the leaf nodes sends m to its children. The number of messages sent by this transaction is simply $n - 1$ which is the number of edges of any tree structure. We can therefore state that the message complexity of this algorithm is $\Theta(n)$. As for time complexity, the maximum time taken for the message m to be received by the farthest node is $O(n)$ since this is the length of the longest possible path of a tree. Note that we have used *BigOh* notation for time complexity as this is the greatest possible time whereas the number of messages transmitted is exactly $n - 1$. A complete binary tree and a linear network are depicted in Fig. 2.9a and b respectively. The number of messages sent by the root process with identifier 0 are $n - 1$, 14 and 6, in both cases. However, time taken for the broadcast operation in (a) is 3 and 6 in (b). In both cases, the time complexity of the algorithm is the height of the tree which is the longest path from the root to a leaf node.

2.7 Chapter Notes

We reviewed fundamental concepts in distributed systems in this chapter. The nodes of the distributed system communicate over a communication network that employs protocols at various layers. The operating system of a distributed system performs

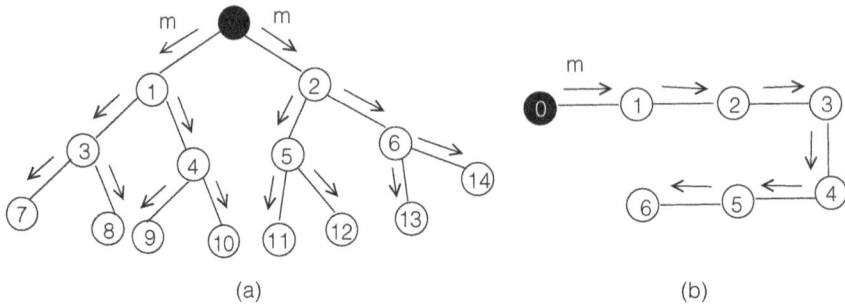

Fig. 2.9 a A complete binary tree b a linear network

additional tasks to that of a traditional operating system. It has to provide efficient communication and synchronization among the nodes, maintain balanced workload over the nodes and provide sharing of resources over the network. A middleware is a software module that uses the distributed operating system to provide general services to distributed applications.

Message passing is the main method of communication among the nodes of a distributed system. This type of operation may be performed synchronously or asynchronously. Channels between the processes may be FIFO or non-FIFO and a FIFO operation may be performed over a non-FIFO channel by the use of sequence numbers attached to messages. Nodes and channels of a distributed system may be modeled conveniently by graphs where vertices represent nodes and edges show the channels between the nodes.

Formal analysis of distributed algorithms may be handled using various tools; one such tool is the FSM that displays the states of a node and its transitions between the states. This model proves to be practical when understanding the operation and realization of a distributed algorithm that is more complicated than a usual one. We also need to prove that a distributed algorithm is correct and the induction and loop invariance methods are commonly used for this purpose.

Complexity of a distributed algorithm may be evaluated in terms of space, time and message complexities. Time complexity has a similar notion as in a sequential algorithm with a slight modification: we need to asses this complexity between the first start time of the algorithm at a node and the termination at the lastly finishing node. The message complexity is the number of messages exchanged between the nodes from the start of the algorithm until its completion. This parameter is commonly expressed in terms of the number of nodes n, and the number of edges m in the graph, when a graph represents the network and provides a measure of network usage during the execution of the algorithm. The total number of rounds is also used when the distributed algorithm works synchronously using rounds.

Exercises

1. Draw the state diagram of a FSM that detects the pattern 10011 in an input binary string. Obtain the FSM table and actions based on the state diagram and implement this FSM in Python.
2. An elevator has up and down buttons and it can access three floors. Work out the FSM state diagram, state table and actions for this elevator and implement its algorithm in Python using FSM.
3. A vending machine accepts 5 or 10 cents only. It has a *release* and a *change* button to release a product worth 20 cents and to give change respectively. Draw the FSM state diagram, state table and implement this machine operation in Python using FSM.
4. Provide the pseudocode of the bubble sort algorithm and propose a loop invariant for this algorithm. Show the validity of the initialization, maintenance and termination conditions for this loop invariant.
5. A distributed algorithm works in rounds initiated by a *root* node. The nodes of this system communicate using a spanning tree with the *root* process located at the root of the tree. Assuming there are *start* round and *end* round messages at each round, work out the message complexity of this algorithm for r rounds.

References

1. K. Erciyes, in *Guide to Graph Algorithms: Sequential, Parallel and Distributed*. Springer Texts in Computer Science Series (2018)
2. D. Harel, Statecharts: a visual formalism for complex systems. Sci. Comput. Progr. **8**(3), 231–274 (1987)

Implementation Models Using Python and *mpi4py* 3

Abstract

This chapter is a brief introduction to the message passing interface module for Python, *mpi4py*, and basic implementation models for distributed algorithms. We review $mpi4py$ module for message based communications in the first part and illustrate its use in distributed algorithms. The second part of this chapter describes asynchronous and synchronous execution models of distributed algorithms with coding templates in Python.

3.1 Introduction

Modelling a distributed computation is needed to provide a framework to be followed when implementing the algorithm. A commonly used execution model for distributed algorithms may be stated as follows:

- A distributed system is commonly and conveniently modelled by an undirected graph where the nodes represent computational units and the edges show the bidirectional communication links.
- Each node in the system has a unique identifier which is commonly used to break symmetries. For example, a node with the largest identifier among its neighbors may be selected to perform a specific task on behalf of its neighbors. Each identifier is represented using at most $\lceil c \log_2 n \rceil$ bits for some constant $c \geq 1$.
- Initially and throughout the distributed computation, each node communicates only with its neighbors.
- Each node is commonly responsible only for computing its part of the output. For example, each node determines its parent and children only when a distributed minimum spanning tree is computed.

- The only means of communication for a node is to exchange messages with its neighbors.
- Synchronous communication is performed in *rounds* where a node receives message(s) from its neighbor(s), performs a computation and sends a message to its neighbors. Note that the order of operations could be different; a round may start by receiving a message of results from the last round, and then sending a message to neighbors and finally performing a computation. This mode of operation is the preferred model of distributed computation in most cases as it provides deterministic steps of computation with known termination instant.
- System is fault-free with no node crashes and lost messages. We will review fault tolerance to recover from faults in Chap. 8.

This model which bears the message-passing, synchronous, fault-free communication among nodes with unique identifiers where a node communicates only with its neighbors is called the $\mathcal{LOCAL}$ model which we will use, unless stated otherwise, for the implementation of most of the distributed algorithms throughout this book. The $\mathcal{CONGEST}$ model adds a restriction to this model by limiting the size of messages to $\Theta(\log n)$ bits.

3.2 Message Passing Interface for Python: *mpi4py*

The message passing interface (MPI) is a general standard that provides a set of routines and communication modes between the processes of distributed and parallel systems. The *mpi4py* module of Python is an adaptation of MPI to Python with similar methods of communication of MPI [1,2]. The first line of a Python program is importing MPI from *mpi4py* after which various methods from MPI can be used. A communication object is first constructed from MPI module which allows various methods of message transfer over this object.

The following code segment starts by creating a communication object called *comm* and then each process invoked can learn its unique identifier using the method *Get_rank* from this object. The total number of processes which is input to *mpi4py* at runtime is obtained using the *Get_size* method. In the simple example in Listing 3.1, the root process with identifier 0 sends a message to all others processes by the *send* method of the *comm* object. Any process other than the root process finds the sum of the numbers up to and including its rank and returns this value to the root process which receives the messages and displays the rank of the sender and the received value as displayed in Listing 3.2. Note that the root accepts message in any order by specifying ANY_SOURCE as the source and ANY_TAG as the tag, thus each run of this code may result in different order of message receptions.

3.2 Message Passing Interface for Python: *mpi4py*

Listing 3.1 MPI Example

```
from mpi4py import MPI
import numpy as np

comm = MPI.COMM_WORLD
rank = comm.Get_rank()
size = comm.Get_size()

msg = [0,0] # sender and data
# master process
if rank == 0:
    for i in range(1, size):
        comm.send(msg, dest=i, tag=i)
    for i in range(1, size):
        recvd = comm.recv(source=MPI.ANY_SOURCE, tag=MPI.ANY_TAG)
        print(" {} sent: {}".format(recvd[0],recvd[1]))

# worker processes
else:
    my_msg = comm.recv(source=0, tag=rank)
    s = 0
    for i in range(0,rank+1):
        s = s + i
    msg = [rank, s]
    comm.send(msg, dest=0, tag=0)
```

Listing 3.2 Output of MPI Example

```
5 sent: 15
6 sent: 21
2 sent: 3
3 sent: 6
4 sent: 10
1 sent: 1
7 sent: 28
```

There are many other communication modes in *mpi4py* such as broadcasting a message to all other processes, scattering a message such that each process receives personal data, gathering personal messages from each process etc. [1,2].

3.2.1 Calculation of π

Another commonly used MPI example is the calculation of the value of π which is approximately equal to $\int_0^1 \frac{4}{1+x^2}$. The area under this function can be calculated by dividing it to n slices with each *mpi4py* process calculating the area in its slice and sending it to the root process for summing as in the Python code of Listing 3.3 [1]. The *broadcast* operation provides each node with the value of n which is the number of slices. The *reduce* operation results in the collection of partial results at the root process. The output of this algorithm is displayed in Listing 3.4.

Listing 3.3 Calculation of Pi with 100 Slices and 10 Processes

```
from mpi4py import MPI
import math

def compute_slice(n, start=0, step=1):
    width = 1.0 / n
    func = 0.0
    for i in range(start, n, step):
        x = width * (i + 0.5)
        func += 4.0 / (1.0 + x**2)
    return func * width

comm = MPI.COMM_WORLD
nprocs = comm.Get_size()
myrank = comm.Get_rank()

if myrank == 0:
    n = 100
else:
    n = None

n = comm.bcast(n, root=0)
mypi = compute_slice(n, myrank, nprocs)
pi = comm.reduce(mypi, op=MPI.SUM, root=0)

if myrank == 0:
    error = abs(pi - math.pi)
    print ("pi is approximately %.16f, ""error is %.16f" % (pi,
        error))
```

Listing 3.4 Output of Pi Calculation

```
pi is approximately 3.1416009869231249, error is
    0.0000083333333318
```

3.2.2 Stop-and-Wait Automatic Repeat Request Protocol

As a more advanced example using FSMs, we will consider the Stop-and-Wait (SaW) data link layer protocol based on sending a frame and receiving a reply before sending the next frame. This protocol is very basic and has a poor performance as every frame sent has to be acknowledged by the receiver, and thus is never used. Figure 3.1 depicts the FSM of this algorithm where the sender process is at IDLE state waiting for a request from Layer 3 and upon receiving this request, prepares frame header and sends the frame to the receiver. It also changes its state to WAIT waiting for a reply from the receiver. Three possible inputs to the sender at this state are the ACK message from the receiver indicating that the frame was received correctly or NACK meaning there was an error, and an internal TIMEOUT message that shows that there is no response from the receiver. Frame retransmission is initiated In both NACK and TIMEOUT inputs. If the input is an ACK message, Layer 3 is informed which may then initiate a next frame transfer and the state is changed to IDLE.

3.2 Message Passing Interface for Python: *mpi4py*

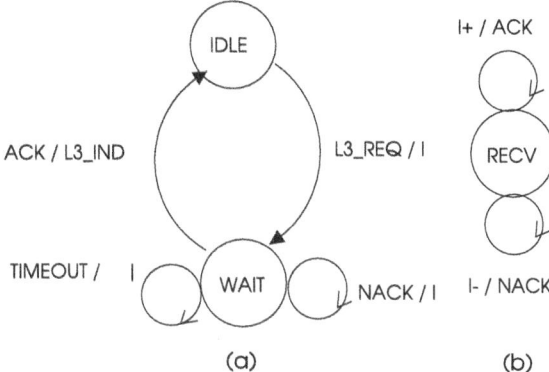

Fig. 3.1 FSM of SaW protocol

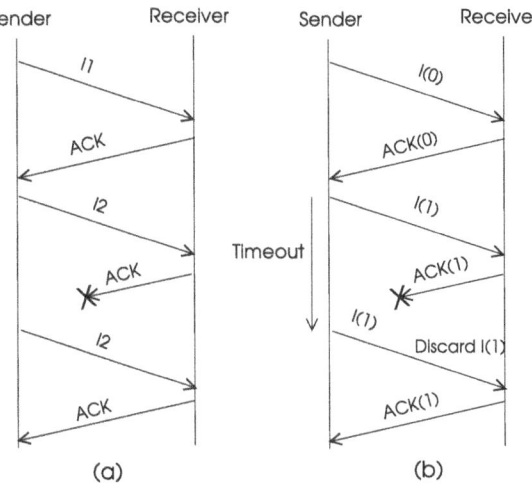

Fig. 3.2 SaW protocol examples **a** without sequence numbers, **b** with sequence numbers

It is possible for the ACK frame sent by the receiver to be lost in the network in which case, the sender will time-out and re-send the previous frame as in Fig. 3.2a. However, the receiver is not aware of this situation and receive the re-transmitted frame as a new one. In order to remedy this erroneous transfer of frames, sequence numbers are attached to frames. The sender sends frames with sequence numbers 0 and 1 only, one after the other. When the ACK frame for frame 1 is lost as above, the sender will re-transmit frame 1 but the receiver will discard this frame as it is expecting frame with sequence number 0 as depicted in Fig. 3.2b.

Table 3.1 Stop-and-wait protocol FSM table

	L3_REQ	ACK	NACK	TOUT
IDLE	act00	–	–	–
WAIT	–	act11	act12	act13

Python Implementation

In order to transform the FSM into Python code, we will have the FSM table for the sender process as shown in Table 3.1 with rows of the table showing the states of the sender and the columns as the inputs. We then form functions for each action entry in this table and place the addresses of these functions in the FSM table as shown in Listing 3.5.

The sender process with rank 0 waits for any type of message and it calls the action defined by its current state and the type of message. The Layer 3 process with rank 2 opens the source code of this file and for each entry in the file, it sends a layer 3 request (L3_REQ) message with the read file data. The sender then sends this data to the receiver which sends an ACK message to the sender. Note that the FSM is run by the sender process only.

Listing 3.5 Stop and Wait Protocol

```
comm = MPI.COMM_WORLD
rank = comm.Get_rank()
n    = comm.Get_size()

# states
IDLE = 0
WAIT = 1

# message types
L3_REQ, ACK, NAK       = 0, 1, 2
TOUT, DATA, READY, FIN = 3, 4, 5, 6

# msg = [type, data]
msg = [-1,-1]
seq_no = 0    # initialize
state = IDLE

def act00():
    global msg, state
    msg = [DATA,data]
    state = WAIT
    comm.send(msg, dest=1,tag=DATA)

def act11():
    global seq_no, state, msg
    seq_no = (seq_no + 1) % 2
    state = IDLE
    msg[0] = READY
    comm.send(msg, dest=2,tag=READY)

def act12():
    comm.send(msg, dest=1,tag=DATA)
```

```python
def act13():
    comm.send(msg, dest=1, tag=DATA)

fsm_tab = [[act00, None, None, None],
           [None, act11, act12, act13]]

if rank == 0:   # sender
    while True:
        msg = comm.recv(source=MPI.ANY_SOURCE, tag=MPI.ANY_TAG)
        typ, data = msg[0], msg[1]
        if typ == FIN:
            break
        fsm_tab[state][typ]()
        msg[0] = FIN
    comm.send(msg, dest=1, tag=1)

elif rank == 1: # receiver
    while True:
        msg = comm.recv(source=MPI.ANY_SOURCE, tag=MPI.ANY_TAG)
        typ, data = msg[0], msg[1]
        if typ == FIN:
            break
        print(data)
        msg[0] = ACK
        comm.send(msg, dest=0, tag=0)

else:   # Layer 3
    f = open("L2.py")
    for data in f:
        data = data.rstrip()
        msg = [L3_REQ, data]
        comm.send(msg, dest=0, tag=0)
        msg = comm.recv(source=0, tag=READY)
    msg[0] = FIN
    comm.send(msg, dest=0, tag=0)
```

Running this program with three processes as layer 3 process, the sender and the receiver results in the printing of the full source code of the algorithm. Stop-and-Wait protocol is inefficient as every packet sent needs to be acknowledged or rejected and is not used for data communications for this reason.

3.3 Execution Modes

The execution modes of a distributed algorithm has two modes of operation: whether the algorithm is started by a single process or multiple processes; and whether the algorithm is synchronous or asynchronous as shown in Table 3.2.

Table 3.2 Distributed algorithm execution modes

	Single initiator	Multiple initiators
Synchronous	SSI	SMI
Asynchronous	ASI	AMI

Commonly, a root process starts the distributed algorithm in single-initiator mode. A synchronous single initiator (SSI) is the most commonly used implementation model as it is deterministic. A synchronous execution of distributed algorithms at the nodes of a distributed system advances in lockstep fashion in rounds. This execution mode commonly requires a spanning tree T built prior to the running of the algorithms. Each round is initiated by a *root* or *initiator* node which sends a *round* message to its children over T which is propagated from an intermediate process to its children until it reaches all leaves of T. When a leaf process finishes what it needs to do at a round, it sends a *round_over* (or *rover*) message to its parent and these messages are convergecast back to the root process which can then initiate the next round. A typical round for a node in this mode is shown in Algorithm 3.1.

Algorithm 3.1 *SSI*

1: **while** some condition **do**
2:    **receive** *round* message
3:    **send** *data* message to neighbors
4:    **receive** *data* message from neighbors
5:    perform local computation
6:    **if** leaf **then**
7:       **send** *round_over* message to parent
8:    **else if** not root **then**
9:       **if** *round_over* received from all neighbors and finished **then**
10:          **send** *round_over* message to parent
11:       **end if**
12:    **else if** all *round_over* messages are received from children and finished **then**
13:       start next round
14:    **end if**
15: **end while**

3.3 Execution Modes

Fig. 3.3 Broadcast and convergecast operations over a spanning tree

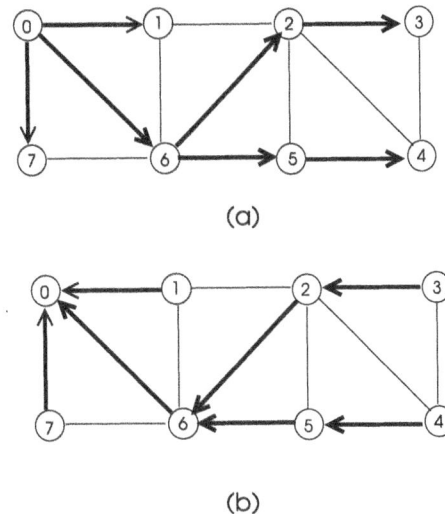

Typically, each node exchanges messages by its neighbors in each round and performs some local operation based on the data it receives. Note that a round is initiated by the root but the end of the round is initiated by leaf processes since these nodes do not need to wait for any child to finish. An intermediate node waits for all of its children to finish and then sends a *round_over* message to its parent when itself also finishes. Also, the results of local computation at round k are transmitted to neighbors only at round $k + 1$. An alternative operation is possible by performing local computations first based on a previous round $k - 1$ for example, and then sending the results to neighbors at round k.

A sample network with graph nodes as distributed algorithm processes is depicted in Fig. 3.3 where *round* messages are broadcast from the root process 0 to all nodes up to leaf processes 1, 3, 4 and 7 over the spanning tree shown in bold. The convergecast of *round_over* messages from leaves to the root is shown in (b) of the same figure. In both cases, the height of the tree, which is $n - 1$ at most for n nodes, determines the number of steps for *round* and *round_over* messages to reach all nodes.

One major issue with this mode of operation, as with all other modes, is the detection of termination. We can have two modes of SSI: SSI with known number of rounds and SSI with undetermined number of rounds.

3.3.1 SSI with Determined Rounds

In various and somehow rare applications, we know the number of rounds to be executed by a SSI algorithm beforehand. This is commonly the case when the distributed algorithm acts like a sequential one, that is, there is a single activity at any round. One such example is the coloring vertices of a graph where a single vertex is colored at each round based on its identity. Vertex coloring is the process of assigning colors to the vertices of a graph such that each vertex receives a color which is an integer that is different than all of its neighbor vertex colors. *Vertex coloring* problem is to use the minimum number of colors to color vertices of a graph. In such applications, we can set the number of rounds to n which is the number of nodes, yielding a time complexity of $O(n)$. Even in this seemingly simple mode of operation, we need to consider the synchronous sending and receiving of messages. Common causes of uncertainties in this mode can be specified as below:

- The sequence of the received messages by a node is arbitrary. A node may receive a *data* message before a *round* message or vice versa.
- Some children of an intermediate node may have finished the round and others may be involved in communication with neighbors.

Based on this reasoning, each node needs to monitor two asynchronous activities: sending/receiving messages to/from neighbors and finishing of a round by the children if it is an internal node of the tree. It should send the *round_over* (*rover*) message to its parent only when these two activities are complete. In the detailed SSI algorithm with known round numbers, we have two logical variables for each node: *neighs_over* that becomes *true* when sending and receiving of messages from neighbors is complete and *child_over* that becomes *true* when round is over for all children. A node has to check each of these flags at each message reception as we cannot estimate the order of messages. The pseudocode of the SSI algorithm with known round numbers (SSI-KRN) considering these details is shown in Algorithm 3.2.

Python Implementation
The pseudocode of Algorithm 3.2 is directly translated into Python code using the Python Message Passing Interface (MPI) module *mpi4py*. We use the graph of Fig. 3.3 for the communication graph and the spanning tree to transfer *round* and *rover* messages. The parents and children of a nodes are declared in *parents* and *children* lists to specify the spanning tree as shown in Listing 3.6. The maximum round number is set to 100,000 and all nodes finish 100,000 rounds by sending and receiving data messages at each round as shown by the output in Listing 3.7.

3.3 Execution Modes

Algorithm 3.2 *SSI* with constant number of rounds

1: **message types:** *round, data, rover*
2: **for** $i = 1$ to *max_round* **do**
3:     *round_over, neighs_over* ← *false*
4:     *neighs_rcvd, rover_rcvd* ← ∅
5:     **if** *me == root* **then**   ▷ root starts a round
6:         *round_num* ← *round_num* + 1
7:         **send** $msg(i, round, round\_num)$ to children
8:         **send** $msg(i, data, round\_num)$ to neighbors
9:     **end if**
10:
11:    **while** *round_over == false* **do**
12:        **receive** message $msg(j)$ ▷ receive any message
13:        **if** *msg.type == round* **and** I am not root **then**
14:            **send** $msg(i, round)$ to children
15:            **send** $msg(i, data)$ to neighbors
16:
17:        **else if** *msg.type == data* **then**
18:            *neighs_rcvd* = *neighs_rcvd* ∪ {*j*}
19:            **if** *neighs_rcvd == neighbors* **then**   ▷ check if all neighbors received
20:                *neighs_over* = *true*
21:                **if** I am leaf **or** *child_over* **then**
22:                    **send** $msg(i, rover)$ to *parent*
23:                **end if**
24:            **end if**
25:
26:        **else**
27:            *rover_rcvd* = *rover_rcvd* ∪ {*j*}
28:            **if** *rover_rcvd == childs* **then**   ▷ check if all children received
29:                *child_over* ← *true*
30:                **if** *neighs_over* **then**
31:                    *round_over* = *true*
32:                    **if** I am not root **then**
33:                        **send** $msg(i, rover)$ to *parent*
34:                    **end if**
35:                **end if**
36:            **end if**
37:        **end if**
38:    **end while**
39: **end for**

Listing 3.6 SSI with Known Round Number

```
from mpi4py import MPI
import numpy as np

comm = MPI.COMM_WORLD
rank = comm.Get_rank()
n    = comm.Get_size()

A = np.array([[0,1,0,0,0,0,1,1],
```

```
                      [1,0,1,0,0,0,1,0],
                      [0,1,0,1,1,1,1,0],
                      [0,0,1,0,1,0,0,0],
                      [0,0,1,1,0,1,0,0],
                      [0,0,1,0,1,0,1,0],
                      [1,1,1,0,0,1,0,1],
                      [1,0,0,0,0,0,1,0]],dtype=int)
children = [[1,6,7],[],[3],[],[],[4],[2,5],[]]
parents  = [0,0,6,2,5,6,0,0]

# message types
ROUND, DATA, ROVER  =  0, 1, 2

# message = [sender, type, round number]
msg = np.array([-1, -1, -1])

rover_rcvd = set()
child = children[rank]
parent = parents[rank]
childs = set(child)
neighs, neighs_rcvd = set(), set()

for i in range(0,n):      # identify neighbors
    if A[rank,i] == 1:
        neighs.add(i)

max_round = 100000 # number of rounds

for round_num in range(0,max_round):
    round_over = False
    neighs_over, child_over  = False, False
    rover_rcvd.clear()
    neighs_rcvd.clear()
    if rank == 0:   # if root, start the next round
        round_num = round_num + 1
        msg = [rank, ROUND, round_num]
        for child in childs: # send ROUND to children
            comm.send(msg, dest=child, tag=ROUND)
        msg[1] = DATA
        for node in neighs:   # send DATA to neighbors
            comm.send(msg, dest=node, tag=DATA)

    while not round_over:
        msg = comm.recv(source=MPI.ANY_SOURCE, tag=MPI.ANY_TAG)
        sender, typ, roun = msg[0], msg[1], msg[2]
        msg[0] = rank
        if typ == ROUND: # send ROUND to children
            if rank != 0:
                for child in childs:
                    comm.send(msg, dest=child, tag=ROUND)
                msg[1] = DATA
                for node in neighs:   # send DATA to neighbors
                    comm.send(msg, dest=node, tag=DATA)

        elif typ == DATA:   # DATA received
            neighs_rcvd.add(sender)
            if neighs_rcvd == neighs: # all neighbors received?
                neighs_over = True
                if len(childs) == 0 or child_over:
                    msg[1] = ROVER   # leaf starts convergecast
                    comm.send(msg, dest=parent, tag=ROVER)
                    round_over = True
```

3.3 Execution Modes

```
72      else:    # ROVER received
73          rover_rcvd.add(sender)
74          if rover_rcvd == childs:  # all children received?
75              child_over = True
76              if neighs_over:
77                  round_over = True
78                  if rank != 0:
79                      comm.send(msg,dest=parent,tag=ROVER)
80 print(" Rank: {} Finished, Round: {}".format(rank,roun))
```

Listing 3.7 Output of SSI wth Known Round Number

```
Rank: 1 Finished, Round: 100000
Rank: 3 Finished, Round: 100000
Rank: 7 Finished, Round: 100000
Rank: 4 Finished, Round: 100000
Rank: 2 Finished, Round: 100000
Rank: 5 Finished, Round: 100000
Rank: 6 Finished, Round: 100000
Rank: 0 Finished, Round: 100000
```

3.3.2 SSI with Determined Rounds Using a Finite State Machine

As demonstrated in Chap. 2, using an FSM simplifies many complicated distributed algorithm implementations. We will now convert the distributed SSI algorithm template of the previous section to the one with an FSM. The message types are the same but we need to define states of nodes. As a simple approach, we define the states of nodes based on their location on the tree as below:

- ROOT: A root node starts the algorithm in single initiator model of distributed algorithms. It does not have a parent but has at least one child.
- INTERM: An intermediate node has a parent and at least one child.
- LEAF: A leaf node has a parent and does not have a child.

A sub-state FINISHED is used to determine the termination of a node. The state diagram using these states is depicted in Fig. 3.4. All nodes terminate when the maximum number of rounds is reached. The FSM state table may be formed as in Table 3.3.

Python Implementation

Python implementation of SSI mode with determined round number using FSM is shown in Listing 3.8. A spanning tree is already built prior to the execution of the algorithm. We first define actions as specified in Table 3.3 which are then placed in the FSM array called fsm obeying the row and column placements in the table. The distributed algorithm at each node simply runs the action at the row entry specified by the current state and the received input. The working of the algorithm is simplified and errors are largely eliminated using this model of implementation, thus, we will be using this approach when the problem is more complicated than usual. The output of this algorithm is displayed in Listing 3.9.

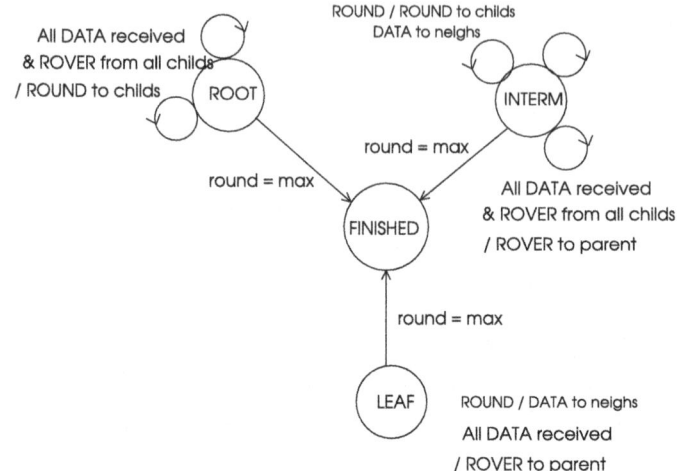

Fig. 3.4 FSM states of SSI with known round numbers

Listing 3.8 SSI with Known Round Number and FSM Template Algorithm

```
from mpi4py import MPI
import numpy as np

comm = MPI.COMM_WORLD
rank = comm.Get_rank()
n    = comm.Get_size()

A = np.array([[0,1,0,0,0,0,1,1],
              [1,0,1,0,0,0,1,0],
              [0,1,0,1,1,1,1,0],
              [0,0,1,0,1,0,0,0],
              [0,0,1,1,0,1,0,0],
              [0,0,1,0,1,0,1,0],
              [1,1,1,0,0,1,0,1],
              [1,0,0,0,0,0,1,0]],dtype=int)

# determine parent and children
children = [[1,6,7],[],[3],[],[],[4],[2,5],[]]
parents  = [0,0,6,2,5,6,0,0]
parent = parents[rank]
child = children[rank]
childs = set(child)

# message types
ROUND    = 0
DATA     = 1
ROVER    = 2

# states
ROOT       = 0
INTERM     = 1
LEAF       = 2
FINISHED   = 3

# message = [sender, type, round number]
```

3.3 Execution Modes

```
36  msg = np.array([-1, -1, -1])
37
38  # sets to monitor message order
39  neighs, neighs_rcvd, rover_rcvd = set(), set(), set()
40
41  # determine states
42  if rank == 0:
43      state = ROOT
44  elif len(childs) != 0:
45      state = INTERM
46  else:
47      state = LEAF
48
49  for i in range(0,n):     # identify neighbors
50      if A[rank,i] == 1:
51          neighs.add(i)
52
53  # Actions
54  def act00(): pass
55  def act01():
56      global msg, round_over, neighs_rcvd, neighs_over
57      neighs_rcvd.add(sender)
58      if neighs_rcvd == neighs: # all neighbors received?
59          neighs_over = True
60          if child_over:
61              round_over = True
62
63  def act02():
64      global round_over, rover_rcvd, child_over
65      rover_rcvd.add(sender)
66      if rover_rcvd == childs: # all children received?
67          child_over = True
68          if neighs_over:
69              round_over = True
70
71  def act10():
72      global  msg, sent_over
73      for child in childs:
74          comm.send(msg, dest=child, tag=ROUND)
75      msg[1] = DATA
76      for node in neighs:     # send DATA to neighbors
77          comm.send(msg, dest=node, tag=DATA)
78      sent_over = True
79
80  def act11():
81      global msg, neighs_over, round_over, neighs_rcvd
82      neighs_rcvd.add(sender)
83      if neighs_rcvd == neighs: # all neighbors received?
84          neighs_over = True
85          if child_over:
86              msg[1] = ROVER
87              comm.send(msg, dest=parent, tag=ROVER)
88              round_over = True
89
90  def act12():
91      global msg, rover_rcvd, child_over, round_over
92      rover_rcvd.add(sender)
93      if rover_rcvd == childs: # all children received?
94          child_over = True
95          if neighs_over and sent_over:
96              msg[1] = ROVER
97              comm.send(msg,dest=parent,tag=ROVER)
98              round_over = True
```

```python
def act20():
    global msg, sent_over
    msg[1] = DATA
    for node in neighs:     # send DATA to neighbors
        comm.send(msg, dest=node, tag=DATA)
    sent_over = True

def act21():
    global msg, round_over, neighs_rcvd, neighs_over
    neighs_rcvd.add(sender)
    if neighs_rcvd == neighs: # all neighbors received?
        neighs_over = True
        if sent_over:
            msg[1] = ROVER
            comm.send(msg, dest=parent, tag=ROVER)
            round_over = True

def act22(): pass

fsm = np.array([[act00,act01,act02],
                [act10,act11,act12],
                [act20,act21,act22]])

max_round = 100000 # number of rounds
for round_num in range(1,max_round+1):
    round_over = False
    neighs_over, child_over, sent_over  = False, False, False
    rover_rcvd.clear()
    neighs_rcvd.clear()
    if rank == 0:
        msg = [rank, ROUND, round_num+1]
        for child in childs:   # ROOT sends ROUND message
            comm.send(msg, dest=child, tag=ROUND)
        msg[1] = DATA
        for node in neighs:    # send DATA to neighbors
            comm.send(msg, dest=node, tag=DATA)
        sent_over = True
    if round_num == max_round:
        break
    round_num = round_num + 1

    while not round_over:
        msg = comm.recv(source=MPI.ANY_SOURCE, tag=MPI.ANY_TAG)
        sender, typ, roun = msg[0], msg[1], msg[2]
        msg[0] = rank
        fsm[state][typ]()

print("Rank: {}, Finished, Round: {}".format(rank,round_num))
```

Listing 3.9 Output of SSI with Known Round Number Algorithm

```
Rank: 0, Finished, Round: 100000
Rank: 1, Finished, Round: 100000
Rank: 3, Finished, Round: 100000
Rank: 4, Finished, Round: 100000
Rank: 5, Finished, Round: 100000
Rank: 2, Finished, Round: 100000
Rank: 6, Finished, Round: 100000
Rank: 7, Finished, Round: 100000
```

3.3 Execution Modes

Table 3.3 SSI with round known numbers state table

	ROUND	DATA	ROVER
ROOT	–	act01	act02
INTERM	act10	act11	act12
LEAF	act20	act21	–

When each round number is displayed for 5 rounds by inserting

```
if typ == ROUND:
         print("{}:{} ".format(rank,round_num),end=" ")
```

after line 144 in Listing 3.12, the output in Listing 3.10 is obtained showing all rounds are processed synchronously and correctly.

Listing 3.10 Detailed Output of SSI with Known Round Number Algorithm

```
Rank: 0, Finished, Round: 5
7:1   7:2   7:3   7:4   7:5   Rank: 7, Finished, Round: 5
3:1   3:2   3:3   3:4   3:5   Rank: 3, Finished, Round: 5
4:1   4:2   4:3   4:4   4:5   Rank: 4, Finished, Round: 5
2:1   2:2   2:3   2:4   2:5   Rank: 2, Finished, Round: 5
5:1   5:2   5:3   5:4   5:5   Rank: 5, Finished, Round: 5
6:1   6:2   6:3   6:4   6:5   Rank: 6, Finished, Round: 5
1:1   1:2   1:3   1:4   1:5   Rank: 1, Finished, Round: 5
```

3.3.3 Synchronous Execution with Undetermined Round Number

A node does not have the number of rounds to execute in most cases and the nodes of the network may finish arbitrarily, depending on the problem addressed. Yet, a finished node that has at least one unfinished node in its subtree has to continue transferring *round* and *rover* messages over the spanning tree. One way to overcome this problem is to have the finished nodes continue sending *rover* messages in *convergecast* mode to their parents. However, the following issues remain to be addressed:

- An unfinished intermediate node of the spanning tree should exclude its finished children and send the round message only to its current children. We therefore need a current children set ($currchilds$) that changes dynamically. An internal node now waits for *rover* messages only from its $currchilds$ set.
- We need to introduce a new message type $rovfin$ sent by a node to its parent only when it has finished and all nodes in its sub-tree have finished. We use this message also to indicate the end of a round. Convergecast of this message to the root means all nodes have finished.

We can now elaborate on the structure of SSI distributed algorithm by imposing synchrony over an asynchronous network by the use of *round* (ROUND), *round_over* (ROVER), and round_over_finished (ROVFIN) messages and form the state table for this mode of operation as in Table 3.4. Note that we have piggybacked *finish* message on top of *rover* message to form *rovfin* message.

The actions of this FSM can be detailed as in Table 3.5 with each action labelled as $(state, input)$ denoting its current state and the input it receives.

We will frequently implement this SSI algorithm template for various problems, sometimes using a FSM with this template when the problem to be addressed requires more elaboration than usual.

Python Implementation

As an example of nodes finishing at different rounds, we consider a network with unique identifiers and each process finishes at the round number equal to its identifier.

Table 3.4 SSI with round known numbers state table

	ROUND	ROVER	ROVFIN
ROOT	–	*act*01	*act*02
INTERM	*act*10	*act*11	*act*12
LEAF	*act*20	–	–

Table 3.5 SSI undetermined using FSM algorithm actions

*act*01 (ROOT, ROVER)	*act*02 (ROOT, ROVFIN)
1. If ROVER∪ ROVFIN received from all children 2. Increment round number 3. Send ROUND(*mw*) msg to current children	1. Mark source as finished 2. If all children are finished 3. Send TERM to all children
*act*10 (INTERN, ROUND)	*act*11 (INTERN, ROVER)
1. Send ROUND to all children 2. Do local processing	1. If ROVER received from all children 2. Send ROVER to parent
*act*12 (INTERN, ROVFIN)	*act*20 (LEAF, ROUND)
1. Add child to finished 2. If all children and me finished 3. State = FINISHED 4. Send FIN to parent	1. Do local processing 2. Send ROVER to parent

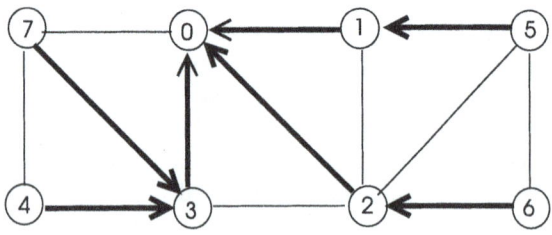

Fig. 3.5 Sample network for SSI algorithm with unknown number of rounds

3.3 Execution Modes

However, an internal process has to wait until all its children finish and itself finishes. We have a spanning tree over which rounds are executed, with a root process that manages the starting and ending of rounds.

Python code is implemented by transferring the actions into functions which are placed at the FSM table accordingly as shown in Listing 3.11. Running the code for the graph of Fig. 3.5 results in the output displayed in Listing 3.12. Note that although node 1 finishes locally at round 1, it has to wait for node 5 to finish at round 5 before it can change its state to finished and send finished message to its parent which is node 0. The root node 0 has to wait for all its children to finish until round 7 to change its state to *finished*. The leaf nodes which are nodes 4, 5, 6 and 7 finish exactly at the round numbers equal to their identifiers as expected since they do not wait for any children.

Listing 3.11 SSI with Unknown Round Number Template

```python
from mpi4py import MPI
import numpy as np

comm = MPI.COMM_WORLD
rank = comm.Get_rank()
n    = comm.Get_size()

A  = np.array([[0,1,1,1,0,0,0,0],
               [1,0,0,0,0,1,0,0],
               [1,0,0,0,0,0,1,0],
               [1,0,0,0,1,0,0,1],
               [0,0,0,1,0,0,0,0],
               [0,1,0,0,0,0,0,0],
               [0,0,1,0,0,0,0,0],
               [0,0,0,1,0,0,0,0]], dtype=int)

# determine parent and children
children = [[1,2,3],[5],[6],[4,7],[],[],[],[]]
parents  = [0,0,0,0,3,1,2,3]
parent = parents[rank]
child = children[rank]
childs = set(child)
sender, typ, roun = 0,0,0

# message types
ROUND, ROVER, ROVFIN  = 0, 1, 2

# states
ROOT, INTERN, LEAF, FINISHED = 0, 1, 2, 3

# message: sender, type, round number
msg = np.array([-1, -1, -1])
rover_rcvd, finish_rcvd = set(), set()
currchilds = childs.copy()
round_over, over, roun = False, False, 0
state2 = -1

if rank == 0:
    state = ROOT
    over = True
elif len(childs) != 0:
    state = INTERN
else:
    state = LEAF
```

```python
def act01():
    global rover_rcvd, round_over, finish_rcvd
    rover_rcvd.add(sender)
    if rover_rcvd.union(finish_rcvd) == childs:
        round_over = True
        rover_rcvd.clear()

def act02():
    global finish_rcvd, currchilds, state2, round_over
    finish_rcvd.add(sender)
    currchilds.remove(sender)
    if finish_rcvd == childs:
        state2 = FINISHED
        round_over = True
    elif rover_rcvd.union(finish_rcvd) == childs:
        round_over = True
        rover_rcvd.clear()

def act10():
    global over, state2
    msg= [rank, ROUND, roun]
    for node in currchilds:
        comm.send(msg, dest=node, tag=ROUND)
    if not over:
        if rank == roun:
            over = True

def act11():
    global rover_rcvd, round_over, finish_rcvd, sender
    rover_rcvd.add(sender)
    if rover_rcvd.union(finish_rcvd) == childs:
        msg = [rank, ROVER, roun]
        comm.send(msg, dest=parent, tag=ROVER)
        rover_rcvd.clear()
        round_over = True

def act12():
    global finish_rcvd, currchilds, state2, rover_rcvd, round_over, sender
    finish_rcvd.add(sender)
    currchilds.remove(sender)
    if finish_rcvd == childs and over:
        state2 = FINISHED
        msg = [rank, ROVFIN, roun]
        comm.send(msg,dest=parent,tag=ROVFIN)
        round_over = True
    elif finish_rcvd.union(rover_rcvd) == childs:
        msg = [rank, ROVER, roun]
        comm.send(msg, dest=parent, tag=ROVER)
        rover_rcvd.clear()
        round_over = True


def act20():
    global round_over, over, state2
    if not over:
        if rank == roun:
            over = True
            state2 = FINISHED
            msg = [rank, ROVFIN, roun]
            comm.send(msg, dest=parent, tag=ROVFIN)
        else:
```

3.3 Execution Modes

```
            msg = [rank, ROVER, roun]
            comm.send(msg, dest=parent, tag=ROVER)
      round_over = True

fsm = np.array([[None,act01,act02],
                [act10,act11,act12],
                [act20,None,None]])

round_num = 0

while state2 != FINISHED:
    round_over = False
    if rank == 0:
        round_num = round_num + 1
        msg = [rank, ROUND, round_num]
        for node in currchilds:
            comm.send(msg, dest=node, tag=ROUND)

    while not round_over:
        msg = comm.recv(source=MPI.ANY_SOURCE, tag=MPI.ANY_TAG)
        sender, typ, roun = msg[0], msg[1], msg[2]
        fsm[state][typ]()

print("Rank: {}, Finished at round: {}".format(rank,roun))
```

Listing 3.12 Output of SSI with Unknown Round Number Template Algorithm

```
Rank: 4, Finished at round: 4
Rank: 5, Finished at round: 5
Rank: 1, Finished at round: 5
Rank: 2, Finished at round: 6
Rank: 6, Finished at round: 6
Rank: 7, Finished at round: 7
Rank: 3, Finished at round: 7
Rank: 0, Finished at round: 7
```

3.3.4 Asynchronous Operation

The asynchronous operation model of distributed computing may be implemented as single or multiple initiators. We have no rounds for synchronization in this mode and any node may start a computation at any time. An important problem in this mode is the determination of termination by all nodes. The algorithms in this model tend to be more complicated than the synchronous ones due to uncertainties in message transfers involved.

As a simple multiple initiator asynchronous distributed algorithm example, we will have the node identifiers of leaves of an existing spanning tree collected at the root node. We have a spanning tree constructed prior to the execution of the algorithm with each node knowing its parent and its children if any. A node can be in three states: *root*, *internal* or *leaf*, all leaves start the algorithm by sending their identifiers to their parents which send these identifiers to their parent. The root process collects identifiers and prints them when all are received through its children as shown in the Python code of Listing 3.13. We use the same graph and the same spanning tree of Fig. 3.3b as the input to this algorithm. The output in Listing 3.14 displays the leaf identifiers received by the root process which include all of the leaves of the spanning tree.

Listing 3.13 Asynchronous Execution with Multiple Initiators

```
ffrom mpi4py import MPI
import numpy as np

comm = MPI.COMM_WORLD
rank = comm.Get_rank()
n    = comm.Get_size()

A = np.array([[0,1,0,0,0,0,1,1],
              [1,0,1,0,0,0,1,0],
              [0,1,0,1,1,1,1,0],
              [0,0,1,0,1,0,0,0],
              [0,0,1,1,0,1,0,0],
              [0,0,1,0,1,0,1,0],
              [1,1,1,0,0,1,0,1],
              [1,0,0,0,0,0,1,0]],dtype=int)

# determine parent and children
children = [[1,6,7],[],[3],[],[],[4],[2,5],[]]
parents  = [0,0,6,2,5,6,0,0]
parent = parents[rank]
child  = children[rank]
childs = set(child)
child_rcvd = set()
leaves = set()
over = False

# states
ROOT   = 0
INTERN = 1
LEAF   = 2

# message: sender, ids
msg = [-1,-1]

if rank == 0:
    state = ROOT
elif len(childs) != 0:
    state = INTERN
else:
    state = LEAF

if state == LEAF: # if leaf start convergecast
    me = {rank}
    msg = [rank, me]
    comm.send(msg, dest=parent, tag=1)
    over = True

while not over:
    msg = comm.recv(source=MPI.ANY_SOURCE, tag=MPI.ANY_TAG)
    sender, ids = msg[0], msg[1]
    leaves = leaves.union(ids)
    child_rcvd.add(sender)
    if child_rcvd == childs: # all children received?
        if state == INTERN: # send ids to parent
            msg = [rank, leaves]
            comm.send(msg, dest=parent, tag=1)
            over = True
        elif state == ROOT: # display all
```

```
59              print("Rank: {}, Leaves: {}".format(rank, leaves))
60              over = True
```

Listing 3.14 Output of SSI with Unknown Round Number Template Algorithm

```
Rank: 0, Leaves: {1, 3, 4, 7}
```

3.4 Chapter Notes

We will commonly be using the synchronous single initiator mode of operation for distributed algorithm implementations. This operation can be further categorized as follows:

- Synchronous Single Initiator with known number of rounds (SSI-KRN): This mode is achieved by a root process broadcasting *round* messages and nodes convergecasting *rover* messages to the root. It is the simplest mode of operation since each node knows the number of rounds to finish beforehand.
- Synchronous Single Initiator with known number of rounds using FSM (SSI-KRN-FSM): This mode operates like the previous mode but we use FSMs to describe and implement the operation of a node. We commonly use this mode when the problem at hand is more complicated than usual.
- Synchronous Single Initiator with unknown number of rounds (SSI-URN): A node may finish in an arbitrary round in this mode. We need to introduce new message types in this case and the implementation code is more complicated than SSI-KRN.
- Synchronous Single Initiator with unknown number of rounds using FSM (SSI-URN-FSM): We will use this mode for more complicated problems with nodes having undetermined finishing times.
- Asynchronous Single Initiator (ASI): We do not have synchronous operation using rounds in this mode. A problem with this approach is determining the termination condition for nodes.
- Asynchronous Single Initiator with FSM (ASI with FSM): There are no synchronous rounds in this mode either, which may be used to deal with a complicated problem that needs to be solved in an asynchronous environment.

Programming Exercises

1. The matrix product of two square matrices A and B of dimension 12 is to be calculated in parallel using *mpi4py*. Write the pseudocode of this algorithm using row partitioning of A and distributing these rows and broadcasting B to 4 processes. Convert the pseudocode to Python code and obtain the resulting product matrix C for randomly generated integer elements of matrices A and B.

Fig. 3.6 Sample graph for Exercise 3

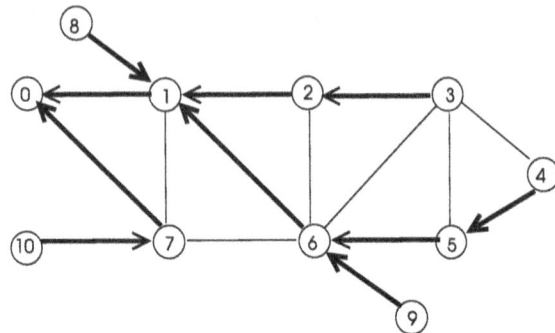

Fig. 3.7 Sample graph for Exercise 5

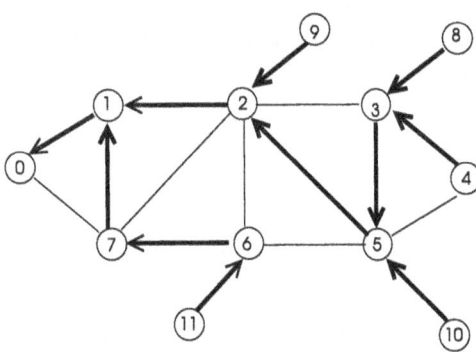

2. A distributed system consists of 10 processes $P_0, ..., P_9$ that are fully connected to each other. These processes exchange messages with each other and then declare the highest identifier. Write this program in Python using *mpi4py* and show that it works.
3. Write a SSI-KRN algorithm in Python assuming a spanning tree of Fig. 3.6 with 0 as the root node already exists and a node that has an identifier equalling the round number sends its degree to its parent starting from the leaves of the tree and then finishes, and the root node prints the degrees of all nodes in the network.
4. Modify SSI-URN-FSM algorithm of Sect. 3.3.3 so that there is a new message called *terminate* which is sent by the root to all processes to indicate that all have finished. Each process waits for this message to terminate. Modify the FSM table of SSI-URN algorithm and implement it in Python using *mpi4py*.
5. Write an SSI-URN-FSM algorithm in Python assuming a spanning tree of Fig. 3.7 with 0 as the root node already exists and each node sends the sum of the identifiers in its subtree and its identifier to its parent starting from the leaves of the tree and then finishes, and the root node prints the sum of all identifiers which should be 66.

References

1. L. Dalcin, R. Paz, M. Storti, MPI for Python. J. Parallel Distrib. Comput. **65**(9), 1108–1115 (2005)
2. L. Dalcin, R. Paz, M. Storti, J. D'Elia, MPI for Python: performance improvements and MPI-2 extensions. J. Parallel Distrib. Comput. **68**, 655–662 (2008)

Part II
Fundamental Algorithms

Time Synchronization 4

> **Abstract**
>
> Time synchronization is needed in a distributed system for various functions such as ordering of events, recording global state, and fault detection and recovery. Physical synchronization of clocks in a distributed system is the process of adjusting the physical clock of a process based on the clock values of other processes. Logical clocks consider virtual clocks which are advanced at each local event or sending and receiving of messages. Vector clock and matrix clock based synchronizations provide adjusting of the clock of a process by observing the clock values of other processes in the system. In this chapter, we review physical clock, logical clock, vector clock and matrix clock synchronization algorithms and implement them in Python using *mpi4py*.

4.1 Introduction

Time synchronization is needed in a distributed system for a number of reasons. We may want to know the physical time of the occurrence of an event at a node or it may be necessary to compare and detect the order of events on two or more machines. Moreover, the events running at nodes may need to be ordered. For example, we may want to edit a file at node *A* and compile the edited file at another node *B*. If the clock at node *B* runs faster than the clock of node *A*, we may compile an old version of the file. In fault detection, the sequence of events that lead to the fault needs to be investigated to diagnose the fault and recover.

Definition 4.1 (*clock drift*) The difference between two clocks at a given time point is called *clock drift*.

Definition 4.2 (*clock skew*) Maximum allowed clock drift is called *clock skew*.

The aim of clock synchronization in a distributed system is to minimize the clock skew among all processes in the system. Round trip time (RTT) is the time interval between sending a message and reception of a reply between two hosts.

4.2 Physical Clocks

Atomic clocks are based on the oscillations of atoms with accuracy as 1 part in 10^{13}. The values of these clocks are broadcast using radio stations and the receiving nodes may adjust their clock values with respect to the broadcast ones. Coordinated universal time (UTC) is the international clock standard that is based on atomic clocks. The UTC value is also broadcast on radio for nodes to synchronize. Fast, perfect and slow clock time changes with respect to UTC time are depicted in Fig. 4.1.

A node in a distributed system may have positive or negative drift with respect to a perfect clock such as the UTC. In *external synchronization*, nodes synchronize their clocks with an external reference clock such as UTC whereas nodes synchronize their clocks with respect to their neighbors, without any external synchronization in *internal synchronization*.

4.2.1 Clock Synchronization with a Central Server

Clock synchronization with a central server method of time synchronization enables the client nodes to synchronize with a central server that maintains the accurate time either from an external trusted source or calculates a reasonable reference time value for example, by averaging local clock values.

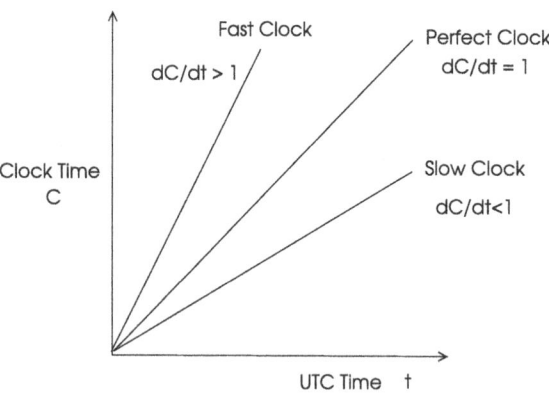

Fig. 4.1 Perfect, fast and slow clocks with respect to UTC

4.2.2 Cristian's Algorithm

Cristian's algorithm is a simple external synchronization algorithm using an accurate server synchronized to a global clock [1]. The clients request time from this server and adjust their clocks accordingly. The operation of this algorithm consists of the following steps below as illustrated in Fig. 4.2.

- Any node that wants to set its clock records its local time T_1 and sends a request message to the server.
- Upon receiving this message, the server timestamps the message with its current local time T_s and sends it to the sending client node.
- The client then records the time of reception T_2 of this message.
- The client can now adjust its clock to be,

$$T_c = T_s + (T_2 - T_1)/2$$

Note that assuming the server responds immediately, the difference of the two recordings of its time in the client is the round trip time (RTT) and halving it compensates for the network delay from the server to the client. In the example operation of this algorithm between a client and a server shown in Fig. 4.2, the client calculates the network delay to be 200 ms and adjusts its clock accordingly.

Python Implementation

The Python code in Listing 4.1 shows the implementation of Cristian's algorithm between a server with rank 0 and client processes with ranks 1, 2 and 3. Processes 2 and 3 need minor corrections whereas process 1 has the same time with the server in this sample run of the algorithm as in the output displayed in Listing 4.2. We need to assume clock times will be very similar as the program is run in one processor with 8 cores to simulate a distributed environment, however, there is convergence to a common value as shown.

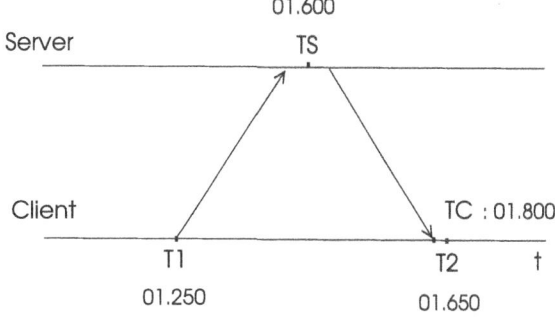

Fig. 4.2 Cristian's algorithm message transfers

Listing 4.1 Cristian's Algorithm

```
from mpi4py import MPI
import numpy as np
import time

comm = MPI.COMM_WORLD
rank = comm.Get_rank()
size = comm.Get_size()

msg = [0,0] # sender and time
# master process

if rank == 0:
    for i in range(1,size): # receive requests
        msg = comm.recv(source=MPI.ANY_SOURCE, tag=MPI.ANY_TAG)
        T_s = time.time()
        sender = msg[0]
        msg[0], msg[1] = rank, T_s
        comm.send(msg, dest=sender, tag=sender)
        print("Root sent time: {} to: {}".format(T_s,sender))


# worker processes
else:
    msg[0] = rank
    T_1 = time.time() # send time
    comm.send(msg, dest=0, tag=0)
    msg = comm.recv(source=0, tag=rank)
    T_2 = time.time()
    T_server = msg[1]
    my_time = T_server + (T_2 - T_1)/2 #correct
    print("Rank: {} uncorrected: {}, corrected: {}".format(rank,
        T_2,my_time))
```

Listing 4.2 Cristian's Algorithm

```
Rank: 1 uncorrected: 1725704445.494636, corrected:
    1725704445.5056047
Root sent time: 1725704445.4945772 to: 1
Root sent time: 1725704445.494625 to: 3
Root sent time: 1725704445.5026972 to: 2
Rank: 3 uncorrected: 1725704445.5027113, corrected:
    1725704445.5020583
Rank: 2 uncorrected: 1725704445.5147295, corrected:
    1725704445.5112882
```

4.2.3 Berkeley Algorithm

The Berkeley algorithm is an internal clock synchronization method that was used for clock synchronization in Unix 4.3 BSD [3]. One of the nodes in the distributed system is selected as the root process to manage the synchronization.

An example operation of Berkeley algorithm with one root node R and three nodes A, B and C is depicted in Fig. 4.3. The root polls the client processes in (a) to receive their clock values. It then calculates the average of all received values and itself as $(15 + 18 + 30)/3 = 21$, disregarding the outlier value sent by node B.

4.2 Physical Clocks

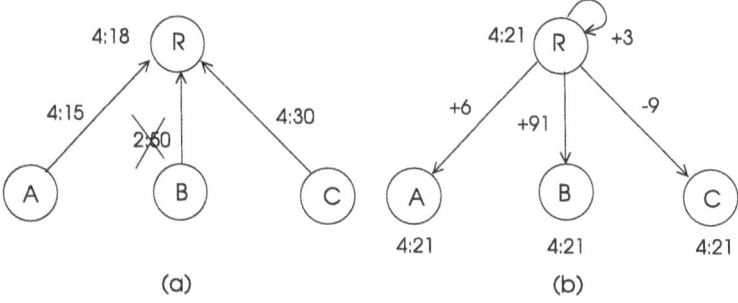

Fig. 4.3 Berkeley algorithm example

The corrections to each node including the outlier node B is sent as differences to adjust their clock values in (b) so that all clocks are set to 4:21. In practice, Berkeley protocol uses an estimate of RTT to obtain a better approximation of average time.

Python Implementation

Python implementation of Berkeley clock synchronization algorithm is given in Listing 4.3 where the server process requests time values from the clients by the *mpi4py broadcast* routine. It then calculates the average value of client clock values and its clock value and sends correction values to clients. Each client adjusts its clock with the correction value in the final step.

Listing 4.3 Berkeley Algorithm

```
from mpi4py import MPI
import numpy as np
import time

comm = MPI.COMM_WORLD
rank = comm.Get_rank()
size = comm.Get_size()

msg = [0, 0] # sender, time values
clocks = np.zeros(size)
clocks_tot = 0
root = 0
# root process
if rank == root:
    clocks[0] = time.time()
    msg[0], msg[1] = rank, clocks[0]
    comm.bcast(msg, root)            # request clock values
    for i in range(1, size):
        msg = comm.recv(source=MPI.ANY_SOURCE, tag=MPI.ANY_TAG)
        sender = msg[0]
        clocks_tot = clocks_tot + msg[1]
        clocks[sender] = msg[1]
    msg[0] = rank
    sumv = sum(clocks)   # find average value
    ave = sumv / size
    for i in range(1, size):   # send for corrections
        msg[1] = clocks[i] - ave
```

```
              comm.send(msg, dest=i, tag=i)
28
              correction = clocks[0] - ave
29
              my_time = time.time()    # current time
30
31
32    # client processes
33    else:
34         comm.bcast(msg, root)  # receive message from root
35         my_time = time.time()    # send my time
36         msg[0], msg[1] = rank, my_time
37         comm.send(msg, dest=0, tag=0)
38         msg = comm.recv(source=0, tag=rank)   # receive correction
39         correction = msg[1]
40         my_time = time.time()    # current time
41    print("Rank: {} correction: {} my time: {}".format(rank,
              correction, my_time))
42    print("Rank: {} corrected time: {}".format(rank,my_time +
              correction))  # update clock
```

Listing 4.4 Berkeley Algorithm

```
Rank: 0 correction: -0.002660036087036133   my time:
    1725704071.1387968
Rank: 0 corrected time: 1725704071.1361368
Rank: 1 correction: -0.0010495185852050781  my time:
    1725704071.1388123
Rank: 1 corrected time: 1725704071.1377628
Rank: 2 correction: 0.0037093162536621094   my time:
    1725704071.1446397
Rank: 2 corrected time: 1725704071.148349
```

4.2.4 Network Time Protocol

The network time protocol is a widely used protocol for time synchronization in the Internet [6]. It is constructed as a tree of servers with the servers at level 0 synchronizing with UTC. Class 1 servers have highly accurate clocks commonly following UTC, Class 2 servers get time only from Class 1 servers and Class 2 servers and Class 3 servers get time from any host. The following is a possible sequence of actions in this protocol as depicted in Fig. 4.4.

1. The client node timestamps a message at time T_1 and sends it to the server node.
2. The server receives this message at time T_2 and then timestamps it at time T_3 and sends it back to the client.
3. The client receives the message that contains all timestamps T_1, T_2 and T_3 at time T_4.

4.2 Physical Clocks

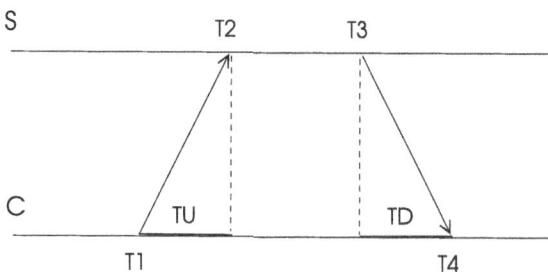

Fig. 4.4 Network time protocol example

Assuming that the clock skew between the client and the server is δ, the following equations can be derived using T_U and T_D shown in Fig. 4.4:

$$T_2 = T_1 + T_U + \delta$$
$$T_4 = T_3 + T_D - \delta$$
$$T_U + T_D = T_2 + T_4 - T_1 - T_3$$

the sum of T_U and T_D is the RTT of packets. Now, subtracting T_4 from T_2 and reorganizing to obtain δ value yields,

$$T_2 - T_4 = T_1 - T_3 + t_u * T_D + 2\delta$$
$$\delta = \frac{T_2 - T_4 - T_1 + T_3 - T_U + T_D}{2}$$

All of the $T_1, \ldots, T_4$ values are recorded and known by the node C and RTT can be estimated experimentally by sending and receiving few test messages resulting in calculation of δ value after which C can correct its clock.

Python Implementation

The Python implementation of NTP is given in Listing 4.5 with a server process of rank 0 and three client processes with ranks 1, 2 and 3. The corrected clock values of the client processes are displayed in Listing 4.6.

Listing 4.5 NTP Algorithm

```
from mpi4py import MPI
import numpy as np
import time

comm = MPI.COMM_WORLD
rank = comm.Get_rank()
size = comm.Get_size()

msg = np.array([0,0,0]) # sender and time values

# root process
if rank == 0:
```

```
13      for i in range(1,size):
14          # receive message from any process
15          msg = comm.recv(source=MPI.ANY_SOURCE, tag=MPI.ANY_TAG)
16          T2 = time.time()
17          sender = msg[0]
18          # print("hello")
19          T3 = time.time()
20          msg[0], msg[1], msg[2] = rank, T2, T3
21          comm.send(msg, dest=sender, tag=sender)
22
23  # client processes
24  else:
25      msg[0] = rank
26      T1 = time.time()
27      comm.send(msg, dest=0, tag=0)
28      msg = comm.recv(source=0, tag=rank)
29      T4 = time.time()
30      T2, T3 = msg[1], msg[2]
31      RTT = T2+T4-T1-T3
32      delta = (T2-T4-T1+T3+RTT)/2
33      print("Rank: {}, skew: {}".format(rank, delta))
34      T5 = time.time()
35      my_time = T3 + delta
36      print("Rank: {}, uncorrected: {}, corrected: {}".format(rank,
            T5,my_time))
37  if rank == 0:
38      print("Rank: {}, time: {}".format(rank,T3))
```

Listing 4.6 Output of NTP Algorithm

```
Rank: 3, skew: -0.9529492855072021
Rank: 3, uncorrected: 1725705376.9568696, corrected:
    1725705375.0470507
Rank: 0, time: 1725705376.96281
Rank: 1, skew: -0.9582563638687134
Rank: 1, uncorrected: 1725705376.9646804, corrected:
    1725705375.0417438
Rank: 2, skew: -0.9595004320144653
Rank: 2, uncorrected: 1725705376.968169, corrected:
    1725705375.0404997
```

4.3 Logical Clocks

Instead of attempting to synchronize nodes of a distributed system by correcting their physical clocks, logical clocks may be used where the value of a logical clock is changed only due to an internal or external event. Thus, a logical clock counts the occurrences of events and is not related to the physical clock of a node and an external event is the sending or reception of a message. If a is the event of sending of a message by a node and b is its reception event by another node, then the following cases of event orderings are possible [4]:

- $a \rightarrow b$, a precedes b
- $a \parallel b$, if neither $a \rightarrow b$ or $b \rightarrow a$

Fig. 4.5 Logical clock example

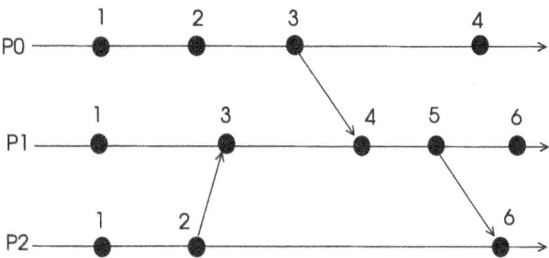

- If $a \rightarrow b$ and $b \rightarrow c$, then $a \rightarrow c$, (transition property)

Let P_i be the process with identifier i with a local clock L_i. The following rules are implemented to increment the value of a logical clock.

- *Local event*: P_i sets $L_i \leftarrow L_i + 1$ at each local event at P_i.
- *Send event*: When P_i sends a message m to P_j, it sets $L_i \leftarrow L_i + 1$ and timestamps the message with L_i ($m(L_i)$).
- *Receive event*: When P_j receives a message m with timestamp L_i from P_i, it sets L_j to $\max(L_i, L_j) + 1$. Incrementing is needed since reception is a local event for process P_j.

A sample process set of three processes P_0, P_1 and P_2 that communicate arbitrarily with the shown logical clock values is depicted in Fig. 4.5.

For any two events $a \rightarrow b$, $L(a) < L(b)$. However, if $L(a) < L(b)$, we can not conclude $a \rightarrow b$ which is the main problem with logical clocks that can be corrected by *vector clocks*.

Python Implementation

A simple Python implementation of logical clocks is presented in Listing 4.7 with functions *send_msg* and *recv_msg* to send and receive messages according to logical clock rules. Running logical clock rules for the example process communication example of Fig. 4.5 results in the same final outputs shown in the figure as displayed in Listing 4.8.

Listing 4.7 Logical Clocks

```
from mpi4py import MPI
import numpy as np

comm = MPI.COMM_WORLD
rank = comm.Get_rank()
size = comm.Get_size()

# msg = [sender, type, clock value]
msg = np.array([-1,-1, -1])
clock = 0
SEND = 1

def tick():
    global clock
    clock = clock + 1

def send_msg(receiver):
    global msg, clock
    clock = clock + 1
    msg[2] = clock
    comm.send(msg, dest=receiver, tag=SEND)


def recv_msg(r):
    global msg, clock
    msg = comm.recv(source=r, tag=MPI.ANY_TAG)
    clock = max(clock,msg[2]) + 1

if rank == 0:
    tick(); tick(); send_msg(1); tick()

if rank == 1:
    tick(); recv_msg(2); recv_msg(0); send_msg(2); tick()

if rank == 2:
    tick(); send_msg(1); recv_msg(1)

print("Rank: {}, clock value: {}".format(rank,clock))
```

Listing 4.8 Output of Logical Clocks Algorithm

```
Rank: 0, clock value: 4
Rank: 1, clock value: 6
Rank: 2, clock value: 6
```

4.4 Vector Clocks

Vector clocks are used to provide a solution to the problem encountered with logical clocks. Each process P_i has a vector $V_i[1, \ldots, n]$ for a system of n processes to store the logical clock values of all processes $P_1, \ldots, P_n$. The entry $v[j]$ in this vector at process P_i shows the best estimate of P_i of the logical time of P_j. Two rules for updating this vector are as follows [2,5]:

- *R1*: At each local event, p_i updates its clock as follows:

$$v[i] = v[i] + 1$$

- *R2*: A process P_i puts its vector V_i in every message it sends to any other process. A process P_j performs the following at each message reception $m(V_j)$ where V_j is the vector of the sender P_j and v_i is the current vector of the receiver process P_i:

    - $V_i[k] = max(V_i[k], V_j[k])$ for $1 \leq k \leq n$. Informally, P_i updates its clock values for the greater of vector entries since P_j may have observed more events of other processes.
    - Implement rule $R1$ since reception of message m is also a local event for process P_i.
    - Deliver message m to the application.

An example implementation of vector clocks between three processes is shown in Fig. 4.6.

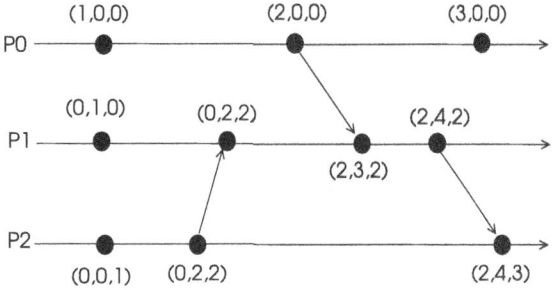

Fig. 4.6 Vector clock example

Python Implementation

Python code for vector clock implementation is shown in Listing 4.9 where the function *vec_tick* increments local clock entry at vector v and is used for a local event. The *vec_send* and *vec_receive* functions implement the vector clock rules for sending and receiving. Running this program with the example scenario of processes of Fig. 4.6 provides the same outputs found manually as displayed in Listing 4.10.

Listing 4.9 Vector Clocks Algorithm

```
from mpi4py import MPI
import numpy as np

comm = MPI.COMM_WORLD
rank = comm.Get_rank()
n = comm.Get_size()

# msg = [sender, type, clock vector]
msg = [-1,-1,[0]*n]
vec_clock = np.zeros((n))
SEND = 1

def vec_tick():
    global vec_clock, rank
    vec_clock[rank] = vec_clock[rank] + 1

def vec_send(receiver):
    global msg, vec_clock
    vec_clock[rank] = vec_clock[rank] + 1
    msg[0] = rank
    msg[1] = vec_clock
    comm.send(msg, dest=receiver, tag=SEND)

def vec_recv(sender):
    global msg, vec_clock
    msg = comm.recv(source=sender, tag=MPI.ANY_TAG)
    clocks = msg[1]
    for i in range(n):
        vec_clock[i] = max(vec_clock[i],clocks[i])
    vec_clock[rank] = vec_clock[rank] + 1

if rank == 0:
    vec_tick(); vec_send(1); vec_tick()

if rank == 1:
    vec_tick(); vec_recv(2); vec_recv(0); vec_send(2)

if rank == 2:
    vec_tick(); vec_send(1); vec_recv(1)
print("Rank: {}, clock value: {}".format(rank,vec_clock))
```

Listing 4.10 Output of Vector Clocks Algorithm

```
Rank: 0, clock value: [3. 0. 0.]
Rank: 1, clock value: [2. 4. 2.]
Rank: 2, clock value: [2. 4. 3.]
```

4.5 Matrix Clocks

The main motivation of a matrix clock based time synchronization is to have a process keep the progress of vector clocks of all other processes in the system. Each process P_i keeps a matrix $M_i[1..n, 1..n]$ with the following properties:

- $M_i[i, i]$ has the logical clock value of P_i.
- $M_i[i, j]$, $j = 1...n$, $j \neq i$ contains the updated clocks of all other processes in the systems as seen by process P_i.
- $M_i[j, k]$, $j = 1...n$, $j \neq i$ displays the clock values of all other processes as known by process P_j which are made known to process P_i.

The following rules are implemented by process P_i when updating the matrix M_i:

- $R1$: P_i updates its local clock value at M_i as below:

$$M_i[i, i] = M[i, i] + 1$$

- $R2$: The matrix M_i is copied to each message sent by P_i.
- $R3$: When process P_i receives a message $m(M_j)$ from a process P_j, it performs the following:
- It updates its local clock values as follows:

  - $M_i[i, k] = max(M_i[i, k], M_j[j, k])$, $k = 1, ..., n$
  - $M_i[k, l] = max(M_i[k, l], M_j[k, l])$, $k, l = 1, ..., n$
  - Run rule $R1$

An example operation of matrix clocks is displayed in Fig. 4.7.

Python Implementation

Matrix clock rules are implemented in the Python code of Listing 4.11 resulting in the final clock values shown in Fig. 4.7 as displayed in Listing 4.12.

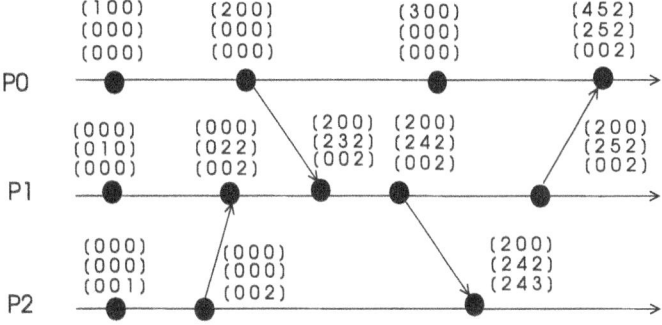

Fig. 4.7 Matrix clock example

Listing 4.11 Matrix Clocks Algorithm

```
from mpi4py import MPI
import numpy as np

comm = MPI.COMM_WORLD
rank = comm.Get_rank()
n = comm.Get_size()

msg = [-1,np.array((n,n))]
mat_clock = np.zeros((n,n))
SEND = 1

def mat_tick():
    global mat_clock, rank
    mat_clock[rank][rank] = mat_clock[rank][rank] + 1

def mat_send(receiver):
    global msg, mat_clock
    mat_clock[rank][rank] = mat_clock[rank][rank] + 1
    msg[0] = rank
    msg[1] = mat_clock
    comm.send(msg, dest=receiver, tag=SEND)


def mat_recv(sender):
    global msg, mat_clock
    msg = comm.recv(source=sender, tag=MPI.ANY_TAG)
    rcvd_clocks = msg[1]
    mat_clock[rank][rank] = mat_clock[rank][rank] + 1
    for i in range (0,n):
        if i == rank:
            continue
        for j in range(n):
            mat_clock[i][j] = max(mat_clock[i][j],rcvd_clocks[i][j
    ])
    for j in range(n):
        mat_clock[rank,j] = max(mat_clock[rank,j],rcvd_clocks[
    sender,j])

if rank == 0:
    mat_tick()
    mat_send(1)
    mat_tick()
    mat_recv(1)

elif rank == 1:
    mat_tick()
    mat_recv(2)
    mat_recv(0)
    mat_send(2)
    mat_send(0)

elif rank == 2:
    mat_tick()
    mat_send(1)
    mat_recv(1)

print("Rank: {}, matrix clock: \n {} ".format(rank,mat_clock))
```

Listing 4.12 Output of Matrix Clocks Algorithm

```
Rank: 1, matrix clock:
 [[2. 0. 0.]
  [2. 5. 2.]
  [0. 0. 2.]]
Rank: 2, matrix clock:
 [[2. 0. 0.]
  [2. 4. 2.]
  [2. 4. 3.]]
Rank: 0, matrix clock:
 [[4. 5. 2.]
  [2. 5. 2.]
  [0. 0. 2.]]
```

4.6 Chapter Notes

Time synchronization in a distributed is needed for nodes to synchronize and coordinate their actions. Many distributed system applications rely on the agreement of nodes in a global time. The notion of global time is difficult to achieve in a distributed system if not impossible. Physical clocks of nodes are not perfect and they drift apart in time due to structures and environmental conditions. Physical clock synchronization may be achieved by internal synchronization of nodes with respect to each other or by synchronization to an external source. We reviewed physical clock synchronization protocols which are Cristian's algorithm, Berkeley Algorithm, and Network Time Protocol. Logical clock synchronization methods assume virtual clocks that are incremented only in local events and *send* and *receive* events. Three main logical clock synchronization methods are Lamport's logical clocks, vector clocks and matrix clocks as we have reviewed. Time synchronization is a well studied topic in distributed systems and recent studies address this problem in mobile ad hoc networks and wireless sensor networks as we will review in Chaps. 12 and 13.

Exercises

1. A client process sends a message m to its NTP server at its time 18 ms. The receiver receives m at its time 24 ms and sends back a reply m' at its time 27 ms by timestamping its reception and sending times. The sender receives this message at its time 25 ms. What is the round trip time (RTT) according to sender and what should be the corrected time of the sender?
2. Find the logical clock values for each event in Fig. 4.8. Run the Python code for logical clocks and compare the values obtained by the program with the values calculated manually.
3. Find the vector clock values for each event in Fig. 4.9. Run the Python code for vector clocks and compare the values obtained by the program with the values calculated manually.

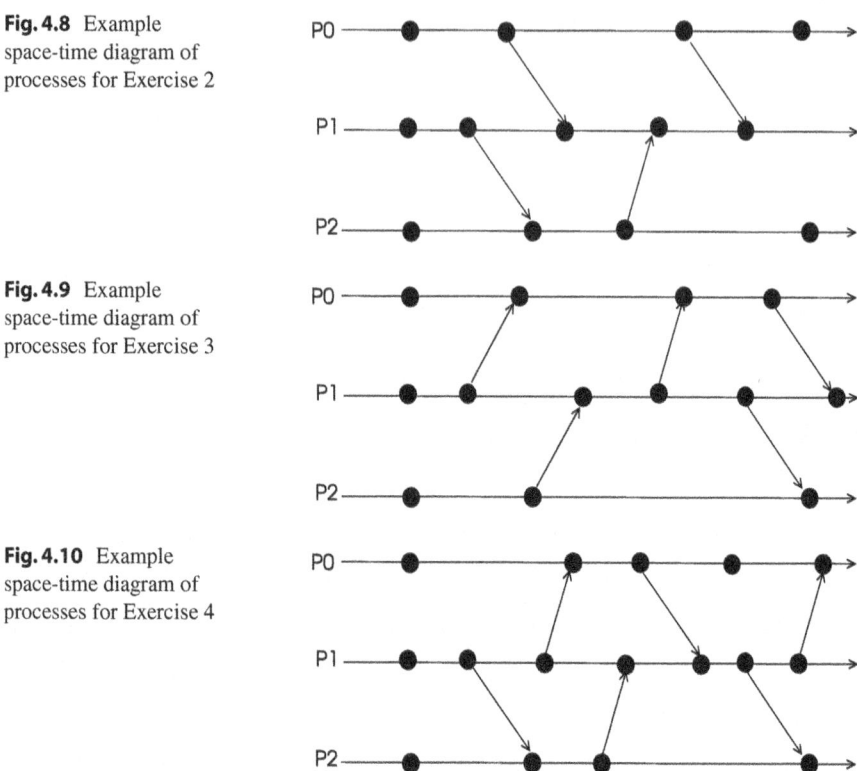

Fig. 4.8 Example space-time diagram of processes for Exercise 2

Fig. 4.9 Example space-time diagram of processes for Exercise 3

Fig. 4.10 Example space-time diagram of processes for Exercise 4

4. Find the matrix clock values for each event in Fig. 4.10. Run the Python code for matrix clocks and compare the values obtained by the program with the values calculated manually.

References

1. F. Cristian, Probabilistic clock synchronization. Distrib. Comput. **3**(3), 146–158 (1989)
2. C.J. Fidge, Timestamps in message-passing systems that preserve the partial ordering, in *Proceedings of the 11th Australian Computer Science Conference (ACSC'88)*, ed. by K. Raymond (1988), pp. 56–66
3. R. Gusella, S. Zatti, The accuracy of clock synchronization achieved by TEMPO in Berkeley Unix 4.3BSD. IEEE Trans. Softw. Eng. SE **15**(7), 847–853 (1989)
4. L. Lamport, Time, clocks, and the ordering of events in distributed systems. Commun. ACM **21**(7), 558–565 (1978)

5. F. Mattern, Virtual time and global states of distributed systems, in *Proceedings of the Workshop on Parallel and Distributed Algorithms* (Elsevier, Chateau de Bonas, 1988), pp. 215–226
6. D.L. Mills, Internet time synchronization: the network time protocol. IEEE Trans. Commun. **39**(10), 1482–1493 (1991)

Distributed Mutual Exclusion 5

Abstract

Distributed mutual exclusion is a fundamental problem in distributed systems since resources are shared and exclusive access to these resources are needed as in a single-node computer system. Algorithms for this purpose may be broadly classified as permission-based or token-based algorithms. A process needs to obtain permission from all other processes to enter its critical section in the former method and the possession of a token entitles a process to enter its CS in the latter method. In this chapter, we review fundamental permission-based and token-based algorithms for distributed mutual exclusion and implement them in Python using *mpi4py*.

5.1 Introduction

Distributed mutual exclusion is a fundamental problem in distributed systems since resources are shared and exclusive access to these resources are needed as in a single-node computer system. A single processor-based system provides mutually exclusive sharing of resources which can be monitored using data structures such as semaphores and locks. These structures are not available in a distributed system that does not have any shared memory, thus, execution of critical sections need to be performed over a communication network by the exchange of messages only.

Distributed mutual exclusion algorithms aim at exclusive resource access in a distributed setting. These algorithms may be broadly classified as permission-based algorithms in which a process that needs to execute a critical section (CS) requests permission from all or a group of processes; and token-based algorithms where the possession of a unique token entitles the holder to enter its CS. We review sample algorithms from these classes, analyse them and provide Python implementations for sample CS execution scenarios in this chapter.

5.2 System Model

We will assume that the distributed system consists of n sites $S_0, ..., S_{n-1}$, $i = 0, ..., (n-1)$ with a single processes P_i running at site S_i and the sole mode of communication is by message passing. A site S_i may be requesting to enter its CS, may be executing its CS or in an idle state. Frequently, a process P_i needs to be aware of the states of other processes in the system and we will find using finite state machines will be convenient in the design of distributed mutual exclusion algorithms.

5.2.1 Requirements

The following properties should be provided by a distributed mutual exclusion algorithm:

- **ME1**, *Safety*: Safety, in general, means bad things will never happen. In this case, safety means only one process should execute its CS at any instant. This property is the simplest requirement from any mutual exclusion algorithm.
- **ME2**, *Liveness*: Liveness, in general, means something good will happen eventually. Starvation is the situation where a process waits infinitely to execute a CS while other processes repeatedly execute CSs. A deadlock condition arises when two or more processes are waiting for each other to execute CS endlessly without any progress. Liveness property of a distributed mutual exclusion algorithm ensures that these two conditions, starvations and deadlocks never happen.
- **ME3**, *Fairness*: Fairness in mutual exclusion is the ability to provide each process a fair opportunity to execute a CS. Enabling process CS entries in the order of request arrivals (FIFO) is a common way to implement fairness in a distributed mutual exclusion algorithm.

5.2.2 Performance Metrics

The following metrics are commonly used to asses the performance of a distributed mutual exclusion algorithm.

- **Message complexity**: The maximum number of messages exchanged for the execution of a critical section.
- **Response time** (R): Time between requesting to be in a critical section and the completion of the CS as displayed in Fig. 5.1 where P_i at site S_i makes a request for a CS and this request is sent over the network by site S_i after which process P_i enters its CS and then finishes.

5.2 System Model

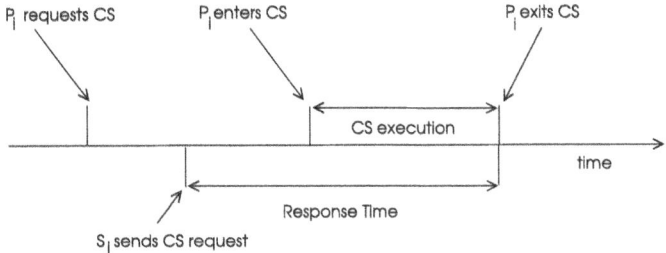

Fig. 5.1 Response time example

Fig. 5.2 Synchronization delay example

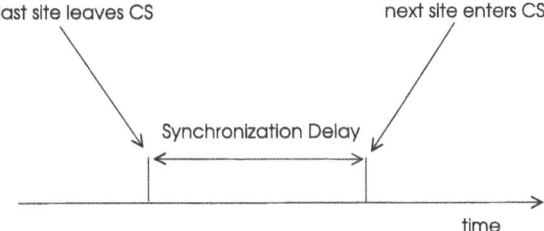

- **Synchronization Delay** (SD): This is the time between completion of a CS by a process and entrance of a CS by the next process as shown in Fig. 5.2 which is denoted by T as one average message transfer time.
- **System throughput** (S): The number of CS executions per second which can be stated as follows with C being the average execution time of the CS:

$$S = \frac{1}{SD + C} \quad (5.1)$$

5.2.3 Algorithm Classes

Distributed mutual exclusion algorithms may be broadly classified according to the method used as follows:

- *Permission-Based Algorithms*: This type of algorithms require exchange of messages among sites to get permission to enter CS as stated. The *request* messages are timestamped to select the earliest request of CS to be fulfilled which means a global clock synchronization is needed.
- *Token-Based Algorithms*: A unique message is exchanged among the sites possession of which entitles the holder to enter its CS as described. Since there is one token in transit, mutual exclusion is guaranteed. A token commonly contains a sequence number to distinguish old and current CS requests.

- *Quorum Algorithms*: The main characteristic of these algorithms is that a process P_i requests permission from a group of sites instead of all of the sites. Any two quorums C_i and C_j share a site C_k which is responsible to monitor mutual exclusion of CS execution.

5.3 Permission-Based Algorithms

Non-token based algorithms are characterised by the agreement of processes on which one of them should enter CS by the exchange of a number of messages. In the simplest case, we can have a central server that decides which process should enter CS based on the reception order of requests sent to it as described in the next section.

5.3.1 Central Server Algorithm

We start with the simple central server algorithm for mutual exclusion. A central node P_c manages the accesses to a shared resource by fulfilling requests if the resource is available and deferring requests until a current process in its CS finishes. The type of messages used in this algorithm are as follows:

- *request*: A process P_i that needs to enter its CS sends this message to P_c.
- *reply*: If the resource is available, P_c replies with this message to the *request* message of P_i so that it can enter its CS.
- *release*: The process P_i sends this message to P_c upon completion of its CS.

The algorithms for the server P_c and a general process P_i may be designed using a FSM as shown in Fig. 5.3. A process P_i can be at IDLE state, waiting for *reply* (REP) message at WAIT state or may be executing its CS at INCS state. The manager process P_c may be IDLE or BUSY meaning some process is executing its CS. A *request* (REQ) message received at BUSY state needs to be queued to be served later when all previous requests are acknowledged.

Mutual exclusion property (ME1) is evident as the central server ensures there is only one process in its CS. Two messages, *request* and *reply*, are needed to enter a CS and exiting a CS takes one message, *release* (REL), for a total of three messages per CS execution. Two messages, *release* and *reply*, are transferred between one

5.3 Permission-Based Algorithms

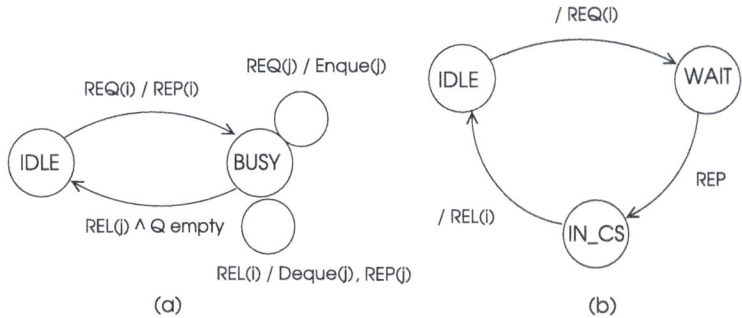

Fig. 5.3 States of **a** central server **b** node of the central server algorithm

process leaving a CS and another one entering CS. Thus, synchronization delay is $2T$ with two messages. As with all distributed algorithms with a central managerial node, this algorithm suffers a bottleneck of messages around the server and the server is a single point of failure.

Python Implementation

Python implementation of the central mutual exclusion is implemented using the FSM of Fig. 5.3 as shown in Listing 5.1. We assume there are four processes in the system with P_0 as the central server and all other processes request CS asynchronously. Different runs of the algorithm may result in different sequence of CS executions by the processes as messages may be received by the central server in any order. An example output of this algorithm is displayed in Listing 5.2. In order to terminate the program, we set the total number of messages to be received by the central server to six; with two messages per CS execution of each process.

Listing 5.1 Central Mutex Algorithm

```
from mpi4py import MPI
import numpy as np

comm = MPI.COMM_WORLD
rank = comm.Get_rank()
size = comm.Get_size()

#states of the server
IDLE, BUSY = 0, 1
msg = [-1,-1]    # rank, type

# message types
REQUEST, REPLY, RELEASE = 0, 1, 2
MAX_ENTRY = 3
Wait_Q = []
state = IDLE

if rank == 0: # server
    for i in range(0,MAX_ENTRY*2):
        msg = comm.recv(source=MPI.ANY_SOURCE, tag=MPI.ANY_TAG)
        sender, typ = msg[0], msg[1]
        msg[0] = rank
```

```
23      if typ == REQUEST:
24          if state == IDLE:
25              msg[1] = REPLY
26              comm.send(msg, dest=sender, tag=REPLY)
27              state = BUSY
28          else:
29              Wait_Q.append(sender)
30      else: # RELEASE received
31          if len(Wait_Q) == 0:
32              state = IDLE
33          else:
34              next_node = Wait_Q.pop(0)
35              msg[1] = REPLY
36              comm.send(msg, dest=next_node, tag=REPLY)
37
38  else: # node
39      msg[0], msg[1] = rank, REQUEST # request CS
40      comm.send(msg, dest=0, tag=REQUEST)
41      msg = comm.recv(source=0, tag=REPLY)
42      print("Rank: {}, in CS".format(rank))
43      msg[1] = RELEASE  # release CS
44      comm.send(msg, dest=0, tag=RELEASE)
```

Listing 5.2 Output of Central Mutex Algorithm

```
Rank: 2, in CS
Rank: 1, in CS
Rank: 3, in CS
```

5.3.2 Lamport's Algorithm

Lamport provided a distributed mutual exclusion algorithm using the logical clocks for site synchronization [2]. This algorithm further assumes that the communication channels deliver messages in FIFO order in a network of completely connected nodes. Message types used are *request* sent by a process P_i to all other processes to request a CS, *release* to inform all processes the CS execution is finished, and *reply* to a CS request. Each site maintains a request queue (Req_Q) to hold CS request messages in the order of their logical time stamps. The following procedures are performed by a process P_i for CS execution:

- *CS Request*:
  - Broadcast a request message with timestamp ts_i, $request(i, ts_i)$, to all sites and place this message in request queue Req_Q_i.
  - If $request(j, ts_j)$ is received from a site S_j, place it in Req_Q_i and send a reply message with a timestamp, $reply(i, ts_i)$, to site S_j.

- *CS Execution*: Enter CS when both of the following conditions are satisfied:
  - **L1**: $reply(j, ts_j)$ messages are received from all other sites.

- **L2**: Own request $request(i, ts_i)$ is at the top of Req_Q_i.

- *CS Release*:
  - Remove $request(i, ts_i)$ from the top of Req_Q_i and broadcast a timestamped release message, $release(i, ts_i)$ to all other sites.
  - If $release(j, ts_j)$ is received from a site S_j, remove its request from request queue Req_Q_i.

Analysis

Theorem 5.1 *Lamport's algorithm achieves mutual exclusion.*

Proof We will prove ME1 for this algorithm using contradiction. Let us assume process P_i at site S_i and process P_j at site S_j are executing their CSs concurrently. This case is possible only when both conditions L1 and L2 are valid for these processes. Thus, both P_i and P_j should have their requests at the top of their request queues by the condition L1 at some time t. Let us further assume that request of P_i has a smaller timestamp than the timestamp of P_j at this point in time. Since communication channels are FIFO, request of P_i must be in the request queue Req_Q_j of process P_j. Thus, request of P_j is at the top of its Req_Q_j when a request with a smaller timestamp is in this queue which is a contradiction. □

Each CS execution using this algorithm needs $(n-1)$ messages for $request$ messages, $(n-1)$ messages for $reply$ messages and $(n-1)$ messages for $release$ messages for a total of $3(n-1)$ messages.

5.3.3 Ricart-Agrawala Algorithm

Ricart-Agrawala (RA) algorithm also relies on logical clocks for site synchronization as in Lamport's algorithm, it also assumes FIFO delivery of messages by the communication channels on a completely connected network of nodes [5]. Time stamped *request* messages, and *reply* messages are used to synchronize CS executions, but the *release* messages are removed in this algorithm providing a significant gain in performance. Each process P_i maintains a vector of deferred requests $RD[n]$ initialized to zeros for every process in the system. If a process P_i defers a CS request by a Process P_j, it sets $RD[j] = 1$ and when P_i sends a reply message to P_j, it sets $P_j = 0$.

Different than Lamport's algorithm, reception of $(n-1)$ *reply* messages from all other processes is needed only for a process to enter its CS. Thus, RA algorithm provides an optimization of Lamport's algorithm by sending a *reply* message only when CS execution to a process is allowed. The following rules are implemented to enter CS, execute CS and exit CS in this algorithm.

- *CS Request*:
  - Send a request message with timestamp ts_i, $request(i, ts_i)$ to all other processes.
  - When a $request(j, ts_j)$ is received from a process P_j, do the following:
    Send a $reply(i)$ message to P_j if not requesting or executing a CS; or requesting CS but time stamp t_j in $request(j, ts_j)$ message is lower than the time stamp t_i sent in own request message $request(i, ts_i)$. Else defer the $reply(i)$ message to P_j and set $RD[j] = 1$.
- *CS Execution*: Enter CS when $reply(j)$ message is received from all other processes.
- *CS Release*: Send $reply(j)$ to each process P_j if $RD[j] = 1$, and then set $RD[j] = 0$ for these processes.

An Example Operation

An example operation of RA algorithm with five processes P_0, ..., P_4 is depicted in Fig. 5.4. A process may be in one of the IDLE, REQ or INCS states denoting idle, CS requesting and inside the CS states. Processes P_0, P_2 and P_4 simultaneously request CS with time stamps 3, 5 and 1 respectively. Since both processes P_1 and P_3 are in IDLE state, they answer with *reply* messages to these requests in (a). Processes P_0 and P_2 send *reply* messages to the requesting processes P_4 as request of P_4 has a lower timestamp than the timestamps of their requests. Process P_4 inserts the requests of $P0$ and P_2 in its RD and can now enter its CS as in (b). Note that the message transfers in (a) and (b) occur concurrently. When $P4$ finishes executing its CS, it sends *reply* messages to the waiting processes in RD in (c) and $P0$ can now enter its CS as it has reply messages from all other processes. Finally, $P0$ finishes its CS and sends reply to the only waiting process $P2$ in its RD which can now execute its CS.

Analysis

Theorem 5.2 *RA algorithm provides mutual exclusion (ME1 property).*

Proof Let us assume that two processes P_i and P_j are both in their CS which would mean they have sent *reply* messages to each other. Therefore, $ts_i < ts_j$ and $ts_j < ts_i$ which is a contradiction. Let us assume the case that P_i has a smaller timestamp and P_i receives P_j's request after it makes its own request. Process P_j can enter its CS concurrently with P_i if it receives a $reply(i, ts_i$ message from P_i before P_i exits

5.3 Permission-Based Algorithms

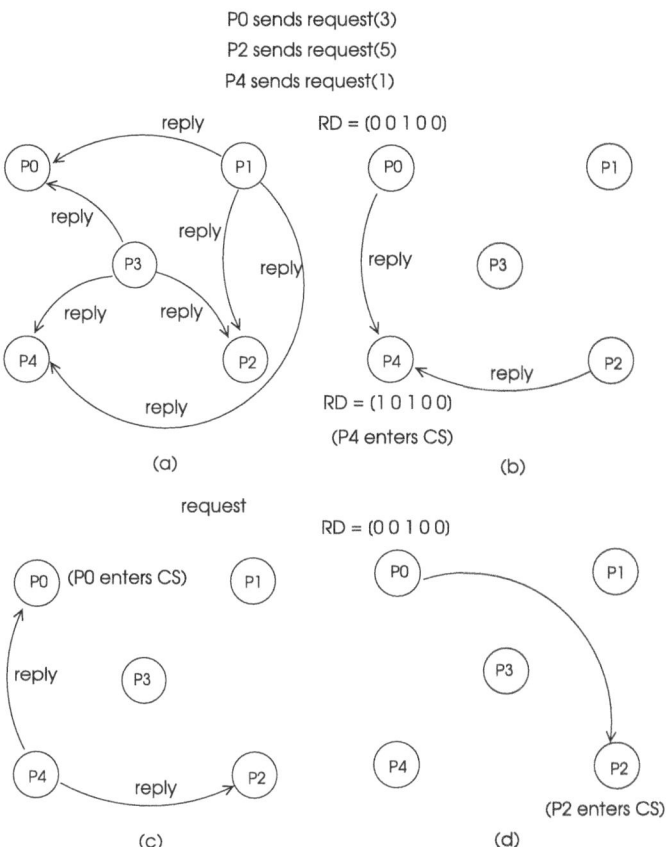

Fig. 5.4 An example operation of RA algorithm with four processes

the CS. This is not possible since the request of P_j, $request(j, ts_j)$, has a greater timestamp than that of P_i's request, therefore a contradiction again. □

A CS execution in RA algorithm requires $(n-1)$ *request* and $(n-1)$ *reply* messages for a total of $2(n-1)$ messages. Synchronization delay is simply one *reply* message transfer time.

Python Implementation

We will implement the RA algorithm in Python for the process execution scenario of Fig. 5.4 where processes P_0, P_2, and P_4 make concurrent CS requests. Any IDLE process simply returns a *reply* message to these requests and any CS requesting process with state REQ compares timestamps in an incoming *reply* message and its own request, sends a *reply* message to the sender if its own timestamp is higher as shown in Listing 5.3. Otherwise, it sets the entry of the sender in RD array. We use a variable *over* to enable termination of the program.

Listing 5.3 RA Algorithm

```python
from mpi4py import MPI

comm = MPI.COMM_WORLD
rank = comm.Get_rank()
n    = comm.Get_size()

IDLE, REQ, INCS = 0, 1, 2  #states of a node
REQUEST, REPLY= 0, 1 # message types
msg = [-1,-1,-1]   # message[sender,type,timestamp]
RD = [0]*n # Requests Deferred List
state = IDLE
replies = set() # set to hold replies
neighs = set([0,1,2,3,4]) # others
neighs.remove(rank)
#print(neighs)

if rank == 0: # P0 sends a request for CS with ts=3
    state = REQ
    my_msg = [rank,REQUEST,3]
    for node in range(1,5):
        comm.send(my_msg, dest=node, tag=REQUEST)

elif rank==4:  # P2 sends a request for CS with ts=1
    state = REQ
    my_msg = [rank,REQUEST,1]
    for node in range(0,5):
        if node != 4:
            comm.send(my_msg, dest=node, tag=REQUEST)

elif rank==2:  # P2 sends a request for CS with ts=5
    state = REQ
    my_msg = [rank,REQUEST,5]
    for node in range(0,5):
        if node != 2:
            comm.send(my_msg, dest=node, tag=REQUEST)

over = False
count = 0
while not over:
    msg = comm.recv(source=MPI.ANY_SOURCE, tag=MPI.ANY_TAG)
    sender, typ, ts_rcvd = msg[0], msg[1], msg[2]
    msg[0] = rank
    if typ == REQUEST: # REQUEST received
        if state == IDLE:
            msg[1] = REPLY
            comm.send(msg, dest=sender, tag=REPLY)
            count = count + 1
            if count == 3:
                over = True
        elif state == REQ:
            if ts_rcvd < my_msg[2]: # check time stamps
                msg[1] = REPLY
                comm.send(msg, dest=sender, tag=REPLY)
            else:
                RD[sender] = 1
    else: # REPLY received
        replies.add(sender)
        if replies == neighs: # enter CS
            print("rank: {}, in CS".format(rank))
            msg[0] = rank
            for i in range(0,n): # send deferred REPLYs
```

```
62              if RD[i] == 1:
63                  msg[1] = REPLY
64                  comm.send(msg, dest=i, tag=REPLY)
65                  RD[i] = 0
66              over = True
```

The output of this algorithm shows the execution sequence of processes with respect to the timestamp value of their requests. As displayed in Listing 5.4, all processes enter their CSs as in the sequence of Fig. 5.4.

Listing 5.4 Output of RA Algorithm

```
rank: 4, in CS
rank: 0, in CS
rank: 2, in CS
```

5.4 Token-Based Algorithms

Token based algorithms are characterised by the possession of a special message called *token* to enter a CS. Mutual exclusion using a token is guaranteed as there is a single token. However, regeneration of a token when it is lost due to the failing of the site that holds it, starvation and deadlock issues still need be addressed. In the simplest form, processes may be configured as a ring and the token is continuously circulated in this ring. Any process that does not require to be in CS, sends the token to its proceeding node. A process that needs to execute a CS holds the token and sends it to the next node upon completion of the CS. Synchronization delay in this method varies from 1 to $(n-1)$ multiples of CS execution time. Safety is guaranteed as there is only one token, however lost of token and generating a new one are the main issues to be dealt with in this approach as stated. Moreover, a process executing CS multiple times while holding the token may cause starvation of other processes. We will review two classical token-based algorithms for mutual exclusion: Suzuki-Kasami algorithm and Raymond's algorithm.

5.4.1 Suzuki-Kasami Algorithm

Suzuki-Kasami token-based algorithm assumes a completely connected structure of nodes and uses the *request* and *token* messages, any node that requires a CS broadcasts a *request* message to all other nodes [6]. The node that has the token sends a *token* message to the sender to allow its access to its CS. A node that receives a *request* message when it is in its CS defers sending the *token* message until it finishes. The following data structures are maintained by each process P_i:

- An array of integers $RN_i[1...N]$ to hold request numbers by processes where $RN_i[j]$ is the current largest sequence number received using *request* message from process P_j.

- An array of integers $LN_i[1...N]$ contained in token where $LN[j]$ is the sequence number of the request that was last executed by P_j.
- A queue Q that is used by the token to trace the identities of processes with pending token requests. A process at the top of Q can enter its CS.

Using these structures, the operation of this algorithm by process P_i at site S_i is as follows:

- *CS Request*:
  - If token is not possessed, increment sequence $RN_i[i]$, set sequence number $sn = RN_i[i]$ and send a $request(i, sn)$ to all other processes.
  - When a $request(j, sn)$ is received from a process P_j, do the following:

    Set $RN_i[j] = max(RN_i[j], sn)$
    If token is at site and if $RN_i[j] = LN[j] + 1$, send token to P_j.

- *CS Execution*: Enter CS when *token* message is received from the token holding process.

- *CS Release*: When a process P_i finishes executing its CS, it does the following:
  - Set $LN[i] = RN_i[i]$ to indicate its CS execution is completed.
  - For any $P_j \notin Q$, append P_j to Q if $RN_i[j] = LN[j] + 1$
  - If $Q \neq \emptyset$, remove a process P_j from the top of Q and send token to P_j.
  - If Q is empty, keep the token.

An Example Operation

An example operation of Suzuki-Kasami algorithm with five processes is shown in Fig. 5.5 where the token holding process is shown in grey and the local RN vectors are displayed next to processes and the token with vector LN and its queue Q is shown inside a rectangle next to the holding process. Initially process P_1 has the token and it has already sent *request* messages so that all processes have have updated their RN vectors as shown in (a). Processes P_4 and P_2 broadcast *request* messages, all nodes update their RN vectors to reflect these requests and the token holding P_1 queues these requests in the token queue Q in (b). Process P_1 finishes its CS, sets its entry in the token vector LN to indicate its termination of the CS, removes P_4 from the top of queue Q and sends *token* to P_4 in (c). At this time, process P_3 broadcasts a *request* message and all nodes update their RN vectors accordingly and the token holding node P_4 queues P_3 in the token queue Q in (d). Process P_4 finishes its CS, sets its entry in token vector LN, removes the first process which is P_2 from the token queue Q and sends the token to P_2 in (e). Lastly, P_2 finishes executing its CS,

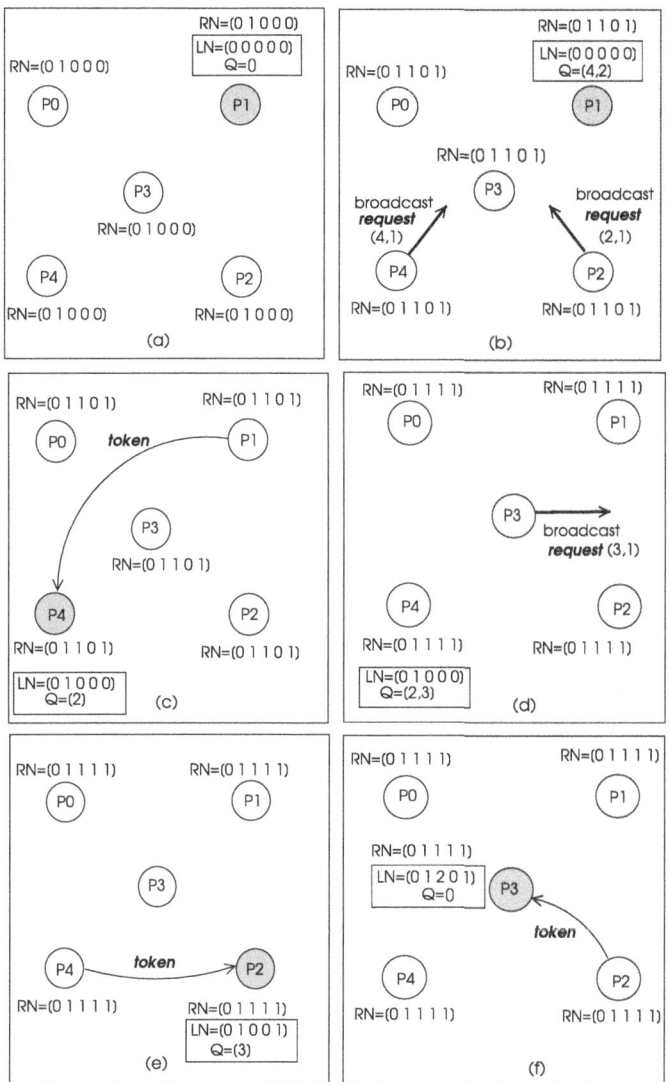

Fig. 5.5 An example operation of Suzuki-Kasami algorithm with five processes

increments its entry in token vector LN, removes P_3 from token queue Q and sends the *token* to P_3 which can now enter its CS.

Analysis

Mutual exclusion (ME1) is guaranteed as there is a unique token possession of which enables the holder to execute its CS. A process requesting to enter its CS sends a *request* message to all other processes, this request will be put in token queue and there will be $(n-1)$ processes in the queue in the worst case resulting in finite time for a process to enter a CS (ME2), thus, starvation is not possible.

Python Implementation

Implementing SK algorithm in Python is realized by the provision of functions for requesting a CS, reception of a *token*, reception of a *request* message and releasing a CS as in Listing 5.5. The scenario of the process actions in Fig. 5.5 is used with process P_1 holding the token initially and processes P_4, P_3 and P_2 make CS requests. The output in Listing 5.6 shows all CS requests are satisfied. Different runs of this algorithm resulted in different sequence of CS executions such as P_3, P_2, P_4 and P_4, P_2, P_3 due to undetermined message delivery times. Wait time of each process is set at $waits$ vector to enable termination which can be configured for a different scenario.

Listing 5.5 Suzuki-Kasami Algorithm

```
from mpi4py import MPI
import time

comm = MPI.COMM_WORLD
rank = comm.Get_rank()
n    = comm.Get_size()

IDLE, REQ, INCS = 0, 1, 2 #states of a node
REQUEST, TOKEN = 1, 2 # message types
allprocs = list(range(0,n))
neighs = set(allprocs) # others
neighs.remove(rank)
RN = [0] * n  # request vector initial state
token = [[0]*n, []] # token with token[0]=LN, token[1]=Q
msg = [-1,-1,-1,token]  # message[sender,type, sn, token]
has_token = False

def CS_Request():
    RN[rank] = RN[rank] + 1 # increment request number
    sn = RN[rank]
    msg = [rank, REQUEST, sn, token] # send request to all
    for node in neighs:
        comm.send(msg, dest=node, tag=REQUEST)

def Token_Recvd():  # token received, enter CS
    global has_token
    has_token = True
    print("rank: {} in CS".format(rank))
    CS_Release()   # release CS

def Request_Recvd(sender,sn): # request received
    global RN, has_token, token
    RN[sender] = max(RN[sender],sn) # send token if posessed
    if has_token and RN[sender] == token[0][sender]+1:
        has_token = False
        msg = [rank,TOKEN,-1,token]
        comm.send(msg, dest=sender, tag=TOKEN)

def CS_Release():
    global token, RN, has_token
    token[0][rank] = RN[rank]     # CS finished
    for node in neighs:
        if node not in token[1]:  # queue any pending requests
```

5.4 Token-Based Algorithms

```
44            if RN[node] == token[0][node]+1:
45                token[1].append(node)
46        if len(token[1]) != 0:       # send token to first in Q
47            node = token[1].pop(0)
48            has_token = False
49            msg = [rank, TOKEN, -1, token]
50            comm.send(msg, dest=node, tag=TOKEN)
51
52 if rank == 1:
53    has_token = True
54 if rank == 2 or rank == 3 or rank == 4:
55    CS_Request()
56
57 count = 0
58 waits = [3,3,3,3,3]  # number of messages to wait
59 while count < waits[rank]:
60    msg = comm.recv(source=MPI.ANY_SOURCE, tag=MPI.ANY_TAG)
61    count = count + 1
62    sender, typ, sn, token1 = msg[0], msg[1], msg[2], msg[3]
63    if typ == REQUEST:
64        Request_Recvd(sender,sn)
65    else:
66        token = token1
67        Token_Recvd()
```

Listing 5.6 Output of RA Algorithm

```
Rank: 3 in CS
Rank: 4 in CS
Rank: 2 in CS
```

5.4.2 Raymond's Token-Based Algorithm

Raymond's token-based (RT) algorithm assumes the existence of a dynamic spanning tree over the communication network of the distributed system [4]. The root of the tree is the current holder of the token and the messages are transferred only over the edges of the spanning tree. At any time, a node has a parent which is oriented towards the node that holds the token. The main idea of this algorithm is to dynamically update the spanning tree such that the current token holder becomes the new root and a request is always forwarded towards the root. In order to handle multiple requests, each process P_i maintains a local queue Req_Q_i to hold any token requests from its subtree.

The working of this algorithm assuming the usual states IDLE, REQ and INCS for being in idle state, token requesting state and in CS state is as follows. When a process needs to execute a CS, it changes its state to REQ and checks whether it has the token by testing its parent. If it has the token, it changes its state to INCS and executes its CS. Otherwise, it stores itself in the Req_Q_i and sends a *request* message to its parent if it is the only process in this queue. Having more than process in this queue means a *request* message has already been sent to the parent, therefore, duplication is avoided by not sending this message again.

CS_Request:

- state = REQ
- **if** parent = NULL **then**

    - state = INCS
    - do CS work.

- **else**

    - Store P_i in Req_Q_i
    - **if** there is only one process in Req_Q_i **then** send $request(i)$ to parent.

When a process P_i finishes executing a CS, it changes its state to IDLE, removes the first entry P_j from Req_Q, sends token to P_j and sets P_j as its parent. If Req_Q is not empty, a *request* message is sent to parent.

CS Release:

- $state$ = IDLE
- **if** $Req\_Q_i \neq$ NULL **then**

    - Remove the head P_j of Req_Q_i
    - Send token to P_j; parent = P_j
    - **if** $Req\_Q_i \neq \emptyset$ **then** send $request(i)$ to parent.

5.4 Token-Based Algorithms

Reception of request$_j$:

- **if** *parent* = NULL **then**

  - **if** state = INCS **then** Append P_j in Req_Q_i
  - **else** send token to P_j; *parent* = P_j

- **else**

  - Append P_i in Req_Q_i
  - **if** there is only one process in Req_Q_i **then** send $request(i)$ to parent

Reception of token$_j$:

- *parent* = NULL
- Remove the head P_j of Req_Q_i
- **if** $P_j = P_i$ **then** *state* = INCS
- **else**

  - send token to P_j
  - parent = P_j
  - **if** $Req\_Q_i \neq \emptyset$ **then** send $request(i)$ to parent.

An example operation of this algorithm in a distributed system with 5 processes $P_0, ..., P_4$ is depicted in Fig. 5.6 where a process holding the token is shown in grey and request and token message transfers are shown with bold arrows. Initially, P_3 has the token. Process P_4 makes a request for CS by sending a *request* message to its parent P_0 and putting itself in its Req_Q. Process P_0 puts this request in its queue and sends a *request* message to the token holder P_3 which puts P_0 in its queue and concurrently P_2 makes a request for *token* to its parent P_3 in (a). This request is queued in its and P_3's queues. Process P_1 makes a request queued in P_0 and P_3 in (b) of the figure. At this point in time, P_3 sends the *token* to the first process in its queue which is P_0, in (c). Process P_0 deletes the first process in its queue and sends the *token* which can now clear its queue and execute its CS in (d). Upon finishing its CS, P_4 sends the *token* to P_0 which is now the token holder and the root of the tree in (e). Process P_0 now deletes the top of its queue and sends the *token* to P_1 which puts the sender P_0 to its queue and becomes the root of the tree and the owner of the *token* in (f), and can now execute its CS. Upon termination of its CS, P_1 sends the *token* to the only process in its queue which is P_0 in (g). Process P_0 has P_3

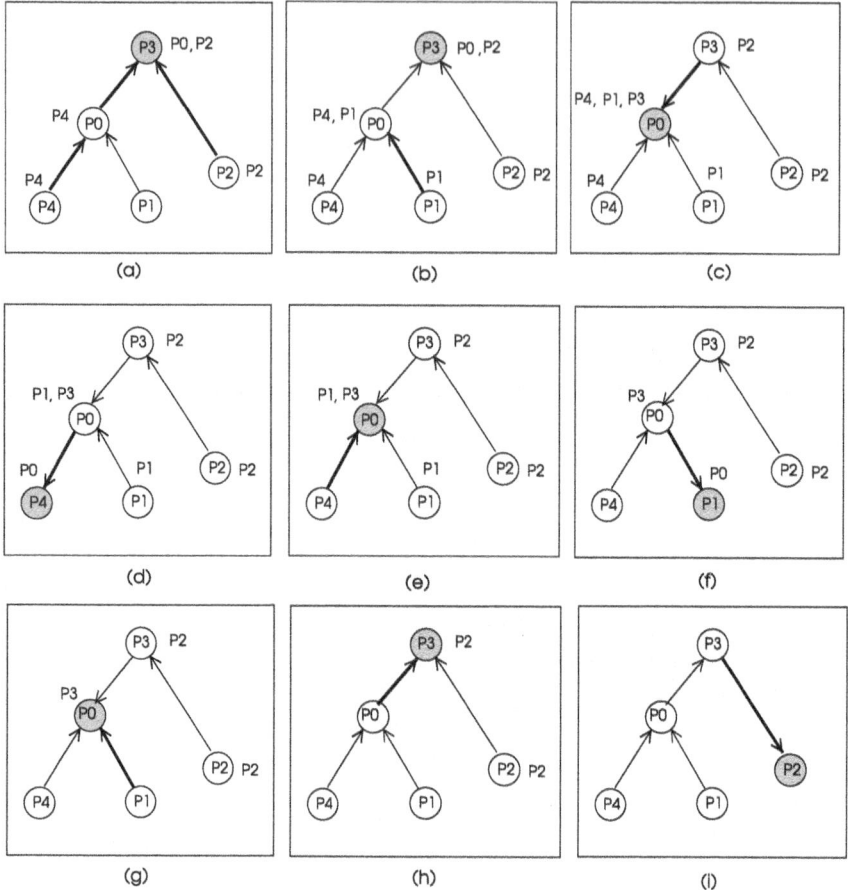

Fig. 5.6 An example operation of Raymond's algorithm with five processes

in its queue, thus, it sends the *token* to P_3 which becomes the holder of the *token* temporarily as it is not requesting a CS entrance in (h). Lastly, process P_2 receives the *token* from P_3 and executes its CS in (i). We can see that the order of requests is obeyed while delivering the token.

Raymond's algorithm provides mutual exclusion as there is exactly one root holding the token at any time. It is also starvation-free since a request eventually reaches the top of a request queue to be processed. The message complexity of this algorithm is $O(d)$ where d is the diameter of the tree. The average diameter of a randomly chosen tree of order n is $O(\log n)$ which is the average message complexity of Raymond's algorithm. The synchronization delay varies under load performing better under heavy load achieving transfer of four messages per CS [4].

5.4 Token-Based Algorithms

Python Implementation

We implement rules of Raymond's algorithm in Listing 5.7 as Python functions for a scenario of where process P_3 is the initial holder of the token and processes P_4 and P_2 make CS requests in sequence. The structure of the tree is modified to always orient towards the token holding node and all CS requests are satisfied as displayed in the output in Listing 5.8.

Listing 5.7 Raymond's Algorithm

```python
from mpi4py import MPI
import time

comm = MPI.COMM_WORLD
rank = comm.Get_rank()
n    = comm.Get_size()

IDLE, REQ, INCS = 1, 2, 3  #states of a node
REQUEST, TOKEN = 1, 2      #message types
msg = [-1,-1]   # message[sender,type]
Req_Q = []  # Requests Queue
state = IDLE
parents = [3, 0, 3, 3, 0]
parent = parents[rank]
sleeps = [ 0, 2, 1, 0, 0 ]

def CS_Request():
    global state, parent, rank, REQ, INCS
    state = REQ
    if parent == rank:  # has token
        state = INCS
        print("rank: {} in CS".format(rank))  # execute CS
        CS_Release()
    else:
        Req_Q.append(rank)
        if len(Req_Q)==1:
            msg = [rank, REQUEST]
            comm.send(msg, dest=parent, tag=REQUEST)

def CS_Release():
    global state, parent, Req_Q
    state = IDLE
    if len(Req_Q) != 0:
        node = Req_Q.pop(0)
        msg = [node, TOKEN]
        parent = node
        comm.send(msg, dest=node, tag=TOKEN)
        if len(Req_Q) != 0:  # more processes on queue
            msg = [rank, REQUEST]
            comm.send(msg, dest=parent, tag=REQUEST)

def Request_Recvd(sender):
    global state, parent
    if parent == rank:
        Req_Q.append(sender)
        msg = [rank, TOKEN]
        node = Req_Q.pop(0)
        parent = node
        comm.send(msg, dest=node, tag=TOKEN)
    else:
        if sender not in Req_Q:
```

```
           Req_Q.append(sender)
       if len(Req_Q) == 1:
           msg = [rank, REQUEST]
           comm.send(msg, dest=parent, tag=REQUEST)

def Token_Recvd():
    global state, parent, Req_Q
    node = Req_Q.pop(0)
    parent = node
    if rank == parent:
        state = INCS
        print("rank: {} in CS".format(rank))
        CS_Release()
    else:
        msg = [rank, TOKEN]
        comm.send(msg, dest=node, tag=TOKEN)
        parent = node
        if len(Req_Q) != 0: # more processes on queue
            msg = [rank, REQUEST]
            comm.send(msg, dest=parent, tag=REQUEST)

time.sleep(sleeps[rank])
if rank==4 or rank==2:
    CS_Request()

count = 0
waits = [4,0,1,3,2]
while count < waits[rank]:
    msg = comm.recv(source=MPI.ANY_SOURCE, tag=MPI.ANY_TAG)
    count = count + 1
    sender, typ = msg[0], msg[1]
    if typ == REQUEST:
        Request_Recvd(sender)
    elif typ == TOKEN:
        Token_Recvd()
```

Listing 5.8 Output of RA Algorithm

```
rank: 4 in CS
rank: 2 in CS
```

5.5 Quorum-Based Algorithms

Quorum based algorithms are characterised by dividing the processes into overlapping subsets (quorums) so that permissions are sought from a subset only, thereby reducing the message complexity.

Maekawa's Algorithm

Maekawa's algorithm is a permission-based algorithm that provides mutual exclusion in a distributed system [3]. It works similar to RA algorithm with a reduced set of processes. Three types of messages used in this algorithm are *request*, *reply* and *release* as in RA algorithm. A process sends a *request* message to only processes in its quorum and it sends a *release* message again to only processes in its

5.5 Quorum-Based Algorithms

quorum. Construction of the quorums specified by the following rules is crucial in the operation of this algorithm:

- M1: There is at least one common process between the request sets of any two processes P_i and P_j, that is:

$$\forall i, \forall j : i \neq j, 1 \leq i, j \leq n :: R_i \cap R_j \neq \emptyset$$

- M2: Every process P_i is a member of its request set R_i:

$$\forall i : i \neq j, 1 \leq i \leq n :: P_i \in R_i$$

- M3: The size of a request set is K:

$$\forall i : i \neq j, 1 \leq i \leq n :: |R_i| = K$$

- M4: A process P_i is contained in exactly K request sets.

Using the projective planes theory, Maekawa showed that $N = K(K + 1)$ which means $K \approx \sqrt{N}$. The detailed working of this algorithm is as follows:

state = IDLE,

- *CS Request*:
  - Send a *request(i)* message to all other processes in the request set R_i.
  - When a *request(j)* is received from a process P_j, it sends a *reply(i)* to P_j if it has not sent a *reply* message to P_j since it received the last *release* message. Otherwise queue the *request(j)* message in *Req_Q*.

- *CS Execution*: Enter CS when *reply(j)* message is received from all other processes in request set R_i.

- *CS Release*:
  - Send *release(i)* to all processes P_j in R_i.
  - When *release(j)* is received from a process P_j, remove the first process from the *Req_Q* and send *reply(i)* message to that process. If *Req_Q* is empty, update state to reflect that no *reply* messages are sent since the receipt of the last *release* message.

Let us consider a process set with 7 processes, $P_0, ..., P_6$. Six request sets with $K = 3$ can be formed as follows:

$$R_0 = 0, 1, 2 \quad R_1 = 1, 3, 5 \quad R_2 = 2, 4, 5 \quad R_3 = 0, 3, 4$$

$$R_4 = 1, 4, 6 \quad R_5 = 0, 5, 6 \quad R_6 = 2, 3, 6$$

Note that we need seven such sets since each process should be a member of its set by M2. Also, sets are selected such that there is at least one process that belongs to any two sets by M1. Let us consider the case when P_1 and P_5 make concurrent request to execute their CSs using their assigned sets. Process P_1 sends *request* messages to P_3 and P_5 in its request set R_1, and P_6 sends *request* messages to P_2 and P_3 in its request set R_6. Assuming P_1 request reaches R_1 before P_6 request reaches R_6, P_3 and P_5 will send *reply* messages to P_1 enabling it to execute its CS. Since P_5 is the common element between the two request sets, it will not send a *reply* message to P_6 deferring its CS execution.

Analysis

Consider the case where P_i and P_j want to enter CS concurrently. There will be a process $P_k = P_i \cap P_j$ and it will not send a *reply* message to both P_i and P_j, ensuring the ME1 property.

Each CS execution needs $\sqrt{N}$ request, $\sqrt{N}$ reply and $\sqrt{N}$ release messages for a total of $3\sqrt{N}$ messages. A process exiting its CS sends a *release* message to its request set R_i and a process in this set sends a *reply* message to another request set with a process waiting to execute a CS. These two sequential message transfers result in $2T$ synchronization delay.

Unfortunately, Maekawa's algorithm is prone to deadlocks. This problem can be solved by the introduction of the following messages:

- *failed*: Sending of this message from process P_i to P_j indicates a negative reply to the request of P_j as P_i has granted permission to a process with a higher request.
- *inquire*: Sent by P_i to P_j to find if P_j has locked all processes in its request set.
- *yield*: Process P_i gives permission to process P_j.

Let us assume that a process P_i at site S_i sends a $request(ts, i)$ to a process P_j at site S_j using this version of the algorithm. A $reply(j)$ message is sent by P_j to P_i if resource is available, as in the first version of the algorithm. If resource is being used by a process P_k, a $failed(j)$ message is sent to P_i if it has a larger timestamp than that the request of P_k. If timestamp of the request message of P_i is lower than that of P_k which is currently holding the resource, P_j sends an $inquire(j)$ message to P_k. If P_k has received a *failed* message from a process in its request set or it has sent a *yield* message to a process in its request set but has not received a new *reply* message from it, it sends a $yield(k)$ to process P_j. When process P_j receives this message, it becomes aware that the resource is released by process P_k, it sends a *reply* message to the process on top of its request queue and places request of P_k

Table 5.1 Comparison of distributed mutual exclusion algorithms

	Message complexity	Synch. delay	Problems
Central	3	$2T$	Single point of failure, bottleneck
Lamport algorithm	$3(n-1)$	T	High number of messages
RA algorithm	$2(n-1)$	T	High number of messages
Suzuki-K algorithm	n	T	Lost/duplicate token
Raymond algorithm	$4 - O(\log n)$	$T(4 - \log n)$	Lost/duplicate token
Maekawa algorithm	$3\sqrt{N}$	$2T$	Deadlock possible

in its request queue. Message complexity of CS execution in the modified algorithm is $O(5\sqrt{n})$ due to extra messages [1].

5.6 Chapter Notes

We reviewed the main distributed mutual exclusion algorithms in this chapter. The three basic types are non-token or permission-based, token-based and quorum algorithms. A node that wants to execute a CS solicits permission from all other nodes in the first class. Lamport's algorithm and Ricart-Agrawala algorithms belong to this class which both rely on logical clock synchronization. A request with a lower timestamp is granted an access to its CS when multiple processes demand CS.

Token-based algorithms have a simpler operation as possession of a token entitles a process to enter its CS. However, outstanding and concurrent requests need be handled as in Suzuki-Kasami algorithm. Raymond's token-based algorithm takes a different approach by considering a dynamic spanning tree over the network. The node that has the token is the root of the tree and whenever token is transferred to another node, that node becomes the new root. Quorum-based algorithms consider asking permission from a subset of nodes when requesting a CS as in Maekawa's algorithm. Message complexities and synchronization delays of the algorithms reviewed are displayed in Table 5.1 where T is the average message transfer time between two processes.

Fig. 5.7 An example process tree for Exercise 3

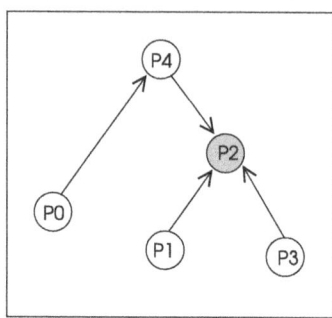

Exercises

1. Write the Python code for Lamport's mutual exclusion algorithm and show that it works for 5 processes $P_0, ..., P_4$ when processes P_2, P_0 and P_3 make concurrent CS requests with timestamps 3, 4, 1 respectively.
2. A distributed system consists of five processes $P_0, ..., P_4$ which use RA algorithm for mutual exclusion. Processes P_3, P_1 and P_4 make concurrent CS requests with timestamps 4, 2, 6 respectively. Display the phases of this algorithm for this scenario until all processes finish executing their CSs. Run Python code for RA algorithm using this scenario.
3. Processes in the distributed system shown in Fig. 5.7 use Raymond's algorithm for mutual exclusion. Process P_2 is the current owner of the token and the root of the tree. Processes P_0 and P_1 make concurrent requests for CS. Show the phases of this algorithm for this scenario until all processes finish executing their CSs. Implement this scenario using the Python code fro Raymond's algorithm.
4. Show the operation of Suzuki-Kasami algorithm with five processes $P_0, ..., P_4$ where P_2 and P_5 make concurrent CS requests when P_3 has the token.
5. Work out the quorums for nine processes $P_0, ..., P_9$ using Maekawa's algorithm.

References

1. A.D. Kshemkalyani, M. Singhal, *Distributed Computing: Principles, Algorithms, and Systems* (Cambridge University Press, 2011)
2. L. Lamport, Time, clocks and ordering of events in distributed systems. Commun. ACM **21**(7), 558–565 (1978)
3. M. Maekawa, A $\sqrt{N}$ algorithm for mutual exclusion in decentralized systems. ACM Trans. Comput. Syst. **3**(2), 145–159 (1985)
4. K. Raymond, A tree based algorithm for distributed mutual exclusion. ACM Trans. Comput. Syst. **7**(1), 61–77 (1989)
5. G. Ricart, A.K. Agrawala, An optimal algorithm for mutual exclusion in computer networks. Commun. ACM **24**(1), 9–17 (1981)
6. I. Suzuki, T. Kasami, A distributed mutual exclusion algorithm. ACM Trans. Comput. Syst. **3**(4), 344–349 (1985)

Global State Analysis

6

Abstract

A global state of a distributed system consists of a collection of the local states of processes in that system along with the states of the communication channels that connect these processes. Global state may be used to enquire and determine system status such as a deadlock or whether all distributed computations have concluded. Distributed snapshot algorithms provide a snapshot of a global state of the system. Termination detection algorithms are commonly used to determine whether a distributed computation has terminated in all nodes of the system. Detection of a deadlock in a distributed system is needed to recover and resume computation. We review fundamental distributed snapshot, termination detection and deadlock detection algorithms and implement them in Python using $mpi4py$ in this chapter.

6.1 Introduction

A global state of a distributed system consists of the collection of local states of processes in that system along with the states of communication channels that connect these processes. Analysis of the global state provides various information to detect whether a distributed computation is functioning as required. One such analysis is to test whether the system is in a deadlock state in which case recovery procedures need be initiated. Yet another important determination of the global state is to check whether a distinct distributed computation has concluded in all processes that are involved. Moreover, generated global state of a distributed system may be used to compute network topology and detect failures in the system.

The global state of a distributed system may be formed by taking local *snapshots* of processes and merging these local states with the states of the channels. Recording of these states should not interfere with the normal functioning of the system. In this chapter, we first describe the system model formally needed to determine the global state of a distributed system followed by a review of distributed snapshot algorithms used to record global states. We then look at ways of determining the termination of a distributed computation in all nodes using the global state investigation. Finally, we describe how global state analysis can be used to detect a deadlock condition in a distributed system.

6.2 System Model

A distributed system consists of a set of n processes $P_0, \ldots, P_{n-1}$, and communication channels between these processes with the following assumptions [3]:

- A process P_i can have only three type of actions: send a message, receive a message and an interval event.
- The local state of a process P_i at any time t, denoted by LS_i, contains all events it has performed since its start. We say $e \in LS_i$ if e is either a send event, a receive event or a local event before LS_i is recorded at time t, otherwise $e \notin LS_i$.
- Let channel C_{ij} be the communication channel between processes P_i and P_j. A *transit message* is a message sent by P_i which is not yet received by P_j.

Delivery of messages through channels can be as first-in-first-out (FIFO) where messages are delivered to the receiver in the order they are sent, or non-FIFO where the receiver collects the messages from a channel in random order. Casual delivery of messages imposes a type of restriction on the delivery of messages by ensuring that if a message m_{ij} is sent before m_{kj} by processes P_i and P_k to process P_j, then reception of these messages by P_j should be in the same order.

Definition 6.1 (*global state*) A global state of a distributed system is the union of all local states of processes in that system. Formally, a global state GS may be stated as follows:

$$GS = \left\{ \bigcup LS_i, \bigcup SC_{ij} \right\}$$

where SC_{ij} is the state of the channel C_{ij} between processes P_i and P_j.

We can now define the global state as follows:

6.2 System Model

Fig. 6.1 Timing diagram of three processes

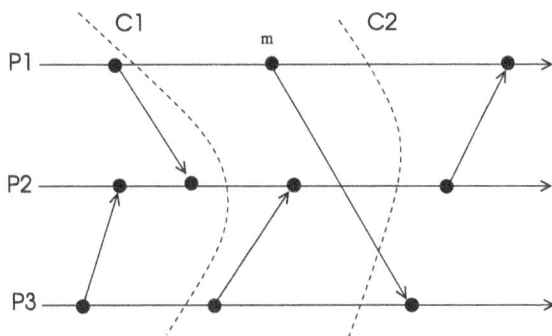

Definition 6.2 (*consistent global state*) A consistent global state should provide the following conditions:

- C1: If a message m_{ij} is sent from process P_i to process P_j and is included in the state LS_i of P_i, then either m_{ij} is included in the state SC_{ij} of channel C_{ij} and delivered to P_j or it is not in SC_{ij} and not recorded in the state LS_j of P_j.
- C2: If a message m_{ij} is not contained in the state LS_i, then it is not contained in the state SC_{ij} of channel C_{ij} and its reception by P_j is not contained in the state LS_j of Process P_j.

In short, a consistent global state ensures that there are no messages in transit over any channel and any message not sent may not be part of the state of the channel it would be sent and the state of the receiver process.

Definition 6.3 (*cut*) A distributed system may be represented as a timing diagram with horizontal lines showing the time and points on the line depict events such as sending or receiving a message from another process. A *cut* in a space-time diagram is a vertical line with exactly one point of intersection at each process time line. A cut divides this diagram into two regions called *past* and *future* representing a global state. Every message sent in the *past* is received in the *past* in a *consistent global state* that is represented by that cut and such a cut is called a *consistent cut*. Otherwise the global state and the cut that represents it are *inconsistent*.

A timing diagram of three processes is depicted in Fig. 6.1 with two cuts C_1 and C_2. Cut C_1 and the global state of this distributed system are consistent as every sent message in its past is received by the receiving processes. However, cut C_2 and the global state it generates are inconsistent since message m sent by process P_1 in its past is received by process P_3 in its future.

Problems to be solved while taking a consistent snapshot in a distributed system are as follows [5]:

- A message m sent before taking the snapshot of process P_i should be recorded in the snapshot, that is $m \in LS_i$, a message sent after recording the snapshot must not be recorded in the snapshot.
- A message m_{ij} received from process P_j by process P_i after taking its snapshot must not be recorded in the snapshot.
- Let message m_{ij} be sent by process P_i after recording its snapshot to process P_j, then, P_j must record its snapshot before processing this message.

6.3 Distributed Snapshot Algorithms

We will assume that the graph representing the distributed system is strongly connected with each directed edge (i, j) representing a communication channel between processes P_i and P_j. We will describe two representative algorithms to record global states for different channel types: Chandy-Lamport algorithm for FIFO channels, Lai-Yang algorithm for non-FIFO channels.

6.3.1 Chandy-Lamport Algorithm

Chandy-Lamport (CL) snapshot algorithm uses two types of messages: computation (*basic*) messages and control messages called *marker* which is used to separate messages in FIFO channels. The main idea of this algorithm is to use *marker* messages to initiate taking the snapshot of the system. Each process sends *markers* exactly once over its adjacent channels. A process receiving a *marker* message takes a snapshot and sends the *marker* in its adjacent channels. The following rules are applied by process P_i to take a snapshot of the system [7]:

- *Marker sending rule*:
  - P_i records its state
  - P_i sends a *marker* to each outgoing channel C through which a marker has not been sent.

- *Marker receiving rule through channel C*:
  - **if** P_i has not recorded its state **then**

    Sets channel state $SC_{ij} = \emptyset$, local state $LS_i = taken$
    Implements the *marker sending rule*.

– **else**

> Let m_{ij} be a message sent by P_i to P_j received through channel C_{ij} after P_j has recorded its state and before P_j received the marker through C_{ij}. Record all such messages in the state of channel C_{ij}.

Since channels are FIFO, any message sent after the *marker* transferred over a channel C_{ij} will not be recorded in the state SC_{ij} of that channel which means condition C2 is fulfilled. A process that receives a message m_{ij} over the channel C_{ij} which precedes a *marker* over the same channel may have recorded its snapshot. In this case, it records m_{ij} in the channel state SC_{ij}. If it has not taken its snapshot, it includes m_{ij} in its snapshot, thus condition C1 is satisfied in both cases.

6.3.2 Lai-Yang Algorithm

Lai-Yang distributed snapshot (LY) algorithm works with non-FIFO channels [6]. Processes are colored either *white* or *red*, initially all processes are white and there is an initiator process that collects local states of processes. LY algorithm works according to the following principles [6]:

- Every message sent and every action performed by a process receives the color of the process.
- A process becomes red when it takes a snapshot.
- A white message is sent before taking a snapshot and a red message is sent after taking the snapshot.
- A white process can take its snapshot arbitrarily but it must do so before receiving a red message.

LY algorithm implements the following rules while forming a global state of the system.

- LY1: Every white process stores all of the white messages it has received along all of its channels in M.
- LY2: A process turning red sends $\{M \cup$ its snapshot$\}$ to the initiator process.
- LY3: The initiator process determines the transit messages of each channel SC_{ij} by taking the difference of the recorded messages in the local state LS_i of process P_i and the received messages recorded in the local state LS_j of process P_j.

A white message m_{ij} is included in the snapshot of process P_j if it receives m_{ij} before taking its snapshot, otherwise m_{ij} is included in the state SC_{ij} of channel C_{ij} which means condition C1 is valid. A red message does not belong to the snapshot of process P_j that receives the message and the channel state, that is, the state of a channel is the difference of two sets of white processes. This algorithm works without using any marker messages, however, each process needs to record all of the messages to form the local snapshot which may require large memory space. This memory requirement may be reduced by storing the newly sent and received messages since the last snapshot as described in [6].

6.4 Termination Detection

A process may be in idle state with no progress or it may be in active state involved in a distributed computation in a distributed system. A distributed system is said to be terminated when all processes are idle and there are no messages in transit over any channel connecting the processes. A fundamental problem in a distributed system is to determine the end of a distributed computation so that the output of the computation may be used correctly. It is also possible that a distributed computation may comprise a number of smaller computations requiring a subcomputation to cease before the next one starts.

6.4.1 Termination on a Ring

In the simplest case, processes may be configured as a ring and an initiator process starts probing the termination status of the system by sending a *token* message to its successor when it has terminated. Any process P_i that receives the *token* passes it to its successor when it has terminated. When the token returns to the initiator, this process determines that distributed computation has terminated. In order to notify all other process of this condition, the initiator now sends another *terminated* message to its successor which is circulated in the ring as the *token* message and when this message is received by the initiator, it determines that all processes know the termination of the distributed computation. The message complexity of this algorithm is $O(n)$, however, token loss and generation and failure of a node are the major problems with this approach as in various other token-based algorithms.

Python Implementation

We will implement this algorithm for the ring structure in Fig. 6.2 where six processes are connected so that any successor of a process P_i has an identity P_j where $j = (i + 1)\%6$ as shown in Listing 6.1. Two types of messages transferred in the first and second round are *token* and *term* (terminated) messages. The root process P_0

6.4 Termination Detection

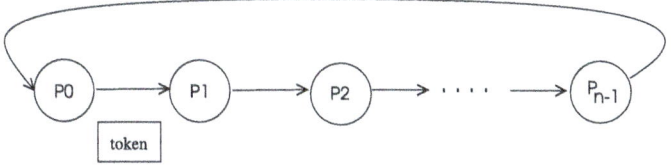

Fig. 6.2 Passing termination token in a ring

starts the first round by sending the *token* message to its successor which passes this message to its successor when it finishes. This process continues until the root receives the *token* it has sent upon which it issues the *term* message to its successor to inform all nodes that the distributed computation has finished. When this message reaches the root, it terminates. All processes display *Terminated* message when they finish as shown in the output of this program in Listing 6.2.

Listing 6.1 Token Ring Termination Algorithm

```
from mpi4py import MPI

comm = MPI.COMM_WORLD
rank = comm.Get_rank()
n    = comm.Get_size()
ROOT = 0

# message types
TOKEN = 1
TERM  = 2

# message: sender, type
msg = [-1, -1]
over = False

if rank == ROOT:
    msg = [rank, TOKEN]
    recvr = (rank + 1) % n
    comm.send(msg, dest=recvr, tag=TOKEN)

while not over:
    msg = comm.recv(source=MPI.ANY_SOURCE, tag=MPI.ANY_TAG)
    sender, typ = msg[0], msg[1]
    if typ == TOKEN:
        if rank == ROOT: # start second round
            msg = [rank, TERM]
        else:
            msg = [rank, TOKEN] # send TOKEN to next
        recvr = (rank + 1) % n
        comm.send(msg, dest=recvr, tag=1)
    elif rank != ROOT:
        msg = [rank, TERM] # send TERM to next
        recvr = (rank + 1) % n
        comm.send(msg, dest=recvr, tag=TERM)
        over = True
    else:
        over = True
print("Rank: {}, Terminated".format(rank))
```

Listing 6.2 Output of Token Ring Termination Algorithm

```
Rank: 1, Terminated
Rank: 2, Terminated
Rank: 3, Terminated
Rank: 4, Terminated
Rank: 5, Terminated
Rank: 0, Terminated
```

6.4.2 Termination Using a Spanning Tree

A spanning tree of a graph is a tree that covers all nodes in the graph. A rooted spanning tree T in a distributed system may be built using a suitable distributed algorithm (see Sect. 9.2). A termination algorithm using a spanning tree consists of the following steps:

- Each leaf process of T has a *token* initially.
- A leaf node sends the token to its parent when it finishes.
- Any intermediate node P_i that receives all tokens from all of its children and has finished itself sends the *token* to its parent. Note that both the nodes in the sub-tree of P_i must have finished and node P_i must have finished to deliver the *token* to its parent.
- The root decides that all nodes in the network have finished when it receives tokens from all of its children.
- It then broadcasts a *terminate* message over the tree T to inform all nodes that the computation is over.

Note that we have implemented a similar termination detection algorithm without tokens when the number of rounds in the SSI model were not known in Chap. 3.

Python Implementation

We will implement the spanning tree-based termination algorithm for eight processes connected with a spanning tree of Fig. 6.3 as shown in Listing 6.3. The Python code starts by assigning parents and children to each process as in the tree of this figure. The leaves have the token and start the algorithm by sending the TOKEN message to their parents which then wait to receive tokens from all of their children and then send the token to their parent. When the root receives tokens from all of its children, it starts the second phase of the algorithm by sending TERM message to its children which is broadcast to children of intermediate node until this message reaches leaves. All nodes display their received set of processes when they terminate. Output of this algorithm showing termination of all nodes is displayed in Listing 6.4.

6.4 Termination Detection

Fig. 6.3 A sample spanning tree to test spanning tree-based termination algorithm

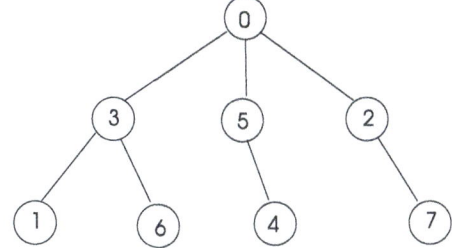

Listing 6.3 Spanning Tree Termination Algorithm

```
from mpi4py import MPI

comm = MPI.COMM_WORLD
rank = comm.Get_rank()
n    = comm.Get_size()

# determine parent and children
children = [[2,3,5],[],[7],[1,6],[],[4],[],[]]
parents  = [0,3,0,0,5,0,3,2]
parent = parents[rank]
child  = children[rank]
childs = set(child)
recvd  = set()

#message types
TOKEN = 1
TERM  = 2

# states
ROOT   = 0
INTERM = 1
LEAF   = 2

# message: sender, type
msg = [-1, -1]

# determine states
if rank == 0:
    state = ROOT
elif len(childs) != 0:
    state = INTERM
else:
    state = LEAF

if state == LEAF: # leaf starts upcast
     msg = [rank, TOKEN]
     comm.send(msg, dest=parent, tag=TOKEN)

over = False
while not over:
    msg = comm.recv(source=MPI.ANY_SOURCE, tag=MPI.ANY_TAG)
    sender, typ = msg[0], msg[1]
    if typ == TOKEN:
        recvd.add(sender)
        if recvd == childs:
          if state == INTERM: # send TOKEN to parent
            msg = [rank, TOKEN]
```

```
48              comm.send(msg, dest=parent, tag=TOKEN)
49          else:    # root starts second round
50              msg = [rank, TERM]
51              for node in childs:
52                  comm.send(msg, dest=node, tag=TERM)
53              over = True     # root terminates
54      else:       # TERM received
55          if state == INTERM:    # send TERM to children
56              msg = [rank, TERM]
57              for node in childs:
58                  comm.send(msg, dest=node, tag=TERM)
59          over = True  # all nodes other than root terminate
60  print("Rank: {}, Received: {} Terminated".format(rank,recvd))
```

Listing 6.4 Output of the Spanning Tree Termination Algorithm

```
Rank: 2, Received: {7} Terminated
Rank: 0, Received: {2, 3, 5} Terminated
Rank: 7, Received: set() Terminated
Rank: 3, Received: {1, 6} Terminated
Rank: 1, Received: set() Terminated
Rank: 5, Received: {4} Terminated
Rank: 6, Received: set() Terminated
Rank: 4, Received: set() Terminated
```

A problem with this algorithm is that a process that has sent a token to its parent to declare that it has finished may receive a message from a neighbor afterwards. Topor provided a correction to the spanning tree-based termination detection algorithm by coloring the processes and the token as described below [10]. Initially each leaf processes possesses a white token and delivery of tokens to the root process is as the original spanning tree based algorithm. A process that has sent a message to another one sends a black token which is delivered to the root which initiates a second round of token delivery knowing there may be unfinished processes. The operating principles of this algorithm is as following:

- Initially, each leaf process has a white token and set S is used to store identifiers of token holding processes. Delivery of tokens to the root is similar to the original spanning tree algorithm.
- A process that sends a message to another one turns black, and it sends a black token to its parent.
- A process sends the token to its parent when it terminates after which it changes its color to white.
- An internal process sends the black token to its parent which is propagated to the root.
- The root receiving a black token determines that there is at least one process that has sent a message to another one. Thus, it restarts the algorithm by broadcasting a *repeat* message.
- Each leaf receiving a *repeat* message starts upcasting its token to its parent.

- The root decides termination if it is idle (terminated), it is white meaning it has not sent any messages to another process and it has received a white token from all of its children.

The best message complexity of this algorithm is $O(n)$ when termination is determined in the first round by sending of tokens over the edges of the spanning tree of $(n-1)$ edges. The worst message complexity is $O(nm)$ where m is the number of computation messages exchanged which occurs when only a computation message is exchanged every time the algorithm is executed.

6.4.3 Huang's Weight Throwing Algorithm

Huang provided a distributed termination algorithm by assigning weights to processes [2]. Processes in this algorithm may be in *idle* or *active* states. A controlling agent is a special process that starts the termination process by dividing its initial weight of unity and sending one part to an arbitrary process in the system. A process receiving weight adds this weight to its weight and a process that becomes *idle* (terminated) sends its weight to the controlling agent. The sum of all weights possessed by all processes in the system is always unity. The controlling agent terminates when its weight becomes unity again and then may inform all processes that the computation is over. Two types of messages are the basic message carrying weight WD, $B(DW)$, and a control message carrying weight DW, $C(DW)$. The following rules are applied in this algorithm.

- H1: A basic message $B(W)$ may be sent by the controlling agent or any active process to another process. The sender divides its weight into $W1$ and $W2$ such that $W = W1 + W2$, assigns its weight to $W1$ and sends $B(W2)$ to the destination process.
- H2: Any process that receives $B(DW)$, adds DW to its weight W and assigns this sum to its current weight. The receiver becomes active if it was idle after receiving this message.
- H3: A process that terminates becomes idle, sends its weight to the controlling agent and assigns its weight to zero.
- H4: The controlling agent, upon receiving $B(DW)$ adds DW to its weight and determines the end of computation if its weight becomes unity.

An example operation of this algorithm with four processes $P_0, ..., P_3$ with P_0 as the controlling agent is displayed in the timing diagram of Fig. 6.4. We assume each process halves its current weight before sending a basic message and process P_0 is

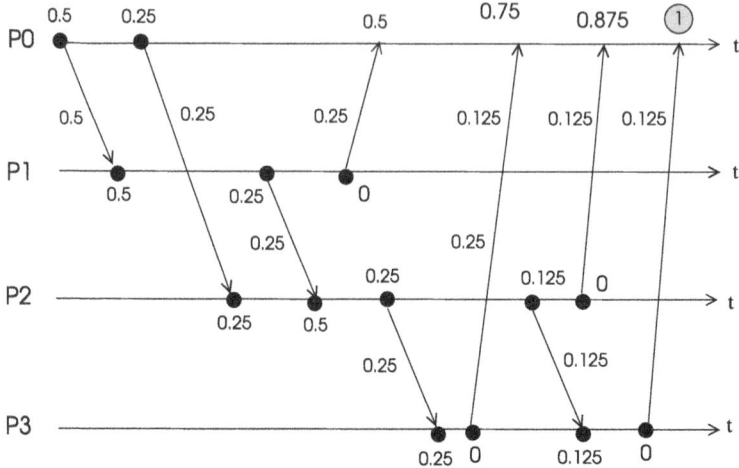

Fig. 6.4 Running of Huang's algorithm in four processes

shown in gray circle when its accumulated weight is unity, thus, all processes have terminated.

Python Implementation

We will implement Huang's algorithm in Python with the process with rank 0 as the controlling agent starting with unity weight. The DW weights and the receiver nodes of basic messages are assigned randomly as displayed in Listing 6.5. We also provide a third message type $term$ which is sent by the controller to all nodes to notify the end of computation. The sample output for five processes is given in Listing 6.6.

Listing 6.5 Huang's Termination Algorithm

```
from mpi4py import MPI
import random
import time

comm = MPI.COMM_WORLD
rank = comm.Get_rank()
n    = comm.Get_size()
CONTROLLER = 0

# states
IDLE, ACTIVE = 1, 2
# message types
BASIC, CONTROL, TERM = 1, 2, 3

# initialization
W = 0
state = IDLE
msg = [-1, -1, -1, -1] # sender, type, weight
over = False

if rank == CONTROLLER:
    W = 1
    DW = round(random.uniform(0,1),2)
```

6.4 Termination Detection

```
24      W = round(W - DW,2)
25      recvr = random.randint(1,n-1)
26      msg = [rank, BASIC, DW, recvr]
27      comm.send(msg, dest=recvr, tag=BASIC)
28
29  while not over:
30      msg = comm.recv(source=MPI.ANY_SOURCE, tag=MPI.ANY_TAG)
31      sender, typ, DW, recvr = msg[0], msg[1], msg[2], msg[3]
32      if typ == BASIC:
33          if state == IDLE:
34              state = ACTIVE
35          W = W + DW
36          ratio = round(random.uniform(0,1),2)
37          DW = round(W * ratio,2)
38          W = round(W - DW,2)
39          recvr = random.randint(1,n-1)
40          msg = [rank, BASIC, DW, recvr]
41          while recvr == rank:
42              recvr = random.randint(1,n-1)
43          comm.send(msg, dest=recvr, tag=BASIC)
44          time.sleep(1)
45          state = IDLE
46          msg = [rank, CONTROL, W, CONTROLLER]
47          W = 0
48          comm.send(msg, dest=CONTROLLER, tag=CONTROL)
49      elif typ == CONTROL:
50          W = W + DW
51          if W == 1:
52              for node in range(1,n):
53                  msg = [rank, TERM, 0, node]
54                  comm.send(msg, dest=node, tag=TERM)
55              over = True
56      else:  # TERM received
57          over = True
58  print("Rank: {}, Terminated".format(rank))
```

Listing 6.6 Output of Huang's Termination Algorithm

```
Rank: 2, Terminated
Rank: 0, Terminated
Rank: 1, Terminated
Rank: 4, Terminated
Rank: 3, Terminated
```

Analysis

Let us assume the following:

- A: Set of weights of all active processes
- B: set of weights of all computation messages in transit
- C : set of weights of all control messages in transit
- W_c: weight of controlling agent

The following invariants hold:

- I_1: $W_c + \sum w \in (A \cup B \cup C) = 1$ (conservation of original weight of the controlling agent)

- I_2: $\forall w \in (A \cup B \cup C)$, $w > 0$ (weights are positive)

Therefore, $\sum_w (A \cup B \cup C) = 0$ if and only if $W_c = 1$ by I_1. $\sum (A \cup B \cup C) = 0$ implies $(A \cup B \cup C = \emptyset)$ by I_2. Thus it must be the case that $A \cup B = \emptyset$ when $W_c = 1$ which signals the termination of all processes. Additionally, if $A \cup B = \emptyset$, $W_c + \sum w \in C = 1$ by I_1. Assuming finite message delays, W_c will eventually be 1, thus, termination will be detected in finite time.

6.5 Deadlock Detection

A deadlock condition arises when two or more processes are waiting for resources held by each other, therefore, no progress can be made. The four simultaneous necessary conditions to exist for a deadlock to arise in a system are as follows:

- *Mutual Exclusion*: Only one process can have access to a resource, that is, resources are not shared.
- *Hold and Wait*: A process must be holding at least one resource while waiting for the release of resources that are currently held by other processes.
- *No Preemption*: Processes can only release resources voluntarily.
- *Circular Wait*: There must be a circular wait sequence of processes such that the requests are ordered in a ring.

6.5.1 Wait-for-Graph

A wait-for-Graph (WFG) may be used to capture the state of the distributed system to detect deadlocks. Processes are the nodes in this directed graph and there is a directed edge from P_i to P_j if P_i is blocked waiting for a resource held by P_j. The distributed system is deadlocked if there is a cycle or a knot in the its WFG since no progress can be made. Such a system snapshot with a deadlock is depicted in Fig. 6.5 where processes P_0, P_3, P_2 and P_5 form a cycle with their requests, thus there is a deadlock, assuming there is only one instance of each resource. Note that process P_1 is also deadlocked although it is not on the cycle, because it needs a resource held by process P_3 and P_3 can not proceed to release the resource because it is deadlocked.

Distributed deadlock models can be classified based the request types made by processes are as follows:

- *Single Resource Model*: A process can have one current request for one resource at any given time. The outdegree of a process in a WFG can be at most 1 in this model, thus a cycle in a WFG representing this request type will indicate a deadlock.

Fig. 6.5 A sample WFG of a deadlock

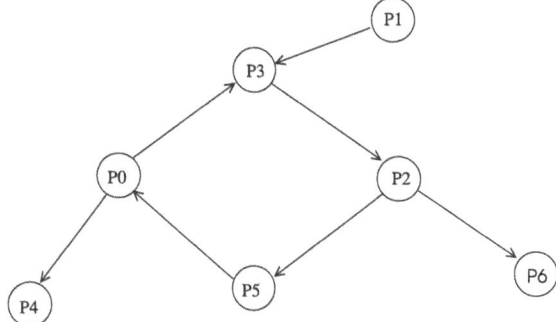

- *The AND Model*: A process can request more than one resource in this model and the request is accepted after all resources are released for this process. A cycle in a WFG with AND model indicates a deadlock. Process P_2 in Fig. 6.5 has two requests and both should be granted for it to continue in the AND model.
- *The OR Model*: A process may request more than one resource, however can continue if only one of the resources it is requesting becomes available. A cycle in such a model does not show a deadlock since release of one of the resources a process is holding will break the cycle. Looking at Fig. 6.5 again, release of the resource held by P_6 to P_2 will break the cycle if WFG represents an OR model.

6.5.2 Handling Deadlocks

The three main methods for handling deadlocks are as follows:

- *Deadlock Prevention*: A process may be given all of the resources it needs so as to avoid it being blocked waiting for a resource. Alternatively, a process holding a resource may be preempted to release the resource it is holding.
- *Deadlock Avoidance*: A resource is provided to a process only if the resulting system state is not deadlocked. A test is carried to assume the requested resource is granted to the process and deadlock condition is then checked. If there is a potential deadlock when request is fulfilled, the request is rejected.
- *Deadlock Detection*: System is checked regularly or whenever a hindrance of progress is detected. A deadlock condition can then be removed by terminating one or more processes involved in the deadlock and returning to a pre-recorded safe state.

The deadlock prevention and avoidance methods are difficult to implement in distributed systems, and assuming deadlocks occur rarely, deadlock detection is the main method of dealing with deadlocks in a distributed setting. Deadlocks in a distributed system may be classified as follows:

- *Resource Deadlock*: This type of deadlock occurs when two or more processes are blocked waiting for resources held by each other, thus preventing any progress.
- *Communication Deadlock*: Processes in this type of deadlock wait for messages from each other when there are no messages in transit on the channels. This situation may be conveniently modelled by a cycle in a WFG breaking of which is possible if at least one of the processes on the cycle gets unblocked. This may happen if at least one of the held resources is released, thus, this type of deadlock may be denoted as OR model.

Once a deadlock is detected, a recovery process needs to be initiated such as terminating one or more processes involved in the deadlock. A *rollback* to a previous safe state of processes in deadlock may then be initiated.

6.5.3 Distributed Deadlock Detection Algorithms

Deadlock detection algorithms in distributed systems may be broadly classified as central, distributed and hierarchical algorithms. A central algorithm has a coordinator which maintains the WFG for the whole system. A process requesting a resource which results in a directed edge to be added to the global WFG sends a message to the coordinator for this update. Likewise, a process releasing a resource sends a message to the coordinator for the deletion of the edge. Upon receiving a message from a process, the coordinator can test the WFG for cycles. Each process can send a single message containing a list of added an deleted edges since the last update periodically to the coordinator to improve performance. When a coordinator detects a cycle, it terminates one of the processes involved in the cycle. A single point of failure and bottleneck of messages to the coordinator are the usual problems as with any central approach.

Coordinators are arranged in a hierarchy in the hierarchical deadlock detection, commonly a coordinator exists for each cluster of nodes. Each coordinator is responsible for the WFG in its cluster and reporting its status to a central coordinator which can determine the deadlock condition. Distributed deadlock detection algorithms allow each process to participate in the detection of deadlock. These algorithms may be classified as follows:

- *Path-Pushing Algorithms*: This class of algorithms provide procedures to build a global WFG of a distributed system. Each process stores its local WFG and when an initiator starts the algorithm, it exchanges its local WFG with its neighbors. Continuing with WFG exchange with neighbors, some processes in the system will eventually obtain the full WFG of the system which can be investigated to detect a deadlock. A process noticing a deadlock will announce this condition to enable starting of a recovery procedure.
- *Edge-Chasing Algorithms*: A cycle in the WFG is sought by sending a special message called *probe* in this class of algorithms. A process investigating a deadlock sends a *probe* message along the edges of its WFG. Receiving the *probe* message

it has sent shows a cycle, thus the existence of a deadlock. Probe messages are transferred only by blocked processes which may be deadlocked, otherwise, active processes discard the *probe* messages.
- *Diffusion Algorithms*: Deadlock detection process is diffused over the WFG of the system in this method. The *query* messages sent by the initiator are distributed over the outgoing edges of the WFG. An active process discards the *query* and *reply* messages, but are echoed by the passive (blocked) processes.
- *Global State Algorithms*: This type of algorithms rely on the global state of the system that is obtained by a snapshot algorithm. This global state may then be investigated for a deadlock condition.

6.5.4 Chandy-Misra-Haas Algorithm

Chandy-Misra-Haas (CMH) algorithm [1] for the AND model is an edge-chasing algorithm to detect a deadlock and as in the general rule with such algorithms, it employs *probe* messages to detect a cycle in WFG. The initiator starts the procedure by sending *probe* messages over outgoing edges of the partial WFG stored in its site. The starting condition could be waiting on a resource and then timing-out or failure of a request for a resource by the initiator. A blocked process receiving a *probe* message transfers it to processes on the outgoing edges of its WFG. Return of the *probe* message to the initiator indicates a cycle and thus a deadlock upon which recovery procedures may be initiated. The terminology and data structures used in this algorithm are as follows [1]:

- A *probe* message is of the form $p(i, j, k)$ where P_i is the initiator and message is sent from process P_j to P_k.
- A process P_i is assumed to be dependent on process P_j if there exists a sequence of processes $Pi, P_{k1}, P_{k2}, ..., P_{km}, P_j$ such that each process except P_j in the sequence is blocked and each process, except P_i, holds a resource for which the previous process in the sequence is waiting.
- Process P_i is locally dependent on process P_j if P_i is dependent on P_j and they are on the same site.
- Each process P_i has a Boolean array, $dependent_i[n]$, where $dependent_i(j)$ is true only if P_j is dependent on P_i. The array $dependent_i[j]$ is false for all processes P_i and P_j initially.

A process P_i that finds to be locally dependent on itself declares a deadlock. Otherwise, if it finds two processes P_j and P_k that reside on two different sites such that P_j is waiting for P_k which means there is an outgoing edge of WFG from P_j to P_k and also if P_i is locally dependent on P_j, it sends a *probe* message to the site of P_k.

On reception of the message $probe(i, j, k)$, if process P_k is blocked and P_k has not replied to all P_j requests, it sets $dependent[i] = true$ making itself and the initiator of the *probe* message dependent. If P_k is the initiator of the *probe* message, meaning the *probe* message has returned, P_k declares a deadlock. Otherwise, *probe* sending rules of the initiator are repeated. The pseudocode of this algorithm is as follows.

- **if** P_i is locally dependent on itself then declare a deadlock
- **else** $\forall P_j$, P_k **send** a $probe(i, j, k)$ to the site of P_k if all of the following holds:
  - P_i is locally dependent on P_k
  - P_j is waiting on P_k
  - P_j and P_k are on different sites

- When a $probe(i, j, k)$ is received, do the following:
  - **if** all of the following is true:

    P_k (the receiver of the probe) is blocked waiting for a resource
    $dependent_k[i] = false$
    P_k has not replied to all requests of P_j

  - **then**

    $dependent_k[i] = true$
    If $k = 1$ then declare P_i is deadlocked
    else $\forall P_x$, P_y **send** $probe(i, x, y)$ to the site of P_y if the following holds:

    · P_k is locally dependent on P_x
    · P_x is waiting on P_y
    · P_x and P_y are on different sites

An advantage of this algorithm is the small size of a *probe* message consisting of three integers only. One *probe* message is transferred over each edge of the WFG for each deadlock detection, therefore, a deadlock of m processes in n sites requires at most $m(n - 1)/2$ messages.

An example operation of this algorithm in three sites S_1, S_2, S_3 and eight processes $P_1, ..., P_8$ is depicted in Fig. 6.6. The initiator process P_1 send the probe $p(1, 4, 7)$ to P_6 which sends it to P_4 and the probe is transferred over the outgoing edges of the WFG to finally reach the initiator P_1 which declares a deadlock.

6.6 Chapter Notes

We first reviewed the properties of the global state of a distributed system and snapshot algorithms to capture the global state. Two representative algorithms we described were Chandy-Lamport algorithm for FIFO channels and Lai-Yang algorithm for non-FIFO channels. Li et al. algorithm works similar to Lai-Yang algorithm and determines the state of a channel by the number of messages in transit over that channel [8]. Mattem provided a distributed snapshot algorithm using vector clocks with an initiator announcing a future vector time when the snapshot is to be taken [9]. Kshemkalyani and Singhal describes a global snapshot algorithm with concurrent initiators in an asynchronous system with FIFO channels in [4]. A detailed review of distributed snapshot algorithms is given in [3].

Two related problems to the global state of a distributed system are the termination detection and deadlock detection both of which require to asses the states of all processes in the system. Determining the termination of a distributed computation is a fundamental problem in distributed systems which is needed to be able to start a new distributed computation. We reviewed three algorithms for this purpose; constructing a ring structure and circulating a token in this ring, using a spanning tree structure by convergecast and broadcast operations over this tree, and by weight throwing. A weight throwing algorithm distributes weights to processes by a special process called a controlling agent and the algorithm terminates when all weights gathered at this agent equals the initial distributed weight value of unity.

Lastly, we described the deadlock problem in a distributed system where processes may be blocked waiting for resources held by each other in resource deadlocks, or messages to be sent in communication deadlocks. The three basic methods to handle deadlocks in a single processor or a distributed system are deadlock prevention, deadlock avoidance and deadlock detection. Allowing deadlocks and then detection for recovery procedures is the common approach to handle deadlocks in a distributed

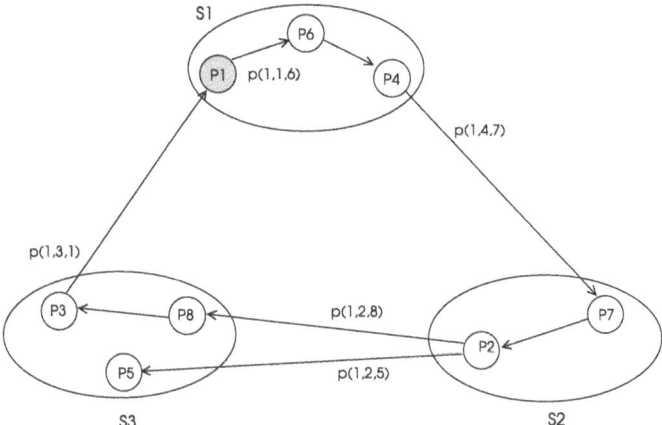

Fig. 6.6 CMH algorithm example operation

Fig. 6.7 Timing diagram for Exercise 1

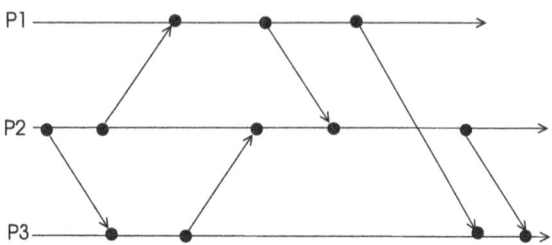

setting. Path-pushing, edge-chasing, diffusion and global state algorithms are the four classes of algorithms for deadlock detection in a distributed system. We reviewed Chandy-Misra-Haas algorithm for the AND model of deadlock request as the final topic in this chapter. There are ongoing research efforts on all of the topics covered; snapshot algorithms, termination detection and deadlock detection in distributed system community.

Exercises

1. Work out consistent and inconsistent states in Fig. 6.7.
2. Implement Chandy-Lamport's distributed snapshot algorithm in Python using $mpi4py$.
3. Label the weights of the nodes in Huang's weight throwing algorithm in Fig. 6.4 where each node sends a quarter of its weight to the receiving node.
4. Implement CHS deadlock detection algorithm in Python using $mpi4py$. Show the operation of this algorithm in the graph of Fig. 6.6 with process P_1 as the initiator.

References

1. K.M. Chandy, J. Misra, L.M. Haas, Distributed deadlock detection. ACM Trans. Comput. Syst. **1**(2), 144–156 (1983)
2. S.T. Huang, Termination detection by using distributed snapshots. Inf. Process. Lett. **32**(3), 113–119 (1989)
3. A. Kshemkalyani, M. Singhal, *Distributed Computing: Principles, Algorithms, and Systems* (Cambridge University Press, 2011)
4. A. Kshemkalyani, M. Singhal, Efficient distributed snapshots in an anonymous asynchronous message-passing system. J. Parallel Distrib. Comput. **73**(5), 621–629 (2013)
5. A.D. Kshemkalyani, M. Raynal, M. Singhal, An introduction to snapshot algorithms in distributed computing. Distrib. Syst. Eng. **2**, 224–233 (1995)
6. T.H. Lai, T.H. Yang, On distributed snapshots. Inf. Process. Lett. **25**, 153–158 (1987)
7. L. Lamport, K.M. Chandy, Distributed snapshots: determining global states of a distributed system. ACM Trans. Comput. Syst. **3**(1), 63–75 (1985)

8. H.F. Li, T. Radhakrishnan, K. Venkatesh, Global state detection in non-FIFO networks, in *Proceedings of the 7th International Conference on Distributed Computing Systems* (1987), pp. 364–370
9. F. Mattem, Efficient algorithms for distributed snapshots and global virtual lime approximation. J. Parallel Distrib. Comput. **18**, 423–34 (1993)
10. R.W. Topor, Termination detection for distributed computations. Inf. Process. Lett. **18**(1), 33–36 (1984)

Coordination 7

Abstract

Nodes of a distributed system need to coordinate to make common decisions and solve a common problem. A leader of a group of processes in a distributed system manages various group activities such as making decisions and routing of messages. A main coordination problem is the election of a leader when the leader stops functioning. Synchronizers are middleware procedures that provide synchronous operation of algorithms in an asynchronous environment. In this chapter, we review leader election algorithms; implement them in Python using *mpi4py* and describe synchronizers.

7.1 Introduction

Nodes of a distributed system need to coordinate to make decisions and solve a common problem. A fundamental coordination problem is the election of a leader from a group of nodes. A leader process in a distributed system of processes residing at the nodes of a network manages the group and is typically responsible for the non-faulty operation of the distributed nodes. We review fundamental leader election algorithms and show their design using finite state machines and implementations with Python and *mpi4py* module.

A synchronous distributed algorithm may be realized more conveniently than an asynchronous algorithm. We will review both asynchronous and synchronous algorithms with processes having unique identifiers which excludes anonymous networks. We will also assume that the size of the network in terms of the number of processes (or nodes) or the diameter of the graph representing the network is known in most of the algorithms described. We will consider the following communication architectures for leader election: a complete graph, a unidirectional ring, a bidirectional ring, an arbitrary graph and a tree.

A synchronizer is a middleware software module that is implemented on top of an asynchronous system to simulate a synchronous execution in a distributed system. We describe main synchronizer methods in the second part of the chapter.

7.2 Leader Election

A leader of a group of computing nodes is needed in various application cases when the leader performs some operation on behalf of all nodes in a group. For example, a leader of a cluster of sensor network nodes may handle routing such that all messages sent to the cluster is sent only to the leader which relays a message to its destination in the cluster.

A leader node may fail due to some fault and a new node should be selected from the non-faulty nodes in the group. Election algorithms perform this task in synchronous or asynchronous execution environments. We will review four classical election algorithms in the next sections, the Bully algorithm, LeLann algorithm, Chang-Roberts algorithms and Hirschberg-Sinclair algorithm.

7.2.1 The Bully Algorithm

The Bully algorithm [3] is based on the idea that whenever failure of a leader is detected by a node, it starts election; the non-faulty node with the highest identifier becomes the leader and announces itself to all nodes in the network. This algorithm assumes the network is fully connected and communication channels are reliable. There are three types of messages in this algorithm as follows:

- ELECT: A live node that detects the leader is not functioning sends this message to all higher identifier nodes than itself.
- REPLY: A node that receives ELECT message from a lower identifier node replies with this message forcing the sender to be out of the election race.
- LEADER: The highest identifier process that times out on its ELECT message to any higher identifier node declares itself as the leader and sends LEADER message to all nodes in t he system.

A possible execution of events in a 9 process system when node 4 suspects the leader 8 is not working and starts an election is depicted in Fig. 7.1a. The higher identifier nodes respond by REPLY message in (b) and they start election by sending ELECT messages to their higher nodes in (c) and REPLY messages are received in (d). The node 7 times out waiting for a reply from node 8 which has crashed and declares itself as the new leader by sending a LEADER message to all nodes in the system in (d).

7.2 Leader Election

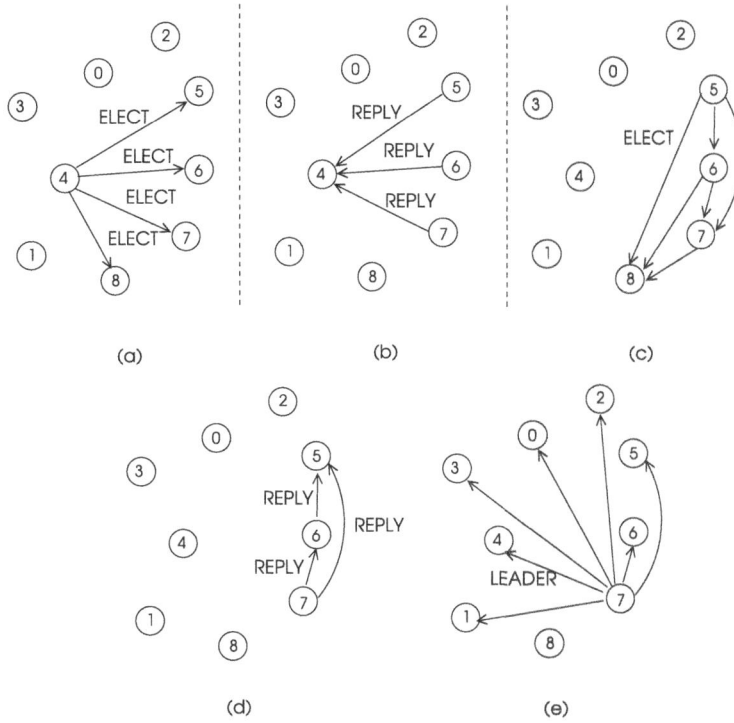

Fig. 7.1 Bully algorithm example

Based on the reasoning above, the FSM states of the Bully algorithm and transitions are are depicted in Fig. 7.2. There are three states of a node as below:

- IDLE: A node in this state has a determined leader.
- W_REPLY: A node in this state has started election and is waiting for REPLY messages.
- W_LEADER: In this state, a node has been taken out of the election by a higher identifier node and is now waiting for the announcement of the leader.

An idle node i may start an election by sending the ELECT message to all higher identifier nodes and then waits for a reply at W_REPLY state. A timeout at this state results in node i to declare itself as the leader and returning to IDLE state. A REPLY to node i means some higher identifier node is non-faulty and node i changes its state to W_LEADER waiting for the LEADER message. However, a time-out at this state means the potential leader has failed and the node i starts election once more. A LEADER message received at states IDLE or W_LEADER results in the determination of the new leader. The state table corresponding to the state diagram

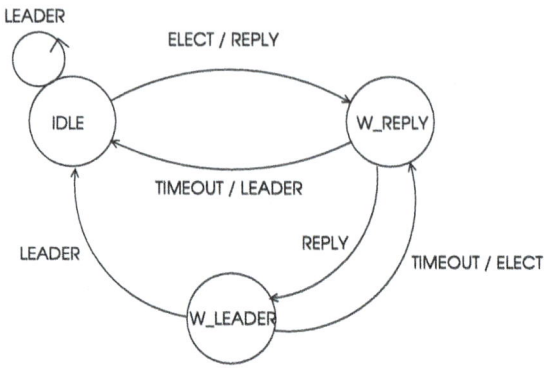

Fig. 7.2 States of the Bully algorithm

Table 7.1 Bully algorithm state table

	ELECT	REPLY	LEADER
IDLE	act00	–	act02
W_REPLY	act10	act11	act12
W_LEADER	act20	–	ac22

Table 7.2 Bully algorithm actions

act00 (IDLE, ELECT)	act02 (IDLE, LEADER)
1. Send REPLY to sender 2. Send ELECT to all higher identifier nodes 3. $state \leftarrow$ W_REPLY	$leader =$ sender of message
act10 (W_REPLY, ELECT)	act11 (W_REPLY, LEADER)
Send REPLY to sender	If REPLY received from all higher nodes 　　$state \leftarrow$ W_LEADER Else if timeout 　　$leader =$ me, send LEADER to all nodes
act20 (W_LEADER, ELECT)	act22 (W_LEADER, LEADER)
Send REPLY to sender	1. $leader \leftarrow$ sender of message 2. $state \leftarrow$ IDLE

of Fig. 7.2 is displayed in Table 7.1. We can rule out some actions such as a node receiving a REPLY message when it is IDLE (Table 7.2).

Correctness is evident as the functioning highest identifier node will always win in this procedure. In the worst case, node 0 may detect that the leader is not functioning sending $n - 1$ ELECT messages and receiving $n - 1$ REPLY messages, node 1 will send $n - 2$ ELECT messages and receive $n - 2$ REPLY messages and so on

7.2 Leader Election

totalling $\sum_{i=1}^{n-1} i$ messages and there will be an additional $n - 1$ messages by the leader declaring itself. Thus, the message complexity of this algorithm is $O(n^2)$.

Python Implementation

We can implement the FSM of Fig. 7.2 with the associated functions in the Python program shown in Listing 7.1. There are few undeterministic cases related to the order of received messages. First, we considered that a process that starts the election should receive replies from all higher processes to enter W_LEADER state which may be needed in a fully synchronous system where each send should be paired with a receive. Secondly, the leader process may declare itself as the leader before an election starting process receives replies from all higher identifier processes. Thus, action 12 results in election to be concluded even in a W_REPLY state of a process, we have this action same as action 22 as they have the same structure. Running of this algorithm in a network of 8 processes is shown where process 4 discovers that the leader has crashed starts the election by sending election messages to processes 5, 6 and 7. Each node determines its leader as node 7 as in the output shown in Listing 7.2.

Listing 7.1 Bully Algorithm

```
from mpi4py import MPI
import numpy as np

comm = MPI.COMM_WORLD
rank = comm.Get_rank()
size = comm.Get_size()

IDLE      = 0 # states
W_REPLY   = 1
W_LEADER  = 2

ELECT   = 0  # message types
REPLY   = 1
LEADER  = 2

leader = -1
msg = np.array([0,0]) # [sender, type]
n_largers = size-1-rank
over = False   # run until over is True
state = IDLE
replied = set() # set of replying nodes


def act00():
    global msg, over, state, leader, sender
    msg[0], msg[1] = rank, REPLY
    comm.send(msg, dest=sender, tag=REPLY)
    if rank != size-1:
        msg[1] = ELECT
        for node in range(rank+1, size):
            comm.send(msg, dest=node, tag=ELECT)
        state = W_REPLY
    else:
        leader = rank
        msg[1] = LEADER
        for node in range(0, size-1):
            comm.send(msg, dest=node, tag=LEADER)
```

```
38          print("Rank: {}, Leader".format(rank))
39          state = IDLE
40          over = True
41
42  def act01():
43      return 0
44
45  def act02():
46      global state, over, leader
47      leader = sender
48      state = IDLE
49      over = True
50
51  def act10():
52      global msg
53      msg[0], msg[1] = rank, REPLY
54      comm.send(msg, dest=sender, tag=REPLY)
55
56  def act11():
57       global state,over, replied
58       replied.add(sender)
59       if len(replied) == n_largers:
60           state = W_LEADER
61
62  def act12():
63      global state, over, leader,leader_found
64      leader = msg[0]
65      state = IDLE
66      over = True
67
68  def act20():
69      global msg
70      msg[0], msg[1] = rank, REPLY
71      comm.send(msg, dest=sender, tag=REPLY)
72
73  def act21():
74      return 0
75
76  def act22():
77      global msg, state, over, leader
78      leader = sender
79      state = IDLE
80      over = True
81
82  actions = np.array([[act00,act01,act02],
83                      [act10,act11,act12],
84                      [act20,act21,act22]])
85
86  if rank == 4:  # start election
87      msg[0], msg[1] = rank, ELECT
88      for node in range(rank+1,size):
89          comm.send(msg, dest=node, tag=ELECT)
90      state = W_REPLY
91
92  while not over:
93      msg = comm.recv(source=MPI.ANY_SOURCE, tag=MPI.ANY_TAG)
94      sender, typ = msg[0], msg[1]
95      actions[state][typ]()
96
97  print("Rank: {}, My Leader:".format(rank),leader)
```

7.2 Leader Election

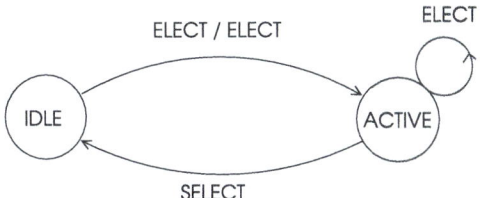

Fig. 7.3 States of CR algorithm

Table 7.3 Token-based algorithm state table

	ELECT	SELECT
IDLE	*act*00	–
ACTIVE	*act*10	act11

Listing 7.2 Output of Bully Algorithm

```
Rank: 0, My Leader: 7
Rank: 1, My Leader: 7
Rank: 2, My Leader: 7
Rank: 4, My Leader: 7
Rank: 5, My Leader: 7
Rank: 3, My Leader: 7
Rank: 7, Leader
Rank: 7, My Leader: 7
Rank: 6, My Leader: 7
```

7.2.2 LeLann Algorithm

We will first present a simple token based algorithm in a unidirectional ring due to LeLann [5]. The main idea of this algorithm is that whenever a node in the ring detects the failure of the current leader, it starts and election by sending the ELECT message to its next node. Any node receiving ELECT message, inserts its identifier in the token and passes it to the next node. When the token traverses all of the nodes, all of the identifiers are stored in it and any node receiving the token second time with its identifier and all identifiers can select the maximum identifier as its leader.

We have the FSM based implementation of this algorithm with a node having two states: IDLE and ACTIVE as shown in Fig. 7.3. There are two message types: ELECT and SELECT in the system and depending on the current state of a node, the operation is determined.

The FSM table for these two states is depicted in Table 7.3 and the actions are shown in Table 7.4.

Table 7.4 Token-based algorithm actions

act00 (IDLE, ELECT)	act01 (IDLE, SELECT)
1. Insert node identifier in token 2. Pass token to next 3. $state \leftarrow$ ACTIVE	NA
act10 (ACTIVE, ELECT)	act11 (ACTIVE; SELECT)
1. Set max id in token to leader 2. Pass token to next 3. $state \leftarrow$ IDLE	1. $leader \leftarrow$ max id in token 2. message type $\leftarrow$ SELECT 3. Pass token to next 4. $state \leftarrow$ IDLE

Python Implementation

The Python implementation using *mpi4py* module simply implements the actions above as shown in Listing 7.3. The message structure has two fields; the sender of the message as the first and the visited node identifiers list as second. We use a Boolean variable called $flag$ that is set at the end of act10 to indicate that a node has finished execution.

Listing 7.3 Token-Based Algorithm

```
from mpi4py import MPI
import numpy as np

comm = MPI.COMM_WORLD
rank = comm.Get_rank()
size = comm.Get_size()

IDLE   = 0   # states
ACTIVE = 1

ELECT  = 0 # messages
SELECT = 1

msg    = [-1,-1,[]]

nexts = [3,5,7,6,0,2,1,4]
prevs = [4,6,5,0,7,1,3,2]

prev = prevs[rank]
nex  = nexts[rank]
leader = -1
flag = True

def act00():
    global msg
    global state
    msg[0] = rank
    msg[2].append(rank)
    comm.send(msg, dest=nex, tag=ELECT)
    state = ACTIVE

def act01(): None

def act10():
```

7.2 Leader Election

```
        if len(msg[2]) == size:
            leader = max(msg[2])
            msg[1] = SELECT
            comm.send(msg, dest=nex, tag=SELECT)
            state = IDLE
            flag = False

def act11():
    global msg, flag, state, leader
    leader = max(msg[2])
    comm.send(msg, dest=nex, tag=ELECT)
    state = IDLE
    flag = False

actions = np.array([[act00,act01],
                    [act10, act11]])
state = IDLE

if rank == 0:
    msg[0] = rank
    msg[1] = ELECT
    msg[2].append(rank)
    comm.send(msg, dest=nex, tag=ELECT)
    state = ACTIVE

while flag:
    msg = comm.recv(source=prev, tag=MPI.ANY_TAG)
    actions[state][msg[1]]()

print("Rank: {}, Leader: {}, Sent: {} to {}"\
    .format(rank,leader,msg,nex))
```

Listing 7.4 Output of Token-Based Algorithm

```
Rank: 3, Leader: 7, Sent: [4, 1, [0, 3, 6, 1, 5, 2, 7, 4]] to 6
Rank: 6, Leader: 7, Sent: [4, 1, [0, 3, 6, 1, 5, 2, 7, 4]] to 1
Rank: 1, Leader: 7, Sent: [4, 1, [0, 3, 6, 1, 5, 2, 7, 4]] to 5
Rank: 5, Leader: 7, Sent: [4, 1, [0, 3, 6, 1, 5, 2, 7, 4]] to 2
Rank: 2, Leader: 7, Sent: [4, 1, [0, 3, 6, 1, 5, 2, 7, 4]] to 7
Rank: 7, Leader: 7, Sent: [4, 1, [0, 3, 6, 1, 5, 2, 7, 4]] to 4
Rank: 4, Leader: 7, Sent: [4, 1, [0, 3, 6, 1, 5, 2, 7, 4]] to 0
Rank: 0, Leader: 7, Sent: [4, 1, [0, 3, 6, 1, 5, 2, 7, 4]] to 3
```

Implementing this algorithm in the ring network of Fig. 7.4 results in the output of Listing 7.4.

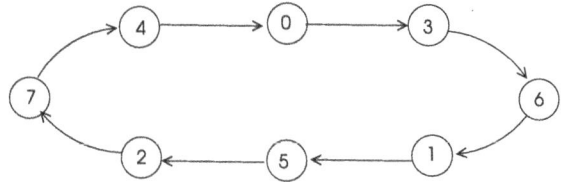

Fig. 7.4 Ring structure for CR algorithm

7.2.3 Chang-Roberts Algorithm

Chang-Roberts (CR) algorithm [2] assumes a ring structure as in LeLann algorithm, however takes a different approach as we will describe. A node that wants to initiate an election starts by sending a token with its identifier in the token to its next node. Any node i receiving the token with identifier j in it, does one of the following:

- If $i > j$, send token to next node.
- If $j > i$, replace j with i in token and send it to next node.
- If $i = j$ then token has traversed all of the network. Declare myself as leader, send LEADER message to next node.

Any node receiving a LEADER message sends it to the next node and this message is not transferred any more when received by the leader node. We will describe the implementation of this algorithm using a state machine and a state table associated with this state machine. A process may be in one of these two states:

- IDLE: A process is at rest and is not aware if an election is in progress or not in this state.
- PART: A process has participated in election in this state.

There are two messages in this algorithm:

- ELECT: A process that finds the current leader is not functioning sends this message to its neighbor.
- LEADER: The elected leader sends this message to announce it is the leader.

The state transitions are depicted in Fig. 7.5. The FSM table for this algorithm is shown in Table 7.5 with rows displaying the states, columns all possible inputs and actions as Table 7.6 entries.

CR algorithm when started by a process next to the highest identifier process needs $n-1$ messages for the ELECT message to be received by the highest identifier node. This node then sends the message with its identifier to be received by itself using n messages and a further n messages are needed for the broadcasting of the

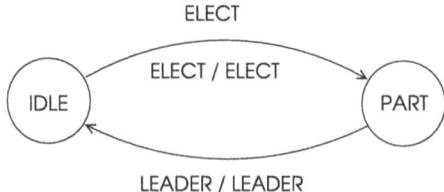

Fig. 7.5 States of CR algorithm

7.2 Leader Election

Table 7.5 CR algorithm state table

	ELECT	LEADER
IDLE	act00	act01
PART	act10	act11

Table 7.6 CR algorithm actions

act00 (IDLE, ELECT)	act01 (IDLE, LEADER)
1. msg(leader) = max(rank, msg(leader)) 2. Send ELECT message to next 3. state ← PART	leader ← sender of message
act10 (PART, ELECT)	act01 (PART, LEADER)
1. If msg(leader)<rank, msg(rank), send ELECT to next 2. If msg(leader)=rank, leader=me; send LEADER to next 3. Otherwise ignore message	1. leader ← sender of message 2. Pass message to next 3. state ← IDLE

leader totalling $3n - 1$ messages. When there are n initiators in decreasing order of identifiers, message of the first one will traverse n nodes, the second one will be transferred $n - 1$ times and the total number of messages with this concurrent initiators is $\sum_{1}^{n} + n = \frac{n(n+1)}{2} + n$ with n times for declaring the leader.

Python Implementation

Note that the main body of the algorithm is only three lines between 64 and 67 where we simply invoke the action at the row corresponding to the state of the process and column corresponding to the received message of Table 7.5 as shown in Listing 7.5. Running of this algorithm in the arbitrarily placed ring of the graph of Fig. 7.4 results in the output displayed in Listing 7.6.

Listing 7.5 CR Algorithm

```
from mpi4py import MPI
import numpy as np

comm = MPI.COMM_WORLD
rank = comm.Get_rank()
size = comm.Get_size()

IDLE = 0 # states
PART = 1
ELECT  = 0 # messages
LEADER = 1
nexts = [3,5,7,6,0,2,1,4]
prevs = [4,6,5,0,7,1,3,2]

prev = prevs[rank]
nex = nexts[rank]
leader = -1
```

```python
msg = np.array([0,0,0])
n = size
flag = True
state = IDLE

def msg_send(typ,data):
    global msg
    msg[0] = rank
    msg[1] = typ
    msg[2] = data
    comm.send(msg, dest=nex, tag=typ)

def act00():
    global msg, state
    cur_leader = max(rank,msg[2])
    msg_send(ELECT,cur_leader)
    state = PART

def act01():
    global msg, flag, state, leader
    leader = msg[2]
    state = IDLE
    flag = False

def act10():
    global msg, state, flag, leader
    if msg[2] > rank:
        comm.send(msg,dest=nex,tag=ELECT)
    elif msg[2] == rank:
        msg_send(LEADER,rank)
        leader = rank
        state = IDLE
        flag = False
        print("Rank: {}, I am Leader".format(rank))

def act11():
    global msg, state, flag, leader
    leader = msg[2]
    state = IDLE
    flag = False
    comm.send(msg,dest=nex,tag=ELECT)

actions = np.array([[act00,act01],
                    [act10,act11]])

if rank == 0:
    msg_send(ELECT,rank)

while flag:
    msg = comm.recv(source=prev, tag=MPI.ANY_TAG)
    actions[state][msg[1]]()
print("Rank: {}, Leader: {}".format(rank,leader))
```

Listing 7.6 Output of LCR Algorithm

```
Rank: 7, I am Leader
Rank: 7, Leader: 7
Rank: 4, Leader: 7
Rank: 0, Leader: 7
Rank: 3, Leader: 7
Rank: 6, Leader: 7
Rank: 1, Leader: 7
```

```
Rank: 5, Leader: 7
Rank: 2, Leader: 7
```

7.2.4 Hirschberg-Sinclair Algorithm

Hirschberg-Sinclair (HS) algorithm is a leader election algorithm that assumes a bidirectional ring of processes [4]. This algorithm uses successive doubling method since the size of the ring is not known by processes. Each process operates in phases $k = 0, 1, 2, ...$ and any process that wants to start the algorithm sends a token in both directions to travel a distance of 2^k. If both tokens return to the initiator, then it continues with phase $k + 1$. The rules of the receiver i of an outgoing token with identifier j are as follows:

- If $j < i$, discard the token.
- If $j < i$, pass it to the next node if end of path is not reached.
- If $j = i$ then declare myself as LEADER.

When the token is traversing inbound to the originator, each process simply sends it to its predecessor towards the originator. Time complexity of this algorithm is $O(n)$ and message complexity is $O(n \log n)$ as there are $\log n$ phases and the number of messages at each phase is $O(n)$.

7.2.5 Leader Election in a Graph

A simple synchronous distributed leader election algorithm that works in rounds for a group of processes connected as a graph can be designed with the following operations at each round.

- Initially each process sets its current leader to its identifier.
- Each process exchanges with its neighbors its current leader identifier.
- Each process selects the maximum identifier received in a round as its current leader.

Clearly, repeating this process for a number of rounds equalling the diameter of the graph will result in the maximum identifier to be stored at each node as the current leader of the network. The time complexity of this algorithm is $O(D)$ where D is the diameter of the graphs since we need to execute D rounds. Since all edges of the graph are traversed at each round, the message complexity is $O(mD)$.

Python Implementation

We will implement this algorithm using the synchronous algorithm template with known number of rounds of Chap. 3. Each *round* message from the root process results in exchange of messages of a node with all of its neighbors as shown in Listing 7.7. Each node then determines its current leader and sends this data to all its neighbors in the next round.

Listing 7.7 Leader Election in a Graph

```
1  from mpi4py import MPI
2  import numpy as np
3
4  comm = MPI.COMM_WORLD
5  rank = comm.Get_rank()
6  n    = comm.Get_size()
7
8  A   =    np.array([[0,1,0,0,0,0,0,0,1,0,0,0],
9                     [1,0,1,0,0,0,0,1,1,0,0,0],
10                    [0,1,0,0,0,0,0,1,1,0,0,1],
11                    [0,0,0,0,0,0,1,0,0,1,0,1],
12                    [0,0,0,0,0,0,0,0,0,0,0,1],
13                    [0,0,0,0,0,0,0,1,0,0,0,0],
14                    [0,0,0,1,0,0,0,1,0,0,0,1],
15                    [0,1,1,0,0,0,1,0,0,0,0,0],
16                    [1,1,1,0,0,1,0,0,0,0,0,0],
17                    [0,0,0,1,0,0,0,0,0,0,0,1],
18                    [0,0,0,0,0,0,0,0,0,0,0,1],
19                    [0,0,1,1,1,0,1,0,0,1,1,0]],dtype=int)
20 children = [[1,8],[2,7],[11],[],[],[],[3],[6],[5],[],[],
21 [4,9,10]]
22 parents  = [0,0,1,6,11,8,7,1,0,11,11,2]
23
24 # message types
25 ROUND = 0
26 DATA  = 1
27 ROVER = 2
28
29 # message: sender, type, round number
30 msg = np.array([-1, -1, -1, -1])
31
32 child  = children[rank]
33 parent = parents[rank]
34 childs = set(child)
35 neighs, neighs_rcvd, rover_rcvd, ids = set(), set(), set(), set()
36
37 for i in range(0,n):  # identify neighbors
38     if A[rank,i] == 1:
39         neighs.add(i)
40
41 max_round = 4  # number of rounds
42 curr_leader = rank
43 ids.add(rank)
44
45 for round_num in range(0,max_round):
46     round_over = False
47     neighs_over, child_over = False, False
48     rover_rcvd.clear()
49     neighs_rcvd.clear()
50     if rank == 0:  # if root, start the next round
51         round_num = round_num + 1
52         msg[0], msg[1], msg[2] = rank, ROUND, round_num
```

7.2 Leader Election

```
53        for child in childs: # send ROUND to children
54            comm.send(msg, dest=child, tag=ROUND)
55        msg[1], msg[3] = DATA, curr_leader
56        for node in neighs:   # send DATA to neighbors
57            comm.send(msg, dest=node, tag=DATA)
58
59    while not round_over:
60        msg = comm.recv(source=MPI.ANY_SOURCE, tag=MPI.ANY_TAG)
61        sender, typ, roun = msg[0], msg[1], msg[2]
62        msg[0] = rank
63        if typ == ROUND: # send ROUND to children
64            if rank != 0:
65                for child in childs:
66                    comm.send(msg, dest=child, tag=ROUND)
67            msg[1], msg[3] = DATA, curr_leader
68            # print(msg)
69            for node in neighs:  # send DATA to neighbors
70                comm.send(msg, dest=node, tag=DATA)
71
72        elif typ == DATA:    # DATA received
73            neighs_rcvd.add(sender)
74            ids.add(msg[3])
75            curr_leader = max(ids)
76            if neighs_rcvd == neighs: # is all received?
77                neighs_over = True
78                if len(childs) == 0 or child_over: # leaf starts convergecast
79                    msg[1] = ROVER
80                    comm.send(msg, dest=parent, tag=ROVER)
81                    round_over = True
82
83        else:   # ROVER received
84            rover_rcvd.add(sender)
85            if rover_rcvd == childs: # all children received?
86                child_over = True
87                if neighs_over:
88                    round_over = True
89                    if rank != 0:
90                        comm.send(msg,dest=parent,tag=ROVER)
91 print("Rank: {}, Round: {}, Leader: {}".format(rank,roun,
       curr_leader))
```

Listing 7.8 Leader Election in a Gaph Algorithm

```
Rank: 5, Round: 4, Leader: 11
Rank: 8, Round: 4, Leader: 11
Rank: 10, Round: 4, Leader: 11
Rank: 4, Round: 4, Leader: 11
Rank: 9, Round: 4, Leader: 11
Rank: 11, Round: 4, Leader: 11
Rank: 3, Round: 4, Leader: 11
Rank: 2, Round: 4, Leader: 11
Rank: 6, Round: 4, Leader: 11
Rank: 7, Round: 4, Leader: 11
Rank: 1, Round: 4, Leader: 11
Rank: 0, Round: 4, Leader: 11
```

Execution of this algorithm in the graph of Fig. 7.6 results in node 11 to be correctly elected as the leader in 4 rounds which is the diameter of this graph, as displayed in Listing 7.8. Note that the spanning tree shown in bold edges in this figure is used for the synchronous round operations.

Fig. 7.6 A sample graph for graph leader election

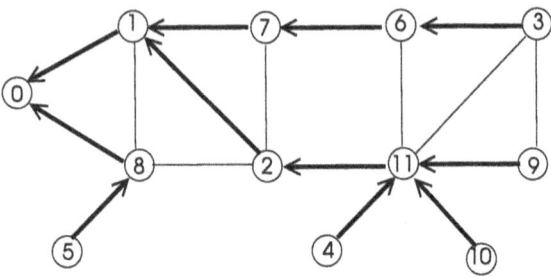

Fig. 7.7 Election in a tree

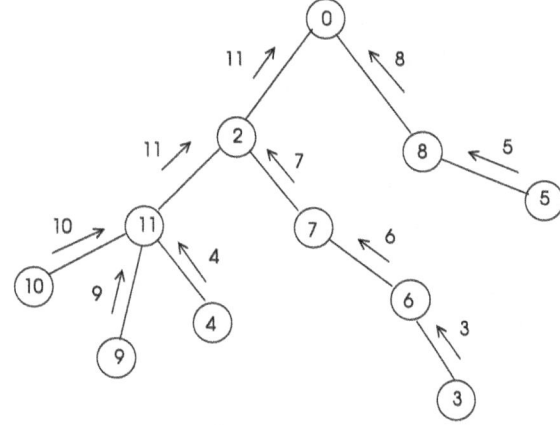

7.2.6 Leader Election in a Tree

Election of a leader in a spanning tree constructed in a network of nodes with unique identifiers may be performed by the rule that each node sends the maximum identifier of the nodes in its subtree including itself to its parent. The root of the tree elects the maximum identifier it receives from its children as the leader and broadcasts this identifier. The following rules are implemented in this algorithm.

- A leaf node sends its identifier to its parent.
- An intermediate node that receives maximum identifiers from its children compares these with its identifier and sends the maximum of these identifiers to its parent.
- This process continues all the way up to the root.
- The root node decides on the leader and broadcasts its identifier to its children.

An example operation of this algorithm is displayed in Fig. 7.7 where the leaf nodes 3, 5, 4, 9 and 10 start the algorithm by sending their identifiers to their parents which send the maximum of the received values and their own identifiers to their parents. The root node 0 decides 11 is the leader and broadcasts this identifier.

7.2 Leader Election

Python Implementation

The above procedure can be translated to Python code as in Listing 7.9 by first assigning children and parents to the nodes as in the spanning tree of Fig. 7.7. The leaves initiate the convergecast process at line 32 and the root decides on the leader and broadcasts its identifier in lines 46–48. Each node finishes with the LDR_KNOWN state. The output displayed in Listing 7.10 shows that node 11 is assigned as leader by all nodes.

Listing 7.9 Tree Algorithm

```
from mpi4py import MPI
import numpy as np

comm = MPI.COMM_WORLD
rank = comm.Get_rank()
n    = comm.Get_size()

children = [[1,8],[2,7],[11],[],[],[],[3],[6],[5],[],[],
            [4,9,10]]
parents  = [0,0,1,6,11,8,7,1,0,11,11,2]

# message types
DATA    = 0
LEADER  = 1

# states
LDR_UNKNOWN = 0
LDR_KNOWN   = 1

# message: sender, type, current leader
msg = np.array([-1, -1, -1])

child  = children[rank]
parent = parents[rank]
childs = set(child)
leaders, rcvd = set(), set()

leaders.add(rank)   # initialize
state = LDR_UNKNOWN
curr_leader = -1

if len(childs) == 0: # leaf node
    msg[0], msg[1], msg[2] = rank, DATA, rank
    comm.send(msg, dest=parent, tag=DATA)

while state != LDR_KNOWN:
    msg = comm.recv(source=MPI.ANY_SOURCE, tag=MPI.ANY_TAG)
    sender, typ, ldr_rcvd = msg[0], msg[1], msg[2]
    if typ == DATA:
        rcvd.add(sender)
        leaders.add(ldr_rcvd)
        if len(rcvd) == len(childs):
            curr_leader = max(leaders)
            msg[0], msg[2] = rank, curr_leader
            if rank == 0:
                for child in childs:
                    msg[1] = LEADER
                    comm.send(msg, dest=child, tag=LEADER)
                    state = LDR_KNOWN
            else:
```

```
                comm.send(msg, dest=parent, tag=DATA)
    else:
        curr_leader = ldr_rcvd
        state = LDR_KNOWN
        if len(childs) != 0:
            for child in childs:
                comm.send(msg, dest=child, tag=LEADER)

print("Rank: {}, Leader: {}".format(rank, curr_leader))
```

Listing 7.10 Output of Tree Algorithm

```
Rank: 0, Leader: 11
Rank: 8, Leader: 11
Rank: 5, Leader: 11
Rank: 1, Leader: 11
Rank: 2, Leader: 11
Rank: 7, Leader: 11
Rank: 9, Leader: 11
Rank: 6, Leader: 11
Rank: 3, Leader: 11
Rank: 10, Leader: 11
Rank: 11, Leader: 11
Rank: 4, Leader: 11
```

7.3 Synchronizers

A synchronizer is a middleware that transforms an asynchronous distributed system to a distributed one. It assumes that the underlying distributed system is non-faulty with no process or node crashes. A synchronizer works in rounds and assumes that a process sends a single message at each round.

A *global synchronizer* ensures that a node p in the distributed system may receive a message for round r only after all processes send their messages in round r. On the other hand, a *local synchronizer* is concerned only with the neighbors of a node p such that p may receive a message in round r only when all of its neighbors have sent their messages at this round.

Definition 7.1 (*safety condition*) A process p is safe in round k if all messages sent by p are received.

Three main types of synchronizers are named α, β and γ synchronizers [1] as described in the next sections.

7.3.1 The α Synchronizer

The α synchronizer is a local synchronizer governed by the following rules:

7.3 Synchronizers

- A process p in round r can start round $r+1$ if all of its neighbors are safe in round r.
- Any process p that receives acknowledgements for all messages it sent informs its neighbors that it is safe.

Informally, the α synchronizer at a node p sends a message to all of the neighbors of p at each round and delivers the incoming neighbor messages to p only when messages from all of the neighbors are received. Let us consider a synchronous distributed algorithm using the SSI model that needs k rounds and employs the α synchronizer. This algorithm will still run k rounds but its message complexity will increase $k \cdot m$ times due to synchronization messages which would not be trivial.

7.3.2 The β Synchronizer

The β synchronizer assumes a rooted spanning tree T is already constructed in the distributed system in which the root functions as the initiator of each round. The convergecast delivery of messages over T is used to collect *round_over* messages from each node of the tree. At each round, a process p other than the root performs the following:

- Wait for *round* message from parent.
- Send message m to all neighbors.
- Wait for *ack* messages from each neighbor.
- Wait for *round_over* message from all children (if any).
- Send *round_over* message to parent.

Essentially, each process guarantees that all of the messages it sent to its neighbors are received and all of the processes in its subtree, if such a subtree exists, have finished and are in safe state. When these conditions are met, it sends *round_over* message to its parent. When *round_over* messages from all of its children are received, the root process may start the next round. Note that this mode of operation is exactly as described in the synchronous single initiator with known number of rounds model of distributed computation in Chap. 3. The message complexity of an algorithm that uses β synchronizer will be $2n-2$ for synchronization messages due to broadcast *round* and convergecast *round_over* messages along the edges of the spanning tree which may be acceptable for many applications. However, the time complexity of the algorithm will increase in proportion to the depth of the spanning tree.

7.3.3 The γ Synchronizer

This type of synchronizer is a combination of α and β synchronizer, making use of both modes of operation with the aim of reducing the time and message complexities

Fig. 7.8 The γ synchronizer network structure

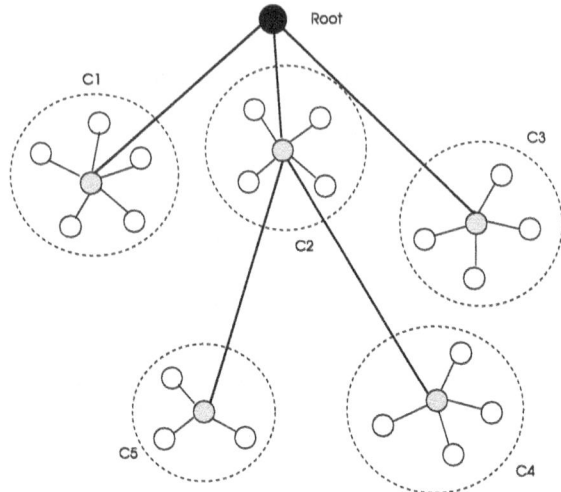

that the algorithm will incur due to employing the synchronizer. The α synchronizer introduces significant message overhead and the β synchronizer results in significant time overhead as we have discussed. The main idea of γ synchronizer is to have a small group of processes implementing the α synchronizer to yield a relatively low number of message exchanges when compared with the whole network and use the β synchronizer over a spanning tree with a low depth which consists only of some privileged nodes.

The network consists of clusters of nodes organized as a spanning tree as depicted in Fig. 7.8. The α synchronizer is used within the cluster and the inter cluster synchronization is performed with the β synchronizer. Each cluster has a *clusterhead* shown in grey in the figure and the synchronization in a cluster is performed under the control of the clusterhead. The clusterheads are connected as the nodes of a spanning tree and when a round within a cluster is over, the clusterheads convergecast *round_over* messages to the root process shown in black, as in the usual operation of a β synchronizer. The diameter of a cluster is typically kept low for ease of communication between the ordinary nodes and the clusterheads.

7.4 Chapter Notes

We reviewed coordination algorithms under two main topics: leader election and synchronizers in this chapter. Leader election is needed at system initialization and whenever a current leader does not function. The main leader election algorithms described are the Bully algorithm, LeLann algorithm, Chang-Roberts algorithm and Hirschberg-Sinclair algorithm. All of these algorithms assume that the processes have unique identifiers and the node with the greatest identifier is the current leader.

7.4 Chapter Notes

Table 7.7 Election algorithms comparisons

	Bully	LeLann	CR	HS
Time complexity	$O(n)$	$O(n)$	$O(n)$	$O(n)$
Message complexity	$O(n^2)$	$O(n^2)$	$O(n)$	$O(n)$

For the communication architecture, the Bully algorithm assumes a fully connected network, LeLann and Chang-Roberts algorithms assume a unidirectional ring and Hirschberg-Sinclair algorithm considers a bidirectional ring. The time and message complexities of these algorithms are compared in Table 7.7.

A synchronizer is a software module that resides between the distributed application and an asynchronous network to simulate a synchronous mode of operation in this structure. The α synchronizer ensures that messages in a round are all received by all processes before the next round by the exchange of messages between neighbors whereas the β synchronizer assumes a previously built spanning tree for broadcasting $round$ and convergecasting $round_{over}$ messages over the edges of this tree. The α synchronizer has low time complexity with significant message complexity whereas the β synchronizer has low message complexity since control messages are sent only over $n - 1$ tree edges but introduces extra time proportional to the depth of the tree formed. The γ synchronizer is implemented in a spanning tree consisting of clusters as its nodes. The synchronizer is executed within a cluster that typically has a low diameter, thus resulting in low message complexity in the cluster that uses α synchronizer and linear number of messages traversing the edges of tree.

Exercises

1. Show the execution steps of the Bully algorithm in a distributed system with 10 processes and leader with identifier 10, when node 6 suspects that the leader is not functioning.
2. Show the execution steps of CR algorithm in a distributed system with 9 processes connected as a unidirectional ring with sequence 3– > 5– > 1– > 0– > 4– > 6– > 8– > 2– > 7– > 5 and nodes 3 and 4 concurrently start election process.
3. Show the execution phases of HS algorithm in a distributed system with 8 processes connected as a ring with sequence 0-3-7-5-1-4-6-2 and nodes 6 and 7 concurrently start election process.
4. Implement the γ synchronizer in Python using $mpi4py$. Assume the network of Fig. 7.8 with five clusters as the input. Show the working of this synchronizer for three rounds: Each node sends its degree, number of its neighbors and the identifiers of its neighbors in rounds 1, 2 and 3 respectively to its clusterhead. The clusterheads transfer this information to the root process which displays them.

References

1. B. Awerbuch, Complexity of network synchronization. J. ACM **32**, 804–823 (1985)
2. E. Chang, R. Roberts, An improved algorithm for decentralized extrema-finding in circular configurations of processes. Commun. ACM **22**(5), 281–283 (1979)
3. H. Garcia-Molina, Elections in a distributed computing system. IEEE Trans. Comp. Syst. C **31**(1), 48–59 (1982)
4. D.S. Hirschberg, J.B. Sinclair, Decentralized extrema-finding in circular configurations of processors. Commun. ACM **23**(11) (1980)
5. G. LeLann, Distributed systems: towards a formal approach, in *Proceedings of the Information Processing '77*, ed. by B. Gilchrist (North-Holland, 1977), pp. 155–160

Fault Tolerance

8

Abstract

A fault in a distributed system is a defect in the software or a hardware component which commonly results in errors and failures. Fault tolerance methods provide correct operation of a system in the presence of faults. Redundancy through replication is a basic method for fault tolerance in a distributed system. Process groups are commonly used to provide replication and orderly group communication is needed for correct operation of replicas. In this chapter, we review basic fault tolerance methods, group communication protocols, implement these protocols in Python using $mpi4py$ and describe the consensus problem in distributed systems.

8.1 Introduction

A distributed system consists of a number of computational elements each of which works independently to achieve a single goal. The correct operation of these nodes may be hindered as a result of some hardware and/or software malfunctioning. A *fault* in a distributed system is defined as a defect in the software or a hardware component which commonly results in errors and failures. An *error* manifests itself by producing incorrect results due to a fault in the distributed system. A *failure* in a distributed system is the state of the system when the required aim is not achieved. Failure in a distributed system may be partial and the entire system may still function correctly. A fault is commonly perceived as a deviation of a function from its design and specification; an error is the manifestation of a fault by an incorrect value, and a failure is the deviation of system functioning from specification. Relationships between fault, error and failure are depicted in Fig. 8.1.

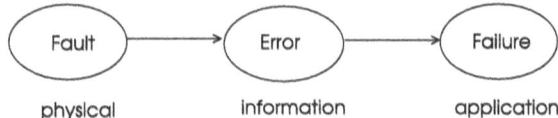

Fig. 8.1 Relationships between fault, error and failure

A fault may arise due to the mistakes in specification or design of a component; defects in components because of manufacturing process, or due to inconvenient operating environment conditions such as radiation or vibration.

A *dependable system* operates as users expect and will not fail under normal use. A dependable system should have the following basic properties:

- *Availability*: The system and its services should be available at all times.
- *Reliability*: The system should run continuously without a failure. A system that fails 1 second every hour has an availability of 99.97 % but is not reliable whereas a system that never crashes but is shut down for a week once every year is 100% reliable but only 98% available.
- *Safety*: The ability of the system to operate without catastrophic failure. This property is needed in hard real-time systems such as nuclear plants where a failure may result in a disaster.
- *Maintainability*: Maintenance of the system and its services should not be difficult or excessively expensive. A highly maintainable system may also have a high degree of availability. Formally, maintainability is the probability of repair in a given time interval.

Fault avoidance method detects faults during design and prevents them by removal. Defects in software are removed by testing and debugging in this approach. Faults are localized and are prevented from disturbing the system operation in *fault masking*. However, it is impossible to avoid faults completely, making it necessary to design and implement additional measures to manage correct system operation when faults occur. *Fault Tolerance* is defined as the ability of the system to function properly even in the presence of failures. This valuable feature is needed in a distributed system to provide correct functioning in the presence of multitude sources of failures when compared to a single computational system. In this chapter, we first review types of faults and problems in distributed systems. We then describe failure detection methods with recovery procedures and process groups that provide replicas of processes for fault tolerance.

8.2 Faults

A fault first needs to be detected, its location to be determined and diagnosed as to understand its nature. *Fault recovery* is the process of resuming normal system operation after the fault. Faults may be broadly classified depending on their source of origination as hardware faults which are due to the malfunctioning of a hardware component such as a processor, memory, communication line etc.; or software faults resulting from a software bug. A hardware fault is commonly the result of a defect in manufacturing, deterioration of a component over a long time or some environmental factor such as radiation, temperature etc. On the other hand, errors in specification and design of a system results in software faults. Faults in a distributed system may be classified to be one of the following types based on their temporal behaviour:

- *Transient Faults*: This type of fault is commonly caused by the environment occurring only once but not usually affecting system operation.
- *Intermittent Faults*: Such a fault disappears and repeats after some time, such as the hardware fault caused by a loose wire.
- *Permanent Faults*: The fault stays until removed or the affected hardware or software unit is replaced.

8.3 Failure Models

Failure models are needed to identify and determine the source of a failure, and initiate a fault recovery processes. Analysis of these models help to design more reliable systems with improved availability and safety. The main failure models are classified as follows:

- *Fail-stop Failures*: A component or a subsystem of a system stops completely loosing its assigned functionality in this type of fault. Other nodes may observe this fault.
- *Crash Failures*: A crash failure is a sudden and complete halt of a system function which may not be observed.
- *Omission Failures*: These failures occur when a subsystem fails to respond or fails to perform a required action in a specified time frame possibly as a result of network failures or software bugs.
- *Temporal Failures*: These failures are related to errors due to time inconsistencies such as clock synchronization.
- *Byzantine Failures*: Such a failure in a system manifests itself by a subsystem that behaves unpredictable and/or malicious by producing and transferring incorrect data to other subsystems and hence causing a total incorrect operation of the system.

For many applications, assuming most faults are fail-stop faults would be adequate to provide fault tolerance to those systems. However, Byzantine failures need be considered and tolerated in life-critical systems since any failure in such systems may result in catastrophic outcomes. A *t-fault tolerant system* works in accordance with its specifications if at most t of its components fail.

8.4 Fault Tolerance Methods

A component is considered faulty once its behaviour is no longer consistent with its specification. A simple method to handle faults and achieve fault tolerance is to replicate hardware and software components so that a replica may be employed when a component fails. Main methods for fault tolerance in a distributed system may be stated as follows:

- *Replication*: Several replicas of software or processes or hardware components are maintained. In the event of a component failure, a replica may be activated. The maintenance of replicas such that they are in exact state of the actual component is needed in this method. Finite state machines may be used to implement software replicas, however, in order to preserve these replicas in identical states, they should receive the messages in the same order. We will address this issue, message ordering and multicast communication, in this chapter when we review group communication.
- *Error Checking and Correction*: This method is employed mostly in communication protocols to eliminate any transmission errors. Cyclic redundancy check is a common error detection mechanism where the message to be sent is appended with error bits so that the receiver of the message dividing the message by a fixed polynomial should obtain a zero remainder if message is received correctly. An incorrect message needs to be re-transmitted.
- *Check Pointing and Roll Back*: The current state of the system which includes process and environment information is stored in a stable storage at regular intervals. The system is recovered from its last recorded state in the event of the failure of a system component.
- *Graceful Degradation*: In some cases, it may not be possible to eliminate the fault completely. When such a fault occurs, it may be convenient to allow the system to function at a reduced capacity rather than completely halting it which is called *graceful degradation*.

8.5 Failure Masking by Redundancy

Redundancy in a fault tolerant system is achieved by providing spare capacity to the system. The main types of redundancy for fault tolerance are the hardware redundancy, information redundancy, software redundancy and time redundancy as described below:

- *Hardware Redundancy*: The system is provided with spare hardware components, for example, spare processors in critical systems such as aeroplanes.
- *Software Redundancy*: Different versions of software are provided so that another version may be used when a software failure occurs. *N-version programming* method for fault tolerance is implemented by running N versions of the same

program in parallel and taking the majority vote of the output to determine the final output.
- *Information Redundancy*: Data is coded to include extra information to provide detection and correction of errors as in computer network communication protocols.
- *Time Redundancy*: Spare time is provided such that running recovery operations and tasks do not contradict system requirements in this type of redundancy method.

8.6 Replication

A server process typically receives *requests* and provides *responses* to these requests and a client is commonly blocked waiting for a response. Replicating a server is a common method for fault tolerance in client/server type of distributed systems. Two basic ways of implementing replicated servers are the *active* and *passive* replications.

8.6.1 Active Replication

All replicas of a server are actively involved in sending a response to a client in this method. The replicas are commonly implemented as a state machine; thus, another name for this type of replication is *state machine replication*. When a client makes a request, all replicas perform the requested operation in parallel and send their responses to the client as shown in Fig. 8.2a. The client receives and processes the first response and ignores the other responses.

When there are multiple client requests, the replicas should receive the client requests in the same order to produce correct results which means there is a need for the ordering of messages as we will review in the next section. Given the same initial state and same client request sequence, the servers will produce the same result. Failure of a replica is not a problem since a client request will be handled by the

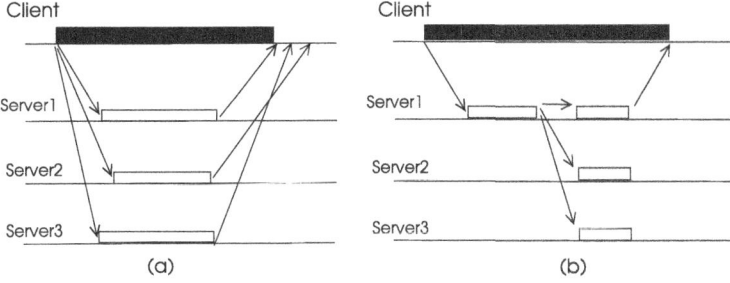

Fig. 8.2 **a** Active replication **b** passive replication

other replicas. Major drawbacks of this method is that replicas consume resources such as memory and processor time and any update of software on a replica should be done in all of them.

8.6.2 Passive Replication

There is a primary server and backup servers in this mode of replication. The client communicates with the primary server only which processes the request and then updates the backup servers with the produced results as depicted in Fig. 8.2b. The primary server can send update messages to backups in any order. When the primary fails, one of the replicas is chosen to replace it. Resource consumption is reduced significantly in this method but the response time increases if there is a failure in the primary.

8.7 Process Groups

Three basic types of communication between the processes of a distributed system are the *unicast, multicast* and *broadcast* communications. The unicast (point-to-point) communication is between a pair of processes, multicast communication is achieved between a single sender and a subset of processes commonly called a *group* and broadcast communication is performed by sending of a message to all processes in the system. A *process group* is a subset of processes with a unique attribute and some common attribute. Members of a process group may be participating in a common activity; or a process group simply denotes the active processes which may not be related, discarding the faulty ones. A commonly implemented example of the former is the active replication using finite state machines method where a message from a client should be sent as a multicast message to the group and ordering of messages from the clients should be preserved. Process groups may be classified based on their structure as follows.

- *Closed or Open Groups*: In closed groups, only the group members may send a message to the group whereas open groups allow non-members to send message to a group as in replicated servers.
- *Peer Groups or Hierarchical Groups*: A peer group allows all members to exchange messages with each other. A distributed *voting* mechanism may be used for a collective decision taken by the group. A hierarchical group has a coordinator that manages message transfers and decision making. As with any central manager node, it forms a single point of failure and a bottleneck of messages.

Groups are commonly dynamic allowing joining of new members and leaving of some of the current members. Group management handling requires the group membership for consistent view of the group members and group communication protocols to provide orderly and reliable delivery of multicast messages to group members.

Group membership management should provide primitive operations to *join*, *leave* a group as well as creating and deleting a group. A process may belong to more than one group needing coordination of two or more group managers. The manager should also notify the group members of a joining/leaving process.

8.7.1 Group Communication

Group communication is needed in various applications: to maintain consistent replicas in a client-server system with replicated servers, cluster management, conferencing and on-line scoreboards where a message is sent to a set of processes. This type of communication may be in peer-to-peer, client-server with replicated servers or hierarchical modes. A broadcast communication involves sending a message to all processes in the system whereas multicast communication, that is, group communication is sending a message to a group of processes. Timely delivery of an incoming message is handled by a multicast protocol which transfers an incoming message first to a queue and then delivers it to the application when certain conditions are met is shown in Fig. 8.3.

Group communication may be implemented with support from the hardware which provides physical multicast addresses. If this is not possible as in the general case, hardware broadcast and software filtering may be used. Group messages are broadcast to all nodes in the system and the non-group members simply discard these messages in this method. The most common method to implement group communication is to provide multicast communication entirely in software using suitable protocols. Two main methods of sending a multicast message this way are the sender sending a multicast message to each member of the group or employing a central coordinator which receives a multicast message and sends it to the members of the

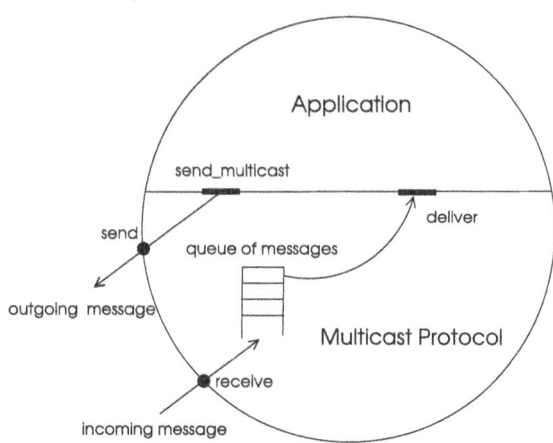

Fig. 8.3 A multicast protocol example operational structure

group on behalf of the sender, thus reducing the burden of the sender. Basic modes of group communication may be stated as follows:

- *Basic Multicast*: A process P_i sends message m to each member of the group G using the primitive *B-multicast(m, G)*. Any process P_j receiving message m simply delivers it to the application.
- *Atomic Multicast*: A required property of a type of group communication is *atomicity* or *atomic multicast* which means a group message is delivered to all members of the group or none. The sender needs to receive acknowledgements from every process to ensure that the multicast message is received by all members of the group after which it can initiate delivery of the multicast message by sending a special message to the group members.

Python Implementation of Atomic Multicast

Python implementation of atomic multicast algorithms with five group processes $P_0, ..., P_4$ is shown in Listing 8.1. There are three message types: MCAST, REPLY and DELIVER. The sender process P_0 sends a multicast message to all group members and waits for REPLY messages. When all replies are received, it sends a DELIVER message to all to initiate delivery to the application. The output in Listing 8.2 shows all group members receive the message correctly.

Listing 8.1 Atomic Multicast Algorithm

```
from mpi4py import MPI

comm = MPI.COMM_WORLD
rank = comm.Get_rank()
n    = comm.Get_size()
SENDER = 0

# message types
MCAST, REPLY, DELIVER = 1, 2, 3
msg = [-1, -1, "data"] # sender, type, data

# initialization
replies = set() # set to hold replies
allprocs = list(range(0,n))
neighs = set(allprocs) # others
neighs.remove(rank)

if rank == SENDER:
    msg = [rank, MCAST, 'Hello World']
    for node in neighs:
        comm.send(msg, dest=node, tag=MCAST)

over = False
while not over:
    msg = comm.recv(source=MPI.ANY_SOURCE, tag=MPI.ANY_TAG)
    sender, typ, data = msg[0], msg[1], msg[2]
    if typ == MCAST:
        data_saved = data
        msg = [rank, REPLY, ""]
        comm.send(msg, dest=sender, tag=MCAST)
    elif typ == DELIVER:
```

8.7 Process Groups

```
32              print("Rank: {}, Received: {}".format(rank,data_saved))
33              over = True
34          else:
35              replies.add(sender)
36              if replies == neighs:
37                  msg = [rank, DELIVER, ""]
38                  for node in neighs:
39                      comm.send(msg, dest=node, tag=DELIVER)
40                  over = True
```

Listing 8.2 Output of Atomic Multicast Algorithm

```
Rank: 3, Received: Hello World
Rank: 2, Received: Hello World
Rank: 4, Received: Hello World
Rank: 1, Received: Hello World
Rank: 5, Received: Hello World
```

- *Reliable Multicast*: Sender is assumed to remain alive and it will re-transmit all undelivered messages in reliable multicast (R-multicast). It waits for reply from all of the group members and re-transmits to members which have not replied after a time-out. R-multicast should provide the following attributes:

  - *Integrity*: A correct process P_i delivers a message m at most once, thus there are no duplicate messages delivered to the application.
  - *Agreement*: If a correct process P_i delivers message m, then all the other correct processes in the group of P_i will eventually deliver m.
  - *Validity*: A correct process P_i sending a message m will eventually deliver m itself. Provision of both validity and agreement ensures liveness that is the case of a multicast message m sent by a process P_i being delivered by all correct processes.

A R-multicast algorithm based on B-multicast algorithm may be stated in the following where all three requirements of reliable multicast are satisfied.

- $received = \{\}$
- *R-multicast* of message m by process P_i to group G:
  $B\text{-}multicast(m,G)$
- Delivery of message m by P_j:

  - **if** $m \notin received$ **then**   # **integrity**

    $received = received \cup \{m\}$
    if $P_j \neq P_i$ **then** $B\text{-}multicast(m,G)$ # **agreement**
    $R\text{-}deliver(m)$ # **validity**

- *Unreliable Multicast*: Some applications such as multicast video may employ *unreliable multicast* which is sending a multicast message and assuming all members of the group receives it.

Another fundamental property of group communication is to preserve the ordering of the messages delivered to the members of the group. Messages sent to a group may be unordered, single-source FIFO delivery implemented, causally ordered, totally ordered or a hybrid method as reviewed in the next sections.

8.7.2 Single Source FIFO Delivery

In single-source FIFO delivery (SFIFO), messages from a single sender are received in the order they are sent, however, there is no restriction in the order of messages from different servers. Formally, if process P_i sends a message m_1 before it sends message m_2 to a process P_j, then P_j does not receive m_2 before it receives m_1. The same condition applies when m is a multicast message to a group. A simple protocol to implement SFIFO delivery using sequence numbers for messages is outlined below. Each process has a sequence number vector SN to maintain the last sequence numbers of the messages sent and received. A list of queues, Q which consists of a queue for each process, is used to store messages coming out of sequence. These messages are not delivered before its predecessor messages arrive; and when the sequence is correct, they are delivered with the incoming message.

- Initially $SN = [0, 0, .., 0]$, $Q = \emptyset$
- Sending multicast message $m(i, sn)$ by P_i to group G:

    - $SN_i[i] = SN_i[i] + 1$
    - $m(sn) = SN[i]$
    - $SFIFO\_send(m, G)$

- Receiving multicast message $m(i, sn)$ by P_j:

    - **if** $m(sn) = SN_j[i] + 1$ **then**:

        $SN_j[i] = SN_j[i] + 1$
        Deliver message to P_j
        Remove any message m_old from $Q[i]$ that now has $sn = SN_j[i] + 1$
        Deliver message m_old to P_j
        $SN_j[i] = SN_j[i] + 1$

    - **else** Queue m in $Q[i]$ until condition is *true*

8.7 Process Groups

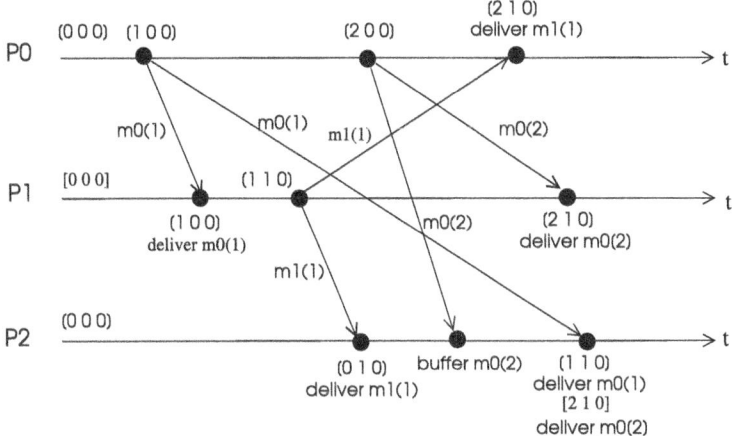

Fig. 8.4 An example of SFIFO algorithm

An Example Operation

Operation of SFIFO protocol in a system with three processes, P_0, P_1 and P_2 is depicted in Fig. 8.4 with SN vectors shown next to sending and receiving message times. Process P_0 sends a multicast message $m0(1)$ with $sn = 1$ to P_1 and P_2. Process P_2 receives the multicast message $m0(2)$ from P_0 prior to receiving $m0(1)$ and buffers this message until it receives $m0(1)$. At that time, it updates its SN vector and delivers both messages in sequence to the application.

Python Implementation

Python implementation of SFIFO protocol with four processes P_0, P_1, P_3 and P_4 is shown in Listing 8.3. Process P_0 sends three messages with unordered sequence numbers of 3, 2, 1 as input to $SFIFO\_send$ function on purpose to test the correctness of the algorithm. Note that the normal operation of $SFIFO\_send$ is shown as comment. Process P_0 sends a message with type TERM with sequence number 4 to signal the end of computation. The output shows the messages are delivered in sequence with the TERM message as the last message to the application as shown in Listing 8.4.

Listing 8.3 SFIFO Algorithm

```python
from mpi4py import MPI

comm = MPI.COMM_WORLD
rank = comm.Get_rank()
n    = comm.Get_size()

Q = [[] for _ in range(n)] # Queue for any out-of-order messages
SN = [0]*n
DATA, TERM = 1, 2
allprocs = list(range(0,n))
neighs = set(allprocs) # others
neighs.remove(rank)
msg = [-1, -1, 0, "data"]  # message[sender, type, sn, data]
data = []
over = False

def SFIFO_send(msg_data, sn):
    global SN
    # SN[rank] = SN[rank] + 1 :  normal operation
    # sn = SN[rank]
    if msg_data == "TERM":
        typ = TERM
    else:
        typ = DATA
    msg = [rank, typ, sn, msg_data]
    for node in neighs:
        comm.send(msg, dest=node, tag=DATA)

def SFIFO_deliver(msg):
    global SN, Q
    sender, typ, sn, data = msg[0], msg[1], msg[2], msg[3]
    if sn == SN[sender] + 1: # check sequence number
        SN[sender] = SN[sender] + 1
        # deliver any other waiting message
        l = len(Q[sender])
        i = 0
        while i < l: # modify Q and check again
            if Q[sender][i][2]  == SN[sender] + 1:
                SN[sender] = SN[sender] + 1
                msg_old = Q[sender].pop(i)
                msg.append(msg_old)
                l = len(Q[sender])
                i =0
            else:
                i = i+1
        return(msg)
    else:
        Q[sender].append(msg)
        return False

if rank == 0: # P0 sends a request for CS with ts=3
    SFIFO_send("Hello03",3)
    SFIFO_send("Hello02",2)
    SFIFO_send("Hello01",1)
    SFIFO_send("TERM", 4)
    over = True

while not over:
    msg = comm.recv(source=MPI.ANY_SOURCE, tag=MPI.ANY_TAG)
    if msg[1] == TERM:
        over = True
```

8.7 Process Groups

```
62     result = SFIFO_deliver(msg)
63     if result != False:
64         print("Rank: {}, {}".format(rank, result))
```

Listing 8.4 Output of SFIFO Algorithm

```
Rank: 2, [0, 1, 1, 'Hello01', [0, 1, 2, 'Hello02'], [0, 1, 3, 'Hello03']]
Rank: 2, [0, 2, 4, 'TERM']
Rank: 3, [0, 1, 1, 'Hello01', [0, 1, 2, 'Hello02'], [0, 1, 3, 'Hello03']]
Rank: 3, [0, 2, 4, 'TERM']
Rank: 1, [0, 1, 1, 'Hello01', [0, 1, 2, 'Hello02'], [0, 1, 3, 'Hello03']]
Rank: 1, [0, 2, 4, 'TERM']
```

8.7.3 Causal Delivery

Casual delivery (CD) protocol implements partial ordering of messages such that if $multicast(m, G) \prec multicast(m', G)$ then every process that delivers message m' will have delivered m. CD of multicast messages uses the concept of vector clocks and the *happened before* relationship we reviewed in Chap. 4. Each process has a sequence number vector SN as in SFIFO algorithm which shows the newest sequence number received from any other process. Any sender process P_i of a CD message increments its SN entry, appends the whole SN vector to the message as V and sends the message to the group G. A receiving process P_j compares its SN_j with the vector V in the received message. The delivery condition is that $SN_j[k] \geq V[k]$, for $k = 0, ..., n - 1$ which is to ensure that P_j has received all of the messages received by P_i as shown in the following pseudocode for processes P_i as the sender, and process P_j as the receiver. Note that this test is equivalent to testing vector clocks with the exception that we are only interested in sending and reception of messages but not in local events in CD of messages.

- Initially $SN_i = [0, 0, ..., 0]$, $Q = \emptyset$
- Sending multicast message $m(i, V)$ by P_i to group G:

  - $SN_i[i] = SN_i[i] + 1$
  - $m(V) = SN$
  - $CD\_send(m, G)$

- Receiving multicast message $m(i, V)$ by P_j:

  - **if** the following are true:

    C1: $V[i] = SN_j[i] + 1$
    C2: $\forall k \neq i : V[k] \leq SN_j[k]$

- **then**

    Deliver m to the application
    Set $SN_j[i] = V[i]$
    Remove any message m_old from Q that now satisfies C1 and C2.
    Deliver m_old to the application
    $SN_j[i] = SN_j[i] + 1$

- **else** Queue m in $Q[i]$ until conditions are $true$

An Example Operation

An example operation of this algorithm with three processes P_0, P_1 and P_2 is shown in Fig. 8.5 where processes P_0, P_2 and P_1 send CD multicast messages in sequence. Process P_1 sends the message $m_1(111)$ to P_0 and P_2, P_2 accepts this message as conditions C1 and C2 are satisfied. However, P_0 does not deliver this message as condition C2 is not satisfied and when it receives message $m_2(101)$, both conditions are satisfied which means both m_2 and queued message m_1 may be delivered to the application.

Python Implementation

Python code that implements CD of multicast messages with four processes $P_0, ..., P_3$ is shown in Listing 8.5. The sending and delivering of CD messages are executed by functions CD_send and $CD\_deliver$ respectively. These routines implement the rules of sending and reception of CD messages we have described. Any CD message that arrives out of order is stored in the queue Q to be delivered when delivery condition which is tested by comparing the vector V in the message with the local

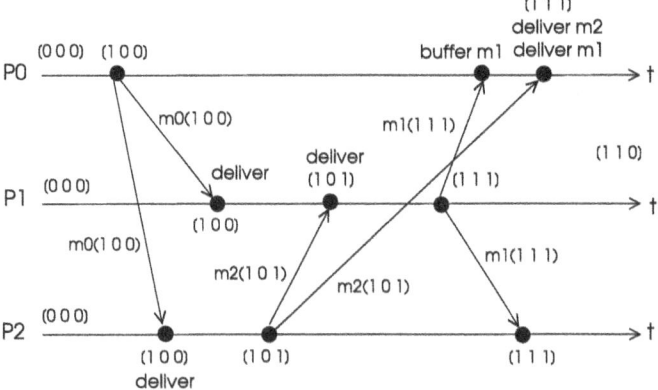

Fig. 8.5 An example operation of the casual delivery algorithm

8.7 Process Groups

vector SN is satisfied. The scenario implemented consists of processes P_0 and P_2 sending two CD multicast messages each and processes P_1 and P_3 sending a single CD multicast message each. A message carries data "Hellosn" where s is the sender and n is the sequence number of the message for this sender. The $waits$ array contains the number of messages to be received by each process for proper termination. The output of this algorithm displayed in Listing 8.6 shows the CD order is satisfied for all processes with each process receiving the messages sent by a sender in the same order.

Listing 8.5 Causal Message Delivery Algorithm

```python
from mpi4py import MPI

comm = MPI.COMM_WORLD
rank = comm.Get_rank()
n    = comm.Get_size()

Q = [[] for _ in range(n)]
SN = [0]*n

DATA, TERM = 1, 2
allprocs = list(range(0,n))
neighs = set(allprocs) # others
neighs.remove(rank)
msg = [-1, 0, [], "data"]   # message = [sender, type, V, data]

def vector_test(P,S):
    for k in range (0,n):
        if k == rank:
            continue
        if P[k] > S[k]:
            return True
    return False

def vector_test2(P,S):
    for k in range (0,n):
        if k == S[rank]:
            continue
        if P[k] > S[k]:
            return False
    return True

def CD_send(msg_data):
    global SN
    SN[rank] = SN[rank] + 1 # normal operation
    msg = [rank, DATA, SN, msg_data]
    for node in neighs:
        comm.send(msg, dest=node, tag=DATA)

def CD_deliver(msg):
    global SN
    sender, typ, V, data = msg[0], msg[1], msg[2], msg[3]
    if V[sender] == SN[sender] + 1 and vector_test(V,SN):
        SN[sender] = V[sender]
        # deliver any other waiting message
        l = len(Q[sender])
        i = 0
        while i < l: # modify Q and check again
            if V[sender] == Q[sender][i][2][sender]+1 and vector_test2(V,Q[sender][i][2]):
                SN[sender] = SN[sender] + 1
```

```
                msg_old = Q[sender].pop(i)
                msg.append(msg_old)
                l = len(Q[sender])
                i = 0
            else:
                i = i + 1
        return(msg)
    else:
        Q[sender].append(msg)
        return False

if rank == 0: # P0 sends a request for CS with ts=3
    CD_send("Hello01")
    CD_send("Hello02")
elif rank == 1:
    CD_send("Hello11")
elif rank == 2:
    CD_send("Hello21")
    CD_send("Hello22")
elif rank == 3:
    CD_send("Hello31")
waits=[4,5,4,5]
count = 0
while count < waits[rank]:
    msg = comm.recv(source=MPI.ANY_SOURCE, tag=MPI.ANY_TAG)
    count = count + 1
    result = CD_deliver(msg)
    if result != False:
        print("Rank: {}, Received: {}".format(rank, result))
```

Listing 8.6 Output of CD Algorithm

```
Rank: 0, Received: [3, 1, [0, 0, 0, 1], 'Hello31']
Rank: 0, Received: [2, 1, [0, 0, 1, 0], 'Hello21']
Rank: 0, Received: [2, 1, [0, 0, 2, 0], 'Hello22']
Rank: 0, Received: [1, 1, [0, 1, 0, 0], 'Hello11']
Rank: 2, Received: [3, 1, [0, 0, 0, 1], 'Hello31']
Rank: 2, Received: [0, 1, [1, 0, 0, 0], 'Hello01']
Rank: 2, Received: [0, 1, [2, 0, 0, 0], 'Hello02']
Rank: 2, Received: [1, 1, [0, 1, 0, 0], 'Hello11']
Rank: 3, Received: [2, 1, [0, 0, 1, 0], 'Hello21']
Rank: 3, Received: [2, 1, [0, 0, 2, 0], 'Hello22']
Rank: 3, Received: [0, 1, [1, 0, 0, 0], 'Hello01']
Rank: 3, Received: [0, 1, [2, 0, 0, 0], 'Hello02']
Rank: 3, Received: [1, 1, [0, 1, 0, 0], 'Hello11']
Rank: 1, Received: [3, 1, [0, 0, 0, 1], 'Hello31']
Rank: 1, Received: [2, 1, [0, 0, 1, 0], 'Hello21']
Rank: 1, Received: [2, 1, [0, 0, 2, 0], 'Hello22']
Rank: 1, Received: [0, 1, [1, 0, 0, 0], 'Hello01']
Rank: 1, Received: [0, 1, [2, 0, 0, 0], 'Hello02']
```

8.7.4 Total Order Multicast

Total order multicast (TOM) requires that all messages are received in the same order by all the receivers. Formally, for any two processes P_i and P_j and any two messages m_1 and m_2 that are delivered to these processes, m_1 is delivered to P_i before m_2 if and only if m_1 is delivered before m_2 to P_j. Thus a total order of

8.7 Process Groups

messages with the same sequence of reception by all processes is provided. This protocol is stronger than the SFIFO and casual delivery protocols. A simple way to implement TOM is to use a central server called *Sequencer* which monitors message transfers as follows. Any process P_i that wants to deliver a multicast message $m(i, G)$ to the group G sends m to the group G and to the *Sequencer*. This central server process has a sequence number S which is incremented at each multicast message reception, included in the *Sequencer* message $M(m, S)$ and broadcast to the group. Each process P_i has a sequence number S_i which is initialized to 0. Any process P_j receiving message m delivers it to the application when *Sequencer* message M is received and the sequence number in this message is the expected sequence number. Note that messages m and M may be in any order and any out of order message received by P_j will be buffered.

- *Sequencer*:
  - Maintains a sequential number S which is initially 0.
  - When a multicast message $m(i)$ is received:

    Set $S = S + 1$
    $SEQ\_send(M(m, S)$ to the group G

- Sending multicast message $m(i)$ by P_i:
  - $TOM\_send(m)$ to the *Sequencer* and to the group G

- Reception of message $m(j)$ from P_j by P_i. Deliver message m to the application when both of the following conditions are $true$:
  - Message $M(m, S)$ is received from the Sequencer.
  - $S = S_i + 1$

Correctness is evident as there is a unique sequence number maintained by the *Sequencer*. As with all algorithms with a privileged process, single point of failure and dense message traffic around the central server are the major drawbacks of this approach as well as performing two *send* operations for each multicast message. A distributed TOM protocol is employed in ISIS system [1] where receiver of a multicast message stores the message in a priority queue and replies with a proposed priority to the sender. The sender process chooses agreed priority and re-sends the multicast message. Upon receiving the final agreed priority, the receiver updates message priority, re-organizes the message queue and delivers all of the deliverable messages to the application.

An Example Operation

An example operation of this algorithm with four processes $P_0, ..., P_3$ is depicted in Fig. 8.6 with sequence numbers displaying the sending and receiving times of

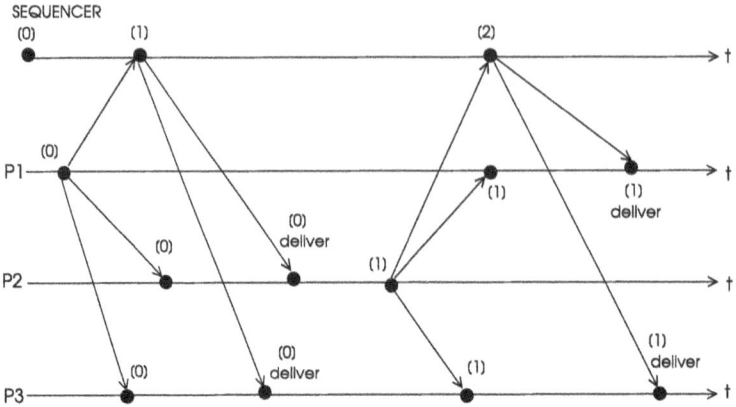

Fig. 8.6 An example operation of TOM algorithm with a sequencer

messages. Processes P_1 and P_2 send TOM messages to both the *Sequencer* process which is P_0 and to all other processes. The messages are delivered to the application when the sequence number of the *Sequencer* message is as expected and the TOM message from the sender is received.

Python Implementation

Python implementation of TOM algorithm with a *Sequencer* is shown in Listing 8.7 for five processes $P_0, \ldots, P_4$ with TOM_send and $TOM\_deliver$ as the routines for sending and delivering TOM messages. Process P_0 is the *Sequencer* and processes P_1, P_2 and P_3 are the sender of TOM messages. Delivering a TOM message to the application requires both the reception of TOM message from the sender and the *Sequencer* message with the correct sequence number. The $TOM\_deliver$ message tests these two conditions and since the order of TOM and Sequencer messages cannot be determined, a TOM message with a pending sequence number is queued in the queue Q to be released when the required *Sequencer* message arrives. The number of messages for a process to to terminate in this scenario is stored in the *waits* array with the *Sequencer* to receive three messages, processes P_1 and P_2 four, two from other processes and two from the *Sequencer* each and six for P_3 which waits three *Sequencer* and three TOM messages. The output of the algorithm is displayed in Listing 8.8 showing total order is satisfied for all processes. For example, "Hello31–Hello21" messages are received in correct sequence by processes P_1 and P_4; and "Hello11–Hello21" messages are received in correct sequence by processes P_3 and P_4.

Listing 8.7 Total Order Multicast Algorithm with a Sequencer

```
1  from mpi4py import MPI
2  import time
3
4  comm = MPI.COMM_WORLD
5  rank = comm.Get_rank()
```

8.7 Process Groups

```python
n       = comm.Get_size()

TOSEQ, FRSEQ, TOM = 1, 2, 3  # message types
SEQUENCER = 0
allprocs = list(range(0,n))
neighs = set(allprocs)  # others
neighs.remove(rank)
msg = [-1, -1, -1, "data"]  # message[sender, type, sn, data]
frseq, seqno, seqsaved = 0, 0, 0
both = [0] *n
TOM_recvd = [0]*n
SEQ_recvd = [0]*n
Q = [[] for _ in range(n)]

def TOM_send(msg_data):
    msg = [rank, TOSEQ, 0, msg_data]
    # print("TOM SENT SEQ",msg)
    comm.send(msg, dest=SEQUENCER, tag=TOSEQ)
    msg[1] = TOM
    for node in neighs:
      if node == SEQUENCER:
          continue
      comm.send(msg, dest=node, tag=TOM)

def TOM_deliver(msg):
    global seqno, boths, frseq, seqsaved
    sender, typ, seq, data = msg[0], msg[1], msg[2], msg[3]
    if typ == FRSEQ:
        if seq == seqno + 1:
            seqno = seqno + 1
        SEQ_recvd[sender] = SEQ_recvd[sender] + 1
    else:
        TOM_recvd[sender] = TOM_recvd[sender] + 1
        Q[sender].append(msg)
    msg = []
    while SEQ_recvd[sender] > 0 and TOM_recvd[sender] > 0:
        msg_old = Q[sender].pop(0)
        msg.append(msg_old)
        SEQ_recvd[sender] = SEQ_recvd[sender] - 1
        TOM_recvd[sender] = TOM_recvd[sender] - 1
    return msg

if rank == 1:
    data = "Hello11"
    TOM_send(data)

elif rank == 2:
    data = "Hello21"
    time.sleep(1)
    TOM_send(data)

elif rank == 3:
    data = "Hello31"
    TOM_send(data)

count = 0
waits = [3,4,4,4,6]
while count < waits[rank]:
    msg = comm.recv(source=MPI.ANY_SOURCE, tag=MPI.ANY_TAG)
    count = count + 1
    sender, typ = msg[0], msg[1]
    if typ == TOSEQ:
        frseq = frseq + 1
```

```
69          msg[1], msg[2] = FRSEQ, frseq
70          for node in neighs:
71              if node == sender:
72                  continue
73              comm.send(msg, dest=node, tag=FRSEQ)
74      else:   # message type is FRSEQ or TOM
75          result = TOM_deliver(msg)
76          if result:
77              print("Rank: {}, Received: {}".format(rank,result))
```

Listing 8.8 Output of TOM Algorithm with a Sequencer

```
Rank: 1, Received: [[3, 3, 0, 'Hello31']]
Rank: 1, Received: [[2, 3, 0, 'Hello21']]
Rank: 3, Received: [[1, 3, 0, 'Hello11']]
Rank: 3, Received: [[2, 3, 0, 'Hello21']]
Rank: 2, Received: [[1, 3, 0, 'Hello11']]
Rank: 2, Received: [[3, 3, 0, 'Hello31']]
Rank: 4, Received: [[1, 3, 0, 'Hello11']]
Rank: 4, Received: [[3, 3, 0, 'Hello31']]
Rank: 4, Received: [[2, 3, 0, 'Hello21']]
```

8.8 Consensus

Agreement in a distributed system is a fundamental requirement needed mainly for fault tolerance when some nodes fail and the remaining nodes need to function correctly. For example, various applications such as the commit decision in a database system where processes either commit or abort a transaction need agreement of processes; blockchain is another application where the processes need consensus on the validity and the order of transactions of a central server, and bitcoin networks are other applications that need to reach consensus. The general assumption of a consensus algorithm in a faulty system is that there are m faulty processes out of n processes and the non-faulty $n - m$ processes should agree on some value.

We can classify consensus algorithms as consensus without any fault, consensus with at most m crash faults and consensus with at most m Byzantine faults in which processes act arbitrarily to produce correct or incorrect results. Consensus in a non-faulty environment is trivial, each process broadcasts its value to all other processes, every node agrees on the minimum (or maximum) of all of the values received, thus agreeing on the same value. A consensus algorithm should provide the following properties:

- *Termination*: Every non-faulty node eventually decides.
- *Agreement*: All non-faulty nodes decide on the same value.
- *Validity*: The decided value must be the input of at least one node.

Agreement in an asynchronous system with even a single process failure is impossible due to Fischer, Lynch and Patterson (FLP) [2] result.

8.8.1 Consensus with Crash Failures

Consensus in a system with at most m crash failures may be achieved by the following algorithm executed by each process P_i in a synchronous execution model with reliable communication channels. Each processes broadcasts its initial value in the first round and in the following rounds, it broadcasts any new value received in the last round. If a single node fails at each round, running the algorithm for $m + 1$ rounds ensures that "there is at least one round where all processes worked correctly and obtained values to achieve consensus". Number of messages transferred at each round is $O(n^2)$, thus, total number of messages in this algorithm is $O(n^2 m)$

- x = local value

  - **for** round 1 to $m + 1$ **do**

      if current x has not been broadcast **then** $broadcast(x)$

  - y_i = value received from P_j in this round
  - $x = min(x, y_j)$

- output x as the consensus value

8.8.2 Byzantine Agreement

A distributed system may have Byzantine processes which may fail arbitrarily sending conflicting or incorrect information to other processes. Reaching agreement in such a system is more difficult than agreement in a system with fail-stop or crash failure processes. Byzantine agreement problem is commonly exemplified by an army consisting of a commander and a number of generals who communicate over reliable channels. The commander can give *attack* (1) or *retreat* (0) to the generals and all generals must agree on the same value to succeed.

A Byzantine army with a commander (C) and two generals $G1$ and $G2$ is shown in Fig. 8.7. The commander is the faulty node in (a) and generals are not able to decide whether to attack or to retreat. General $G2$ is faulty in (b) of the figure and general $G1$ can not decide as it has two inputs as attack and retreat.

However when there is one commander and three generals, generals can decide correctly by taking the majority of the commands they receive as depicted in Fig. 8.8a where the commander is faulty and general $G2$ is faulty in (b). Lamport proved that agreement on a correct value is possible when there are m Byzantine processes in a distributed system that has at least $3m + 1$ processes. It was also shown that this agreement problem has no solution, that is, agreement cannot be reached if $n < 3m + 1$.

Oral Message Algorithm

We will assume communication channels are reliable with no message losses, faulty nodes cannot send unidentified messages and they may not remain silent, also o communications is synchronous. Oral message (OM) algorithm is a recursive algorithm to reach consensus in a Byzantine system of m faulty processes out of $n = 3m + 1$ processes, The following are assumed in this algorithm [3]:

- A1. Every message that is sent is delivered correctly.
- A2. The receiver of a message knows who sent it.
- A3. The absence of a message can be detected.

OM algorithm based on these assumptions has the following steps:

- S: source process, P_i: process i
- Base Case: $(OM(0))$
  - Source node S sends its value to every other process.
- $OM(m), m > 0$
  1. Source node S sends its value to every other process

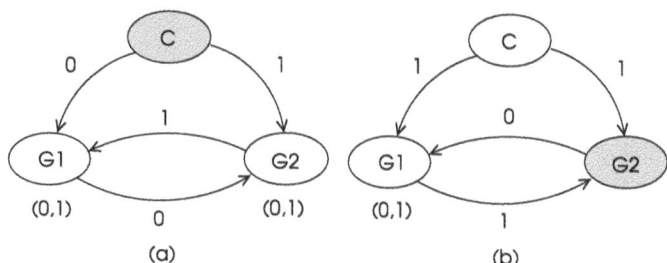

Fig. 8.7 A Byzantine system with three processes

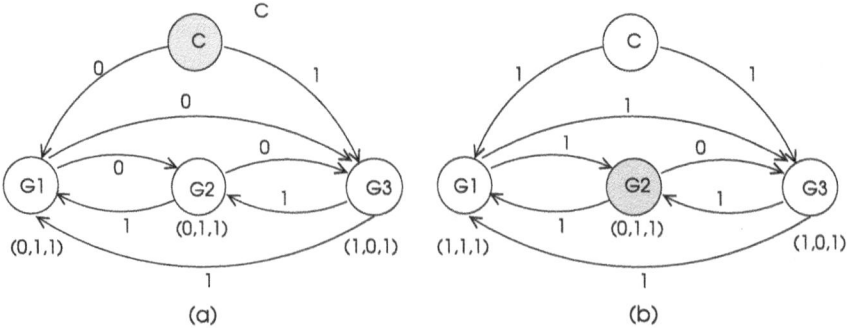

Fig. 8.8 A Byzantine system with three processes

> 2. Let v_i be the value received by each process P_i. If P_i receives no value, it sets $v_j = 0$. Each P_i acts as the source S and activates the algorithm $OM(m-1)$ by sending v_i to $n-2$ all other processes.
> 3. For each P_i and each P_j $(i \neq j)$ let v_j be the value P_i received from P_j in step 2. If P_i receives no value, it sets $v_j = 0$. Process P_i computes $majority(v_1, ..., v_{n-1})$ and decides on that value.

OM algorithm works recursively where OM(m) activates $n-1$ separate runs of the algorithm OM($m-1$) which in turn activates $n-2$ runs of OM($m-2$) etc. Thus, there will be $(n-1)$ messages in the first stage, $(n-1)(n-2)$ messages in the second stage and $(n-1)(n-2)...(n-(m+1))$ messages in the $(m+1)$th stage for a total of $O(n^{m+1})$ messages.

8.9 Chapter Notes

We reviewed three distinct but related topics in fault tolerance which are Replication, Group Communication and Consensus in this chapter. Fault tolerance is the ability of a system to function correctly in the presence of faults. An evident method to provide fault tolerance in a distributed system is through redundancy which can be accomplished by replicating the computations or data. We briefly introduced replication of servers in a client-server type of distributed system. This type of replication is commonly achieved by implementing servers as state machines. The consistency of the replicas can be achieved by ordered message delivery to them and group communication is a convenient method to achieve this purpose. A group is a subset of processes that have a unique name. The main methods of ordered message delivery using group communication are FIFO delivery, causal delivery and total order multicast delivery protocols as we briefly described. Consensus in a distributed system is the agreement of the system processes on a common value. A Byzantine process may act arbitrarily making consensus in such a system difficult. Agreement in asynchronous systems with even a single crash failure is impossible [2]. We described consensus and agreement in the presence of Byzantine processes as the last topic of the chapter.

Exercises

1. Label sequence vector values when processes of Fig. 8.9 exchange messages using SFIFO algorithm.
2. Label sequence vector values when processes of Fig. 8.10 exchange messages using CD algorithm.
3. Test TOM Python algorithm for six processes $P_0, ..., P_5$ and show all messages are received in the same order by all processes for the following events: P_0, P_2 and P_5 send TOM messages with their identifiers.

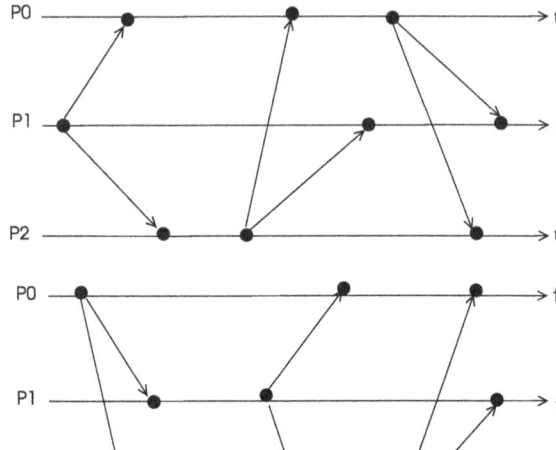

Fig. 8.9 Message transfers using SFIFO multicast for Exercise 1

Fig. 8.10 Message transfers using CD multicast for Exercise 2

4. Write the Oral message algorithm in Python using $mpi4py$ for five processes $P_0, \ldots, P_4$ where P_0 is the commander and P_3 is the betrayer. Draw the diagram of this Byzantine system when commander gives $attack$ order. Verify by the output of the algorithm that all processes other than process P_3 agree on $attack$ value.

References

1. K. Birman, T. Joseph, Reliable communication in the presence of failures. ACM Trans. Comput. Syst. **5**(1), 47–76 (1987)
2. M.J. Fischer, N.A. Lynch, M.S. Paterson, Impossibility of distributed consensus with one faulty process. J. ACM **32**(2), 374–382 (1985)
3. L. Lamport, R. Shostak, M. Pease, The Byzantine generals problem. ACM Trans. Programm. Lang. Syst. **4**(3), 382–401 (1982)

Part III
Distributed Graph Algorithms

Trees and Traversals 9

Abstract

Constructing spanning trees of a graph has various applications such as building a communication network over which the messages can be transferred efficiently. In this chapter, we review basic distributed tree building procedures which are general spanning tree, breadth-first-search tree and depth-first-search tree algorithms and provide their implementations in Python using *mpi4py*.

9.1 Introduction

A tree is an acyclic graph, given a graph $G = (V, E)$, *a spanning tree T* of G contains all of the vertices of G and a subset of its edges. Spanning trees provide a convenient communication subgraph of a computer network. The number of edges a spanning tree covering n nodes is $n - 1$.

A constructed rooted spanning tree in a distributed system consisting of n nodes may be used for a number of communication modes. The root process may broadcast a message to its children and each internal node may send this message to its children resulting in the reception of a copy of the message by all nodes. Convergecast of message of each node at root node is also possible, this time in the reverse direction from the leaves to the root. The breadth-first-search tree of an undirected unweighted graph provides shortest distances to the root node and the depth-first-search in a graph searches nodes as deep as possible and provides a spanning tree of visited nodes.

We review basic operation of these algorithms; spanning tree, broadcast and convergecast over a spanning tree, constructing a BFS tree and a DFS tree, and provide Python codes using *mpi4py* in this chapter.

9.2 Spanning Tree Construction

An arbitrary spanning tree of a graph can be constructed by the root node using flooding of messages. The distributed spanning tree construction algorithm has three types of messages: *probe*, *ack* and *reject*. Any node that receives *probe* message for the first time sets the sender as its parent and then sends a *probe* message with its identifier to all of its neighbors other than its parent as shown in Algorithm 9.1 [1]. If a node already has an assigned parent, it sends *reject* message to the sender. The algorithm at each node continues until a node receives *ack* or *reject* messages from all of its neighbors as checked at line 6 of the algorithm.

Algorithm 9.1 *Spanning_Tree*

1: **Input**: $G = (V, E)$ an unweighted graph
2: **Output**: $T = (V, E')$, a spanning tree of G
3: **if** $me = root$ **then**
4:     **send** *probe* to all my neighbors
5: **end if**
6: **while** $(childs \cup others) \neq neighbors$ **do**
7:     **receive** msg from a neighbor v
8:     **switch** msg.type:
9:         **case** *probe*:
10:             **if** $parent = \perp$ **then**
11:                 $parent \leftarrow v$
12:                 **send** *probe* to all neighbors except v
13:             **else**
14:                 **send** $reject$ to v
15:             **end if**
16:         **case** *ack*: $childs \leftarrow childs \cup \{v\}$
17:         **case** *rej*: $others \leftarrow others \cup \{v\}$
18: **end while**

Analysis

Theorem 9.1 *Algorithm 9.1 correctly builds a spanning tree and has $O(m)$ message complexity.*

Proof Each node u will be visited at least once and thus will have a designated parent at the end of the algorithm. If a node u receives at least one *ack* message from any of its neighbors, it will assign those nodes as its children, otherwise it will be a leaf node. Thus, each node other than the root will be an internal node or the leaf of the spanning tree. A node u will never have two parents since u will not change its parent once this is assigned, preventing any cycles in the structure to be formed. Thus, the final structure is acyclic and a tree. Since every node will be visited and be denoted as an internal or a leaf node in the end, the resulting structure is a spanning tree. The algorithm at each node terminates when each neighbor of a node is designated as its

9.2 Spanning Tree Construction

children or as unrelated. Thus, we have shown that the resulting structure is a tree, it is a spanning tree and the distributed algorithm at each node terminates.

Each edge in the graph is traversed at most twice, once in each direction. Therefore, the message complexity of this algorithm is $O(m)$. □

Python Implementation

The Python code with *mpi4py* module in Listing 9.1 implements Algorithm 9.1 using the same type of messages and the same flow control. The adjacency matrix A has neighborhood information and each process can find its neighbors by the row indexed by its rank from this matrix and storing its neighbors at set *neighs*. The sets *childs* and *others* are used to keep the children and unrelated neighbors of a node respectively. The message structure is an array of two integers with the first integer holding the identifier of the sender and the second one is the type of the message.

Listing 9.1 Spanning Tree Construction

```
from mpi4py import MPI
import numpy as np

comm = MPI.COMM_WORLD
rank = comm.Get_rank()
n    = comm.Get_size()

PROBE, ACK, REJ = 1, 2, 3
parent = -1
msg    = np.array([-1,-1])
neighs, childs, others = set(), set(), set()

A = np.array([[0,1,0,0,1,1,0,0],
              [1,0,1,1,1,0,0,0],
              [0,1,0,1,0,0,1,0],
              [0,1,1,0,1,0,1,1],
              [1,1,0,1,0,1,0,0],
              [1,0,0,0,1,0,0,0],
              [0,0,1,1,0,0,0,1],
              [0,0,0,1,0,0,1,0]], dtype=int)

for j in range(0,n): # set neighbors
    if A[rank,j] == 1:
        neighs.add(j)

if rank == 0: # root starts ST
    parent = 0
    msg[0], msg[1] = rank, PROBE
    for node in neighs:
        comm.send(msg, dest=node, tag=PROBE)

while childs.union(others) != neighs:
    msg = comm.recv(source=MPI.ANY_SOURCE, tag=MPI.ANY_TAG)
    sender, typ = msg[0], msg[1]
    msg[0] = rank
    if typ == PROBE:
        if parent == -1:
            parent = sender
            neighs.remove(sender)
            msg[0], msg[1] = rank, ACK
            comm.send(msg, dest=sender, tag=ACK)
```

```
42              msg[1] = PROBE
43              for node in neighs:
44                  comm.send(msg,dest=node,tag=PROBE)
45          else:
46              msg[1] = REJ
47              comm.send(msg, dest=sender, tag=REJ)
48
49      elif typ == ACK:
50          childs.add(sender)
51
52      else:
53          others.add(sender)
54
55  print("Rank: {}, Parent: {}, Childs: {}, Others: {}".format(rank,
         parent,childs,others))
```

Listing 9.2 Output of Spanning Tree Algorithm

```
Rank: 0, Parent: 0, Childs: {1, 4, 5}, Others: set()
Rank: 5, Parent: 0, Childs: set(), Others: {4}
Rank: 1, Parent: 0, Childs: {2, 3}, Others: {4}
Rank: 4, Parent: 0, Childs: set(), Others: {1, 3, 5}
Rank: 2, Parent: 1, Childs: {6}, Others: {3}
Rank: 3, Parent: 1, Childs: {7}, Others: {2, 4, 6}
Rank: 7, Parent: 3, Childs: set(), Others: {6}
Rank: 6, Parent: 2, Childs: set(), Others: {3, 7}
```

The running of this code in the sample graph of Fig. 9.1 resulted in four different spanning trees displayed in the figure with the output shown in Listing 9.2 corresponding to the tree in (b) of this figure.

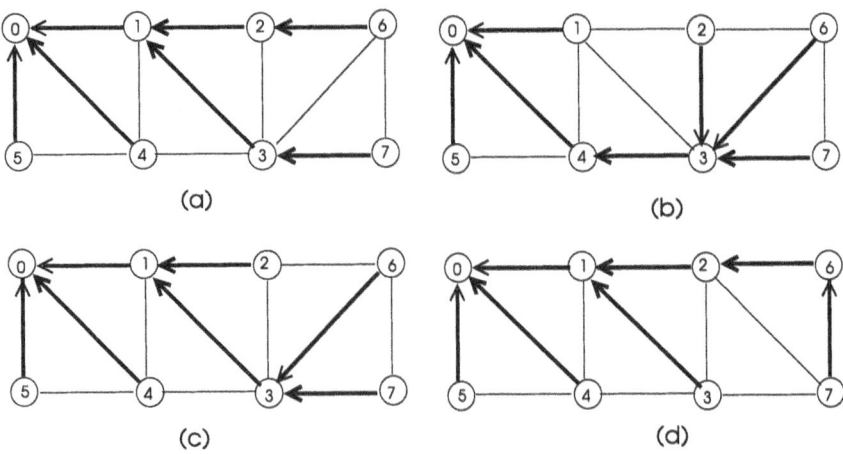

Fig. 9.1 Different runs of Algorithm 9.1 in a sample graph

9.2.1 Broadcast over a Spanning Tree

Broadcast operation results in the storage of a message from a single source to all nodes in a distributed system. A simple way for broadcast is to use flooding in which any node other than the source node sends the message it receives to all other nodes in the system. However, this method is not efficient as it results in duplicate messages.

9.2.2 Broadcast Without Acknowledgement

A simple and effective way for broadcast is to use an already built spanning tree and send the broadcast message only over the edges of this tree. Each node simply forwards the message to its descendants as shown in Algorithm 9.2. Total number of messages transferred over the spanning tree edges is $n - 1$ as each tree edge is traversed exactly once.

Algorithm 9.2 $Broadcast$

1: **Input**: $G = (V, E)$, an undirected graph
2: **Output**: copy of $bcast\_msg$ at each node
3: $T \leftarrow$ a spanning tree of graph $G = (V, E)$
4: **if** $me = source$ **then**
5:     send $bcast\_msg$ to all my children
6: **else**
7:     **receive** $bcast\_msg$ from my parent
8:     **if** I have children **then**
9:         send $bcast\_msg$ to all my children
10:    **end if**
11: **end if**

Python Implementation

We can have two different ways of implementing Algorithm 9.2 in Python, the first one is the direct implementation of Algorithm 9.2 without acknowledgements as shown in Listing 9.3. We will use the spanning tree of Fig. 9.2 for the broadcast and convergecast algorithms. Each node P_i in the network has a previously defined parent as the entry i in the *parents* list and the children of a node P_i are listed in *childs* list corresponding element and the broadcast message is "Hello". The output of this algorithm displayed in Listing 9.4 shows that all nodes receive the broadcast message.

Fig. 9.2 A sample graph spanning tree for broadcast and convergecast algorithms

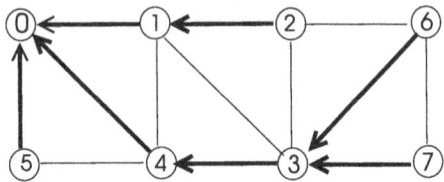

Listing 9.3 Broadcast Without Acknowledgement Algorithm

```
1  import mpicom as m
2
3  children = [[4,5,1],[2],[],[7,6],[3],[],[],[]]
4  parents  = [0,0,1,4,0,0,3,3]
5
6  childs = children[m.rank]
7  parent = parents[m.rank]
8  B_CAST = 1
9
10 if m.rank == 0:
11     b_msg = ["Hello"]
12     for child in childs:
13         m.comm.send(b_msg, dest=child, tag=B_CAST)
14 else:
15     my_msg = m.comm.recv(source=parent, tag=B_CAST)
16     print("Rank:{}, Received {} from {}".format(m.rank,my_msg,
       parent))
17     if len(childs) != 0:
18         for child in childs:
19             m. comm.send(my_msg, dest=child, tag=B_CAST)
```

Listing 9.4 Output of Broadcast Without Acknowledgement Algorithm

```
Rank:5, Received ['Hello'] from 0
Rank:4, Received ['Hello'] from 0
Rank:3, Received ['Hello'] from 4
Rank:7, Received ['Hello'] from 3
Rank:6, Received ['Hello'] from 3
Rank:1, Received ['Hello'] from 0
Rank:2, Received ['Hello'] from 1
```

9.2.3 Broadcast with Acknowledgement

We require that the source node is notified of the delivery of the broadcast message to all nodes in the distributed system in the second implementation. We have an acknowledgement message (*ack*) this time and sending of *ack* messages is initiated by the leaf nodes of the spanning tree when they receive the broadcast message. Any node that receives *ack*s from all of its children sends an *ack* message to its parent and the algorithm terminates when the source process receives *ack*s from all of its children as in Algorithm 9.3.

9.2 Spanning Tree Construction

Algorithm 9.3 *Broadcast with Acknowledgement*

1: **Input**: $G = (V, E)$, an undirected, unweighted graph
2: **Output**: copy of *bcast_msg* at each node
3: **message types** *bcast, ack*
4: $T \leftarrow$ a spanning tree of graph $G = (V, E)$
5: **if** $i = root$ **then**
6:     **send** *bcast_msg* to all my children
7: **end if**
8: **while** $acked \neq childs$ **do**
9:     **receive** *bcast_msg* from my parent
10:    **if** $msg(j).type = bcast$ **then**
11:       **if** I have children **then**
12:         **send** *bcast_msg* to all my children
13:       **else**
14:         **send** *ack* to *parent*
15:       **end if**
16:    **else**
17:       $acked \leftarrow acked \cup \{j\}$
18:    **end if**
19: **end while**
20: **if** $i \neq root$ **then**
21:     **send** *ack* to *parent*
22: **end if**

Python Implementation

Python code for this algorithm can be formed as in Algorithm 9.3 by carefully considering the position of nodes in the spanning tree. We use the logical variable *over* to test whether a node should finish running as shown in Listing 9.5. This flag for an intermediate node u is set to *true* value when u receives *ack* messages from all of its children after which sends an *ack* to its parent. A leaf node sends an *ack* message to its parent immediately after it receives the broadcast message which contains the identifiers of all nodes in the system and sets the variable *over* to true as in lines 33–36.

Listing 9.5 Broadcast with Acknowledgement Algorithm

```
from mpi4py import MPI
import numpy as np

comm = MPI.COMM_WORLD
rank = comm.Get_rank()
size = comm.Get_size()

# message types
B_CAST   = 1
ACK      = 2
over     = False
msg      = np.array([-1,-1, 99]) # msg = [rank, type, data]

children = [[4,5,1],[2],[],[7,6],[3],[],[],[]]
parents  = [0,0,1,4,0,0,3,3]
```

```
16  acked = set()
17  childs = children[rank]
18  parent = parents[rank]
19  childs = set(childs)
20
21  if rank == 0:
22      b_msg = [0,1,2,3,4,5] # msg data
23      msg = [rank, B_CAST, b_msg]
24      for child in childs:   # broadcast
25          comm.send(msg, dest=child, tag=B_CAST)
26
27  while not over:
28      msg = comm.recv(source=MPI.ANY_SOURCE, tag=MPI.ANY_TAG)
29      sender, typ, data = msg[0], msg[1], msg[2]
30      if typ == B_CAST:
31          print("Rank: {}, Received: {}".format(rank,msg))
32          msg[0] = rank
33          if len(childs) == 0: # leaf node
34              msg[1] = ACK      # send ACK to parent
35              comm.send(msg,dest=parent,tag=ACK)
36              over = True
37          else:
38              for child in childs:
39                  comm.send(msg, dest=child, tag=B_CAST)
40      else:
41          acked.add(sender)
42          if acked == childs:
43              msg = [rank, ACK, 0]
44              if rank != 0:
45                  comm.send(msg,dest=parent,tag=ACK)
46              else:
47                  print("Rank: {}, all done".format(rank))
48                  over = True
```

Output of this algorithm displayed in Listing 9.6 shows that all nodes receive the broadcast message and acknowledge it since the termination condition for the root process is the reception of *ack* messages from all of its children.

Listing 9.6 Output of Broadcast with Acknowledgement Algorithm

```
Rank: 6, Received: [3, 1, [0, 1, 2, 3, 4, 5]]
Rank: 5, Received: [0, 1, [0, 1, 2, 3, 4, 5]]
Rank: 2, Received: [1, 1, [0, 1, 2, 3, 4, 5]]
Rank: 7, Received: [3, 1, [0, 1, 2, 3, 4, 5]]
Rank: 1, Received: [0, 1, [0, 1, 2, 3, 4, 5]]
Rank: 3, Received: [4, 1, [0, 1, 2, 3, 4, 5]]
Rank: 4, Received: [0, 1, [0, 1, 2, 3, 4, 5]]
Rank: 0, all done
```

9.2.4 Convergecast over a Spanning Tree

The convergecast is the operation of gathering of individual messages from all nodes at a single destination, commonly the root of the spanning tree. Any leaf node initiates this procedure by sending its data to its parent and any intermediate node receiving all data from all of its children combines its data with received data and sends the whole data to its parent as in Algorithm 9.4. The root process receives data from

9.2 Spanning Tree Construction

every node in the end. Total number of messages sent over the edges of the spanning tree is $n - 1$ as in the broadcast algorithm without acknowledgement.

Algorithm 9.4 *Convergecast*

1: **Input**: $G = (V, E$ a graph
2: **Output**: Clusters $C = \{C_1, C_2, ..C_k\}$ of G
3: $T \leftarrow$ a spanning tree of graph $G = (V, E)$
4: **if** $me = leaf$ **then**
5:    send my_msg to my parent
6: **else**
7:    **receive** $ccast\_msg$ from all my children
8:    $ccast\_msg \leftarrow ccast\_msg \cup my\_msg$
9:    **if** $me \neq root$ **then**
10:       **send** $ccast\_msg$ to my parent
11:    **end if**
12: **end if**

Python Implementation

We can implement this algorithm in Python using the test graph of Fig. 9.2 as in Listing 9.7. Each leaf node sends its rank to its parent which converges these values with its rank and sends the combined message to its parent. The root process prints the contents of the message. The output of this algorithm displayed in Listing 9.8 shows that the root process receives all of the node messages. Note that we have already used a convergecast process in Algorithm 9.3 for broadcast with acknowledgement operation. We use a different approach for message reception by an internal node and the root node though; these nodes wait explicitly for messages from their children at lines 21–22 in the specified sequence of their children list at line 9 rather than receiving a message in any sequence.

Listing 9.7 Convergecast Algorithm

```
from mpi4py import MPI
import numpy as np

comm = MPI.COMM_WORLD
rank = comm.Get_rank()
size = comm.Get_size()


C_CAST = 1
children = [[4,5,1],[2],[],[7,6],[3],[],[],[]]
parents  = [0,0,1,4,0,0,3,3]

childs = children[rank]
parent = parents[rank]
msg = []

if len(childs) == 0: # leaf node
    msg = [rank]
    comm.send(msg, dest=parent, tag=C_CAST)
```

```
19      print("Rank: {}, Leaf Message: {}, Sent to Parent: {}".format(
            rank,msg,parent))
20  else:
21      for child in childs:
22          new_msg = comm.recv(source=child, tag=C_CAST)
23          msg.extend(new_msg)
24      if rank != 0:
25          msg.append(rank) # append rank in msg
26          print("Rank: {}, Message: {}, Sent to Parent: {}".format(
            rank,msg,parent))
27          comm.send(msg, dest=parent, tag=C_CAST)
28      else:
29          print("Rank: 0, All Received: ",msg)
```

Listing 9.8 Output of Convergecast Algorithm

```
Rank: 7, Leaf Message: [7], Sent to Parent: 3
Rank: 2, Leaf Message: [2], Sent to Parent: 1
Rank: 1, Message: [2, 1], Sent to Parent: 0
Rank: 5, Leaf Message: [5], Sent to Parent: 0
Rank: 6, Leaf Message: [6], Sent to Parent: 3
Rank: 3, Message: [7, 6, 3], Sent to Parent: 4
Rank: 4, Message: [7, 6, 3, 4], Sent to Parent: 0
Rank: 0, All Received:  [7, 6, 3, 4, 5, 2, 1]
```

9.3 Distributed Breadth-First-Search

The breadth-first-search (BFS) algorithm of an undirected graph G started from a source node s visits all nodes that are at distance 1, labels them as level 1 nodes, then visits all nodes at distance 2 labelling them as level 2 nodes and so on until all nodes in a connected graph are visited. The output of this algorithm is a BFS tree with the assignment of the parent and children of each vertex in this tree. The BFS algorithm starting from a root node v finds the shortest paths from v to all vertices when the graph is unweighted. The layer value of a vertex from the root denotes its distance to the root in this case. The distributed BFS algorithm is executed by all nodes of the network and the result is the parent and children values of all nodes in the system as in the sequential case. We can implement this algorithm asynchronously or synchronously as described in the next sections.

9.3.1 Asynchronous Distributed BFS

An asynchronous distributed BFS algorithm may be formed with the following steps. The layer value at a node at any instant is used to show the shortest number of hops it currently has to the root process. The source (root) node starts the process by sending a *layer* message containing the next layer value to all of its neighbors. Any node that receives a *layer* message compares its current layer value with that contained in the message. If the message layer value is smaller than its own value, it sets its layer

9.3 Distributed Breadth-First-Search

value to the message value and sets its current parent to the sender of the message as in Algorithm 9.5 [1]. It then sends the new layer value, to all of its neighbors so that they can adjust their layer values. Note that layer value and consequently, the identifier of its parent may change during the operation of this algorithm. Clearly the number of changes of these values will not exceed the diameter d of the graph G which is the maximum number of hops between any two nodes in G. Note that the value of d should be provided to each node at the beginning of the algorithm which requires calculation of d and broadcasting this value to all nodes.

Algorithm 9.5 *Asynchronous Distributed BFS*

1: **Input**: $G = (V, E)$, an undirected graph
2: **Output**: A BFS tree of G
3: **message types** $layer, ack, reject$
4: $parent \leftarrow \perp, my\_layer \leftarrow \infty, count \leftarrow 1, d \leftarrow$ diameter of G
5: **if** $i = root$ **then**
6:    **send** $layer(1)$ to $N(root)$
7: **end if**
8: **while** $count \leq d$ **do**
9:    **receive** $bcast\_msg$ from my parent
10:    **if** $msg(j).type = layer(l)$ **then**
11:       **if** $my\_layer > l$ **then**
12:          $count \leftarrow count + 1$
13:          $parent \leftarrow j$
14:          $my\_layer \leftarrow l$
15:          **send** $layer + 1$ to $N(i) \setminus \{j\}j$
16:          **send** ack to j
17:       **else**
18:          **send** $reject$ to j
19:       **end if**
20:    **else if** $msg(j).type = ack(l)$ **then**
21:       $childs \leftarrow childs \cup \{j\}$
22:    **else**
23:       $others \leftarrow others \cup \{j\}$
24:    **end if**
25: **end while**

Theorem 9.2 *The number of steps of this algorithm is $O(d)$ and it requires $O(nm)$ messages.*

Proof All of the layer messages will reach all nodes in d steps where d is the diameter of the graph. A node v may change its layer value $n - 2$ times along the longest path and at each update, it will send $deg(v)$ messages to its neighbors. Total number of messages transferred along the edges will then be:

$$\sum_{v=1}^{n} n \cdot deg(v) = O(nm) \qquad (9.1)$$

Python Implementation

Python code given in Listing 9.9 implements Algorithm 9.5 obeying the algorithm steps. The diameter of the network displayed in the sample figure is three which is the maximum number of possible layer value changes for a node and this is the termination condition for a node in the main *while* loop. Since the number of messages received for each node varies, we have a receiving function *recv_safe* which tests whether any message is available a number of times with a delay of one second each time, using the *mpi4py* function *Iprobe* which returns *false* immediately if there are no messages. A node decides to terminate if there are no messages received for a definite time interval.

Listing 9.9 Asynchronous Distributed BFS Graph Algorithm

```
from mpi4py import MPI
import numpy as np
import time

comm = MPI.COMM_WORLD
rank = comm.Get_rank()
n    = comm.Get_size()

LAYER, ACK, REJ = 1, 2, 3   # message types

parent = -1
msg    = np.array([-1,-1,-1,-1])  # sender, type, layer, value
neighs, childs, others, finished = set(), set(), set(), set()

A = np.array([[0,1,0,0,1,1,0,0],
              [1,0,1,1,1,0,0,0],
              [0,1,0,1,0,0,1,0],
              [0,1,1,0,1,0,1,1],
              [1,1,0,1,0,1,0,0],
              [1,0,0,0,1,0,0,0],
              [0,0,1,1,0,0,0,1],
              [0,0,0,1,0,0,1,0]], dtype=int)

for j in range(0,n):   # find neighbors
    if A[rank,j] == 1:
        neighs.add(j)
my_layer = 99

def recv_safe():  # wait for a while to check message
    count = 0
    res = comm.Iprobe(source=MPI.ANY_SOURCE, tag=MPI.ANY_TAG)
    while res == False and count < 6:
        time.sleep(1)
        res = comm.Iprobe(source=MPI.ANY_SOURCE, tag=MPI.ANY_TAG)
        count = count + 1
    if res == False:
        msg = [-1,-1,-1,-1]
    else:
```

9.3 Distributed Breadth-First-Search

```
            msg = comm.recv(source=MPI.ANY_SOURCE, tag=MPI.ANY_TAG)
    return(msg)

if rank == 0:  # root starts BFS
    my_layer, parent = 0, 0
    msg = [rank, LAYER, my_layer,1]
    for node in neighs:
            comm.send(msg, dest=node, tag=LAYER)

d = 3          # max number of messages to receive
counts = 0
while counts < d:
    msg = recv_safe()
    if msg[3] == -1:  # if no more messages, quit
        break
    sender, typ, layer = msg[0], msg[1], msg[2]
    if typ == LAYER:
        if my_layer > layer + 1: # if layer changes, inform neighbors
            counts = counts + 1
            my_layer = layer + 1
            old = parent        # save previous parent
            parent = sender
            msg = [rank, ACK, 0, 1]
            comm.send(msg, dest=parent, tag=ACK)
            if old != -1:  # include previous parent in neighs
                neighs.add(old)
            msg = [rank, LAYER, my_layer,1]
            for node in neighs:
                if node == parent:
                    continue
                comm.send(msg, dest=node, tag=LAYER)
        else:
            msg = [rank, REJ, 0, 1]
            comm.send(msg, dest=sender, tag=REJ)

    elif typ == ACK:
            childs.add(sender)

    elif typ == REJ:
            others.add(sender)

print("Rank: {}, Parent: {}, Layer: {}, Children: {},\t\tOthers: {}
        ".format(rank,parent,my_layer,childs, others))
```

Listing 9.10 Output of Asynchronous Distributed BFS Algorithm

```
Rank: 3, Parent: 1, Layer: 2, Children: {7},      Others: {2, 4, 6}
Rank: 5, Parent: 0, Layer: 1, Children: set(),    Others: {4}
Rank: 4, Parent: 0, Layer: 1, Children: set(),    Others: {1, 3, 5}
Rank: 0, Parent: 0, Layer: 0, Children: {1, 4, 5}, Others: set()
Rank: 1, Parent: 0, Layer: 1, Children: {2, 3},   Others: {4}
Rank: 7, Parent: 3, Layer: 3, Children: set(),    Others: {6}
Rank: 2, Parent: 1, Layer: 2, Children: {6},      Others: {3}
Rank: 6, Parent: 2, Layer: 3, Children: set(),    Others: {3, 7}
```

The output in Listing 9.10 provides the parent, children and unrelated neighbors denoted as *Others* as the output of each node. Running the Python code for the sample graph of Fig. 9.3 resulted in the BFS tree shown by bold arrows in (a) with layer values displayed next to the nodes. A different run of the algorithm resulted in the BFS tree shown in (b) of the same figure. Note that nodes 1, 4 and 5 will always

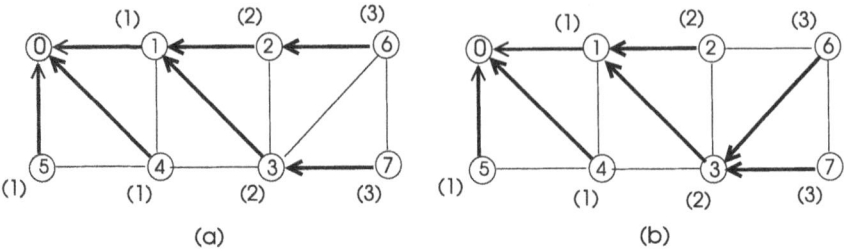

Fig. 9.3 Asynchronous BFS algorithm results in a sample graph

be at layer 1 connected to node 0 with the same BFS tree edges. However, node 3 may have node 1 or 4 as parent, and node 6 may have node 2 or 3 as parent as can be shown by different runs of the algorithm.

9.3.2 Synchronous Distributed BFS

We can have a synchronous distributed BFS algorithm that forms layers of the BFS tree in synchronous rounds. At each round r, a new layer that is at a distance of r hops from the root is discovered. The root process starts the algorithm by sending the PROBE message with round number 1 to all of its neighbors. The following steps are performed during the execution of this algorithm.

1. Any node receiving the PROBE message for the first time, sets its layer to layer + 1 in the PROBE message, sets its parent to the sender and responds with ACK to parent. It also becomes a leaf node by changing its state to LEAF and removes the parent from its neighbors.
2. When a leaf node of the partial tree T' receives a ROUND message, it sends PROBE message to all of its neighbors except its parent.
3. A leaf node that receives an ACK from a node v, adds v to its children. If it receives a REJ message from a node v, it adds v to its non-child set *others*.
4. When a leaf node receives ACKs and REJs from all of its neighbors, round is over.
5. A leaf node finishes when it receives REJ messages from all of its neighbors. This message is convergecast to the root along the tree.
6. An intermediate node forwards the PROBE message to its children and it also sends PROBE message to its undiscovered neighbors.
7. An intermediate node convergecasts a ROVER message when it receives ROVER from all of its children.
8. An intermediate node finishes when it receives FIN message from all of its children.
9. The root and the algorithm terminates when the root receives FIN message from all of its children.

9.3 Distributed Breadth-First-Search

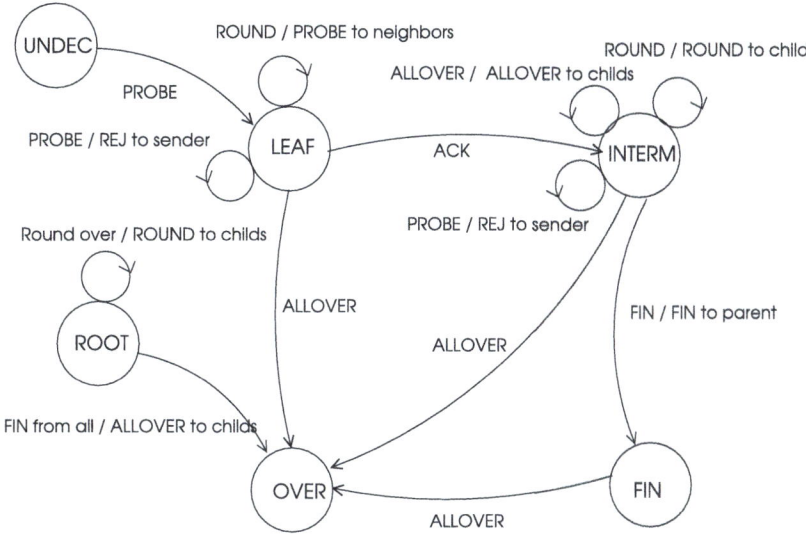

Fig. 9.4 FSM diagram of SBFS algorithm

Table 9.1 State table of synchronous BFS algorithm

	PROBE	ACK	REJ	ROVER	FIN	ALLOVER	ROUND
ROOT	–	act01	–	act03	act04	–	–
UNDEC	act10	–	–	–	–	–	–
INTERM	act20	–	–	act23	–	act25	act26
LEAF	act30	act31	act32	–	–	act35	act36
FINISHED	act40	–	–	–	–	act45	–

The steps of this algorithm requires a detailed design and thus, we will use FSM based design for the implementation of the synchronous BFS algorithm. We will use a combination of the position of the node in the BFS tree and its running state to denote the states as in Fig. 9.4.

The states specified in this diagram are ROOT, INTERM and LEAF to describe the position of a node in the tree and UNDEC, OVER and FINISHED denoting the undecided, active part over and all finished states respectively of the node in terms of its running state. The FSM table for these states is depicted in Table 9.1.

The message types used in this algorithm are listed as follows:

- ROUND: Broadcast by the root node to all nodes that are on the partial BFS tree formed.
- PROBE: Any LEAF node that receives a ROUND message will send PROBE message to all its neighbors except its parent to discover new nodes.

Table 9.2 SBFS algorithm ROOT actions

*act*01 ACK	*act*03 ROVER
1. Add sender to *childs* 2. If all neighbors sent, round is over	If all ROVER/FIN received, round is over
*act*04 FIN	
1. Add sender to *finished* 2. If all *childs* finished, send ALLOVER to *childs* 3. Else if *finished* and *roundover* = *childs*, round is over, *state* ← OVER	

- ACK: Sent by a newly discovered node to the sender which now becomes its parent.
- REJ: An already discovered node sends REJ message to the sender.
- ROVER: Sent by a node that has received replies from all its neighbors and descendants. This message is used to convergecast the finishing of the round to the root node.
- FIN: The execution of a node is finished and this message is convergecast to the root to declare all nodes finish execution.
- ALLOVER: This message is broadcast by the root node to all nodes that every node has finished execution.

An internal node on the partial BFS tree formed is involved in a number of different operations; it should forward ROUND message to all of its children and when it receives ROVER from all of its children, it should convergecast this message to its parent. On the other hand, it should keep track of the finished nodes in its subtree and when all of the nodes in its subtree are finished, a FIN message is sent to its parent. Another issue of concern is whether a node that has finished execution should be made aware that all nodes in the system have finished or not. When all FIN messages are convergecast to the root, it broadcasts an ALLOV message so that every node receiving this message is informed that all nodes in the network have finished execution as displayed in Table 9.2. The actions performed at states INTERM, LEAF and FINISHED are shown in Tables 9.3, 9.4 and 9.5 respectively.

All of these considerations may be handled by clearly specifying the steps of the actions displayed in Table 9.1.

Python Implementation

The Python implementation of the synchronous BFS algorithm involves conversion of the actions to Python code and running the FSM algorithm as shown in Listing 9.11.

9.3 Distributed Breadth-First-Search

Table 9.3 SBFS algorithm INTERM actions

*act*20 PROBE	*act*23 ROVER
Send REJ to *sender*	If all ROVER received, round is over
*act*24 FIN	*act*25 ROUND
1. Add sender to *finished* 2. If all *childs* finished, send FIN to *parent* 3. Else if *finished* and *roundover* = *childs*, send ROVER to parent	1. Send ALLOVER to *childs* 2. *state* ← OVER
*act*26 ALLOVER	
Send ROUND to *childs*	

Table 9.4 SBFS algorithm LEAF actions

*act*30 PROBE	*act*31 ACK
Send REJ to *sender*	1. If all received, round is over 2. *state* ← *INTERM*
*act*32 REJ	*act*35 ALLOVER
1. Add sender to *others* 2. If *other* = *neighbors* 3. *state* ← *FINISHED*	*state* ← OVER
*act*36 ROUND	
Send PROBE to neighbors except parent	

Table 9.5 SBFS algorithm FINISHED actions

*act*40 (FINISHED, PROBE)	*act*45 (INTERM, ROVER)
Send REJ to *sender*	1. Send ALLOVER to *childs* 2. *state* ← OVER, round is over

Listing 9.11 Synchronous BFS Construction

```
from mpi4py import MPI
import numpy as np

comm = MPI.COMM_WORLD
rank = comm.Get_rank()
size = comm.Get_size()
# message types
PROBE, ACK, REJ, ROVER, FIN, ALLOVER, ROUND  = 0, 1, 2, 3, 4, 5, 6
# states
ROOT, UNDEC, INTERM, LEAF, FINISHED, OVER = 0, 1, 2, 3, 4, 5
parent, layer = -1, -1
# message (sender, type, round, layer)
msg     = np.array([-1,-1,-1,-1])
neighs, childs2, childs, currchilds, others, finished, r_over = set
    (), set(), set(), set(), set(), set(), set()

```

```
17  A = np.array([[0,1,0,0,1,1,0,0],
18                 [1,0,1,1,1,0,0,0],
19                 [0,1,0,1,0,0,1,0],
20                 [0,1,1,0,1,0,1,1],
21                 [1,1,0,1,0,1,0,0],
22                 [1,0,0,0,1,0,0,0],
23                 [0,0,1,1,0,0,0,1],
24                 [0,0,0,1,0,0,1,0]],dtype=int)
25
26  for j in range(0,size): # set neighbors
27      if A[rank,j] == 1:
28          neighs.add(j)
29  state = UNDEC
30
31  def actpass(): pass
32
33  def act01():
34      global msg, round_num, r_over, round_over, childs
35      childs2.add(sender)
36      if childs2 == neighs:
37          round_over = True
38
39  def act03():
40      global msg, r_over, round_over
41      r_over.add(sender)
42      if r_over.union(finished) == childs:
43          round_over = True
44
45  def act04():
46      global msg, state, round_over, finised, childs, currchilds
47      currchilds.remove(sender)
48      finished.add(sender)
49      if finished == childs:
50          state = OVER
51          round_over = True
52          msg[0], msg[1] = rank, ALLOVER
53          for child in childs:
54              comm.send(msg, dest=child, tag=ALLOVER)
55      elif r_over.union(finished) == childs:
56          round_over = True
57
58  def act10():
59      global msg, round_over,state,neighs,parent, sender, round_num,
         layer, roun, parent
60      parent, layer = sender, msg[3] + 1
61      neighs.remove(parent)
62      msg[0], msg[1] = rank, ACK
63      comm.send(msg, dest=parent, tag=ACK)
64      state = LEAF
65
66  def act20():
67      global msg
68      msg[0], msg[1] = rank, REJ
69      comm.send(msg, dest=sender, tag=REJ)
70
71  def act23():
72      global msg, r_over, round_over
73      r_over.add(sender)
74      msg[0] = rank
75      if r_over.union(finished) == childs:
76          comm.send(msg,dest=parent,tag=ROVER)
77          round_over = True
78  def act24():
```

9.3 Distributed Breadth-First-Search

```
79      global finished, msg, over, state, r_over, childs, round_over,
        currchilds
80      finished.add(sender)
81      r_over.add(sender)
82      currchilds.remove(sender)
83      msg[0] = rank
84      if finished == childs:
85          state = FINISHED
86          msg[1] = FIN
87          comm.send(msg,dest=parent,tag=FIN)
88          round_over = True
89      elif finished.union(r_over) == childs:
90          msg[1] = ROVER
91          comm.send(msg,dest=parent,tag=ROVER)
92          round_over = True
93  def act25():
94      global msg, state
95      msg[0] = rank
96      for child in childs:
97          comm.send(msg, dest=child, tag=ALLOVER)
98          state = OVER
99  def act26():
100     global msg
101     msg[0] = rank
102     for child in currchilds:
103         comm.send(msg, dest=child, tag=ROUND)
104
105 def act30():
106     global msg
107     msg[0], msg[1] = rank, REJ
108     comm.send(msg, dest=sender, tag=REJ)
109 def act31():
110     global msg, state, round_over, childs, currchilds
111     childs.add(sender)
112     currchilds.add(sender)
113     msg[0] = rank
114     if neighs == currchilds.union(others,finished):
115         msg[1] = ROVER
116         comm.send(msg,dest=parent,tag=ROVER)
117         state = INTERM
118         round_over = True
119 def act32():
120     global msg, state, others, round_over
121     others.add(sender)
122     msg[0] = rank
123     if others == neighs:
124         msg[1] = FIN
125         comm.send(msg,dest=parent,tag=FIN)
126         state = FINISHED
127         round_over = True
128     elif neighs == currchilds.union(others,finished):
129         msg[1] = ROVER
130         comm.send(msg,dest=parent,tag=ROVER)
131         round_over = True
132         if len(childs)!= 0:
133             state = INTERM
134
135 def act35():
136     global state
137     state = OVER
138 def act36():
139     global msg
140     msg[0], msg[1], msg[3] = rank, PROBE, layer
```

```
        for node in neighs:
            comm.send(msg, dest=node, tag=PROBE)

def act40():
    global msg
    msg[0], msg[1] = rank, REJ
    comm.send(msg, dest=sender, tag=REJ)

def act45():
    global msg, state, round_over
    msg[0] = rank
    for child in childs:
        comm.send(msg, dest=child, tag=ALLOVER)
    state = OVER
    round_over = True

actions = np.array([[actpass,act01,actpass,act03,act04,act05,
    actpass],
                    [act10,actpass,actpass,actpass,actpass,actpass,
    actpass],
                    [act20,actpass,actpass,act23,act24,act25,act26],
                    [act30,act31,act32,actpass,actpass,act35,act36],
                     [act40,actpass,actpass,actpass,actpass,act45,
    actpass]])
over = False
round_num = 0

if rank == 0:
    parent, layer = None, 0
    round_num = 0
    state = ROOT
    neighs2 = neighs.copy()
    currchilds = neighs.copy()
    childs = neighs.copy()

while state != OVER:
    round_over = False
    r_over.clear()
    if rank == 0:
        if round_num == 0:
            typ = PROBE
        else:
            typ = ROUND
        round_num = round_num + 1
        msg[0], msg[1], msg[2], msg[3] = rank, typ, round_num, layer
        for child in currchilds:
            comm.send(msg, dest=child, tag=ROUND)
    while not round_over:
        msg = comm.recv(source=MPI.ANY_SOURCE, tag=MPI.ANY_TAG)
        sender, typ, roun = msg[0], msg[1], msg[2]
        actions[state][typ]()
print("Rank: {}, Parent: {}, Layer: {}, Childs: {}, Others: {}".
    format(rank,parent,layer,childs,others))
```

Listing 9.12 Output of Synchronous BFS Algorithm

```
Rank: 0, Parent: None, Layer: 0, Childs: {1, 4, 5}, Others: set()
Rank: 4, Parent: 0, Layer: 1, Childs: set(), Others: {1, 3, 5}
Rank: 1, Parent: 0, Layer: 1, Childs: {2, 3}, Others: {4}
Rank: 2, Parent: 1, Layer: 2, Childs: {6}, Others: {3}
Rank: 5, Parent: 0, Layer: 1, Childs: set(), Others: {4}
Rank: 3, Parent: 1, Layer: 2, Childs: {7}, Others: {2, 4, 6}
Rank: 6, Parent: 2, Layer: 3, Childs: set(), Others: {3, 7}
Rank: 7, Parent: 3, Layer: 3, Childs: set(), Others: {6}
```

Using the sample graph of Fig. 9.1 results in the BFS trees shown in (a) and (c) of the figure as the asynchronous BFS algorithm as displayed in Listing 9.12. Note that trees (b) and (d) of this figure will never be output since these are not BFS trees.

9.4 Distributed Depth-First-Search

A depth-first-search (DFS) algorithm starts from a source node s, visits a neighbor v of node s then a neighbor w of v and continues in this manner by going as deep as possible. When there are no unvisited neighbors of a node u, the algorithm returns to the node that first visited node u.

The distributed DFS algorithm we will implement uses a special message called *token* that is exchanged between the nodes. The source node s starts the algorithm by sending it to an arbitrarily selected neighbors u which marks s as its parent in the DFS tree to be formed. The node u than selects a random neighbor v and sends the *token* to it. This operation continues until all nodes are visited by the *token* and when all neighbors of a node has received the *token*, it is sent back to the node it was first received. We do not have global data and we need to keep track of visited nodes which can be accomplished by storing the visited nodes inside the *token* as shown in Algorithm 9.6 [1].

Theorem 9.3 *Asynchronous distributed DFS algorithm correctly builds a DFS tree rooted at the root node in $2n - 2$ time using $2n - 2$ messages.*

Proof Each node is visited at least once and a parent is assigned at the first visit. The parent of a node remains the same once assigned, thus the resulting structure is a spanning tree. Traversing of the token in fact simulates the sequential algorithm where each edge is visited twice once in each direction. The first traversal of an edge (u, v) from node u is when node v is discovered and node u is assigned as its parent. The second traversal of the same edge is from node v to u when v has all of the neighbors visited and a return to parent u is made. Therefore, total time is the sum of these steps which is $2(n - 1) = 2n - 2$ as the DFS tree will have $n - 1$ edges. Similarly, total number of messages is also $2n - 2$. □

Algorithm 9.6 *Asynchronous Distributed DFS*

1: **Input**: $G = (V, E)$, an undirected graph
2: **Output**: A DFS tree of G
3: **message types** $token$
4: $parent \leftarrow \perp$, $visited \leftarrow \emptyset$
5: **if** $i = root$ **then**
6:    $parent \leftarrow i$
7:    **select** $j \in N(i)$
8:    **send** $token(1)$ to j
9: **end if**
10: **while** $true$ **do**
11:    **receive** $token(j, visited)$
12:    **if** $parent = \perp$ **then**
13:       $parent \leftarrow j$
14:    **end if**
15:    **if** $\exists j \in N(i) \setminus \{token.visited\}$ **then**
16:       **select** $j \in N(i) \setminus \{token.visited\}$
17:       **send** $token(visited \cup \{i\})$ to j
18:    **else if** $i == root$ **then**
19:       exit
20:    **else**
21:       **send** $token(visited \cup \{i\})$ to $parent$
22:    **end if**
23: **end while**

Python Implementation

Python code for the token-based distributed DFS formed using Algorithm 9.6 as guidance is displayed in Listing 9.13. The test graph of Fig. 9.5 is used as the input to this algorithm.

Listing 9.13 Token-Based DFS Algorithm

```
from mpi4py import MPI
import numpy as np

comm = MPI.COMM_WORLD
rank = comm.Get_rank()
size = comm.Get_size()

TOKEN = 1
parent = -1
n = size
msg = [-1,-1,-1]
neighs = []
token = []

A   = np.array([[0,1,0,0,1,1,0,0],
                [1,0,1,1,1,0,0,0],
                [0,1,0,1,0,0,1,0],
                [0,1,1,0,1,0,1,1],
                [1,1,0,1,0,1,0,0],
                [1,0,0,0,1,0,0,0],
                [0,0,1,1,0,0,0,1],
```

```
                        [0,0,0,1,0,0,1,0]],dtype=int)
neighbors = A[rank,:]
for i in range(0,n):
    if neighbors[i] == 1:
        neighs.append(i)
flag = True

if rank == 0:  # root starts DFS
    parent = 0
    next_node = neighs.pop(0)
    msg[0], msg[1] = rank, [rank]
    comm.send(msg, dest=next_node, tag=TOKEN)

while flag:
    msg = comm.recv(source=MPI.ANY_SOURCE, tag=TOKEN)
    token = msg[1]
    next_node = -1
    if parent == -1:
        parent = msg[0]
        token.append(rank)
    for node in neighs:   # find next node to visit
        if node not in token:
            next_node = node
            break
    if next_node != -1:   # found
        msg[0], msg[1] = rank, token
        comm.send(msg, dest=next_node, tag=TOKEN)
    else:                 # not found
        if rank == 0:     # all done
            print("I am root, all done",msg[1])
            flag = False
        else:             # return to parent
            flag = False
            print("Rank: {} finished, token {} sent to parent {}"
            .format(rank,token,parent))
            msg[0] = rank
            comm.send(msg, dest=parent, tag=TOKEN)
```

Listing 9.14 Output of Token-Based DFS Algorithm

```
Rank: 5 finished, token [0, 1, 2, 3, 4, 5] sent to parent 4
Rank: 4 finished, token [0, 1, 2, 3, 4, 5] sent to parent 3
Rank: 7 finished, token [0, 1, 2, 3, 4, 5, 6, 7] sent to parent 6
Rank: 6 finished, token [0, 1, 2, 3, 4, 5, 6, 7] sent to parent 3
Rank: 3 finished, token [0, 1, 2, 3, 4, 5, 6, 7] sent to parent 2
Rank: 2 finished, token [0, 1, 2, 3, 4, 5, 6, 7] sent to parent 1
Rank: 1 finished, token [0, 1, 2, 3, 4, 5, 6, 7] sent to parent 0
Root, all done [0, 1, 2, 3, 4, 5, 6, 7]
```

Running Python code for Algorithm 9.6 results in the DFS tree shown in Fig. 9.5. Note that different runs of this algorithm may produce different DFS trees.

9.5 Chapter Notes

Trees are fundamental data structures in algorithm design and implementations. We reviewed main distributed tree construction procedures in this chapter with Python

Fig. 9.5 DFS tree built by Algorithm 9.6 Python code in a sample graph

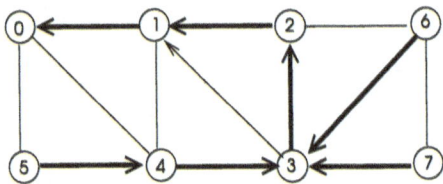

implementations. The basic spanning tree may be realized by a root node starting the algorithm by sending a *probe* message and any other node that receives this message for the first time assigns the sender as its parent and sends it to all neighbors except the parent. Broadcast, broadcast with acknowledgement and convergecast operations may be performed over a constructed spanning tree.

Asynchronous distributed BFS algorithm has a similar structure to the spanning tree algorithm based on flooding but it allows changing the parent if a shorter path to the root is discovered by a new *probe* message. The synchronous version of this algorithm works in rounds in which a new layer from the root node is assigned at each round. It should be noted that broadcast and convergecast operations over a BFS tree will improve parallelism and thus performance will be enhanced by reduced execution times. Lastly, we described an asynchronous distributed DFS algorithm which is based on passing a token between the nodes, simulating the sequential algorithm. Detailed review of all of these algorithms to construct trees can be found in [1,2].

Programming Exercises

1. Run Algorithm 9.5 Python code in the graph of Fig. 9.6 to form a BFS tree asynchronously, starting from node 0 as the root node, for three times and note all of the BFS trees formed.
2. Run the synchronous BFS algorithm Python code in the graph of Fig. 9.6 taking node 0 as the root node for three times and note all of the BFS trees formed.
3. Run Algorithm 9.6 Python code to form a DFS in the graph of Fig. 9.7 taking node 0 as the root node for three times and note all of the DFS trees formed.
4. Tarry's algorithm [3] is used to form a spanning tree of a graph using a token. This algorithm is based on two rules:

   - Send the token to any neighbor exactly once.
   - If this is not possible for any neighbor, meaning token has been sent to all, return the token to parent.

   Write this algorithm in Python using *mpi4py*, implement it in the graph of Fig. 9.8 with node 0 as the initiator and obtain its output. Work out the time and message complexities of this algorithm.

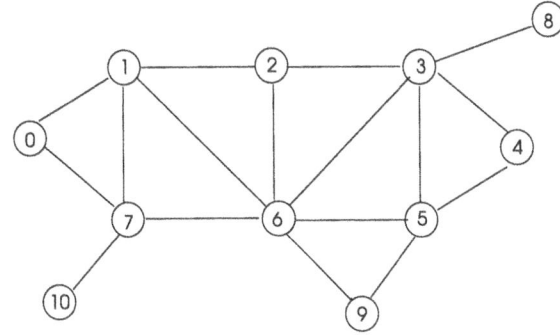

Fig. 9.6 Sample graph for Exercises 1 and 2

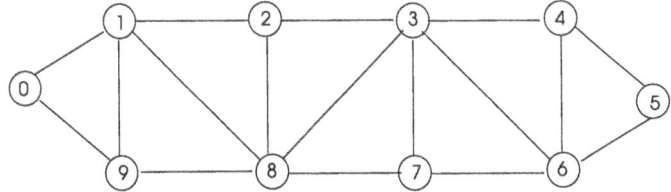

Fig. 9.7 Sample graph for Exercise 3

Fig. 9.8 Sample graph for Exercise 4

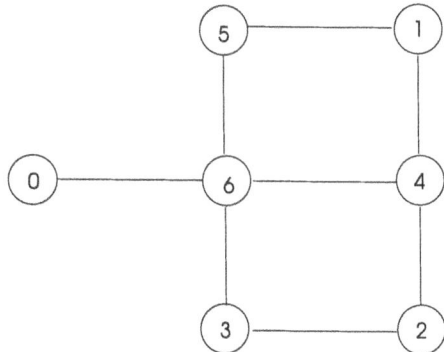

References

1. K. Erciyes, *Distributed Graph Algorithms for Computer Networks*. Springer Computer Communications and Networks Series, vol. 10 (Springer, Berlin, 2013), pp. 14471–51720
2. K. Erciyes, *Guide to Graph Algorithms: Sequential, Parallel and Distributed*. Springer Texts in Computer Science Series (2018)
3. G. Tarry, Le Problem Des Labyrinthes. Nouvelles Annales de Mathematique 14 (1895)

Weighted Graphs 10

Abstract

This chapter provides a review of distributed algorithms to be used in weighted graphs. Finding the minimum spanning tree is a fundamental problem in such graphs. Another main problem is finding shortest paths between the nodes of the graph when the graph is used to represent a computer network. Matching in a weighted graph aims to find a total maximum weight of non-adjacent edges. We describe distributed algorithms for minimum spanning trees, routing and weighted matching and their implementations in Python in this chapter.

10.1 Introduction

An edge-weighted graph (or simply a weighted graph) $G = (V, E, w, w : E \to \mathbb{R})$ has real numbers associated with its edges. Note that vertices may also have weights to denote a parameter such as the capacity of a node etc. The weights of edges are commonly used to represent some parameter such as the capacity of a link connecting the two nodes at the endpoints of an edge. A weighted graph G modelling a computer network has edge weights typically showing the cost of sending messages between the two nodes in the network. Weighted graphs may be used to model various real-life phenomena such as the affinity between two persons in a social network.

We will review three fundamental distributed system problems in networks represented by weighted graphs: minimum spanning trees, routing and weighted matching in the remaining of this chapter.

10.2 Minimum Spanning Trees

A minimum spanning tree (MST) T of a weighted graph $G = (V, E, w : E \to \mathbb{R})$ has a total minimum weight among all spanning trees of G. MSTs have numerous applications such as finding clusters that are group of nodes close to each other in a graph, network installations with minimum wire length etc. Finding MST of a graph using sequential, parallel or distributed algorithms is a well studied topic in computer science [4].

One of the first algorithms to construct an MST of a graph is due to Kruskal which first sorts the edges with respect to their weights from lowest to highest [7]. Then, starting from the lowest edge, each edge is included in the partial MST T' as long as it does not make a cycle with the existing edges in T'. This algorithm finds a unique MST of G when edge weights are distinct and has a time complexity of $O(m \log m)$ due to sorting process. However, the time complexity may be reduced to $O(m \log n)$ using suitable data structures [4]. Working of Kruskal's algorithm is depicted in Fig. 10.1a with the iteration steps shown in parenthesis.

The *Reverse Delete Algorithm* takes a different approach by initializing the MST T to the all edges of the graph G and then sorting the edges of G from highest to lowest weights. The algorithm iteratively removes an edge from T as long as this removal does not disconnect the remaining G.

Prim's algorithm is a classical MST algorithm that starts from an arbitrarily selected vertex v and includes the minimum weight outgoing edge (MWOE) from v in the partial MST T' [10]. The rest of the algorithm follows the same principle: a MWOE e from the vertices in T' is always selected to be included in the MST if e does not generate a cycle in T', until all vertices are included in T'. Time complexity of this algorithm is $O(m \log n)$ making use of convenient data structures. The correctness and analysis of all of the described three algorithms can be found in [4]. Implementation of Prim's algorithm in a sample graph starting from vertex 4 is shown in Fig. 10.1b with the iteration steps given in parenthesis.

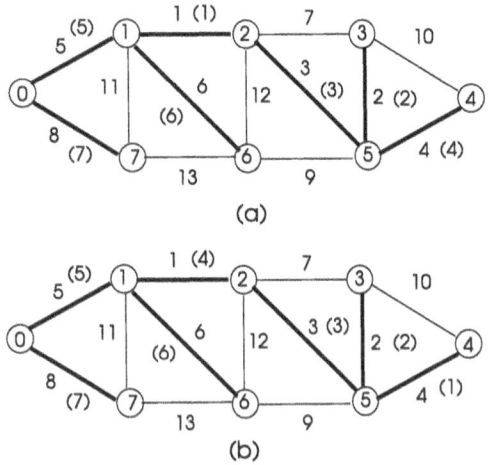

Fig. 10.1 a Kruskal's algorithm b Prim algorithm

10.2 Minimum Spanning Trees

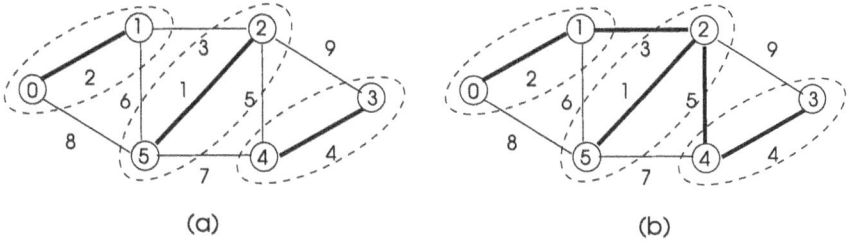

Fig. 10.2 Running of Boruvka's MST algorithm in a simple weighted graph

Boruvka's MST algorithm is based on the observation that the minimum weight edge incident to a node in a graph belongs to an MST of the graph [1]. It performs the following steps to build an MST of a weighted graph.

- **Input**: A connected weighted graph $G = (V, E, w)$
- **Output**: An MST of G
- For each vertex v in G find the smallest incident edge $e = (u, v)$.
- Build a forest with these edges.
- Contract these edges to get a smaller graph G'.
- Contract components of G' using the smallest weight edge between them.
- Continue until there is only one component left.

Each iteration of this algorithm takes $O(m)$ time to complete and the number of vertices contracted are at least halved at each step resulting in $O(m \log n)$ time for the algorithm. Implementation of Boruvka's algorithm in a simple graph concludes in two rounds as depicted in Fig. 10.2. The three components formed in the first round by contracting each node with its lightest edge are shown in dashed sets in (a) and the final MST which is constructed by merging components with the lightest edges between them is illustrated in (b).

10.2.1 A Synchronous Distributed Algorithm

Prim's algorithm, although sequential in nature, can be transformed into a synchronous distributed one with the following logic. A selected root process controls the synchronization at each round by starting the round and checking its end. At each round, the leaves of the partial MST tree T' report their MWOEs to their parents which are convergecast over T' to the root node which decides on the lowest e of MWOEs and informs the leaves over T' so that e is included by its parent in T'. The following are implemented at each round with the specified message types:

- The root starts the round r by sending a *round* message to its children over the partial MST T'. In the first round, it simply sends its lightest incident edge to the node that it is connected with its MWOE.

- An internal node of T' forwards the *round* message to its children. If it receives the identifier of a MWOE (u, v) belonging to itself u in the *round* message, it sets v as its child and notifies v by the *round* message.
- An internal node of T' receives *reply* messages with MWOEs from its children. It finds the lowest MWOE (u, v) including its MWOE and sends (u, v) to its parent during convergecast operation.
- If it receives the id of a MWOE (u, v) belonging to itself u in a *round* message, it changes its state to internal node and notifies the other end v of the MWOE by the *round* message. It also sends its MWOE to its parent in a *reply* message.
- An idle node v that receives a *round* message from the root, any internal or any leaf node knows that it is included in the MST. It sets the sender node u as its parent and sends its MWOE to its parent.
- The root node finds the minimum of MWOEs received including its MWOE. It then broadcasts this edge in round $r + 1$. If the MWOE (u, v) belongs to the root u, it sends a *round* message only to node v.

The pseudocode of this algorithm is displayed in Algorithm 10.1. Note that exactly one MWOE will be included in each round and since the number of edges of MST will be $n - 1$ for n nodes, we need $n - 1$ rounds. However, since the root assigns the lightest edge to itself to partial MST T' in the first round, it sends the *round* message $n - 2$ times over the partial MST tree T'.

Running of this algorithm as it builds an MST T' progressively is depicted in Fig. 10.3. The first edge included by the root node 0 is (0, 1) and the leaf nodes that have the lightest edge at each iteration are shown by double circles with the newly added edge to partial MST T' in parenthesis.

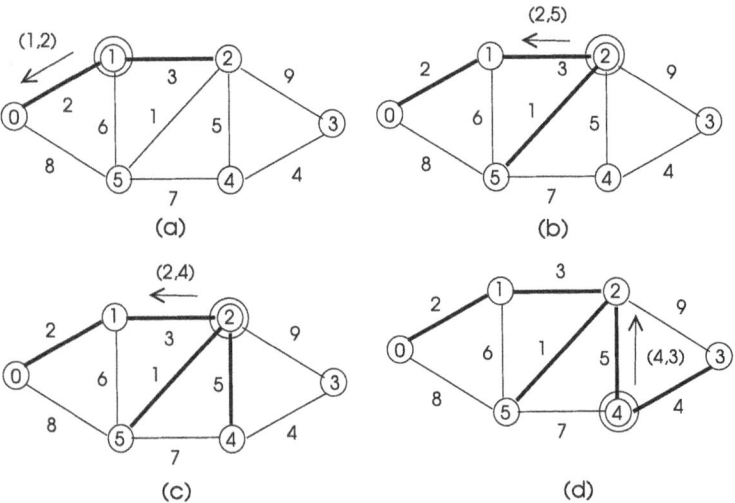

Fig. 10.3 Running of distributed Prim algorithm in a sample network

10.2 Minimum Spanning Trees

Algorithm 10.1 *Distributed Prim Algorithm*

1: **Input**: $G = (V, E, w)$ a weighted graph
2: **Output**: MST T of G
3: **states**: $idle, root, internal, leaf$
4: **message types**: $round, reply, info$
5: **if** $me = root$ **then**
6:    let (u, v) be the lightest incident edge
7:    $T' \leftarrow \{(u, v)\}$
8:    **for** $i = 1$ to $n - 2$ **do**
9:       **send** $round(u, v)$ to children over T'
10:       **receive** $reply(x, y)$ from all children over T'
11:       $(u, v) \leftarrow$ lightest of all received (x, y) edges
12:       $T' \leftarrow T' \cup \{(u, v)\}$
13:    **end for**
14: **else if** $state = leaf$ **then**
15:    **receive** $round(u, v)$ message
16:    **if** (u, v) is incident **then**
17:       send $round$ message to v
18:       assign v as a child
19:       $state \leftarrow internal$
20:    **end if**
21:    $(x, y) \leftarrow$ the lightest edge
22:    **send** $reply(x, y)$ to parent over T'
23: **else if** $state = internal$ **then**
24:    **if** (u, v) is incident **then**
25:       send $round$ message to v
26:       add v to children
27:    **end if**
28:    **receive** $reply(x, y)$ messages from children
29:    **send** the lightest (x, y) in $reply$ message to parent
30: **else**   ▷ Idle node v
31:    **receive** $round(u, v)$ message over edge (u, v)
32:    $v \leftarrow parent$
33:    $state \leftarrow leaf$
34:    **send** $info$ message to all neighbors except parent
35: **end if**

FSM Design

We will use the synchronous communication with known number of rounds model of Sect. 3.3.1 to implement distributed Prim algorithm. The following message types are used in this implementation.

- ROUND: Sent by the *root* process and broadcast over the current partial MST T'. Piggybacking is used such that the MWOE decided to be appended to T' by the root is inserted in the next ROUND message to inform the nodes of T'.
- INFO: When a node that is undiscovered is included in T', it informs all of its unmarked neighbors so that it is excluded in possible future searches of a MWOE by them.

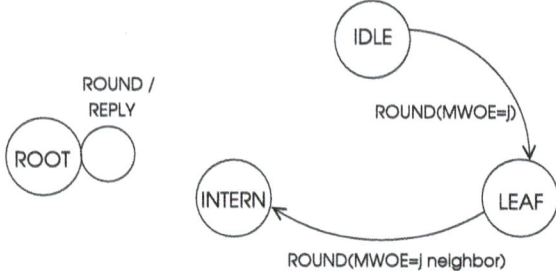

Fig. 10.4 Distributed Prim algorithm FSM table

Table 10.1 Distributed Prim algorithm state table

	ROUND	REPLY	INFO
ROOT	–	act01	act02
IDLE	act10	–	act12
INTERNAL	act20	act21	act22
LEAF	act30	–	act32

- REPLY: This is the convergecast message carrying the MWOEs over the nodes of T' to the root. Note that any intermediate node of T' upcasts only the lowest MWOE of its subtree to its parent.

The nodes can be modelled using an FSM where each node other than the root starts in IDLE state. The ROOT process is responsible to start each round, gather MWOEs from the leaves and internal nodes and decide on the MWOE. The FSM states depicted in Fig. 10.4 are specified blow.

- IDLE: An undiscovered node is in this state.
- LEAF: A node that is discovered becomes a leaf of T'.
- INTERN: A node u that has a leaf node v with MWOE (u, v) becomes an internal node.

The actions for this FSM are described in Table 10.1.

Python Implementation

The actions of Table 10.2 are transferred to Python code in Listing 10.1. The sample graph of Fig. 10.1 is used as the input to this algorithm. We need to consider the following when Python code is designed:

- The newly included node v which was in IDLE state turns into LEAF state needs to inform all of its neighbors by the INFO(v) message so that a neighbor w excludes the edge (v, w) from its outgoing edges in future MWOE searches. Otherwise, (w, v) edge will form a cycle if designated as MWOE of the node w.

10.2 Minimum Spanning Trees

Table 10.2 Distributed Prim algorithm actions

*act*01 (ROOT, REPLY)	*act*10 (IDLE, ROUND)
1. If REPLY received from all children	1. $state \leftarrow$ LEAF
2. Find smallest MWOE mw	2. $parent \leftarrow sender$
3. If $mw(u, v)$ is incident	3. Delete (u, v) from outgoing edges
4. Increment round number	4. Send INFO msg to all outgoing neighbors
5. Send ROUND(mw) msg to v	5. Find incident MWOE mw
6. Delete (u, v) from outgoing edges	6. Send REPLY(mw) to $parent$
7. Add v to children	
8. Find next smallest MWOE mw	
9. Increment round number	
10. Send ROUND(mw) msg to children	
*act*20 (INTERN, ROUND)	*act*21 (INTERN, REPLY)
1. If $mw(u, v)$ is incident	1. If REPLY received from all children
2. Send ROUND(mw) msg to v	2. Find smallest MWOE mw including mine
3. Delete (u, v) from outgoing edges	3. Send REPLY(mw) to $parent$
4. Add v to children	
5. Send ROUND msg to all children	
*act*30 (LEAF, ROUND)	
1. If MWOE $mw(u, v)$ is incident	
2. Send ROUND(mw) msg to v	
3. Delete (u, v) from outgoing edges	
4. Add v to children	
5. $state \leftarrow$ INTERN	
6. Find smallest MWOE mw	
7. Send REPLY(mw) to $parent$	

- When a node w at IDLE state receives an INFO message from a neigbor v meaning node v is now a LEAF of MST, node w does not exclude edge (w, v) from its future MWOE searches but adds it to its candidate MWOE list ($mwoe\_cands$). However, it has to delete all entries of this list from its outgoing edges if node w is assigned as the other end of MWOE by a leaf node.
- The number of messages to be received by a node varies; for this reason, we have a function $recv\_safe$ which waits for a duration and returns false if there are no messages. In this case, we need more ROUND messages than the expected $n - 1$ as there may be empty returns to the root process. In fact, 12 rounds suffices which is $(n - 2) * 2$, as there are $n - 2$ rounds excluding the first round by the root and the REPLY message by a newly discovered IDLE process is received in the next round by a leaf process.

The output obtained in Listing 10.2 shows the step-by-step building of MST which is the same as in Fig. 10.1. The major drawback of this algorithm is that it works sequentially adding only one MWOE to MST in each round.

Listing 10.1 Distributed Prim Algorithm

```python
from mpi4py import MPI
import numpy as np
import sys
import time

comm = MPI.COMM_WORLD
rank = comm.Get_rank()
n    = comm.Get_size()
f, MWOE = 99, -1

A = np.array([[f,5,f,f,f,f,f,8],
              [5,f,1,f,f,f,6,11],
              [f,1,f,7,f,3,12,f],
              [f,f,7,f,10,2,f,f],
              [f,f,f,10,f,4,f,f],
              [f,f,3,2,4,f,9,f],
              [f,6,12,f,f,9,f,13],
              [8,11,f,f,f,f,13,f]], dtype=int)

dists, neighs = A[rank,:], set()
childs, parent, T, out_neighs = set(), -1, [], []
#states
ROOT, IDLE, INTERNAL, LEAF   = 0, 1, 2, 3
# message types
ROUND, REPLY, INFO = 0, 1, 2
# message format: sender, type, round number, [mwoe start, mwoe end
    , mwoe weight]
msg = [-1, -1, -1, [-1,-1,-1]]
reply_rcvd, mwoe_rcvd, mwoe_cands = set(), [], []
max_round, over = 6, False

for j in range(0,n):     # identify neighbors
    if dists[j] != f:
        neighs.add(j)
        out_neighs.append([rank,j,int(dists[j])])

my_mwoe = min(out_neighs,key=lambda x:x[2])
mwoe_min = [99,99,99]

def recv_safe(): # wait for a while to check message
    count = 0
    res = comm.Iprobe(source=MPI.ANY_SOURCE, tag=MPI.ANY_TAG)
    while res == False and count < 6:
        time.sleep(1)
        res = comm.Iprobe(source=MPI.ANY_SOURCE, tag=MPI.ANY_TAG)
        count = count + 1
    if res == False:
        return res
    else:
        msg = comm.recv(source=MPI.ANY_SOURCE, tag=MPI.ANY_TAG)
    return(msg)

def mwoe_incident(mw):     # mwoe is adjacent
    global msg, out_neighs, childs, my_mwoe, round_num
    sys.stdout.flush()
    childs.add(mw[1])
    msg = [rank,INFO, round_num,mw]
    for node in out_neighs: # inform neighbors
        target = node[1]
        if target == parent:
            continue
```

10.2 Minimum Spanning Trees

```python
            comm.send(msg, dest=target, tag=INFO)
    if mw in out_neighs:
        out_neighs.remove(mw)
    if len(out_neighs) > 0:    # update mwoe
        my_mwoe = min(out_neighs,key=lambda x:x[2])
    else:
        my_mwoe = [99,99,99]

def act01():
    global sender, my_mwoe, mwoe_min,mwoe,mwoe_rcvd, reply_rcvd, T,
      round_num, msg,childs, over, out_neighs
    reply_rcvd.add(sender)
    mwoe_rcvd.append(mwoe_msg)
    if reply_rcvd == childs:
        mwoe_rcvd.append(my_mwoe)
        mwoe_min = min(mwoe_rcvd,key=lambda x:x[2])
        T.append(mwoe_min)
        if mwoe_min == my_mwoe:
            mwoe_incident(my_mwoe)
        print("T: {}".format(T))
        sys.stdout.flush()
        mwoe_rcvd.clear()
        reply_rcvd.clear()
        round_over = True

def act10():
    global sender, msg, state, parent, out_neighs, over, my_mwoe,
      mwoe_cands
    sender, typ, round_num, mwoe_msg = msg[0], msg[1], msg[2],msg
      [3]
    state  = LEAF
    parent = sender
    d = A[rank][sender]
    mw = [rank,sender,int(d)]
    msg = [rank, INFO, round_num, mw]
    for node in out_neighs:
        target = node[1]
        if target == parent:
            continue
        comm.send(msg, dest=target, tag=INFO)
    if mw in out_neighs:
        out_neighs.remove(mw)
    for cand in mwoe_cands:
        if cand in out_neighs:
            out_neighs.remove(cand)
    if len(out_neighs) > 0:
        my_mwoe = min(out_neighs,key=lambda x:x[2])
    else:
        my_mwoe = [99,99,99]
    msg = [rank, REPLY, round_num, my_mwoe]
    comm.send(msg, dest=parent, tag=REPLY)

def act02():
    global out_neighs, msg, sender, my_mwoe
    sender, typ, round_num, mwoe_msg = msg[0], msg[1], msg[2],msg
      [3]
    d = A[rank][sender]
    edge = [rank,sender,int(d)]
    if edge in out_neighs:
        out_neighs.remove(edge)

def act20():
    global out_neighs, msg, my_mwoe, mwoe_msg
```

```python
            msg[0] = rank
            for child in childs:
                comm.send(msg, dest=child, tag=ROUND)
            if mwoe_msg == my_mwoe:
                mwoe_incident(my_mwoe)

def act21():
    global sender, mwoe, my_mwoe, msg, mwoe_rcvd, msg, reply_rcvd,
    over, parent, out_neighs
    reply_rcvd.add(sender)
    mwoe_rcvd.append(mwoe_msg)
    if reply_rcvd == childs:   # all mwoe's received ?
        if len(out_neighs) > 0:      # update mwoe
            my_mwoe = min(out_neighs, key=lambda x:x[2])
        else:
            my_mwoe = [99,99,99]
        mwoe_rcvd.append(my_mwoe)      # append my mwoe
        mwoe_min = min(mwoe_rcvd, key=lambda x:x[2]) # find min mwoe
        msg = [rank,REPLY,round_num,mwoe_min]   # insert min_mwoe in REPLY
        comm.send(msg, dest=parent, tag=REPLY) # send REPLY to parent
        reply_rcvd.clear()
        mwoe_rcvd.clear()
        round_over = True

def act30():
    global msg, out_neighs, state, mwoe,my_mwoe, childs, over
    sender, typ, roun, mwoe_msg = msg[0], msg[1], msg[2],msg[3]
    if mwoe_msg == my_mwoe:   # is min  mwoe adjacent?
        mwoe_incident(my_mwoe)
        state = INTERNAL     # change state to INTERN
    else:
        if len(out_neighs) > 0:
            my_mwoe = min(out_neighs, key=lambda x:x[2]) # send my mwoe to parent
        else:
            my_mwoe = [99,99,99]
        msg = [rank, REPLY, round_num, my_mwoe]
        comm.send(msg, dest=parent, tag=REPLY)


act22 = act02
act32 = act02

def act12():
    global mwoe_cands
    d = A[rank][sender]
    edge = [rank,sender,int(d)]
    mwoe_cands.append(edge)

actions = np.array([[None,act01,act02],
                    [act10,None,act12],
                    [act20,act21,act22],
                    [act30,None,act32]])

state = IDLE
round_over = False
round_num = -1

if rank == 0:   # root append the first mwoe
   state = ROOT
   my_mwoe = min(out_neighs,key=lambda x:x[2])
```

10.2 Minimum Spanning Trees

```
179     mwoe_min = my_mwoe
180     T.append(my_mwoe)
181     print("T: {}".format(T))
182     mwoe_incident(my_mwoe)
183
184 for round_num in range(1,12):
185     round_over = False
186     if rank == 0:
187         msg = [rank,ROUND,round_num,mwoe_min]
188         for child in childs:
189             comm.send(msg, dest=child, tag=ROUND)
190
191     while not round_over:
192       msg = recv_safe()
193       if msg == False:   # if no more messages, quit
194          break
195       sender, typ, round_num, mwoe_msg = msg[0], msg[1], msg[2],msg
            [3]
196       actions[state][typ]()
197 if rank == 0:
198     print("ROOT: THIS IS FINAL T:",T)
```

Listing 10.2 Output of Distributed Primr Algorithm

```
T: [[0, 1, 5]]
T: [[0, 1, 5], [1, 2, 1]]
T: [[0, 1, 5], [1, 2, 1], [2, 5, 3]]
T: [[0, 1, 5], [1, 2, 1], [2, 5, 3], [5, 3, 2]]
T: [[0, 1, 5], [1, 2, 1], [2, 5, 3], [5, 3, 2], [5, 4, 4]]
T: [[0, 1, 5], [1, 2, 1], [2, 5, 3], [5, 3, 2], [5, 4, 4], [1, 6,
    6]]
T: [[0, 1, 5], [1, 2, 1], [2, 5, 3], [5, 3, 2], [5, 4, 4], [1, 6,
    6], [0, 7, 8]]
ROOT: THIS IS FINAL T: [[0, 1, 5], [1, 2, 1], [2, 5, 3], [5, 3, 2],
    [5, 4, 4], [1, 6, 6], [0, 7, 8]]
```

10.2.2 Gallager-Humblet-Spira Algorithm

Gallager-Humblet-Spira (GHS) algorithm is a distributed MST algorithm considered as one of the main MST algorithms due to its parallel execution mode of MST construction [5]. The nodes of the distributed system progressively form *fragments* that are partial MSTs. These fragments merge forming larger fragments using the principle implemented in Boruvka's algorithm and the MST is formed as a single fragment eventually.

Let us consider two MSTs, $T_1 = (V_1, E_1)$ and $T_2 = (V_2, E_2)$ with $V_1, V_2 \in V$ and $V_1 \cap V_2 = \emptyset$. As in Boruvka's algorithm, the GHS algorithm finds the least cost edge e that connects a vertex in V_1 to a vertex in V_2 forming the new MST fragment $T_3 = T_1 \cup T_2 \cup e$ covering all of the nodes $V_1 \cup V_2$. This algorithm has both synchronous and asynchronous versions. We will first review the synchronous version.

10.2.2.1 Synchronous GHS Algorithm

Synchronous GHS working in rounds can be considered as a distributed version of Boruvka's algorithm. Each node starts as a fragment in the first phase and then gradually fragments are merged until there is only one fragment. Determining the least cost edge e in a fragment is handled by an elected leader in each fragment. Another problem to be resolved is to decide whether the edge e is between two different fragments or not, which is solved by assigning the same name to all nodes in one fragment. A single round of this algorithm works as follows [8]:

- *Finding the MWOE of the Fragment*:

  – The root (leader) of the fragment broadcasts the message $find\_MWOE$.
  – A node receiving this message checks its neighbors in the order of increasing weights. If the fragment identifier is different than its identifier, the edge is labeled as MWOE and is convergecast to the root. Testing of neighbors will be made from the last edge tested in the last phase since the fragment members will belong to the same fragment throughout the algorithm.

- *Merging Fragments Over MWOE*:

  – The leader broadcast $merge((u, v))$ message where MWOE is the least cost of all MWOEs convergecast.
  – A node u that has upcast m sends $request$ message to the node v to combine with its fragment.
  – If node v has also sent a $request$ message to node u, then they agree to merge through the edge (u, v). Otherwise, if there is only one request from one side, this message is ignored. However, the edge (u, v) is marked by the receiver of the $request$ message.
  – The node with the higher identifier becomes the leader of the fragment.
  – The new leader broadcast a $new\_fragment$ message to the combined fragments.
  – Each node updates its parent, children and the new fragment identifier which is the identifier of the new leader.

Analysis

Total number of rounds is $O(\log n)$ as total number of fragments will be at least reduced by half by the merge operation of neighbor fragments in the worst case. Each round of this algorithm takes $O(n)$ time as in the case of a linear network. Thus, the total time for this algorithm is $O(n \log n)$. The broadcast and convergecast messages at each round are over the fragment tree edges with $O(n)$ messages resulting in in $O(n \log n)$ messages in total. Searching MWOE by nodes is done at most once for each edge except for the last checked node resulting in $O(m)$ messages.

Therefore, message complexity of this algorithm is the sum of these two operations as $O(m + n \log n)$.

10.2.2.2 Asynchronous GHS Algorithm

The asynchronous version of GHS algorithm also assumes each node as a fragment initially, and the algorithm terminates when there is only one fragment as the synchronous version. Each fragment is labelled by an integer denoted as its *level*. Initially, each node is a fragment with level 0. Two procedures for joining two fragments are defined as follows:

- *Merge*: Two fragments of the same level L are merged to form a new fragment of level $L + 1$ named with the least cost edge e joining them.
- *Absorb*: A fragment of level L_i is absorbed by a fragment of higher level L_j by a least cost edge e between them, and the new fragment is assigned level L_2 with the name of fragment at level L_2.

The following message types are used in this algorithm [3]:

- *initiate*: Broadcast from the leader to find MWOE.
- *report*: Convergecasts responses to *initiate* messages to the leader.
- *test*: Check whether an edge is outgoing from the fragment.:
- *connect*: Used to merge components over MWOE between them.
- *changeroot*: Sent from the leader to the endpoint of MWOE.

Test-Accept-Reject Protocol

A node in this algorithm may be in *Sleeping* and *Find* states denoting initial state of a node and searching for MWOE state respectively; a node is in state *Found* at all other times. An edge in the network graph may be in *Branch* state if it belongs to the MST, *Rejected* if it is not part of the MST, and *Base* state if it is not decided to be neither a branch or rejected edge. The *Test-Accept-Reject* protocol of the algorithm works as follows using the following message types [3]:

- A node i receiving an *initiate* message sends $test(F_i, L_i)$ message where F_i is its fragment identifier and L_i is its level, over its minimum weight *basic* edge.
- On reception of message $test(F_i, L_i)$ by node j:

    - If $F_i = F_j$, *reject* message is sent to node i as edge belongs to the same fragment.
    - If $F_i \neq F_j$ and $L_i \leq L_j$, *accept* message is sent to node i.
    - If $F_i \neq F_j$ and $L_i \geq L_j$, no reply is sent until this condition changes.

- On reception of a *reject* message from node j, node i marks edge as *rejected* and sends *test* message to its next incident minimum weight *basic* edge.
- A node i sends *report* message to its leader after receiving responses from all neighbors the *initiate* message was sent.
- The leader selects the lowest MWOE and sends *changeroot* message to the node that is incident to the MWOE.
- The node with the adjacent MWOE sends $connect(L_i)$ message to its MWOE neighbor node j in fragment F_j.

Merging Fragments

Two fragments F_i and F_j at level L having the same MWOE connecting nodes i and j, both send connect messages over MWOE (i, j). The edge (i, j) now becomes the *core* of the new combined fragment of level $L + 1$ and *initiate* message is broadcast in this new fragment. When levels of two fragments F_i and F_j are different, for example $L_i < L_j$, F_i is absorbed by F_j and the node j incident to the MWOE at fragment F_j sends the *initiate* message to all nodes in F_i. Asynchronous GHS algorithm computes an MST of a weighted graph G in $O(n \log n)$ time using $O(m \log n)$ messages [3].

10.3 Routing

Routing is the process of sending a message between a source node and a destination node using least cost links in a computer network. When the graph is represented as a weighted graph, this problem is commonly referred to as the *shortest path problem*. The single source shortest path (SSSP) problem is finding shortest paths from a single source to all destinations in the network whereas in all-pairs-shortest-paths (APSP) procedure, our aim is to establish paths between each pair of node pairs. We will review basic SSSP algorithms and shortest implement one that is convenient for distributed processing in this section.

Dijkstra's SSSP algorithm has a similar structure to Prim's MST algorithm as we continuously search for a least cost path from a single source by progressively building a spanning tree rooted at the source vertex [2]. The main difference is that we search for the total cost of the path instead of the MWOE as in Prim's MST algorithm. This algorithm consists of the following steps:

1. **Input**: A weighted graph $G = (E, V, w)$ and a source vertex s.
2. **Output**: Shortest path distances to s and shortest path tree T rooted at s
3. **for all** node $v \in V \setminus \{s\}$
4.   set distance d_v to ∞ except neighbors of s which are set to edge weights to s
5. **while** $V \neq \emptyset$

6.   **find** v_m with minimum distance
7.   **for all** $(vm, u) \in E$ **do**
8.   **if** $d_u > d_{v_m} + w(u, v_m)$ **then**
9. $d_u > d_{v_m} + w(u, v_m)$
10. $T \leftarrow T \cup \{v_m\}$
11. $V \leftarrow V \setminus \{v_m\}$

The algorithm starts by setting distances of all vertices to the source vertex s to infinity except the neighbors of s which are simply set to the weights of edges joining them to s. Thereafter, a vertex v_m with minimum distance is selected, the distances of a neighbor u of v_m is updated if reaching s through v_m has a lower distance than the current distance of vertex u. This process continues until all vertices are processed resulting in a time complexity of $O(n^2)$ considering two nested loops, however, number of operations can be reduced to $O(n \log n)$ using suitable data structures [3].

10.3.1 Bellman-Ford Algorithm

Dijkstra's SSSP algorithm relies on accumulative distances from a source node and hence, edges with negative weights will produce wrong results. However, some real-life applications such as currency trading and minimum work flows may have negative weight edges. Bellman-Ford (BF) algorithm overcomes this complication using the dynamic programming method. This algorithm calculates distances to a source node u and forms a distance tree (DT) rooted at this node by progressively performing relaxation at each iteration. The root node runs $n - 1$ rounds which is the longest path in the network and updates distances at each iteration of the *for* loop by comparing the distance of a node u to its previous distance to the source node s as shown in Algorithm 10.2 [3]. If a node u is found to be closer to the node s over neighbor node v in an iteration, its distance and its parent in the tree DT is updated as in the lines 9 and 11 of this algorithm. The time complexity of this algorithm is $O(nm)$ considering $n - 1$ loop iterations and the possibility of at most m edge checkings in each loop.

10.3.1.1 Distributed Synchronous Bellman-Ford Algorithm

A distributed synchronous BF algorithm working in rounds can be designed with the following logic [4]: A spanning tree T is built prior to algorithm execution over which the synchronous *round* messages are sent by a special node called the *root*. Each node u exchanging its current distance to a source node s with the *update* message in a round updates its distance to the node s if a neighbor v is closer to s than itself. It assigns its distance as the distance of v to s, $d(s, v)$, plus its distance to v, $d(u, v)$, and also assigns v as its new parent as in the sequential algorithm. This process is repeated for $n - 1$ times by the *root* node, which is the longest path in the network. Messages may be delivered in any order due to undeterministic network behaviour, thus, we have the Boolean variable *round_recvd* which ensures that the *round* message is received before updating distances. Another Boolean variable *round_over* is used as in SSI algorithms in order to start convergecast of *round_over* messages to the root

Algorithm 10.2 *Bellman-Ford SSSP*

1: **Input**: $G = (V, E, w)$ a weighted graph
2: **Output**: Shortest path distances to s and shortest path tree T rooted at s
3: **for all** $v \in V \setminus \{s\}$ **do**   ▷ initialize
4:     $d_u \leftarrow \infty$
5:     $p_u \leftarrow \emptyset$
6: **end for**
7: **for** $k = 1$ to $n - 1$ **do**   ▷ update distances
8:     **for all** $(u, v) \in E$ **do**
9:         **if** $d_u > d_v + w(u, v)$ **then**
10:             $d_u \leftarrow d_v + w(u, v)$
11:             $p_u \leftarrow v$
12:         **end if**
13:     **end for**
14: **end for**
15: **for all** $(u, v) \in E$ **do**   ▷ check negative cycle
16:     **if** $d_u + w(u, v) > d_v$ **then**
17:         **return** $false$
18:     **end if**
19:     **return** $true$
20: **end for**

node. A single round k of this algorithm for node u is displayed in Algorithm 10.3 [4]. Time complexity of this algorithm is $O(n)$ rounds for a total of $O(nm)$ messages.

Algorithm 10.3 *Distributed Syncronous Bellman-Ford Algorithm*

1: **Input**: $G = (V, E, w)$ a weighted graph and a source node u, a spanning tree T
2: **Output**: Shortest distances to all nodes from u and a distance tree DT
3: int $u, v, my\_dist, dist$
4: **boolean** $round\_over \leftarrow False, round\_recvd \leftarrow False$
5: **while not** $round\_over$ **do**
6:     **receive** $(msg(v))$
7:     **switch** $msg(v).type$
8:         **case** $round(k)$: **send** $update(k, my\_dist)$ to $N(u)$
9:                 $round\_recvd \leftarrow True$
10:        **case** $update(v, k, dist)$: $recvd \leftarrow recvd \cup \{v\}$
11:             **if** $recvd = N(u) \wedge round\_recvd$ **then**
12:                 **for all** $v \in N(u)$
13:                     **if** $my\_dist > dist(s, v) + dist(u, v)$ **then**
14:                       $my\_dist \leftarrow dist(s, v) + dist(u, v)$
15:                     $parent \leftarrow v$
16:                 $round\_over \leftarrow True$
17: **end while**

10.3 Routing

Python Implementation

The synchronous BF algorithm is implemented in Listing 10.3 by transferring the pseudocode of Algorithm 10.3 to Python code.

Listing 10.3 Synchronous Distributed Bellman-Ford Algorithm

```python
from mpi4py import MPI
import numpy as np

comm = MPI.COMM_WORLD
rank = comm.Get_rank()
n    = comm.Get_size()

ROUND   = 0   # message types
UPDATE  = 1
ROVER   = 2

# msg = [sender, type, round number, [neighbor id, neighbor
    distance]
msg = [-1,-1, -1,[-1,-1]]

# tree info
children = [[1,6],[2,5],[3],[],[],[4],[]]
parents  = [0,0,1,2,5,1,0]
childs = children[rank]
parent = parents[rank]
childs = set(childs)
neighs, data_recvd, rover_recvd = set(), set(), set()

# distance matrix
e = 99
A  = np.array([[0,8,e,e,e,e,1],
               [8,0,3,e,e,6,2],
               [e,3,0,7,e,8,e],
               [e,e,7,0,1,5,e],
               [e,e,e,1,0,9,e],
               [e,6,8,5,9,0,4],
               [1,2,e,e,e,4,0]])
dists = A[rank,:]

for i in range(0,n):    # identify neighbors
    if dists[i] != 99 and dists[i] != 0:
        neighs.add(i)

round_num = 0
pred = -1

my_dist = [rank,int(dists[0])] # initialize distance to 0
if int(dists[0]) != 99:      # if neighbor of 0, set 0 as parent
    pred = 0

for i in range(0,n):
    round_over, update_over = False, False
    rover_recvd.clear()
    data_recvd.clear()
    currdis = []
    if rank == 0: # root starts the round
        round_num = round_num + 1
        msg[0], msg[1], msg[2] = rank, ROUND, round_num
        for child in childs:
            comm.send(msg, dest=child, tag=ROUND)
        msg = [rank,UPDATE,round_num, my_dist]
```

```python
            for node in neighs:      # send to neighbors
                comm.send(msg, dest=node, tag=UPDATE)

        # new round
        while not round_over:
            msg = comm.recv(source=MPI.ANY_SOURCE, tag=MPI.ANY_TAG)
            sender, typ, roun, neigh_dist = msg[0], msg[1], msg[2], msg[3]
            if typ == ROUND:   # send ROUND to children
                if rank != 0:
                    msg[0] = rank
                    for child in childs:
                        comm.send(msg, dest=child, tag=ROUND)
                    msg[0], msg[1], msg[3] = rank, UPDATE, my_dist
                    for node in neighs:      # send UPDATE to neighbors
                        comm.send(msg, dest=node, tag=UPDATE)

            elif typ == UPDATE:
                data_recvd.add(sender)
                currdis.append(neigh_dist)
                if data_recvd == neighs:   # update distance to 0
                    for node in currdis:
                        if my_dist[1] > (node[1] + int(dists[node[0]])):
                            my_dist[1] = (node[1] + int(dists[node[0]]))
                            pred = node[0]
                    update_over = True
                    if rover_recvd == childs:
                        if rank != 0:
                            msg[0], msg[1] = rank, ROVER
                            comm.send(msg, dest=parent, tag=ROVER)
                        round_over = True

            elif typ == ROVER:   # check if round is received
                rover_recvd.add(sender)
                if rover_recvd == childs:
                    if update_over:
                        if rank != 0:
                            msg[0], msg[1] = rank, ROVER
                            comm.send(msg, dest=parent, tag=ROVER)
                        round_over = True

dists[rank] = 0
print("         Rank {}, Distance to 0: {}, Parent: {}".format(rank, my_dist[1], pred))
```

Listing 10.4 Output of Synchronous Distributed Bellman-Ford Algorithm

```
Rank 4, Distance to 0: 11, Parent: 3
Rank 3, Distance to 0: 10, Parent: 5
Rank 6, Distance to 0: 1, Parent: 0
Rank 5, Distance to 0: 5, Parent: 6
Rank 2, Distance to 0: 6, Parent: 1
Rank 1, Distance to 0: 3, Parent: 6
Rank 0, Distance to 0: 0, Parent: 0
```

Running the distributed algorithm in the sample graph of Fig. 10.5 results in the shortest path spanning tree rooted at node 0 with the displayed node distances to node 0 in Listing 10.4. Note that the spanning tree used for communication is specified in

Fig. 10.5 A sample graph to test distributed synchronous Bellman-Ford algorithm

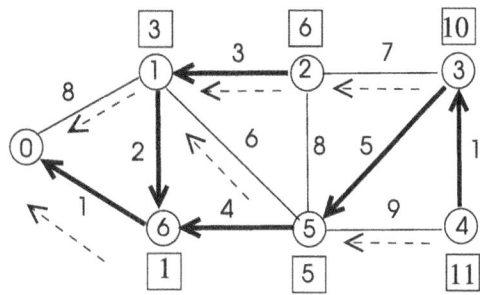

lines 16 and 17 and shown as dashed arrows in the figure whereas the output distance tree DT shown in bold in Fig. 10.5 displays the shortest paths to the source node 0.

10.3.2 Chandy-Misra Algorithm

Chandy and Misra provided an asynchronous SSSP algorithm with an idea similar to Bellman-Ford algorithm. The algorithm however may be augmented by termination detection using convergecasting reply messages from nodes that change their distances. Two types of messages used are UPDATE and ACK. Initially, the distance of each node to the source node u is ∞. The node u starts the algorithm by sending UPDATE message to each neighbor j with the distance $w(u, j)$. Any node i that receives an UPDATE message containing a distance that is lower than its distance to node u, changes its parent to sender, increments the number of acknowledgements to wait (ack_weight) to the number of its neighbors $-$ 1 excluding its parent. Whenever an ack message is received, ack_weight is decremented and if this number is equal to the number of ACK messages waited, the node can terminate the algorithm as shown in Algorithm 10.4. The number of messages transmitted is unbounded which is the major problem with this algorithm.

10.4 Matching

A matching of a graph $G = (V, E)$ is a subset of its edges such that these edges do not share any endpoints. In other words, these edges form an independent edge set of the graph.

10.4.1 Unweighted Matching

The number of matched edges is considered in unweighted matching of a graph as defined below.

Algorithm 10.4 *Chandy-Misra Algorithm*

```
1: Input: G = (V, E, w) a weighted graph and a source node u
2: Output: Shortest paths to all nodes from u
3: N(i) =← neighbors of i, parent ←⊥, acks_rcvd ← 0, acks_weight ← 0, my_dist ← ∞,
4: if i = u then
5:     for all j ∈ N(i) do
6:         send dist(w(u, j)) to j
7:         acks_weight ← |N(i)|
8:     end for
9: end if
10: while ¬over do
11:    receive (msg(j))
12:    switch msg(j).type
13:        case update(d):
14:            if my_dist > d then
15:                my_dist ← d
16:                if parent ≠ j then parent = j
17:                for all j ∈ N(i)
18:                    send update(my_dist + w(i, j)) to j
19:                    acks_weight ← acks_weight + |N(i)| − 1
20:        case ack(j):
21:            acks_rcvd ← acks_rcvd + 1
22:            if acks_rcvd = acks_weight then
23:                send ack to parent
24:                over ← true
25: end while
```

Definition 10.1 Given a graph $G = (V, E)$, a matching $M \subseteq E$ consists of edges such that any edge $(u, v) \in M$ does not have common endpoints with any other edge in M. The size of a *maximal matching* (MM) can not be enlarged any further and a *maximum matching* (MaxM) of a graph has the largest size among all matchings of a graph.

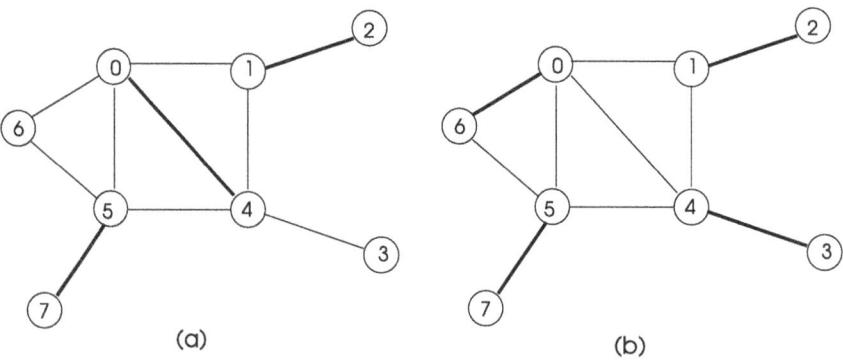

Fig. 10.6 **a** Maximal matching, **b** maximum matching

10.4 Matching

A maximal matching of size 3 and a maximum matching of size 5 are depicted in Fig. 10.6a and b respectively as bold edges.

A simple greedy algorithm can be formed which selects an edge e of a graph G, includes it in the matching and removes all adjacent edges of e from G. This process continues until all edges are removed from the graph as shown in Algorithm 10.5.

Algorithm 10.5 *Maximal Matching*

1: **Input**: $G = (V, E)$ an unweighted graph
2: **Output**: MM M of G
3: $S = \leftarrow E$
4: $M = \leftarrow \emptyset$
5: **while** $S \neq \emptyset$ **do**
6:     Pick any $e \in S$
7:     $M \leftarrow M \cup \{e\}$
8:     $S \leftarrow S \setminus \{e \cup \text{all adjacent edges of } e\}$
9: **end while**
10: **return** M

10.4.2 Weighted Matching

Given a weighted graph $G = (V, E, w : E \to \mathbb{R})$ which has weights as real numbers associated with its edges, a *weighted matching* of G consists of independent edges as in unweighted matching. In this case, our aim is to find a matching M that has a total minimum or maximum weight (MaxWM) of edges. A simple algorithm to find a weighted matching can be designed by always picking the largest weight (heaviest) free edge at each iteration which is simply done by modifying line 6 of Algorithm 10.5. The maximal matching obtained in a sample weighted graph is

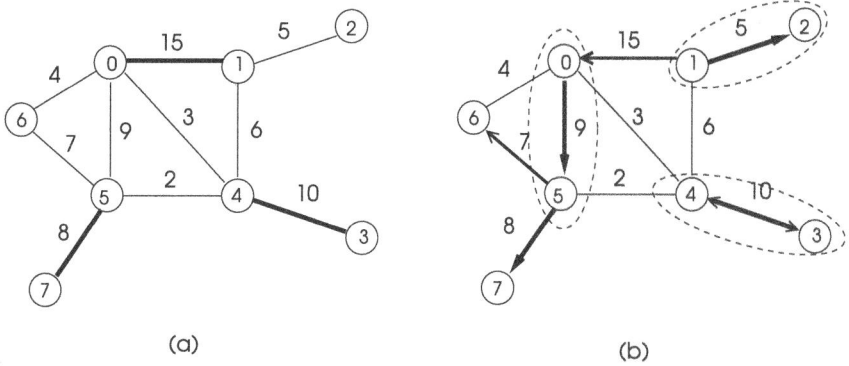

Fig. 10.7 Running of **a** Greedy matching, **b** Preis algorithm

shown in Fig. 10.7a using this procedure which results in a total weight of 33 which is the MaxWM for this graph.

10.4.2.1 Preis' Algorithm

A locally heaviest edge of a node u in a graph is defined as the edge that has the highest weight incident to the node u. Preis proposed an algorithm [9] that picks a local heaviest edge at each iteration again by modifying line 6 of Algorithm 10.5. The selection of vertices may be done at random. Running of this algorithm in the same sample graph of Fig. 10.7a may result in the MWM in (b) of this figure shown in dashed ellipses where each locally heaviest edge is shown pointing to its source node. The total weight of the matching obtained by this sample run of Preis algorithm is 24.

10.4.2.2 Hoepman's Algorithm

Hoepman provided a distributed version of Preis algorithm using a simple protocol [6]. The main idea of this algorithm is to include an edge (u, v) in MWM when this edge is the heaviest edge for both of the nodes u and v. This decision is to be agreed by both nodes by the exchange of messages. There are two types of messages: *request* to solicit whether the incident heaviest edge (u, v) of a node u is also the heaviest edge of node v; and *drop* message to notify neighbors when a matched edge is found. The set R holds the received *request* messages and N is the set of current neighbors of a node u that are not saturated (matched). The *request* message is sent by a node u to node v at the other end of its heaviest edge (u, v). If node v also sends a *request* message to node u, the edge (u, v) is marked as a matching edge by both nodes after which they inform all their neighbors to delete common edges between them by sending a *drop* message.

The termination condition for the algorithm shown in Algorithm 10.6 is when the neighbor set N becomes empty. Two possibilities for this condition is either an incident matching edge (u, c) is found and thus N should be cleared as in line 27 of the algorithm, or when all neighbors of a node u are saturated and they are deleted from the set N one by one which may result in N being empty as in the line 14 of the algorithm.

Running of this algorithm in a simple weighted network graph is depicted in Fig. 10.8. Note that the working of this algorithm is asynchronous without the need for rounds. Total weight of matching by this implementation is 44 where the maximum weighted matching of this graph is 45 with edges (0, 8), (4, 6), (1, 2), (5, 7) included in the matching.

Python Implementation

We can transform the pseudocode of Algorithm 10.6 into Python code as in the code of Listing 10.5. Each node u extracts its neighbor distance information as

10.4 Matching

Algorithm 10.6 *Hoepman's Algorithm*

1: **Input**: $G = (V, E, w)$ a weighted graph
2: **Output**: MWM $M = M_0 \cup ... \cup M_{n-1}$ of G
3: $N =\leftarrow$ neighbors of u
4: $R =\leftarrow \emptyset, M =\leftarrow \emptyset$
5: $c \leftarrow candidate(u, N)$ ▷ pick heaviest incident edgetate
6: **if** $c \neq \bot$ **then**   ▷ if found, send request
7:    bfsend *request* to c
8: **end if**
9: **while** $N \neq \emptyset$ **do**
10:    **receive** message m from v
11:    **if** $m.type = request$ **then**   ▷ if *request* is received, put sender in R
12:      $R \leftarrow R \cup \{v\}$
13:    **else**   ▷ message type is *drop*
14:      $N \leftarrow N \setminus \{v\}$
15:      **if** $c = v$ **then**   ▷ request refused
16:        $c \leftarrow candidate(u, N)$ ▷ choose another edge
17:        **if** $c \neq \bot$ **then**
18:          **send** *request* to c
19:        **end if**
20:      **end if**
21:    **end if**
22:    **if** $c \neq \bot$ and $c \in R$ **then**   ▷ a matching edge is found
23:      **for all** $w \in N \setminus \{c\}$ **do**
24:        **send** *drop* to w
25:      **end for**
26:      $M_u \leftarrow \{(u, c)\}$
27:      $N \leftarrow \emptyset$
28:    **end if**
29: **end while**

its corresponding row from the distance matrix A. In practice, this information is commonly readily available in a computer network by the exchange of data link layer messages. The set *neighs* holds the identifiers of the current neighbors of the node u. Each node iteratively searches its current free neighbors to pair for matching and sends a REQ message to the node opposite its heaviest edge until there are no more free neighbors left or a matching is found. Figure 10.8 is used as the input to this algorithm and the output shown in Listing 10.6 displays the matched edges in accordance with the matched edges in the figure.

Listing 10.5 Hoepman's Algorithm

```
from mpi4py import MPI
import numpy as np

comm = MPI.COMM_WORLD
rank = comm.Get_rank()
size = comm.Get_size()

REQ, DROP = 1, 2
```

```
msg     = np.array([-1,-1])
neighs, R = set(), set()
M = []      # matched edges

A   = np.array([[0,12,0,0,0,5,0,0,18,0],
                [12,0,8,4,3,9,0,0,0,6],
                [0,8,0,4,0,0,0,0,0,0],
                [0,4,2,0,1,0,0,0,0,0],
                [0,3,0,1,0,7,15,0,0,0],
                [5,9,0,0,7,0,0,4,0,0],
                [0,0,0,0,15,0,0,0,0,0],
                [0,0,0,0,0,4,0,0,0,0],
                [18,0,0,0,0,0,0,0,0,0],
                [0,6,0,0,0,0,0,0,0,]],dtype=int)

for j in range(0,size): # find neighbors
    if A[rank,j] != 0:
        neighs.add(j)
W = A[rank,:]           # get weights into weight array

if not np.all((W == 0)): # find candidate
    msg[0], msg[1] = rank, REQ
    c = np.argmax(W)
    comm.send(msg,dest=c,tag=REQ)

while len(neighs) != 0:
    msg = comm.recv(source=MPI.ANY_SOURCE, tag=MPI.ANY_TAG)
    sender, typ = msg[0], msg[1]
    msg[0] = rank
    if typ == REQ: # REQ received
        R.add(sender)
    else:                   # DROP received
        neighs.remove(sender)
        if c == sender: # if already sent to sender, remove sender
            W[c] = 0
            if not np.all((W == 0)): # find another edge
                c = np.argmax(W)
                msg[1] = REQ
                comm.send(msg,dest=c,tag=REQ) #send REQ to candidate

    if not np.all((W == 0)) and c in R:  # send DROP to neighbors
        neighs2 = neighs.copy()     # except the sender
        neighs2.remove(c)
        msg[1] = DROP
        for node in neighs2:
            comm.send(msg,dest=node,tag=DROP)
        neighs.clear()
        M =((rank,c))     # store matched edge

print("Rank: {}, Matched Edge: {}".format(rank,M))
```

Listing 10.6 Output of Hoepman's Algorithm

```
Rank: 6, Matched Edge: (6, 4)
Rank: 8, Matched Edge: (8, 0)
Rank: 0, Matched Edge: (0, 8)
Rank: 4, Matched Edge: (4, 6)
Rank: 5, Matched Edge: (5, 1)
Rank: 9, Matched Edge: []
```

```
Rank: 7, Matched Edge: []
Rank: 1, Matched Edge: (1, 5)
Rank: 3, Matched Edge: (3, 2)
Rank: 2, Matched Edge: (2, 3)
```

10.5 Chapter Notes

A weighted graph has edges labeled with real numbers denoted as weights. These weights are used to represent some parameter such as the difficulty of reaching a node from another node as in a graph representing a computer network and sometimes, displaying the similarity between the nodes as in a social network.

We reviewed main problems that are modelled by weighted graphs which are constructing minimum spanning trees (MSTs), routing in computer networks and weighted matching in this chapter. Although there are well known algorithms to build MSTs sequentially, this problem is not trivial in a distributed environment as we reviewed. The GHS algorithm for this purpose provides an MST in a weighted graph using three phases. The classical sequential routing algorithms in a weighted graph representing a computer network are provided by Dijkstra and Bellman-Ford. The latter is more suitable for distributed processing as it makes use of neighbor information and forms routes iteratively by improving the previously found routes.

A matching of an unweighted graph consists of independent edges which do not share any endpoints. The weighted matching problem is to find a matching in a weighted graph with the largest (or least) total weight among all matchings of the graph. The greedy algorithm for this purpose always picks the highest weight available edge e at each iteration, deleting all adjacent edges to e from the graph and continuing until graph does not contain any more edges. This algorithm achieves 2- approximation to the maximum matching and runs in $O(n \log m)$ time. Preis provided an algorithm that picks locally heaviest edge at each iteration with the same approximation ratio as the greedy algorithm but improving time complexity to $O(m)$. Hoepman presented a distributed version of Preis algorithm using a simple protocol. We reviewed all of these algorithms and provided Python implementation of Hoepman's algorithm.

Programming Exercises

1. Show step-by-step implementation of Distributed Prim algorithm in the graph of Fig. 10.3 with vertex 0 as the source node. Check whether you obtain the same result using Kruskal's MST algorithm.
2. Show step-by-step implementation of Distributed Bellman-Ford algorithm in the graph of Fig. 10.8 with vertex 0 as the source node. Check whether you obtain the same result using Dijkstra's SSSP algorithm.
3. A simple way to obtain a distributed APSP algorithm is to distribute neighborhood information to all nodes and then, each node implements Dijkstra's SSSP algo-

216   10 Weighted Graphs

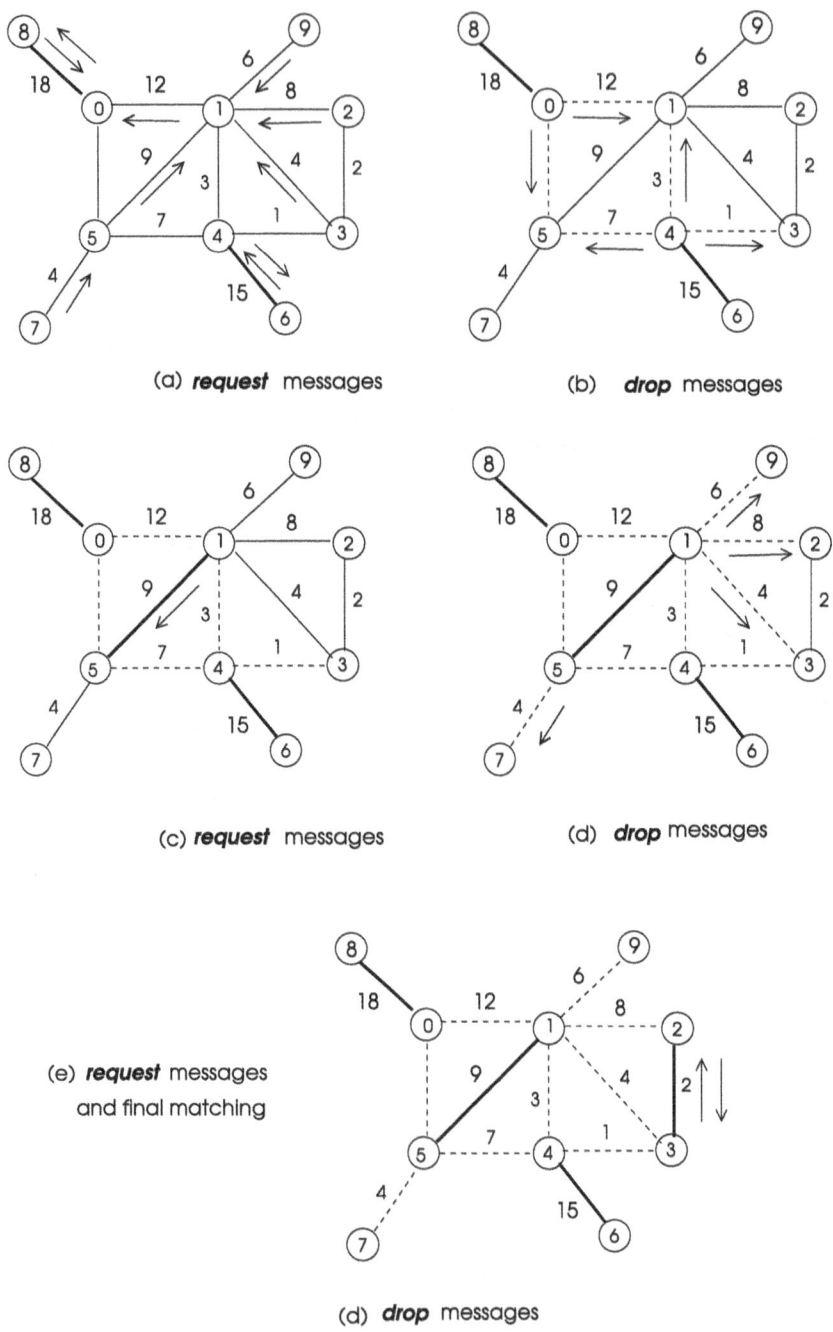

Fig. 10.8 Running of Algorithm 10.6 in a sample network

rithm to find SSSP routes. Write this algorithm in Python and test its operation in the graph of figure.
4. An SSI distributed weighted matching algorithm works in synchronous rounds. A node with the highest rank at each round selects its heaviest incident edge to be included in the matching and informs all its neighbors so that they are excluded from the matching process in the next rounds. Design this algorithm, write its pseudocode and implement in Python using $mpi4py$. Obtain the results using this algorithm for the graph of figure and check whether these results are the same as the ones obtained manually.
5. Design an An SSI distributed weighted matching algorithm in which a node that has the heaviest incident edge (u, v) at a round decides to include (u, v) in matching and informs its neighbors of this decision so that they are excluded in future rounds. The node with the higher identifier at the endpoints of the edge (u, v) is the deciding process. Design this algorithm, write its pseudocode and implement in Python using $mpi4py$. Run this algorithm for the graph of Fig. 10.8 and check whether these results are the same as the ones obtained manually.
6. Implement Preis algorithm in Python and find the results for the graph of figure.

References

1. O. Boruvka, About a certain minimal problem. Prce mor. prrodoved. spol. v Brne III (in Czech, German summary) 3:37–58 (1926)
2. E.W. Dijkstra, A note on two problems in connexion with graphs. Numerische Mathematik **1**, 269–271 (1959)
3. K. Erciyes, *Distributed Graph Algorithms for Computer Networks*. Springer Computer Communications and Networks Series, vol. 10 (Springer, Berlin, 2013), p. 1447151720
4. K. Erciyes, *Guide to Graph Algorithm: Sequential, Parallel and Distributed*. Springer Texts in Computer Science Series (2018)
5. R. Gallagher, P. Humblet, P. Spira, A distributed algorithm for minimumweight spanning trees. ACM Trans. Programm. Lang. Syst. **5**(1), 66–77 (1983)
6. J.H. Hoepman, *Simple Distributed Weighted Matchings*. Technical report (Nijmegen Institute for Computing and Information Sciences (NIII), 2004)
7. J.B. Kruskal, On the shortest spanning subtree of a graph and the traveling salesman problem. Proc. Am. Math. Soc. **7**, 48–50 (1956)
8. G. Pandurangan, P. Robinson, M. Scquizzato, The distributed minimum spanning tree problem. Bull. EATCS **125** (2018)
9. R. Preis, Linear time 1/2-approximation algorithm for maximum weighted matching, in *general graphs, in Symposium on Theoretical Aspects of Computer Science (STACS) 1999*. ed. by C. Meinel, S. Tison, LNCS, vol. 1563, (Springer, Berlin, 1999), pp.259–269
10. R.C. Prim, Shortest connection networks and some generalizations. Bell Syst. Tech. J. **36**(6), 1389–1401 (1957)

Graph Decomposition 11

Abstract

Graph decomposition algorithms are used to form special subgraphs with some property that may be used for various applications such as routing in mobile networks. Vertex coloring is the process of assigning colors to the vertices of a graph such that every vertex receives a color that is different than its neighbors. An independent set is a subset of vertices of a graph that are not adjacent. A dominating set of a graph is a subset of its vertices with the property that each vertex in the graph is either in this set or a neighbor of a node in this set. Coloring vertices with minimum number of colors, finding a maximum independent set and a minimum dominating set are all NP-Hard problems. We review heuristic coloring, vertex cover, maximal independent set and minimal dominating set problems as in [1] in this chapter with provided Python codes using $mpi4py$.

11.1 Vertex Coloring

Coloring refers to coloring vertices or edges and sometimes both vertices and edges of a graph. Vertex coloring is the process of assigning color to the vertices of a graph such that each vertex receives a different color than its neighbors.

Definition 11.1 (*vertex coloring*) Vertex coloring of a graph $G = (V, E)$ is the function $\phi : V \rightarrow C$ where $C = \{0, 1, 2, ...\}$ such that color of a vertex $c(v)$ is different than any color that is assigned to its neighbors.

Coloring vertices have various applications, one very simple one being the coloring the countries in a map. When each vertex of a graph has a unique identifier as an integer, one can easily color each vertex with its identifier resulting in n colors for a graph with n vertices. However, a fundamental requirement is to use as few colors as

Fig. 11.1 Running of random coloring algorithm

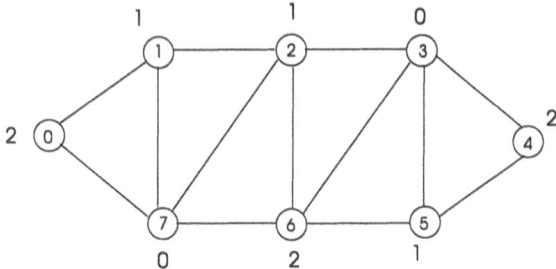

possible to color the vertices in the vertex coloring problem which is NP-Hard [2]. Thus, various heuristics of making use of rank of a vertex or degree of a vertex can be used for this purpose.

A simple sequential algorithm selects a vertex at random, colors it with the lowest possible color that is not used by its neighbors and continues until all vertices are colored as shown in Fig. 11.1 where vertices 3, 7,1, 5, 4, 6, 0, 2 are selected in sequence. Clearly, this algorithm is correct as we obey vector coloring property at each step. The time required is simply $\Theta(n)$ as a new vertex is colored at each iteration of the algorithm.

Distributed Vertex Coloring

A simple synchronous distributed algorithm working in rounds can be designed with the following intuition: At each round, the vertex with the round number is colored with a minimum color that does not conflict with the colors of its neighbors. Pseudocode of this algorithm can be stated below with the following steps at each round for node i.

1. $color \leftarrow -1$
2. Receive *round number* in the round message.
3. **If** *round number* $= i$ **then**
4.   color $c \leftarrow$ minimum color different than neighbors
5.   Inform neighbors of my color c
6. **Else If** color $c = -1$ and *round number* is one of my neighbor identities
7.   Receive neighbor color c from that neighbor.
8.   Remove c from my available color list.

The only message exchange at each round is between the node that has the identity that is equal to the round number and its neighbors. Since nodes are numbered $0, ..., n-1$, all nodes will be colored in n steps.

Python Implementation

We will implement this algorithm using the SSI model with a single initiator starting each round as shown in Listing 11.1. A spanning tree is built prior to the execution of the algorithm with the root process having 0 as identifier to execute synchronous

11.1 Vertex Coloring

rounds. The messages used, as in general SSI model with known round numbers, are below:

- ROUND: Initiated by the root process to start a round.
- DATA : Exchanged by active processes during a round.
- ROVER: Initiated by the leaf nodes of the spanning tree to convergecast to the root that the round is over. Each intermediate node upcasts this message to its parent when all of its children have sent ROVER to itself and it has finished processing at the current round.

Listing 11.1 Vertex Color Algorithm Sequential Simulation

```
from mpi4py import MPI
import numpy as np

comm = MPI.COMM_WORLD
rank = comm.Get_rank()
n = comm.Get_size()

ROUND, COLOR, ROVER, FIN = 0, 1, 2, 3 #message types

msg = np.array([-1,-1, -1, -1])        # initialize message
children = [[1,7],[2],[],[],[],[4],[3,5],[6]]  # initialize
    spanning tree
parents = [0,0,1,6,5,6,7,0]

finished, round_end = set(), set()
childs = children[rank]
parent = parents[rank]
childs = set(childs)
neighs, received = set(), set()
colors = {}

A=np.array([[0,1,0,0,0,0,0,1],    # adjacency matrix
            [1,0,1,0,0,0,0,1],
            [0,1,0,1,0,0,1,1],
            [0,0,1,0,1,1,1,0],
            [0,0,0,1,0,1,0,0],
            [0,0,0,1,1,0,1,0],
            [0,0,1,1,0,1,0,1],
            [1,1,1,0,0,0,1,0]],dtype=int)
neighbors = A[rank,:]
s = []
for i in range(0,n):    # identify neighbors
    if neighbors[i] == 1:
        neighs.add(i)
        colors.update([(i,-1)])
count = n - 1           # initialize
round_num = 0
color = -1
changed = False
if 0 in neighs:    # initialize root color
    colors[0] = 0

if rank == 0:
    color = 0

while count > 0:
    neighs_over, childs_end, round_over = False, False, False
```

```
47      round_end.clear()
48
49      if rank == 0:      # root starts a round
50         round_num = round_num + 1
51         msg[0], msg[1], msg[2] = rank, ROUND, round_num
52         for child in childs:
53            comm.send(msg, dest=child, tag=ROUND)
54
55      while not round_over:
56         msg = comm.recv(source=MPI.ANY_SOURCE, tag=MPI.ANY_TAG)
57         sender, typ, roun, neigh_color=msg[0], msg[1], msg[2], msg[3]
58         msg[0] = rank
59         if typ == ROUND:
60            if len(childs) != 0: # intermediate node
61               for child in childs:
62                  comm.send(msg, dest=child, tag=ROUND)
63            else:              # leaf node
64               childs_end = True
65
66            if rank == roun:
67               for key,value in colors.items():#find an unused color
68                  s.append(value)
69               s.sort()
70               found = False
71               for i in range(1,len(s)):
72                  if s[i] - s[i-1] > 1:
73                     color = s[i-1] + 1
74                     found = True
75                     break
76               if not found:
77                  color = max(s) + 1
78               colors[rank] = color
79               msg[1] = COLOR
80               msg[3] = color
81               for node in neighs:
82                  comm.send(msg, dest=node, tag=COLOR)
83               changed = True
84
85            if len(childs) == 0 and roun not in neighs:
86               msg[1] = ROVER
87               comm.send(msg,dest=parent,tag=ROVER)
88               round_over = True
89
90         elif typ == COLOR:
91            colors[sender] = neigh_color
92            changed = True
93            if childs_end:          # childs finished?
94               if rank != 0:
95                  msg[1] = ROVER
96                  comm.send(msg, dest=parent, tag=ROVER)
97               round_over = True
98
99         elif typ == ROVER:  # check if round is received
100           round_end.add(sender)
101           if round_end == childs:
102              childs_end = True
103              if roun == rank:
104                 if changed:
105                    round_over = True
106                 elif roun in neighs:
107                    if changed:
108                       round_over = True
109                 else: round_over = True
```

11.2 Vertex Cover

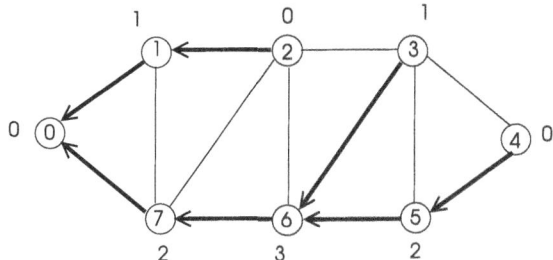

Fig. 11.2 Coloring of a sample graph by the distributed vertex coloring algorithm

```
110              if rank != 0:
111                  comm.send(msg,dest=parent,tag=ROVER)
112       count = count -1
113
114  print("Rank: {}, Color: {}".format(rank,color))
```

Listing 11.2 Output of Vertex Color Algorithm Sequential Simulation

```
Rank: 3, Color: 1
Rank: 4, Color: 0
Rank: 5, Color: 2
Rank: 6, Color: 3
Rank: 7, Color: 2
Rank: 2, Color: 0
Rank: 1, Color: 1
Rank: 0, Color: 0
```

Running of this algorithm in the simple graph of Fig. 11.2 using the spanning tree shown in bold lines results in the colors shown as the output in Listing 11.2 which are consistent with the colors found in the graph manually. As the sequential algorithm, the distributed algorithm is correct since we obey the vertex coloring rule at each round. The time complexity of this algorithm is $\Theta(n)$ as there are exactly n rounds. The message complexity is $O(n\Delta)$ since there will be $\Delta(G)$ messages sent from the active node to its neighbors at each round.

11.2 Vertex Cover

A vertex cover of a graph is a subset of its vertices where any edge is incident to at least one vertex in this set.

Definition 11.2 (*vertex cover*) A vertex cover of a graph $G = (V, E)$ is the set of vertices $V' \in V$ such that $\forall (a, b) \in E$, a or b or both are in V'.

Constructing a vertex cover of a graph has various implications, for example, placing markets in a region so that every road leads to at least one market. Vertex cover with the minimum order (MinVC) among all vertex covers of a graph is an

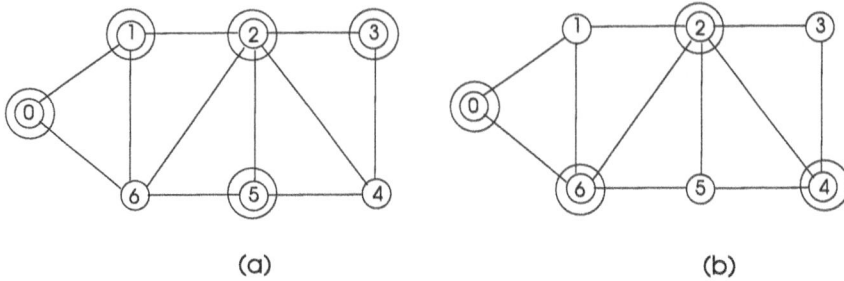

Fig. 11.3 Running of distributed rank based algorithm in a sample graph

NP-Hard problem [2] and thus, various heuristics are commonly used to find minimal vertex cover (MVC) where removal of a vertex from the cover distorts the vertex cover property. A MVC and a MinVC of a graph with orders 5 and 4 are depicted in Fig. 11.3a and b respectively where vertices in the cover are shown by double circles.

A random sequential algorithm to find the vertex cover of a graph selects a vertex v at random from the graph, includes v in the cover, removes v and all its incident edges from the graph, and continues until there are no more edges left. This algorithm requires $O(n\Delta(G))$ steps as n steps for selecting a vertex and $\Delta(G)$ steps of removing edges from this vertex. A different approach selects the highest degree vertex at each step to include in the vertex cover. Unfortunately, this approach results in an unbounded approximation ratio of $\Theta(\log n)$ to the order of minimum vertex cover, thus deviation from the optimal result increases as the number of vertices increases.

In a synchronous distributed setting, our aim is to provide symmetry breaking in each round using some property of the nodes. One approach is to use the identifiers of nodes for this purpose and always select the highest identifier node among all its neighbors to include in the cover.

Working of this algorithm in a simple graph is shown in Fig. 11.4 where a vertex cover of order 6 shown in double circles is obtained in 3 rounds at (c) of the figure. A vertex cover with order 4 constructed using highest degree first heuristic is shown in (d).

11.2.1 Sequential Algorithm Simulation

A distributed vertex cover algorithm working in synchronous rounds, *SeqSim_Vcov*, using SSI model with known round numbers may be designed where a node with the identifier equal to the round number is included in the cover, similar to the vertex color algorithm simulation. There are three states of a node as UNDEC, INCOV and NOTCOV denoting undecided, in cover and not in cover states. A node will finish as INCOV or NOTCOV states at the end of the algorithm as described in the following pseudocode for node i.

11.2 Vertex Cover

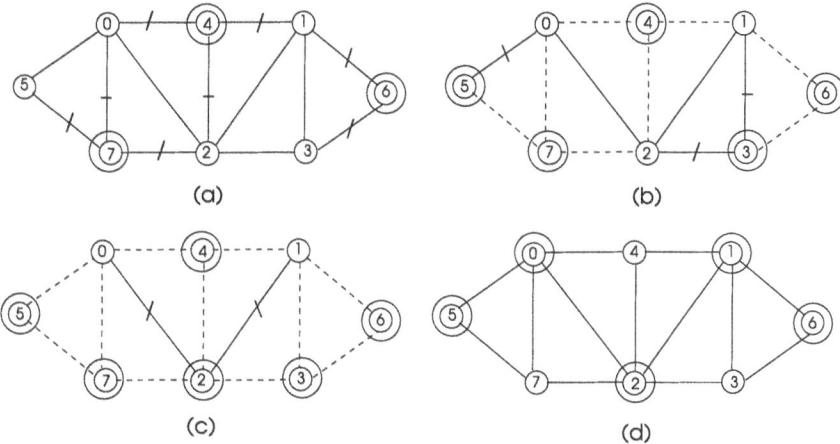

Fig. 11.4 Running of distributed rank based vertex cover algorithm in a sample graph

1. $state \leftarrow$ UNDEC, current edges $\leftarrow$ neighbors.
2. Receive *round number* in the round message.
3. **If** *round number* $= i$ and current edges $\neq \emptyset$ **then**
4. $\quad state \leftarrow$ INCOV
5. $\quad$ Send *state* to current neighbors
6. **Else If** *state* $=$ UNDEC and *round number* is one of my neighbor identities
7. $\quad$ Receive neighbor *state* from that neighbor.
8. **If** neighbor state = INCOV or NOTCOV
9. $\quad$ Remove neighbor edge from current edges.

A node learning that its neighbor has changed its state to INCOV or NONCOV state removes the neighbor from its current neighbors and thus its incident edge to that neighbor.

Python Implementation 1: Sequential Simulation

We implement $SeqSim\_Vcov$ algorithm with the above steps in Python using the SSI model. The synchronization messages are ROUND, DATA and ROVER as shown in Listing 11.3.

Listing 11.3 Vertex Cover Algorithm Sequential Simulation

```
from mpi4py import MPI
import numpy as np

comm = MPI.COMM_WORLD
rank = comm.Get_rank()
n    = comm.Get_size()

A   =   np.array([[0,0,0,1,1,1,0,0,1,0],
                  [0,0,0,0,0,1,1,1,1,1],
                  [0,0,0,0,0,0,1,1,0,0],
                  [1,0,0,0,1,0,0,0,1,0],
```

```
                        [1,0,0,1,0,0,0,0,0,0],
                        [1,1,0,0,0,0,0,0,1,1],
                        [0,1,1,0,0,0,0,1,0,1],
                        [0,1,1,0,0,0,1,0,0,0],
                        [1,1,0,1,0,1,0,0,0,0],
                        [0,1,0,0,0,1,1,0,0,0]],dtype=int)

# sender, type, round number, sender state
msg = [-1,-1, -1, -1]
children = [[3,4,5,8],[6,7],[],[],[],[9],[],[2],[1],[]]
parents  = [0,8,7,0,0,0,1,1,0,5]

# message types
ROUND  = 0
DATA   = 1
ROVER  = 2

# states
UNDEC   = 0
INCOV   = 1
NOTCOV  = 2
states = ['UNDEC','INCOV','NOTCOV']
child = children[rank]
parent = parents[rank]
childs = set(child)
neighs, neighs_rcvd, rover_rcvd = set(), set(), set()

for i in range(0,n):    # identify neighbors
    if A[rank,i] == 1:
        neighs.add(i)
currneighs = neighs.copy()

state = UNDEC
MAX_ROUND = 10 # number of rounds

for round_num in range(-1,MAX_ROUND):
    round_over = False
    neigh_over, child_over = False, False
    rover_rcvd.clear()
    neighs_rcvd.clear()
    if rank == 0:   # if root, start the next round
        round_num = round_num + 1
        msg[0], msg[1], msg[2] = rank, ROUND, round_num
        for child in childs: # send ROUND to children
            comm.send(msg, dest=child, tag=ROUND)
        if round_num == 0:
            state = INCOV
            msg[1], msg[3] = DATA, state
            for node in currneighs:    # send DATA to neighbors
                comm.send(msg, dest=node, tag=DATA)
            currneighs.clear()

    while not round_over:
        msg = comm.recv(source=MPI.ANY_SOURCE, tag=MPI.ANY_TAG)
        sender, typ, roun, ne_state = msg[0],msg[1],msg[2],msg[3]
        msg[0] = rank
        if typ == ROUND: # send ROUND to children
            if rank != 0 and len(childs) != 0:
                for child in childs:
                    comm.send(msg, dest=child, tag=ROUND)

            if rank == roun:
                neigh_over = True
```

11.2 Vertex Cover

```
              # if I have uncovered edges
              if len(currneighs) != 0:
                  state = INCOV
                  msg[1], msg[3] = DATA, state
                  for node in currneighs: # send DATA to neighbors
                      comm.send(msg, dest=node, tag=DATA)
                  currneighs.clear()
              if (len(childs) == 0):
                  msg[1] = ROVER
                  comm.send(msg, dest=parent, tag=ROVER)
                  round_over = True

          elif  roun not in currneighs:
                  neigh_over = True
                  if (len(childs) == 0) and rank != roun:
                      msg[1] = ROVER
                      comm.send(msg, dest=parent, tag=ROVER)
                      round_over = True

      elif typ == DATA:    # DATA received
          neigh_over = True
          if rank != 0:
              if len(childs) == 0 or child_over:
              # leaf starts convergecast
                  msg[1] = ROVER
                  comm.send(msg, dest=parent, tag=ROVER)
                  round_over = True
          currneighs.remove(sender)
          if len(currneighs) == 0:
              state = NOTCOV

      else:    # ROVER received
          rover_rcvd.add(sender)
          if rover_rcvd == childs: # all children received?
              child_over = True
              if roun not in currneighs:
                  neigh_over = True
              if neigh_over:
                  round_over = True
                  if rank != 0:
                      comm.send(msg,dest=parent,tag=ROVER)

print(" Rank: {} State: {}".format(rank,states[state]))
```

Listing 11.4 Output of Vertex Cover Algorithm Sequential Simulation

```
Rank: 3 State: INCOV
Rank: 4 State: NOTCOV
Rank: 6 State: INCOV
Rank: 9 State: NOTCOV
Rank: 2 State: INCOV
Rank: 5 State: INCOV
Rank: 7 State: NOTCOV
Rank: 1 State: INCOV
Rank: 8 State: NOTCOV
Rank: 0 State: INCOV
```

Running of this algorithm using the spanning tree in bold lines in Fig. 11.5 results in the output shown in Listing 11.4. This algorithm runs in $\Theta(n)$ time using $O(n\Delta(G))$ messages since active nodes are the node with identity equalling round number and its adjacent nodes as in $SeqSim\_Vcol$ algorithm.

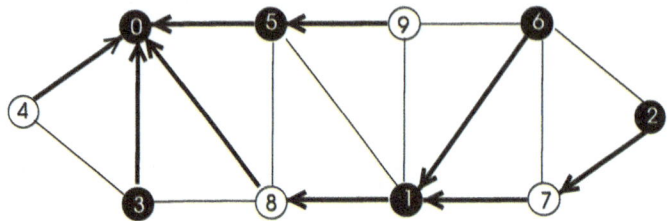

Fig. 11.5 Running of vertex cover sequential simulation algorithm in a sample graph

11.2.2 The Rank-Based Distributed Algorithm

We will use the rank of vertices to implement minimal vertex cover algorithm called *Rank_Vcov* algorithm. Since we do not know when a node decides to be in cover or not, we need to implement a different strategy than the sequential simulation. We need to consider the following:

- We know have two additional types of messages:

  - FINISHED: A node that determines its state sends FINISHED to its parent but continues broadcasting ROUND to its children and convergecasting ROVER message to its parent whenever there is at least one active process in its subtree.
  - TERMINATE: Broadcast by the root process to initiate termination of all processes when the root receives FINISHED from all of its children.

- Message exchange takes place in parallel among active nodes which have uncovered edges.
- Any undecided node that has at least one uncovered incident edge checks whether it has the highest rank among all its active neighbors and if it has, it decides to be INCOV state and informs all its active neighbors.

Python Implementation

We will implement algorithm *Rank_Vcol* with the above considerations in Python using the SSI model with unknown number of rounds as was described in Sect. 3.3.3. We need to have additional logical variables $finished\_childs$, $finished\_all$ and $terminated$ to denote whether children of a node has finished, itself and its children have finished and it is terminated consecutively. These new variables are used since messages from neighbors to a node may arrive in any arbitrary order and we need to make sure that all steps are performed before a round is over and before a node finishes as shown in Listing 11.5.

11.2 Vertex Cover

Listing 11.5 Rank-Based Distributed Vertex Cover Algorithm

```python
from mpi4py import MPI
import numpy as np

comm = MPI.COMM_WORLD
rank = comm.Get_rank()
n    = comm.Get_size()

# states
UNDEC   = 0
INCOV   = 1
NOTCOV  = 2

# message types
ROUND     = 0
DATA      = 1
ROVER     = 2
FINISHED  = 3
TERMINATE = 4

# sender, type, round number, sender state
msg = np.array([-1,-1, -1, -1])


A =     np.array([[0,0,0,1,1,1,0,0,1,0],
                  [0,0,0,0,0,1,1,1,1,1],
                  [0,0,0,0,0,0,1,1,0,0],
                  [1,0,0,0,1,0,0,0,1,0],
                  [1,0,0,1,0,0,0,0,0,0],
                  [1,1,0,0,0,0,0,0,1,1],
                  [0,1,1,0,0,0,0,1,0,1],
                  [0,1,1,0,0,0,1,0,0,0],
                  [1,1,0,1,0,1,0,0,0,0],
                  [0,1,0,0,0,1,1,0,0,0]],dtype=int)

# sender, type, round number, sender state
msg = [-1,-1, -1, -1]
children = [[3,4,5,8],[6,7],[],[],[],[9],[],[2],[1],[]]
parents  = [0,8,7,0,0,0,1,1,0,5]

child  = children[rank]
parent = parents[rank]
childs = set(child)
neighs, neighs_rcvd, rover_rcvd, finish_rcvd = set(), set(),
set(), set()
removed_neighs = set()
removed_childs = set()
states = ['UNDEC','INCOV','NOTCOV']

for i in range(0,n):     # identify neighbors
    if A[rank,i] == 1:
        neighs.add(i)

currneighs = neighs.copy()
currchilds = childs.copy()
round_num = 1
max_count = 4
state = UNDEC
finished_childs, finished_all, terminated = False, False, False

while not terminated:
    round_over, neighs_over, childs_over = False, False, False
    neighs_sent = False
```

```
63       rover_rcvd.clear()
64       neighs_rcvd.clear()
65       removed_neighs.clear()
66       removed_childs.clear()
67
68       if rank == 0:
69          msg[0], msg[1], msg[2] = rank, ROUND, round_num
70          for child in currchilds:
71             comm.send(msg, dest=child, tag=ROUND)
72          if state==UNDEC:
73             msg[1], msg[3] = DATA, state
74             for node in currneighs:
75                comm.send(msg, dest=node, tag=DATA)
76             neighs_sent = True
77          else:
78             neighs_over = True
79             neighs_sent = True
80
81       while not round_over:
82          msg = comm.recv(source=MPI.ANY_SOURCE, tag=MPI.ANY_TAG)
83          sender, typ, roun, ne_state  = msg[0] msg[1],msg[2],msg[3]
84          msg[0] = rank
85          if typ == ROUND:  # active node ROUND received
86                if len(currchilds) != 0:  # intermediate node
87                   for child in currchilds:
88                      comm.send(msg, dest=child, tag=ROUND)
89                else:              # leaf node
90                   childs_over = True
91                if state != UNDEC:  # node already determined
92                   neighs_over = True
93                   neighs_sent = True
94                   if len(childs)==0:
95                      childs_over = True
96                      msg[1] = ROVER
97                      comm.send(msg, dest=parent, tag=ROVER)
98                      round_over = True
99                   else:
100                     neighs_sent, neighs_over = True, True
101               else:            # node undetermined
102                  if rank > max(currneighs):
103                     state = INCOV
104                     round_saved = roun
105                     if len(currchilds) == 0:
106                        childs_over = True
107                        finished_all = True
108                        msg[1] = FINISHED
109                        comm.send(msg,dest=parent,tag=FINISHED)
110                  msg[1], msg[3] = DATA, state
111                  for node in currneighs:
112                     comm.send(msg, dest=node, tag=DATA)
113                  neighs_sent = True
114               if neighs_over and childs_over:
115                  if rank != 0:
116                     msg[1] = ROVER
117                     comm.send(msg, dest=parent, tag=ROVER)
118                  round_over = True
119
120         elif typ == DATA:  # DATA received
121               neighs_rcvd.add(sender)
122               if ne_state == INCOV or ne_state == NOTCOV:
123                  if sender in currneighs:
124                     removed_neighs.add(sender)
125
```

11.2 Vertex Cover

```
                    if neighs_rcvd == currneighs:
                        neighs_over = True
                        if neighs_sent:
                            # childs finished?
                            if len(childs)==0 or childs_over:
                                if rank != 0:
                                    msg[1] = ROVER
                                    comm.send(msg, dest=parent, tag=ROVER)
                                round_over = True

            elif typ == ROVER:   # ROVER received
                rover_rcvd.add(sender)
                if rover_rcvd == currchilds:
                   childs_over = True
                   if neighs_over and neighs_sent: # neighs finished
                      round_over = True
                      if rank != 0:
                          msg[1] = ROVER
                          comm.send(msg,dest=parent,tag=ROVER)


            elif typ == FINISHED: # a child finished
                finish_rcvd.add(sender)
                removed_childs.add(sender)
                if finish_rcvd == childs:
                    finished_childs = True
                    if state != UNDEC:
                        finished_all = True
                        if rank != 0:
                            msg[1] = FINISHED
                            comm.send(msg,dest=parent,tag=FINISHED)
                        else:
                            msg[1] = TERMINATE
                            for child in childs:
                                comm.send(msg, dest=child, tag=TERMINATE)
                            round_over = True
                            terminated = True

            else:   # TERMINATE received
                    if len(childs) != 0:
                        for child in childs:
                            comm.send(msg, dest=child, tag=TERMINATE)
                    terminated = True
                    round_over = True
        round_num = round_num + 1
        currneighs = currneighs-removed_neighs
        currchilds = currchilds-removed_childs
        # all edges covered?
        if len(currneighs) == 0 and state == UNDEC:
            state = NOTCOV
            round_saved = roun
            if len(currchilds) == 0:
                finished_all = True
                msg[1] = FINISHED
                comm.send(msg,dest=parent,tag=FINISHED)
print(" Rank: {}, State: {} at Round: {}"
.format(rank,states[state],round_saved))
```

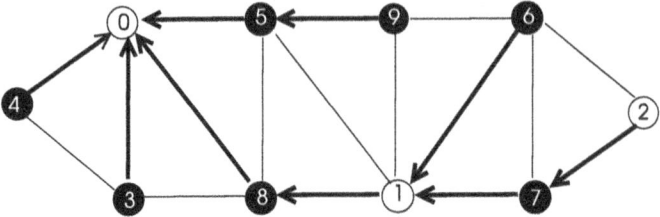

Fig. 11.6 Running of maximum identity vertex cover algorithm in a sample graph

Listing 11.6 Output of Rank-Based Distributed Vertex Cover Algorithm

```
Rank: 0, State: NOTCOV at Round: 2
Rank: 8, State: INCOV  at Round: 1
Rank: 3, State: INCOV  at Round: 2
Rank: 1, State: NOTCOV at Round: 2
Rank: 4, State: INCOV  at Round: 1
Rank: 5, State: INCOV  at Round: 2
Rank: 2, State: NOTCOV at Round: 2
Rank: 7, State: INCOV  at Round: 1
Rank: 9, State: INCOV  at Round: 1
Rank: 6, State: INCOV  at Round: 2
```

Running this algorithm in the graph of Fig. 11.6 provided the outputs shown in Listing 11.6 with the round that state is determined; the vertex cover nodes are shown in black in the graph.

11.3 Maximal Independent Sets

An independent set of a graph $G = (V; E)$ is a subset of its vertices that do not share any adjacent vertices.

Definition 11.3 (*independent set*) An independent set I of a graph $G = (V, E)$ is the set of vertices $I \in V$ with the condition that $\nexists (u, v) \in E$ such that u and $v \in I$.

A maximal independent set (MIS) can not be enlarged any further by the addition of any vertex and a maximum independent set (MaxIS) is a maximal independent set with the maximum order among all MISs of a graph. Finding MaxIS is an NP-Hard problem with no known polynomial time algorithms [2], thus, various heuristics are commonly employed. An MIS and MaxIS of orders 4 and 5 are shown in Fig. 11.7a and (b) respectively in double circles.

A simple sequential algorithm to form an MIS selects a node v of a graph G at random, includes it in the MIS, deletes v and its adjacent vertices from G and continues until all vertices are removed. Instead of selecting a vertex at random, we can select the lowest degree vertex at each iteration as our aim is to have an independent set as large as possible.

11.3 Maximal Independent Sets

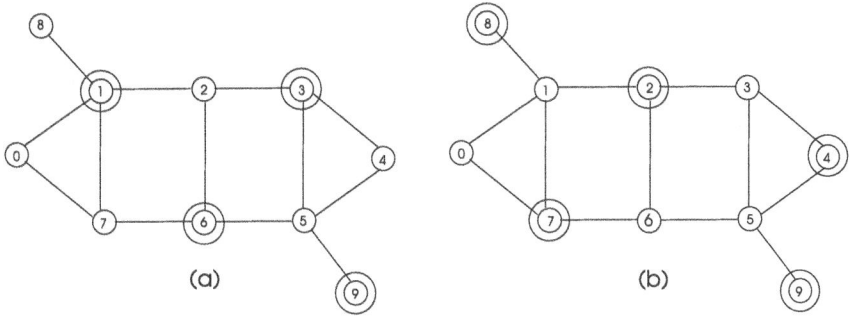

Fig. 11.7 a An MIS b a MaxIS of a sample graph

11.3.1 A Distributed MIS Algorithm Simulating Sequential Operation

An algorithm ($SeqSim\_MIS$) that simulates sequential execution based on node identifiers may be designed with the below steps considering node states as UNDEC, INMIS and NOTMIS denoting node states as undecided, in MIS and not in MIS consecutively,

1. $state \leftarrow$ UNDEC
2. Receive *round number* in the round message.
3. **If** *round number* $= i$ and
4.   **If** $state =$ UNDEC **then**
5. $state \leftarrow$ INMIS
6.   Send *state* to current neighbors
7. **Else If** $state =$ UNDEC and *round number* is one of my neighbor identities
8.   Receive neighbor *state* from that neighbor.
9.   **If** neighbor $state =$ INMIS
10. $state \leftarrow NOTMIS$

The messages exchanged are among the node with the identity equal to the current round number and its neighbors as in sequential simulation algorithms.

Python Implementation

We implement $SeqSim\_MIS$ algorithm in Python with the above steps below as shown in Listing 11.7. The ROVER messages are convergecast to the root process which starts the next round until round $n - 1$, when all nodes determine their states.

Listing 11.7 MIS Algorithm Sequential Simulation

```
from mpi4py import MPI
import numpy as np

comm = MPI.COMM_WORLD
rank = comm.Get_rank()
n    = comm.Get_size()

A =       np.array([[0,0,0,1,0,1,0,0,1,1],
                    [0,0,1,0,0,1,1,0,1,0],
                    [0,1,0,0,0,0,1,1,0,0],
                    [1,0,0,0,0,0,0,1,1],
                    [0,0,0,0,0,1,1,0,0,0],
                    [1,1,0,0,1,0,0,0,1,0],
                    [0,1,1,0,1,0,0,1,0,0],
                    [0,0,1,0,0,0,1,0,0,0],
                    [1,1,0,1,0,1,0,0,0,0],
                    [1,0,0,1,0,0,0,0,0,0]],dtype=int)

# sender, type, round number, sender state
msg = [-1,-1, -1, -1]
children = [[3,5,8,9],[2,6],[7],[],[],[4],[],[],[1],[]]
parents  = [0,8,1,0,5,0,1,2,0,0]

# message types
ROUND    = 0
DATA     = 1
DEGREE   = 2
ROVER    = 3

# states
UNDEC   = 0
INMIS   = 1
NOTMIS  = 2
states = ['UNDEC','INMIS','NOTMIS']

child = children[rank]
parent = parents[rank]
childs = set(child)
neighs, neighs_rcvd, rover_rcvd = set(), set(), set()

for i in range(0,n):      # identify neighbors
    if A[rank,i] == 1:
        neighs.add(i)
#print(rank,neighs,parent,childs)

state = UNDEC
MAX_ROUND = 10 # number of rounds

for round_num in range(-1,MAX_ROUND):
   round_over = False
   neigh_over, child_over   = False, False
   rover_rcvd.clear()
   neighs_rcvd.clear()
   if rank == 0:   # if root, start the next round
       round_num = round_num + 1
       msg[0], msg[1], msg[2] = rank, ROUND, round_num
       for child in childs: # send ROUND to children
           comm.send(msg, dest=child, tag=ROUND)
       if round_num == 0:
           neigh_over = True
           state = INMIS
```

11.3 Maximal Independent Sets

```python
                msg[1], msg[3] = DATA, state
                for node in neighs:    # send DATA to neighbors
                    comm.send(msg, dest=node, tag=DATA)

        while not round_over:
            msg = comm.recv(source=MPI.ANY_SOURCE, tag=MPI.ANY_TAG)
            sender, typ, roun, ne_state = msg[0],msg[1],msg[2],msg[3]
            msg[0] = rank
            if typ == ROUND: # send ROUND to children
                if rank != 0 and len(childs) != 0:
                    for child in childs:
                        comm.send(msg, dest=child, tag=ROUND)
                if roun == rank:
                    neigh_over = True
                    if state == UNDEC:
                        state = INMIS
                    msg[1], msg[3] = DATA, state
                    for node in neighs:    # send DATA to neighbors
                        comm.send(msg, dest=node, tag=DATA)
                    if (len(childs) == 0):
                        msg[1] = ROVER
                        comm.send(msg, dest=parent, tag=ROVER)
                        round_over = True
                elif roun not in neighs:
                    neigh_over = True
                    if (len(childs) == 0) and rank != roun:
                        msg[1] = ROVER
                        comm.send(msg, dest=parent, tag=ROVER)
                        round_over = True

            elif typ == DATA:    # DATA received
                if state == UNDEC and ne_state == INMIS:
                    state = NOTMIS
                neigh_over = True
                if rank != 0:
                    if len(childs) == 0 or child_over:
                        msg[1] = ROVER
                        comm.send(msg, dest=parent, tag=ROVER)
                        round_over = True

            else:    # ROVER received
                rover_rcvd.add(sender)
                if rover_rcvd == childs: # all children received?
                    child_over = True
                    if roun not in neighs:
                        neigh_over = True
                    if neigh_over:
                        round_over = True
                        if rank != 0:
                            comm.send(msg,dest=parent,tag=ROVER)
print(" Rank: {} State: {}".format(rank,states[state]))
```

Listing 11.8 Output of MIS Algorithm Sequential Simulation

```
Rank: 3 State: NOTMIS
Rank: 6 State: NOTMIS
Rank: 4 State: INMIS
Rank: 5 State: NOTMIS
Rank: 9 State: NOTMIS
Rank: 7 State: INMIS
Rank: 2 State: NOTMIS
Rank: 1 State: INMIS
Rank: 8 State: NOTMIS
Rank: 0 State: INMIS
```

Fig. 11.8 A sample graph to run the sequential simulation

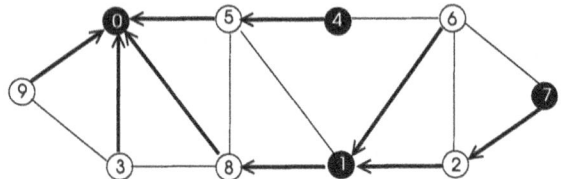

Execution of this algorithm in the sample graph of Fig. 11.8 results in the output shown in Listing 11.8 with the MIS nodes shown in black. Every run of this algorithm produces the same set of nodes in MIS as eligible nodes starting from node 0 to $n-1$ are included sequentially in the MIS of the network. Number of rounds executed is n and each edge of the graph is traversed at most four times, twice by ROUND messages and twice by DATA messages at each round resulting in $O(nm)$ message complexity.

11.3.2 Highest Rank First MIS Algorithm

The greatest identifier node of a graph among its neighbors is included in the MIS in this algorithm which is represented by a FSM displayed in Fig. 11.9. The working of this algorithm in a round is as follows:

- The root process initiates a round by the ROUND message.
- Upon receiving a ROUND message, if a node finds that it has the highest identifier among its *current* undecided neighbors, it enters INMIS state.
- Each node exchanges messages with its neighbors informing them about its current state.

Fig. 11.9 States of synchronous distributed MIS algorithm

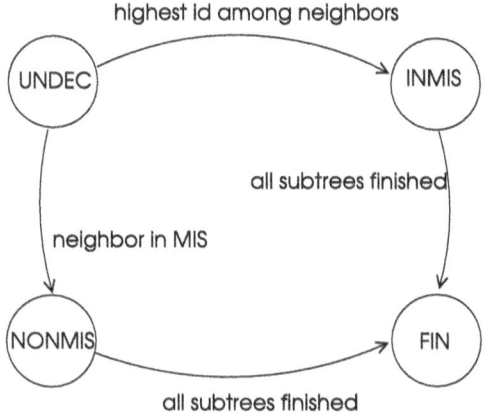

11.3 Maximal Independent Sets

- If a node finds a neighbor declaring to be in INMIS state, it sets its out_flag to be true, deferring informing its state to the next round. This is needed since we allow only one message exchange in a round.

11.3.3 Lowest Degree First MIS Algorithm

A synchronous distributed MIS algorithm that works in rounds may be designed using the lowest degree property. At each round, a vertex v with the lowest degree among all its neighbors is selected to be in the MIS and all of its neighbors with adjacent edges are then removed from the graph. This process continues until the graph becomes empty. The pseudocode of a single round of this algorithm is shown below.

1. $state \leftarrow$ UNDEC
2. Receive ROUND message.
3. **If** state = UNDEC and degree is lowest among current neighbors **then**
4. $state \leftarrow$ INMIS
5.   Send $state$ to current neighbors
6.   Receive $state$ from current neighbors
7. **If** a neighbor state = INMIS **then**
8. $state \leftarrow$ NOTMIS.

This process continues until every node is labeled with INMIS or NONMIS state. We now have FINISHED and TERMINATE messages as in the other SSI algorithm with undetermined number of rounds.

Running of this algorithm in the graph of Fig. 11.10 results in the MIS of order 5 shown in the figure where MIS nodes are displayed in double circles and the removed adjacent nodes are shown as dashed, with the MIS formed only in one step. The lowest identifiers are selected when there is a tie of vertex degrees.

We can now specify the details of the synchronous MIS algorithm called *Lowest_MIS* that uses lowest degree property. The algorithm is initiated by a *root* process which uses identifiers of nodes to break symmetries. We assume a spanning tree T is constructed prior to the running of this algorithm to transfer ROUND messages along the branches of T from parent to child and convergecast messages ROVERs are transferred from the children to parent to indicate round is over as in broadcast and convergecast algorithms. The states are specified as below:

- UNDEC: A node is undecided in this state.
- INMIS : A node decides to be in MIS since it has the lowest degree among all of its neighbors.
- NONMIS: A node decides to be not in MIS since a neighbor has declared to be in MIS.

Fig. 11.10 Lowest degree MIS algorithm implementation in a sample graph

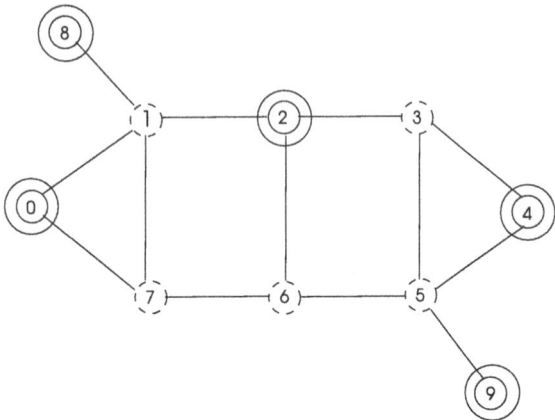

Python Implementation

The Python implementation of this algorithm is simply transferring the described logic to the code shown in Listing 11.9. It is possible that a node may receive a DATA message prior to the ROUND message because of the inherent asynchrony in the message passing system. Whenever such unexpected DATA message arrives, we remove the sender from the *unrecvd* list to prevent sending the same message twice during message exchange when ROUND message comes later. The output of this algorithm with nodes decided to be in MIS or not is displayed in Listing 11.10 which is in accordance with the MIS nodes found manually using the lowest degree heuristic in the graph of Fig. 11.11 with bold lines showing spanning tree edges.

Listing 11.9 Lowest Degree First MIS Algorithm

```
from mpi4py import MPI
import numpy as np
import math

comm = MPI.COMM_WORLD
rank = comm.Get_rank()
n    = comm.Get_size()

# states
UNDEC, INMIS, NONMIS = 0, 1, 2
stats = ['UNDEC', 'INMIS', 'NOTMIS']
# message types
ROUND, DATA, ROVER = 1, 2, 3

# message: sender, type, round number, state, degree
msg = np.array([-1, -1, -1, -1, -1])

A  =   np.array([[0,1,0,0,0,0,0,0,0],
                 [1,0,1,0,0,0,0,1,0],
                 [0,1,0,1,0,1,1,0,0],
                 [0,0,1,0,1,1,0,0,0],
                 [0,0,0,1,0,0,0,0,0],
                 [0,0,1,1,0,0,0,0,0],
                 [0,0,1,0,0,0,0,1,0],
                 [0,1,0,0,0,0,1,0,1],
```

11.3 Maximal Independent Sets

```
                        [0,0,0,0,0,0,0,1,0]],dtype=int)
children = [[1],[2,7],[3,5],[4],[],[],[],[6,8],[]]
parents  = [0,0,1,2,3,2,7,1,7]
rover_rcvd = set()
child = children[rank]
parent = parents[rank]
childs = set(child)
neighs, neighs_rcvd, degrees, states = set(), set(), set(), set()

for i in range(0,n):    # identify neighbors
   if A[rank,i] == 1:
        neighs.add(i)

round_num = 0
state = UNDEC
states.add(state)
degree = len(neighs)
degrees.add(degree)

max_round = math.ceil(math.log2(n))  # number of rounds

for round_num in range(0,max_round):
   round_over = False
   neighs_over, child_over  = False, False
   rover_rcvd.clear()
   neighs_rcvd.clear()
   if rank == 0:   # if root, start the next round
        round_num = round_num + 1
        msg= [rank, ROUND, round_num, -1, -1]
        for child in childs: # send ROUND to children
           comm.send(msg, dest=child, tag=ROUND)
        msg = [rank, DATA, round_num, state, degree]
        for node in neighs:    # send DATA to neighbors
           comm.send(msg, dest=node, tag=DATA)

   while not round_over:
        msg = comm.recv(source=MPI.ANY_SOURCE, tag=MPI.ANY_TAG)
        sender, typ, roun, send_state, send_deg = msg
        msg[0] = rank
        if typ == ROUND: # send ROUND to children
           for child in childs:
                comm.send(msg, dest=child, tag=ROUND)
           msg = [rank, DATA, round_num, state, degree]
           for node in neighs:   # send DATA to neighbors
                comm.send(msg, dest=node, tag=DATA)

        elif typ == DATA:   # DATA received
           neighs_rcvd.add(sender)
           states.add(send_state)
           degrees.add(send_deg)
           if neighs_rcvd == neighs: # is all received?
                if INMIS in states and state == UNDEC:
                    state = NONMIS
                elif state== UNDEC and degree == min(degrees):
                    state = INMIS
                neighs_over = True
                if len(childs) == 0 or child_over: # leaf starts convergecast
                    msg = [rank, ROVER, round_num, -1, -1]
                    comm.send(msg, dest=parent, tag=ROVER)
                    round_over = True

        else:   # ROVER received
```

```
88              rover_rcvd.add(sender)
89              if rover_rcvd == childs: # all children received?
90                  child_over = True
91              if neighs_over:
92                  round_over = True
93                  if rank != 0:
94                      comm.send(msg,dest=parent,tag=ROVER)
95  print("Rank: {}, State: {}".format(rank,stats[state]))
```

Listing 11.10 Output of Lowest Degree First MIS Algorithm

```
Rank: 5, State: INMIS
Rank: 8, State: INMIS
Rank: 4, State: INMIS
Rank: 3, State: NOTMIS
Rank: 2, State: NOTMIS
Rank: 7, State: NOTMIS
Rank: 1, State: NOTMIS
Rank: 6, State: INMIS
Rank: 0, State: INMIS
```

11.4 Dominating Sets

A dominating set of a graph $G = (V, E)$ is a subset of its vertices such that any vertex of the graph is either in this set or adjacent to a vertex in this set.

Definition 11.4 (*dominating set*) A dominating set D of a graph $G = (V, E)$ is the set of vertices $D \in V$ such that any $v \in V$ is either in D or a neighbor of a vertex in D.

A minimal dominating set (MDS) can not be enlarged any further by the addition of any vertex and a minimum dominating set (MinDS) is a minimal dominating set with the minimum order among all MDSs of a graph. Finding MinDS is an NP-Hard problem with no known polynomial time algorithms [2], thus, various heuristics are commonly employed. A connected dominating set (CDS) has paths consisting of member vertices between any two vertices in the set. An MDS of order 4 and a CDS which is also minimal of order 5 are shown in Fig. 11.12a and b respectively in double circles.

Fig. 11.11 Running of *Lowest_MIS* algorithm in a sample graph

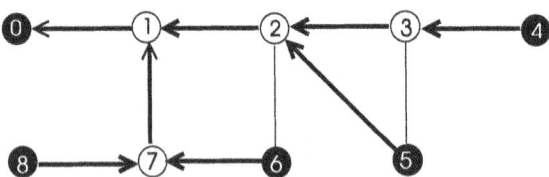

11.5 Chapter Notes

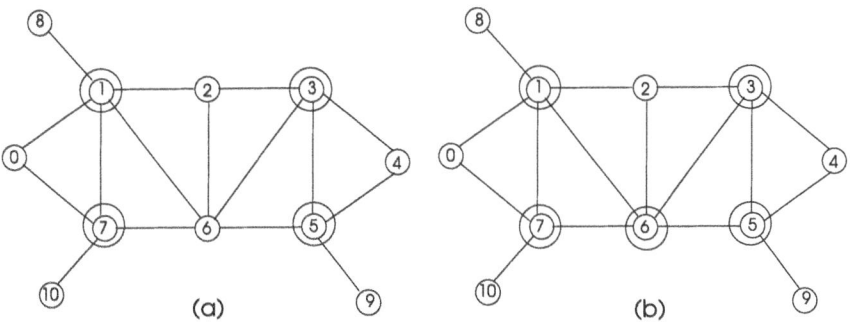

Fig. 11.12 a A minimal dominating set b a connected minimal dominating set

A simple algorithm to find MDS of a graph may use colors to denote membership to MDS: a node is colored black if it is in MDS and white if its not in MDS. The *span* of a node is defined as the number of white nodes including itself. The algorithm *Span_MDS* using the span concept works a follows.

1. Initialize each vertex with its span
2. **while** there are white nodes
3.   Color the maximum span node v black
4.   Color any white neighbors of v grey
5.   Decrement span of any grey or white neighbors of v

Working of this algorithm in a sample graph is depicted in Fig. 11.13 with the initial spans labeled next to vertices in (a) and the final MDS is depicted in (d); the vertex with the highest identifier is selected to be in MDS when there is a tie. A MDS may be used to build a backbone for routing in an ad hoc wireless network. We will defer design and implementation of a distributed MDS in Python to Chap. 12 when we review implementing a routing backbone in mobile ad hoc networks.

11.5 Chapter Notes

We described basic graph decomposition algorithms in this chapter. A vertex coloring algorithm assigns colors to vertices such that each vertex receives a different color than all of its neighbors. Vertex coloring problem is to use as few colors as possible in this process. We reviewed an algorithm that simulates sequential operation by assigning a color in each round to the node with identity that is the same as the round number. A distributed algorithm may use ranks or the degrees of vertices as privileged nodes to decide their colors.

A vertex cover of a graph is the set of its vertices such that each edge in the graph is incident to at least one vertex in this set and vertex cover problem is finding

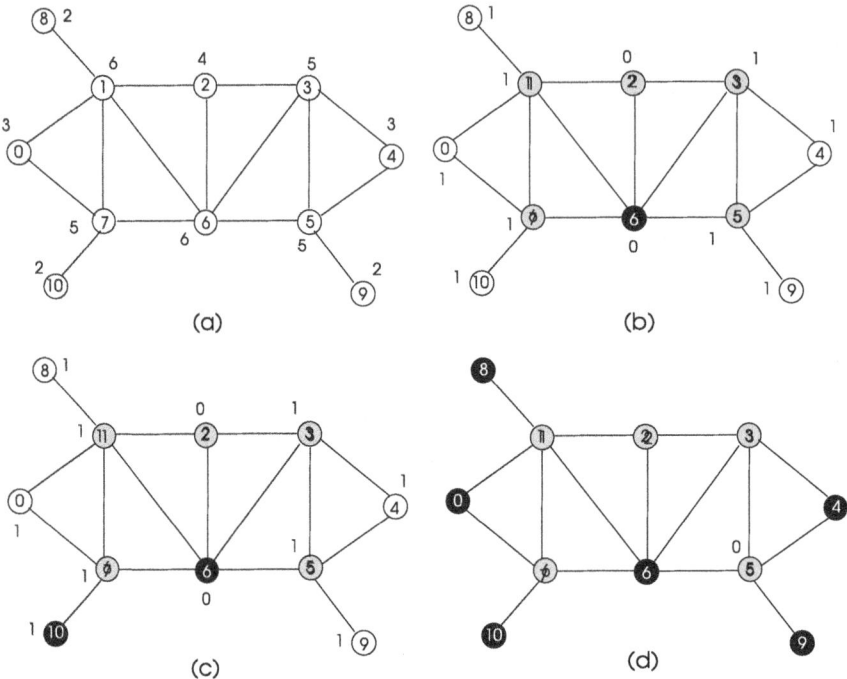

Fig. 11.13 Running of *Span_MDS* algorithm in a sample graph

a minimum order set which is NP-Complete in its decision version. We described and implemented an algorithm that simulates sequential operation by giving decision permission to the vertex with the identifier equalling the round number. We then showed the implementation of a rank based distributed algorithm that provides possible parallel decisions to vertices with highest ranks among their neighbors. A maximal independent set of a graph is a subset of its vertices such that there are no adjacent vertices in this set. We reviewed and implemented an algorithm that simulates sequential algorithm as the above described algorithms and described an algorithm that uses lowest-degree-first heuristic to find MIS. Lastly, a domination set of a graph is a subset of its vertices such that each vertex of the graph is in this set or adjacent to a vertex in this set.

Programming Exercises

1. Design a distributed vertex color algorithm using the SSI model with undetermined number of rounds where a vertex that has the highest degree among its neighbors decides to select a legal color. Write the pseudocode of this algorithm, implement it in Python using *mpi4py*, obtain its output for the graph of Fig. 11.2 and compare this output with the sequential vertex color simulation algorithm for this graph.

2. Design a vertex cover algorithm with the maximum degree first heuristic using SSI model where a vertex with the highest degree among its neighbors decide to be in the cover and informs its neighbors of this decision. Write this algorithm in Python using $mpi4py$ and use the graph of Fig. 11.5 as the input to this algorithm. Test the results of this algorithm with the ones obtained in Sect. 11.2.1.
3. Implement highest rank MIS algorithm of Sect. 11.3.2 in Python using $mpi4py$ and the SSI model and obtain the results of this algorithm for the graph of Fig. 11.12. Show that these results are the same obtained manually for this graph.
4. Propose a distributed version of a span-based MIS algorithm of Sect. 11.4. Write its pseudocode and show its step-by-step implementation in the graph of Fig. 11.13.

References

1. K. Erciyes, *Distributed Graph Algorithms for Computer Networks*. Springer Computer Communications and Networks Series (2013)
2. M.S. Garey, D.S. Johnson, *Computers and Intractability: A Guide to the Theory of NP Completeness* (Freeman, New York, 1979)

Part IV
Applications

Mobile Ad hoc Networks

12

> **Abstract**
>
> A Mobile Ad hoc Network (MANET) consists of mobile wireless nodes that operate autonomously. Topology control in a MANET provides construction of communication network links over wireless communication channels. Grouping of MANET nodes called *clustering* in a MANET is commonly employed to divide the nodes into small groups with a clusterhead in each group to manage the group activities. Efficient routing of messages in a MANET is needed for fast, reliable and effective communications. In this chapter, we describe algorithms for topology control, clustering and routing in MANETs and implement them in Python using *mpi4py*.

12.1 Introduction

A wireless ad hoc network (WANET) consists of wireless nodes that communicate without a fixed infrastructure. The nodes of a WANET are typically randomly deployed in an area. These nodes can communicate directly with neighbor nodes that are within their communication range and multi-hop communication is used for nodes that are not within direct access to each other. Data packets may be transferred over multiple wireless nodes until they reach their destinations in this mode of communication.

Ad hoc wireless networks have numerous applications such as in-home networking, wireless local area networks, networks for disaster relief etc. The main types of ad hoc wireless networks are the following:

- Mobile Ad hoc Networks (MANETs): A MANET consists of wireless nodes that operate autonomously which can move randomly. Each node in a MANET acts as a router and routing is one of the main tasks in a MANET with dynamic topology.

- Wireless Sensor Networks (WSNs): A WSN is an ad hoc network consisting of sensor nodes commonly used to monitor some external phenomenon. The WSN nodes are deployed in the vicinity of the event that is to be observed. Data collected by sensor nodes is transmitted to a central node called *sink* for further processing and analysis. A sensor node has limited computation capacity and battery power.
- Wireless Mesh Networks (WMN): A WMN consists of wireless nodes organized in a mesh topology. Each node may be a client, a server or a gateway. Topology of a WMN is commonly static with clients as laptops, cellular phones and other wireless devices. This type of wireless network is less prone to failures than others since alternative routes when a server fails are usually possible.

There are certain advantages to be gained in employing a WANET for an application. We describe topology control, clustering and routing algorithms in a MANET in this chapter.

12.2 Models

A model of an ad hoc wireless network provides a simplified representation which may be used to build more complex structures and algorithms for the required functionality in the network.

12.2.1 Communication Models

The unit disk graph (UDG) model of an ad hoc wireless network considers each node as having a transmission range of unity and an edge between two nodes u and v is formed in this model if $d(u, v)$ is less than or equal to unity as depicted in Fig. 12.1a. Quasi unit disk graph (QUDG) model is a modified version of UDG model assuming the wireless node has two radii, r and unity. An edge between two nodes u and v in this model means $d(u, v) \leq r$ and there may be an edge between these nodes if $r < d(u, v) \leq 1$ a shown in Fig. 12.1b.

12.2.2 Mobility Models

The dynamically moving nodes of a MANET may be simulated by various models. The *entity model* assumes that nodes move independently and the *group mobility model* considers the movements of nodes as groups. The latter can be classified as follows [1]:

- *Random Waypoint Model*: Each node is identified by velocity and pause parameters in this model. A node moves at constant velocity towards destinations and pause for a determined pause time at the destination before its next move. Assigning

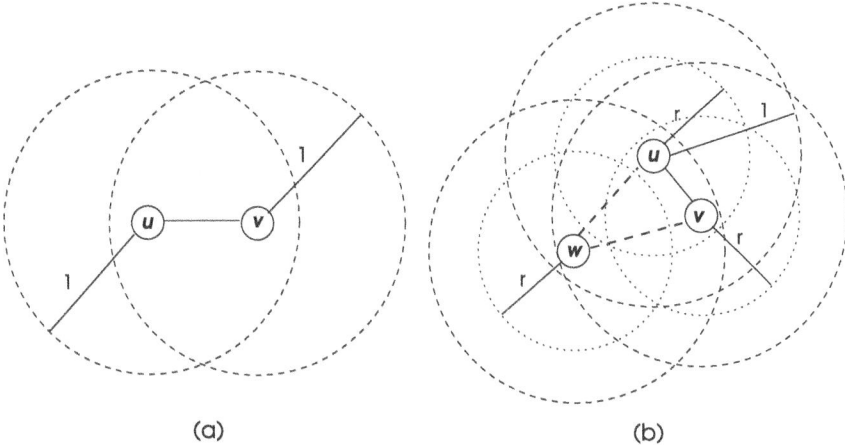

Fig. 12.1 a UDG b QUDG models

small velocity and long pause values means a slowly changing topology and a large velocity with short pause results in a highly dynamic topology.
- *Random Direction Model*: A node has a designated direction rather than a destination in this model and it moves in this direction until it reaches a boundary and then waits there for the duration of a pause in this model.
- *Gauss-Markov Model*: The current velocity of a node at time slot t is determined by using its velocity at the previous time slot $t - 1$ in this model. Various submodels of this model are developed using the randomness of the movement of nodes.

12.3 Topology Control

Topology control in an ad hoc wireless network aims at obtaining and using a subset of existing communication links for data transfer. For example, forming a spanning tree is one such method where the number of communication links among n nodes of a network is reduced to $n - 1$ from the number of edges m where $m \gg n$. A wireless node propagates signals in all directions but only the destined nodes in the topologically reduced communication graph should receive and process the incoming message.

12.3.1 k-Nearest Neighbor Graph

The nearest neighbor relationship in a wireless network is not symmetric as a node u that is closest to a node v may have a node w closest to itself. Thus, the closest neighbor graph formed using this relationship is a digraph. A k-nearest neighbor graph of a node is a set containing the k closest neighbors to the node for a given integer k. We can have a simple procedure we will call *KNN algorithm* for a node to determine its k nearest neighbors as below.

1. Find distances to all neighbors.
2. Sort distances.
3. Assign the first k neighbors as outgoing neighbors.
4. Send outgoing neighbor identifiers to neighbors.

Note that a wireless node needs to broadcast its k nearest neighbors to all of its neighbors due to unsymmetrical positioning of nodes using this property.

Python Algorithm

We can form the distributed Python code using the steps of the described algorithm above by assuming that each node knows the distances to its neighbors, which is obtained from the adjacency matrix of the network graph.

Listing 12.1 k-Nearest Neighbor Algorithm

```
from mpi4py import MPI
import numpy as np

comm = MPI.COMM_WORLD
rank = comm.Get_rank()
n    = comm.Get_size()

A =      np.array([[0,4,0,0,0,0,0,0,2,0,0],
                   [4,0,0,0,1,0,0,0,3,4,0,0],
                   [0,0,0,4,6,4,0,3,0,0,0,5],
                   [0,0,4,0,0,4,5,0,3,0,0,0],
                   [0,1,6,0,0,0,0,0,2,0,0,4],
                   [0,0,4,4,0,0,0,0,0,0,0,0],
                   [0,0,0,5,0,0,0,0,4,7,1,0],
                   [0,0,3,0,0,0,0,0,0,0,0,3],
                   [0,3,0,3,2,0,4,0,0,4,0,0],
                   [2,4,0,0,0,0,7,0,4,0,6,0],
                   [0,0,0,0,0,0,1,0,0,6,0,0],
                   [0,0,5,0,4,0,0,3,0,0,0,0]],dtype=int)

# message type
OUTNEIGH = 0
NONE     = 1
INFO     = 2

n_neighs = 0

# message: sender, type
msg = np.array([-1, -1])
neighs, in_neighs, out_neighs = set(), set(), set()
dists = []
```

12.3 Topology Control

```
32  k = 2
33
34  for i in range(0,n):    # identify neighbors
35      if A[rank,i] != 0:
36          neighs.add(i)
37          n_neighs = n_neighs + 1
38          dists.append((i,A[rank,i]))
39
40  dists.sort(key=lambda x:x[1])
41  msg[0] = rank
42
43  for i in range(0,k):    # form neighbor list
44      out_neighs.add(dists[i][0])
45
46  for i in range(0,n_neighs):    # inform neighbors
47      if i < k:
48          msg[1] = OUTNEIGH
49      else:
50          msg[1] = NONE
51      comm.send(msg, dest=dists[i][0], tag=INFO)
52
53  for i in range(0,n_neighs):    # learn whether I am neighbor
54      msg = comm.recv(source=MPI.ANY_SOURCE, tag=INFO)
55      sender, typ = msg[0], msg[1]
56      if typ == OUTNEIGH:
57          in_neighs.add(sender)
58
59  print("Rank: {}  in neighbors: {}, out neighbors: {}".format(rank,
        in_neighs,out_neighs))
```

Listing 12.2 Output of k-Nearest Neighbor Algorithm

```
Rank: 5   in neighbors: set(), out neighbors: {2, 3}
Rank: 3   in neighbors: {2, 5}, out neighbors: {8, 2}
Rank: 6   in neighbors: {10}, out neighbors: {8, 10}
Rank: 2   in neighbors: {3, 5, 7}, out neighbors: {3, 7}
Rank: 7   in neighbors: {2, 11}, out neighbors: {2, 11}
Rank: 11  in neighbors: {7}, out neighbors: {4, 7}
Rank: 4   in neighbors: {8, 1, 11}, out neighbors: {8, 1}
Rank: 8   in neighbors: {1, 3, 4, 6}, out neighbors: {1, 4}
Rank: 0   in neighbors: {9}, out neighbors: {9, 1}
Rank: 1   in neighbors: {0, 9, 4, 8}, out neighbors: {8, 4}
Rank: 9   in neighbors: {0, 10}, out neighbors: {0, 1}
```

For the ad hoc wireless network of Fig. 12.2 with distances shown as edge weights, the outgoing and incoming neighbors are output as shown in the code. This simple algorithm uses (m) messages in total as each edge is traversed once.

12.3.2 Gabriel Graphs

A *Gabriel graph* (GG) is a topology control method formed by applying the following rule: an edge between nodes u and v is contained in GG if there are no vertices in the disk with the diameter as the edge between u and v as shown in Fig. 12.3a.

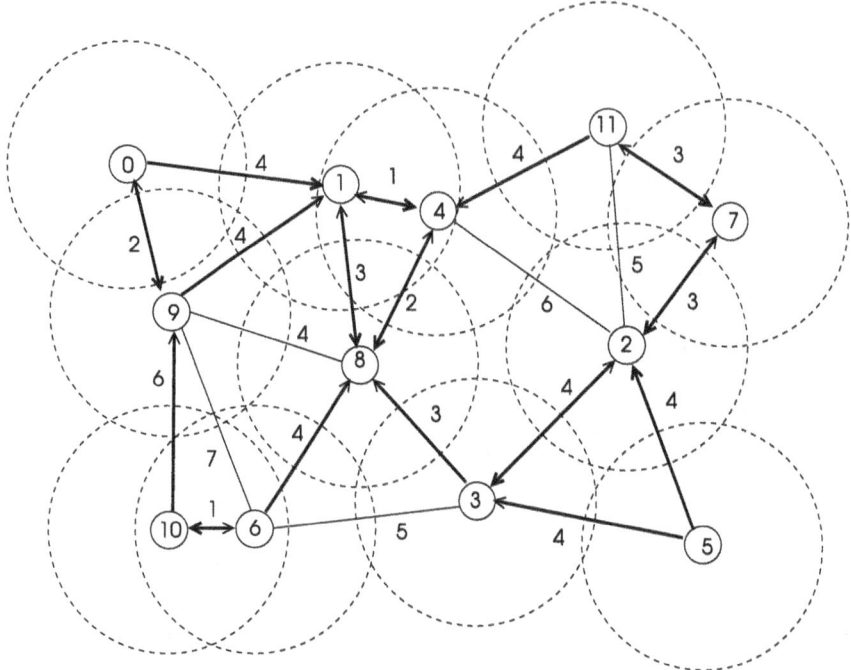

Fig. 12.2 A sample wireless network to test KNN algorithm

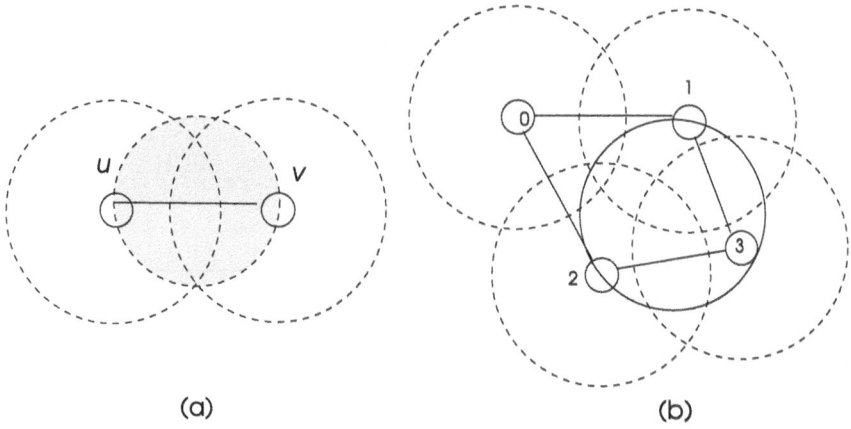

Fig. 12.3 a A Gabriel graph of two nodes **b** a Gabriel graph of 4 nodes

12.3 Topology Control

Formally, given a Gabriel graph $GG = (V, E)$ and a pair of nodes $u, v \in V$, there exists an edge between u and v if there does not exist $w \in V$ such that [1]:

$$d(u, w)^2 + d(v, w)^2 \leq d(u, v)^2 \quad (12.1)$$

which is in fact checking the geometrical property that any triangle with one edge as the diameter and a vertex w on the circumference of the circle is a right-angled triangle with w as the right angle. Thus, if w is in the circle, the above equation yields a true result. Note that Eq. 12.1 provides bidirectional neighborhood. The following steps of the algorithm may be stated:

1. Find distances of all neighbors.
2. Find distances of each neighbor to its neighbors.
3. Implement Eq. 12.1 and determine final neighbors.
4. Send final neighbor identifiers to neighbors.

Python Algorithm

We implement the above procedure in Python by again assuming that distances of immediate neighbors are already known by the use of beacon messages as displayed in Listing 12.3. These distances are obtained from the adjacency matrix by each node as in the wired network algorithms. The output obtained using the graph of Fig. 12.2 as input is listed in Listing 12.4.

Listing 12.3 Gabriel Graph Algorithm

```
from mpi4py import MPI
import numpy as np

comm = MPI.COMM_WORLD
rank = comm.Get_rank()
n    = comm.Get_size()

A   =    np.array([[0,4,0,0,0,0,0,0,2,0,0],
                   [4,0,0,1,0,0,0,3,4,0,0],
                   [0,0,0,4,6,4,0,3,0,0,5],
                   [0,0,4,0,0,4,5,0,3,0,0],
                   [0,1,6,0,0,0,0,2,0,0,4],
                   [0,0,4,4,0,0,0,0,0,0,0],
                   [0,0,0,5,0,0,0,4,7,1,0],
                   [0,3,0,0,0,0,0,0,0,0,3],
                   [0,3,0,3,2,0,4,0,4,0,0],
                   [2,4,0,0,0,7,0,4,0,6,0],
                   [0,0,0,0,0,1,0,0,6,0,0],
                   [0,0,5,0,4,0,0,3,0,0,0]], dtype=int)

# message types
INFO   = 0
NEIGHS = 1

n_neighs = 0
neighs, final_neighs = set(), set()
neighs2_tmp, neighs2, dists, dists_all = [], [], [], []

for i in range(0,n):    # identify neighbors
    if A[rank,i] != 0:
```

```
            neighs.add(i)
            n_neighs = n_neighs + 1
            dists.append((i,A[rank,i]))

# msg sender, type, n_neighs, neighs list
msg = [rank, INFO, n_neighs, dists]

for i in range(0,n_neighs):       # inform neighbors
    comm.send(msg, dest=dists[i][0], tag=INFO)
for i in range(0,n_neighs):       # learn their neighbors
    msg = comm.recv(source=MPI.ANY_SOURCE, tag=INFO)
    sender,typ,n_rneighs,rneighs = msg[0],msg[1],msg[2],msg[3]
    dists_all.append((sender,rneighs))
    for i in range(0,n_rneighs):
        neighs2_tmp.append(rneighs[i][0])
    neighs2_tmp.remove(rank)
    neighs2.append((sender, n_rneighs-1, neighs2_tmp))
    neighs2_tmp = []

for i in range(0,n_neighs):
    u_and_v = set()
    v_neighs = neighs2[i][2]
    v = neighs2[i][0]
    u_and_v = set.intersection(set(neighs),set(v_neighs))
    for w in u_and_v:
        if (pow(A[rank][w],2) + pow(A[v][w],2)) <= pow(A[rank][v
            ],2):
            final_neighs.add(v)
print("Rank: {},  Neighs2:{}".format(rank,final_neighs))
```

Listing 12.4 Output of Gabriel Algorithm

```
Rank: 7,    Neighs2:set()
Rank: 11,   Neighs2:{2}
Rank: 4,    Neighs2:set()
Rank: 2,    Neighs2:{11}
Rank: 5,    Neighs2:set()
Rank: 3,    Neighs2:{6}
Rank: 0,    Neighs2:set()
Rank: 1,    Neighs2:{8}
Rank: 6,    Neighs2:{9, 3}
Rank: 8,    Neighs2:{1}
Rank: 9,    Neighs2:{6}
Rank: 10,   Neighs2:set()
```

12.3.3 Relative Neighborhood Graphs

Relative Neighborhood Graph (RNG) method of topology control assumes that two vertices u and v are connected if there are no other vertices in the intersection region of the UDGs of u and v as shown in Fig. 12.4. Formally, given a RNG graph $G = (V, E)$, an edge $(u, v) \in E$ if,

$$d(u,v) \leq max(d(u,w), d(v,w)), \forall w \in (N(u) \cap N(v)) \qquad (12.2)$$

An algorithm to find the RNG of a given set of ad hoc wireless network nodes can be formed similar to that of Gabriel graphs algorithm, this time implementing

12.3 Topology Control

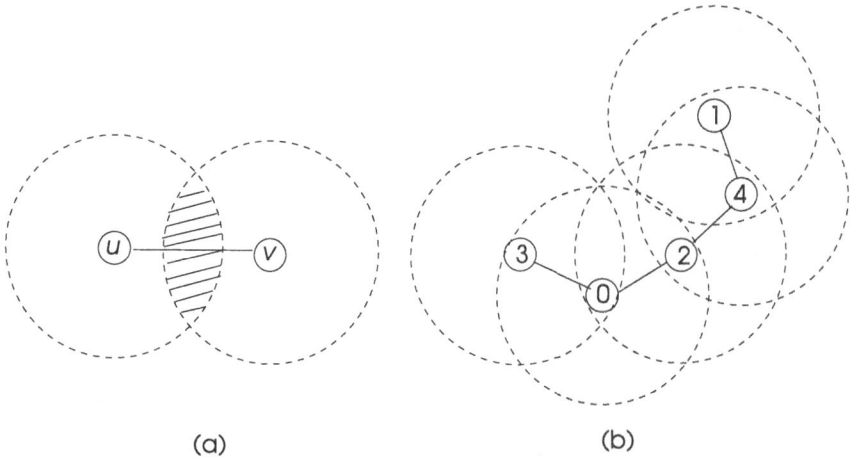

Fig. 12.4 a Two nodes connected by RNG b RNG graph of 5 nodes

Fig. 12.5 An example Yao graph

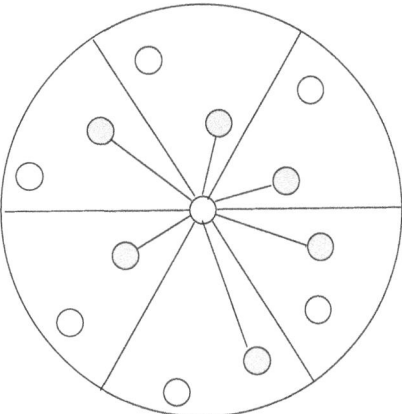

Eq. 12.2 instead of Eq. 12.1. Python implementation for this algorithm is left as an exercise (see Exercise 1).

12.3.4 Yao Graphs

A Yao graph for topology control is formed by dividing the 2D plane around a wireless node into k cone-based regions with $k \geq 6$. A closest neighbor v of a node u is selected in each cone as the neighbor to communicate displayed in grey, and an edge (u, v) is formed in the graph as shown in Fig. 12.5. For equidistant nodes in the same cone, the lower identity node is selected as the final neighbor.

12.4 Clustering

Clustering is the process of grouping nodes of an ad hoc wireless network such that nodes in each cluster are closely located to each other. Commonly, a clusterhead (CH) for a cluster is assigned to perform managerial activities within the cluster. An important function to be handled by a CH is the routing of messages where a message to a cluster member u is relayed to the CH of u which delivers it to the node u. Clusters may overlap and a *gateway* node may belong to two or more clusters at the same time.

Clustering in ad hoc wireless networks is mainly used for routing as noted and also in medium access protocols. A backbone for routing is formed by CHs and gateway nodes to transfer messages as depicted in Fig. 12.6 where a message is transferred between a source node u and a destination node v over the path shown by a dashed curve through the backbone structured using CHs and gateway nodes.

A *k-cluster* contains nodes that can reach each other with a path of at most k steps. A *k-hop cluster* consists of nodes that are within k hops to the CH. Optimal clustering where each cluster has balanced number of nodes and optimal selection of CHs which are at similar distances to member nodes are both NP-hard. For this reason, various heuristics such as selecting a CH with the lowest/highest identifier or highest degree are commonly employed.

12.4.1 Lowest ID Algorithm

Gerla and Tsai provided a clustering algorithm for ad hoc wireless networks using the identifiers of nodes [2]. A node in such a network periodically broadcasts its identity and receives the identities of its neighbors. When this message exchange is finished, the following steps of the algorithm by each node is performed to elect the CH [1,2].

- A node decides to be a CH if it does not hear a node with a higher identifier than itself.

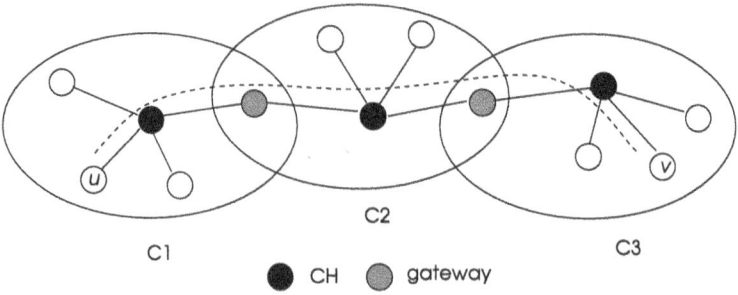

Fig. 12.6 Routing using CHs and gateway nodes

12.4 Clustering

- The lowest identifier neighbor that a node hears is marked by the node as its CH, unless that node voluntarily gives up its position as a CH.
- A node that hears two or more CHs becomes a gateway that joins two clusters.

Each node is in one of ordinary, gateway or CH states at the end of this algorithm.

Python Implementation

We will first describe an incomplete version of this algorithm in Python with the stated steps as shown in Listing 12.5. The wireless network of Fig. 12.7 is used as the test network with the given adjacency matrix. We assumed that each node knows the identity of its neighbors using its associated row in the adjacency matrix as in the previous algorithms. Each node decides to be the CH if it has the lowest identifier among its neighbors, otherwise it is an ordinary node. This decision is transferred to all neighbors and any node except the CH which receives a CH message from a neighbor, assigns its CH as the identity of the sending neighbor; and a node that receives two CH messages assigns itself as the gateway node. The state of a node is ORDINARY, I_CHEAD or GATEWAY at the end of the algorithm and three messages to change states are ORD and CHEAD. The output from this algorithm is as shown in Fig. 12.7 with three clusters C_1, C_2 and C_3 and nodes 6 and 7 ending as gateways as displayed in Listing 12.6. Note that we need all nodes exchange messages of their states for proper synchronization. This simple implementation requires $O(m)$ messages since each edge is used once for message transfer, assuming neighbor identifiers are known by periodic exchange of messages by lower layer network protocols.

Listing 12.5 Lowest ID Algorithm

```
from mpi4py import MPI
import numpy as np

comm = MPI.COMM_WORLD
rank = comm.Get_rank()
n    = comm.Get_size()

A =        np.array([[0,0,1,0,0,0,0,1,0,0,0],
                     [0,0,0,0,1,1,1,1,0,1,0],
                     [1,0,0,0,0,0,0,1,0,0,0],
                     [0,0,0,0,0,0,1,0,1,0,1],
                     [0,1,0,0,0,0,0,0,0,0,0],
                     [0,1,0,0,0,0,0,0,0,0,0],
                     [0,1,0,1,0,0,0,0,1,0,1],
                     [1,1,1,0,0,0,0,0,0,0,0],
                     [0,0,0,1,0,0,1,0,0,0,0],
                     [0,1,0,0,0,0,0,0,0,0,0],
                     [0,0,0,1,0,0,1,0,0,0,0]], dtype=int)

# message types
ORD   = 0
CHEAD = 1
MSG   = 2

# states
ORDINARY = 0
I_CHEAD  = 1
```

```
28  GATEWAY      = 2
29
30  states = ["ORDINARY", "I_CHEAD", "GATEWAY"]
31  # message: sender, type
32  msg = np.array([-1, -1])
33  cheads = set()
34  neighs = set()
35
36  for i in range(0,n):     # identify neighbors
37      if A[rank,i] == 1:
38          neighs.add(i)
39  msg[0] = rank
40  state = ORDINARY
41
42  if rank < min(neighs):   # test if chead
43      msg[1] = CHEAD
44      state = I_CHEAD
45      cheads.add(rank)
46  else:
47      msg[1] = ORD
48  for node in neighs:      # inform neighbors
49      comm.send(msg,dest=node,tag=MSG)
50
51  for node in range(0,len(neighs)):  # receive neighbor messages
52      msg = comm.recv(source=MPI.ANY_SOURCE, tag=MSG)
53      sender, typ = msg[0], msg[1]
54      if typ == CHEAD:
55          cheads.add(msg[0])
56      if len(cheads) > 1:
57          state = GATEWAY
58
59  print("Rank: {}, State: {}, Chead: {}".format(rank,states[state],
        cheads))
```

Listing 12.6 Output of Lowest ID Algorithm

```
Rank: 8, State: ORDINARY, Chead: {3}
Rank: 10, State: ORDINARY, Chead: {3}
Rank: 3, State: I_CHEAD, Chead: {3}
Rank: 0, State: I_CHEAD, Chead: {0}
Rank: 2, State: ORDINARY, Chead: {0}
Rank: 4, State: ORDINARY, Chead: {1}
Rank: 5, State: ORDINARY, Chead: {1}
Rank: 6, State: GATEWAY, Chead: {1, 3}
Rank: 7, State: GATEWAY, Chead: {0, 1}
Rank: 9, State: ORDINARY, Chead: {1}
Rank: 1, State: I_CHEAD, Chead: {1}
```

Although the algorithm described seems to work correctly, there is one problem which can be demonstrated by considering the network of Fig. 12.8a. There would be three clusters as can be detected visually shown by dashed circles in this network. However, although node 1 is the minimum identifier neighbor of nodes 4, 7 and 10, it can not declare itself as the CH since it is a neighbor of node 0. The same situation applies for cluster C_3 and node 2 does not identify itself as a CH being the neighbor of node 0. Nodes 4, 7 and 10 will not hear a CH message from node 1 and similarly nodes 5, 8 and 9 will not receive a CH message from node 2. The worst situation would be when a number of nodes with decreasing identifiers are in a linear configuration as in Fig. 12.8b.

12.4 Clustering

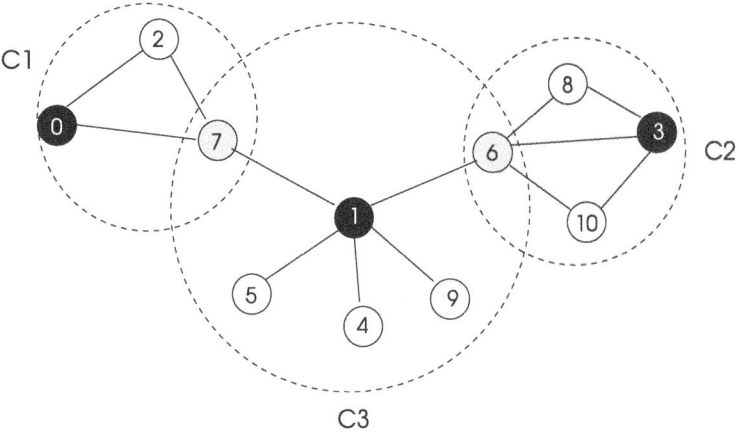

Fig. 12.7 A sample wireless network for LW1 clustering algorithm

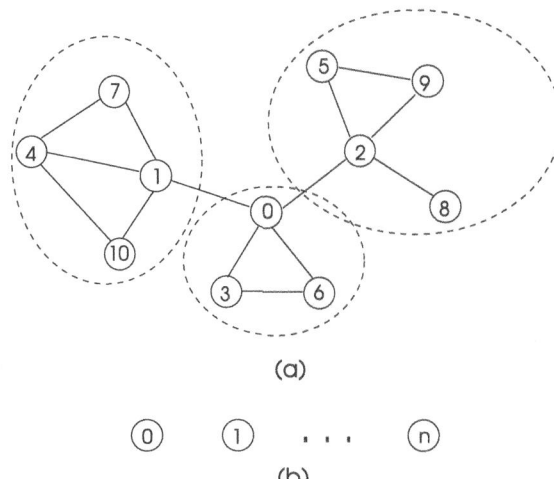

Fig. 12.8 A sample wireless network that is problematic for LW1 clustering algorithm

One way to deal with this problem is by providing two phases of the algorithm; the first phase is implemented as the first version and when this phase is over, any node that does not receive a CH message knows that its CH is its minimum identifier neighbor and assigns this neighbor as its CH. However, the assigned neighbor should be made aware that it is now the CH and this notification can be done by another round of messages in the second phase as in the Python code in Listing 12.7. We now have YOU_CHEAD message sent by the nodes without CHs in the first phase to their assigned neighbors. Implementing this algorithm for the network of Fig. 12.8 results in CHs and clusters displayed in Listing 12.8. The CHs formed in the second phase are now declared as new CHs.

Listing 12.7 Modified Lowest ID Algorithm

```python
from mpi4py import MPI
import numpy as np

comm = MPI.COMM_WORLD
rank = comm.Get_rank()
n    = comm.Get_size()

A = np.array([[0,1,1,1,0,0,1,0,0,0,0],
              [1,0,0,0,1,0,0,1,0,0,1],
              [1,0,0,0,0,1,0,0,1,1,0],
              [1,0,0,0,0,0,1,0,0,0,0],
              [0,1,0,0,0,0,0,1,0,0,1],
              [0,0,1,0,0,0,0,0,1,0],
              [1,0,0,1,0,0,0,0,0,0,0],
              [0,1,0,0,1,0,0,0,0,0,0],
              [0,0,1,0,0,0,0,0,0,0,0],
              [0,0,1,0,0,1,0,0,0,0,0],
              [0,1,0,0,1,0,0,0,0,0,0]],dtype=int)

# message types
PHASE1 = 0
PHASE2 = 1

# message sub types
ORD       = 0
CHEAD     = 1
YOU_CHEAD = 2

# states
ORDINARY  = 0
I_CHEAD   = 1
GATEWAY   = 2
NEW_CHEAD = 3

states = ["ORDINARY", "I_CHEAD", "GATEWAY", "NEW_CHEAD"]
# message: sender, type, sub type
msg = np.array([-1, -1, -1, -1])
neighs,phase1_recvd,phase2_recvd,cheads=set(),set(),set(),set()
c_members = set()
terminated, phase1_over, phase2_over = False, False, False
state = ORDINARY
n_neighs = 0
cheads, neighs = set(), set()

for i in range(0,n):    # identify neighbors
    if A[rank,i] == 1:
        neighs.add(i)
msg[0], msg[1]= rank, PHASE1
state = ORDINARY
terminated = False
new_chead = -1
min_neigh = min(neighs)
if rank < min_neigh: # test if CH
    msg[2] = CHEAD
    state = I_CHEAD
    cheads.add(rank)
    c_members.update(neighs)
else:
    msg[2] = ORD
for node in neighs:     # start Phase 1
    comm.send(msg,dest=node,tag=PHASE1)
```

12.4 Clustering

```
while not terminated:
    msg = comm.recv(source=MPI.ANY_SOURCE, tag=MPI.ANY_TAG)
    sender, typ1, typ2 = msg[0], msg[1], msg[2]
    if typ1 == PHASE1:
        if typ2 == CHEAD:
            cheads.add(msg[0])
        # check if sender is min neighbor
        if state == ORDINARY and sender==min_neigh and typ2==ORD:
            new_chead = sender
            cheads.add(sender)
        phase1_recvd.add(sender)
        if phase1_recvd == neighs:
            phase1_over = True
            msg[0], msg[1]= rank, PHASE2
            for node in neighs:   # start phase 2
                msg[2] = ORD
                if node == new_chead:  # inform new CH
                    msg[2]= YOU_CHEAD
                comm.send(msg,dest=node,tag=PHASE1)

    else:   # type = PHASE2
        phase2_recvd.add(sender)
        # if a neighbor elects me, change state
        if typ2 == YOU_CHEAD:
            if state != NEW_CHEAD:
                state = NEW_CHEAD
            c_members.add(sender)
        if phase2_recvd == neighs:
            phase2_over = True
    if phase1_over and phase2_over:
        if len(cheads) > 1:
            state = GATEWAY
        terminated = True

print("Rank: {}, State: {}, Chead: {}, Members: {}".format(rank,
    states[state], cheads, c_members))
```

Listing 12.8 Output of Modified Lowest ID Algorithm

```
Rank: 3, State: ORDINARY, Chead: {0}, Members: set()
Rank: 6, State: ORDINARY, Chead: {0}, Members: set()
Rank: 8, State: ORDINARY, Chead: {2}, Members: set()
Rank: 5, State: ORDINARY, Chead: {2}, Members: set()
Rank: 9, State: ORDINARY, Chead: {2}, Members: set()
Rank: 2, State: NEW_CHEAD, Chead: {0}, Members: {8, 9, 5}
Rank: 0, State: I_CHEAD, Chead: {0}, Members: {1, 2, 3, 6}
Rank: 4, State: ORDINARY, Chead: {1}, Members: set()
Rank: 1, State: NEW_CHEAD, Chead: {0}, Members: {10, 4, 7}
Rank: 10, State: ORDINARY, Chead: {1}, Members: set()
Rank: 7, State: ORDINARY, Chead: {1}, Members: set()
```

12.4.2 Lowest ID Algorithm Version 2

The LI1 algorithm may provide overlapping clusters as was displayed in the example networks. Lowest identifier algorithm second version (LI2) was proposed by Lin and Gerla [5] to partition a network into non-overlapping clusters, thereby eliminating gateway nodes. The basic assumption in this algorithm as in LI1 is that a node knows the identities of its neighbors as provided by lower layer protocols. The algorithm LI2 is intended for non-overlapping cluster construction and works similar to LI1 initially by each node setting its CH to an incoming CH message from its lowest identifier node. Different than LI1 however, a node decides to create a cluster itself if it does not hear a CH message from any of its neighbors at the end of phase 1. If it hears a CH message from two or more neighbors, it selects the lowest identity one as its CH, thereby becoming a gateway and thus preventing overlapping clusters.

12.4.3 Highest Degree First Algorithm

The highest connectivity algorithm (HCA) proposed by Gerla and Tsai [2] uses the degree of nodes as the heuristic to select the CHs. A node that has the highest degree among its neighbors is selected as the CH in this algorithm and the identifiers of nodes may be used to break a tie. We will first describe an incomplete description of this algorithm; since a node will not know the degrees of its neighbors, we need two phases. Nodes exchange their degrees with their neighbors in the first phase to learn their neighbor degrees and based on this information, a node can decide to be CH or an ordinary node. As in the LW1 algorithm, each node should inform its neighbors of its decision using the following steps.

- *Phase1*: Exchange neighbor degrees with neighbors.
- Decide to be a CH or ordinary node based on neighbor degrees.
- *Phase2*: Exchange the decision with neighbors.
- If ordinary and have more than one CH, decide to be a gateway node.

Python Implementation

The Python algorithm follows the steps outlined above to implement the HDF algorithm. Each node finishes as one of I_CHEAD, ORDINARY or GATEWAY states in the end as shown in Listing 12.9. The output of this algorithm for the network of Fig. 12.9 is given in Listing 12.10.

Listing 12.9 Highest Degree First Algorithm

```
from mpi4py import MPI
import numpy as np

comm = MPI.COMM_WORLD
rank = comm.Get_rank()
n    = comm.Get_size()

A    =    np.array([[0,1,0,0,0,0,0,0,0,0,0,1,1],
                    [1,0,0,0,0,0,0,0,0,0,0,0,0],
                    [0,0,0,1,0,0,0,0,1,0,0,0,0],
                    [0,0,1,0,0,0,1,0,1,0,0,0,0],
                    [0,0,0,0,0,1,1,0,0,0,0,0,0],
                    [0,0,0,0,1,0,1,1,0,0,0,0,0],
                    [0,0,0,1,1,1,0,1,0,0,0,0,0],
                    [0,0,0,0,0,1,1,0,0,0,0,0,0],
```

12.4 Clustering

```
                    [0,0,1,1,0,0,0,0,0,1,1,1,0],
                    [0,0,0,0,0,0,0,0,1,0,1,0,0],
                    [0,0,0,0,0,0,0,0,1,1,0,0,0],
                    [1,0,0,0,0,0,0,0,1,0,0,0,0],
                    [1,0,0,0,0,0,0,0,0,0,0,0,0]], dtype=int)

# message types
PHASE1  = 0
PHASE2  = 1

# message sub types
ORD     = 0
CHEAD   = 1
GATEWAY = 2

# states
ORDINARY = 0
I_CHEAD  = 1
GATEWAY  = 2

states = ["ORDINARY", "I_CHEAD", "GATEWAY"]

# message: sender, type, subtype, number of neighbors
msg = np.array([-1, -1, -1, -1])
neighs, phase1_recvd, phase2_recvd, cheads=set(),set(),set(),set()
terminated, phase1_over, phase2_over = False, False, False
recvd_degs = []
state = ORDINARY
n_neighs = 0

for i in range(0,n):    # identify neighbors
    if A[rank,i] == 1:
        neighs.add(i)
        n_neighs = n_neighs + 1

msg[0], msg[1], msg[2], msg[3] = rank, PHASE1, ORD, n_neighs
# start phase 1
for node in neighs:     # inform neighbors
    comm.send(msg,dest=node,tag=PHASE1)

while not terminated:
    msg = comm.recv(source=MPI.ANY_SOURCE, tag=MPI.ANY_TAG)
    sender, typ1, typ2, n_rneighs = msg[0],msg[1],msg[2], msg[3]
    if typ1 == PHASE1:
        phase1_recvd.add(sender)
        recvd_degs.append((sender,n_rneighs))
        if phase1_recvd == neighs: # process phase 1 results
            phase1_over = True
            recvd_degs.append((rank,n_neighs))
            recvd_degs.sort(key=lambda x:x[1], reverse=True)
            max_node = recvd_degs[0]
            msg[0], msg[1] = rank, PHASE2
            if max_node[0] == rank: # if highest degree declare
                msg[2] = CHEAD       # CHEAD
                state = I_CHEAD
            else:
                msg[2] = ORD         # else ORD
            for node in neighs:     # inform neighbors
                comm.send(msg,dest=node,tag=PHASE1)

    else:   # type = PHASE2
        phase2_recvd.add(sender)
        if typ2 == CHEAD:
```

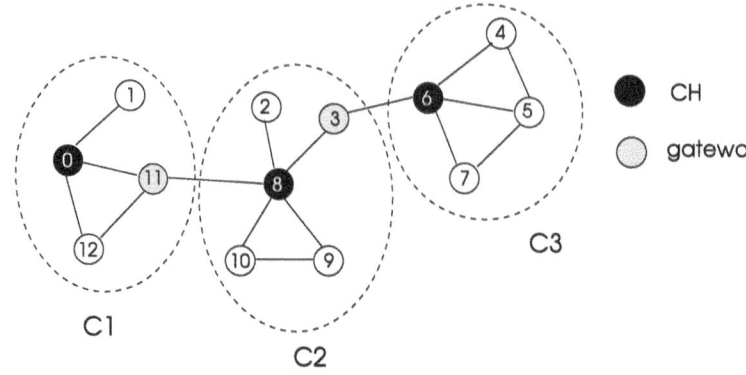

Fig. 12.9 A sample wireless network to test HDF clustering algorithm

```
79                cheads.add(int(sender))
80           if phase2_recvd == neighs:
81               phase2_over = True
82           if phase1_over and phase2_over: # process phase 2 results
83               if len(cheads) > 1:   # if 2 or more CH
84                   state = GATEWAY   # state is GATEWAY
85               terminated = True
86
87 print("Rank: {}, State: {}, Chead: {}".format(rank,states[state],
        cheads))
```

Listing 12.10 Output of Highest Degree First Algorithm

```
Rank: 1,  State: ORDINARY, Chead: {0}
Rank: 0,  State: I_CHEAD,  Chead: set()
Rank: 12, State: ORDINARY, Chead: {0}
Rank: 10, State: ORDINARY, Chead: {8}
Rank: 2,  State: ORDINARY, Chead: {8}
Rank: 4,  State: ORDINARY, Chead: {6}
Rank: 5,  State: ORDINARY, Chead: {6}
Rank: 9,  State: ORDINARY, Chead: {8}
Rank: 11, State: GATEWAY,  Chead: {0, 8}
Rank: 3,  State: GATEWAY,  Chead: {8, 6}
Rank: 8,  State: I_CHEAD,  Chead: set()
Rank: 7,  State: ORDINARY, Chead: {6}
Rank: 6,  State: I_CHEAD,  Chead: set()
```

However, as with the LI1 algorithm, the algorithm may detect only one cluster among few due to the ordering of clusters of CHs from higher to lower with CHs connected as in Fig. 12.10. Node v can not be a CH as node u has a higher degree and node w similarly finishes as an ordinary node due to being a neighbor of node v. This situation can be corrected by adding another phase to the algorithm where a node that is not informed of a CH in phase 2 declares its highest degree neighbor as a CH (see Exercise 3).

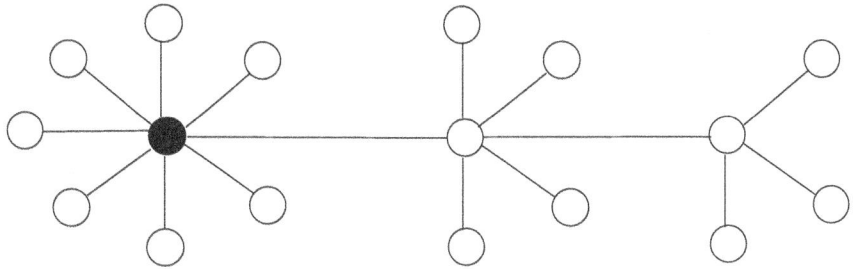

Fig. 12.10 A sample wireless network that is problematic for HDF clustering algorithm

12.5 Ad hoc Routing

Routing in MANETS poses additional problems to routing in wired networks. The topology of the network changes dynamically causing a need to take routing decisions in short intervals, also, the bandwidth and the energy of nodes are limited, error rates are high, making calculation of routes difficult.

12.5.1 Proactive Routing Protocols

Proactive routing protocols are characterized by the calculation of best routes between source and destination node pairs prior to sending of messages. These protocols are thus table-driven with the routes stored as table entries at each node.

Destination sequenced distance vector (DSDV) routing protocol is proactive, based on distributed Bellman-Ford algorithm with some modifications [7]. The count-to-infinity problem posed by this algorithm is overcome by the use of sequence numbers. A wireless node employing this protocol maintains a table with each entry exposing the destination, number of hops to reach there and a sequence number. The tables are exchanged periodically and the local tables are updated as in Bellman-Ford algorithm to find the optimal routes. Frequent updating of routing tables as the topology changes presents significant overheads which is the main disadvantage of this protocol.

12.5.2 Reactive Routing Protocols

These protocols calculate the routes on demand only when needed. The dynamic source routing (DSR) protocol uses source-based-routing where the calculated route which includes the intermediate routes and the destination is included in the message [4]. Each intermediate node then simply forwards the received packet to the next node provided in the packet header. The size of the route included in the packet may be significantly large for a large network and thus, this protocol is aimed for small to medium networks with diameter less than 10 hops.

In Ad hoc On Demand Distance Vector routing protocol (AODV), routes are discovered only when needed as in other reactive protocols [8]. A node u that wants to send a message to a node v initiates its enquiry by sending a request route (RREQ) packet to its neighbors if such a route does not exist in its routing table. An intermediate node receiving RREQ packet sets up a reverse link for this route and floods RREQ to all of its neighbors. Eventually, the RREQ packet reaches the destination node v which then replies by the node reply packet (RREQ) back to the source node. The route is now established and all further data packets follow this route. Temporarily Ordered Routing Protocol (TORA) is another reactive routing protocol designed for highly dynamic MANETs [6].

A protocol may act both as proactive and reactive. One such protocol is the Zone Routing Protocol (ZRP) where each node has a predefined zone around it [3]. Proactive routing is used for any destination node within the zone and reactive routing is used by constructing routes on demand for communication with nodes outside the zone.

12.5.3 A Connected Dominating Set Based Algorithm

Wu and Li proposed a distributed algorithm (WLA) to construct a connected dominating set (CDS) in an ad hoc wireless network. This algorithm works in two phases; nodes exchange their neighborhood information in the first phase and any node that finds it has two non-adjacent neighbors changes its color to black to indicate it is a potential CDS member. Having two unconnected neighbors v and w of a node u is the heuristic used since node u is currently the only connection between nodes v and w. However, there may be more black nodes assigned in this phase than needed and the following pruning rules are applied to finally decide the color of a node by reducing the number of black nodes.

- *Rule 1*: If a black node u discovers that a higher identifier neighbor black node covers its entire closed neighborhood, then it gives up being in CDS by changing its color to white as formalized below:
  If $\exists v \in N(u) | color(v) = black$ and $N[u] \subseteq N[v])$ with $id(u) < id(v)$, then $color(u) = white$.
- *Rule 2*: If the open neighborhood of a black node u is covered by the union of the neighbors of its two black neighbor nodes with both having identifiers higher than u, then node u changes its color to white, thereby resigning from the CDS stated formally below:
  If $\exists v, w \in N(u)(|color(v), color(w) = black$ and $N(u) \subseteq (N(v) \cup N(w))$ with $id(u) < id(v)$ and $id(u) < id(w)$, then $color(u) = white$.

Running of this algorithm in the simple graph of Fig. 12.11 results in the dominating set nodes shown in black after phase 1 in (a), and the final MCDS after phase 2 is displayed in (b). Nodes with at least two unconnected neighbors in (a) are the nodes 2, 3, 4 and 5. Node 2 is deleted from MCDS in (b) since its closed neighborhood

12.5 Ad hoc Routing

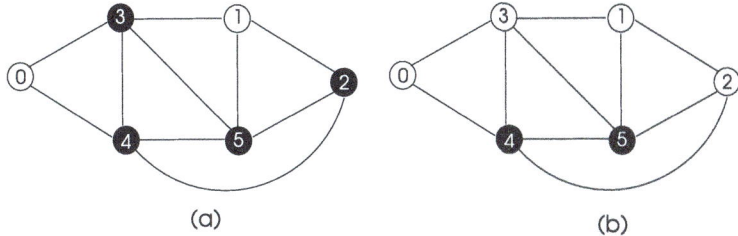

Fig. 12.11 A sample wireless network to test Wu's algorithm, **a** network after phase 1 **b** network after phase 2

{1, 5} is covered by the closed neighborhood of a higher rank node 5 by Rule 1. Node 3 is removed from MCDS by Rule 2 as its open neighborhood {0, 4, 5, 1} is covered by node 5 covering nodes {1, 4} and node 4 covering nodes {0, 5} union of which covers the whole open neighborhood, and the identifiers of both nodes are higher than node 3.

Python Implementation

WLA may be implemented in two phases using the stated rules above. Each node starts with white color and exchanges its neighborhood information with neighbors in the first phase after which a node decides to be a potential CDS member by changing its color to black if it has at least two unconnected neighbors. The decided color are exchanged in the second phase and the two pruning rules are applied to determine the final colors as shown in the code of Listing 12.11.

Listing 12.11 Wu's Algorithm

```
from mpi4py import MPI
import numpy as np
import sys

comm = MPI.COMM_WORLD
rank = comm.Get_rank()
n    = comm.Get_size()

A =     np.array([[0,0,0,1,1,1,1,0],    # adjacency matrix
                  [0,0,1,0,0,1,0,1],
                  [0,1,0,0,1,1,0,1],
                  [1,0,0,0,0,1,1,0],
                  [1,0,1,0,0,1,0,0],
                  [1,1,1,1,1,0,0,0],
                  [1,0,0,1,0,0,0,0],
                  [0,1,1,0,0,0,0,0]],dtype=int)
# message types
PHASE1 = 0
PHASE2 = 1

# message sub types
BLACK = 0
WHITE = 1

n_neighs, n_b_neighs = 0, 0
color = WHITE
```

```python
neighs, phase1_recvd, phase2_recvd = set(), set(), set()
neighs2 = []
b_neighs_open, b_neighs_closed = [], []  # black neighbors open and
    closed neighborhood
paired_nodes = []
result = ['BLACK', 'WHITE']
terminated, phase1_over, phase2_over = False, False, False

for i in range(0,n):    # identify neighbors
    if A[rank,i] == 1:
        neighs.add(i)
        n_neighs = n_neighs + 1

# msg sender, type, n_neighs, neighs list, color
msg = [-1, -1, -1, [-1]*n_neighs, -1]

msg = [rank, PHASE1, n_neighs, neighs, color]  # start phase 1
neighsl = list(neighs)

for i in range(0,n_neighs):                    # inform neighbors
    comm.send(msg, dest=neighsl[i], tag=PHASE1)

while not terminated:
    msg = comm.recv(source=MPI.ANY_SOURCE, tag=MPI.ANY_TAG)
    sender,typ,n_rneighs,rneighs,node_color=msg[0],msg[1],msg[2],
    msg[3], msg[4]
    if typ == PHASE1:                   # phase 1 message received
        neighs2.append([sender,n_rneighs,rneighs])
        phase1_recvd.add(sender)
        if phase1_recvd == neighs:
            phase1_over = True
            flag = False
            for i in range(0,n_neighs): # determine color
                for j in range(i+1,n_neighs):
                    if neighs2[i][0] not in neighs2[j][2]:
                        color = BLACK
                        flag = True
                        break
                if flag:
                    break
            print("Rank: {}, Color after phase 1: {}".format(rank,
    result[color]))
            msg = [rank,PHASE2,n_neighs,neighs,color]
            # start phase 2
            for i in range(0,n_neighs):  # inform neighbors
                comm.send(msg, dest=neighsl[i], tag=PHASE2)

    else:   # type = PHASE2
        phase2_recvd.add(sender)
        if node_color == BLACK:
            b_neighs_open.append([sender,n_rneighs,rneighs])
            rneighs.add(sender)
            b_neighs_closed.append([sender,n_rneighs,rneighs])
            n_b_neighs = n_b_neighs + 1
        if phase2_recvd == neighs:
            phase2_over = True
        if phase1_over and phase2_over:       # start applying rules
            if color == BLACK:
                flag = False                   # apply R1
                neighs_closed = neighs.copy() # get closed
    neighborhood
                neighs_closed.add(rank)
                for i in range(0,n_b_neighs):
```

12.5 Ad hoc Routing

```
                    if neighs_closed.issubset(b_neighs_closed[i][2]) \
                        and b_neighs_closed[i][0] > rank:
                        color = WHITE
                        flag = True
                        break

                if not flag:                       # apply R2
                    # build pair of node neighbors
                    for i in range(0,n_b_neighs):
                        for j in range(i+1,n_b_neighs):
                            twos_tmp = set(b_neighs_closed[i][2]).union(set(b_neighs_closed[j][2]))
                            twos = list(twos_tmp)
                            paired_nodes.append((b_neighs_closed[i][0], b_neighs_closed[j][0],twos))
                    length = int(n_b_neighs*(n_b_neighs-1)/2)
                    for i in range(0, length):
                        if (neighs.issubset(paired_nodes[i][2])) and ((paired_nodes[i][0] > rank and paired_nodes[i][1] >rank)):
                            color = WHITE
                            break
            terminated = True

print("Rank: {}, Final Color: {}".format(rank, result[color]))
```

Implementing this algorithm manually in the sample graph of Fig. 12.12a results in the output shown in Fig. 12.12b. Note that node 4 changes its color to white using Rule 1 since its closed neighborhood is covered by a higher identity black node 5 and node 0 exits CDS by Rule 2 as its neighborhood is covered by black neighbor nodes 3 and 5, thus becomes white again. Running Python code results in the same MCDS nodes as (a) after phase 1 and as (b) after phase 2 as displayed by the output of Listing 12.12.

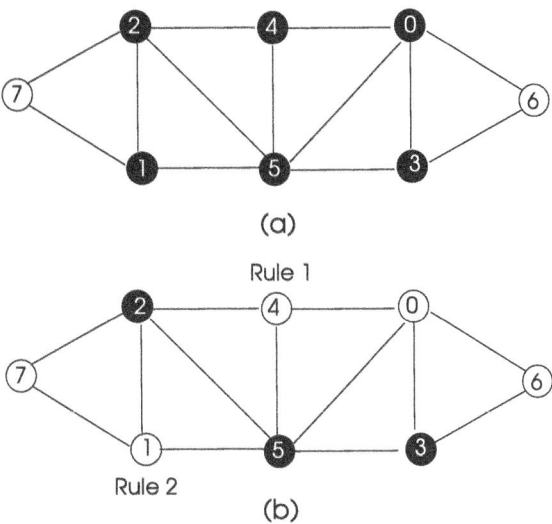

Fig. 12.12 A sample wireless network to test Wu's algorithm, **a** network after phase 1 **b** network after phase 2

Listing 12.12 Output of Wu's Algorithm

```
Rank: 0, Color after phase 1: BLACK
Rank: 0, Final Color: WHITE
Rank: 4, Color after phase 1: BLACK
Rank: 4, Final Color: WHITE
Rank: 1, Color after phase 1: BLACK
Rank: 1, Final Color: WHITE
Rank: 3, Color after phase 1: BLACK
Rank: 3, Final Color: BLACK
Rank: 5, Color after phase 1: BLACK
Rank: 5, Final Color: BLACK
Rank: 6, Color after phase 1: WHITE
Rank: 6, Final Color: WHITE
Rank: 2, Color after phase 1: BLACK
Rank: 2, Final Color: BLACK
Rank: 7, Color after phase 1: WHITE
Rank: 7, Final Color: WHITE
```

12.6 Chapter Notes

We reviewed ad hoc wireless networks with focus on MANETs in this chapter mainly from the view of distributed algorithms. Topology control is an important area of investigation in ad hoc wireless networks since there may be many neighbors within the transmission range of a node in a wireless broadcast communication medium and selection of neighbor nodes for communication using a model is needed to reduce message processing. We reviewed main topology control methods in a MANET as k-nearest neighbor, Gabriel graphs, Relative Neighborhood graphs and Yao graphs with Python implementations of most.

Clustering in a MANET is the process of grouping nodes that are close to each other and has practical implementations for various tasks such as routing. We described two algorithms for this purpose with their implementations in Python. Routing algorithms and protocols provide efficient message transfers between a source node and a destination node. Routing in MANETs is very much investigated in research community resulting in many routing protocols. We described few fundamental routing protocols that are used in MANETs and lastly, we reviewed a connected dominating set construction algorithm which may be employed for routing in MANETs. One of the main areas of research in MANET computing is the design of efficient routing and media access control protocols.

Programming Exercises

1. Write the pseudocode of a distributed algorithm to implement topology control in an ad hoc wireless network using RNGs. Implement this algorithm in Python using $mpi4py$ by taking the graph of Fig. 12.2 as input.
2. Work out the final states of the nodes in the sample graph of Fig. 12.13 by implementing the LW1 algorithm on this graph.

Fig. 12.13 A sample network for Exercise 2

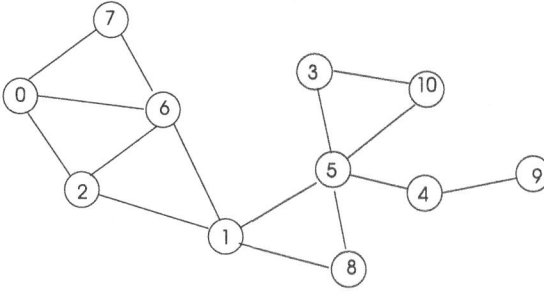

Fig. 12.14 A sample network for Exercise 4

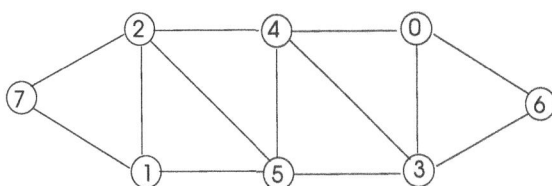

3. Extend the Python code for HDF algorithm of clustering by adding phase 3 so that the problem of the network of Fig. 12.9 is solved.
4. Show the execution steps of Wu's algorithm in the network of Fig. 12.14 by specifying the pruning rules implemented.

References

1. K. Erciyes, *Distributed Graph Algorithms for Computer Networks*. Computer Communications and Networks Series (Springer, Berlin, 2013)
2. M. Gerla, J.T.C. Tsai, Multicluster, mobile, multimedia radio network. Wirel. Netw. **1**, 255–265 (1995)
3. Z.J. Haas, M.R. Pearlman, *The Zone Routing Protocol (ZRP) for Ad hoc Networks*. IETF Internet draft (1998)
4. D.B. Johnson, D.A. Maltz, Dynamic source routing in ad hoc wireless networks, in *Mobile Computing*, ed. by T. Imielinski, H. Korth, chapter 5 (Kluwer Academic, Dordrecht, 1996), pp. 153–181
5. C.R. Lin, M. Gerla, Adaptive clustering for mobile wireless networks. IEEE J. Sel. Areas Commun. **15**(1), 1265–1275 (1997)
6. V.D. Park, S. Corson, *Temporally-Ordered Routing Algorithm (TORA), Version 1, Functional Specification*. IETF Internet draft (1997)
7. C.E. Perkins, P. Bhagwat, Highly dynamic destination-sequenced distance-vector routing (DSDV) for mobile computers. Comput. Commun. Rev. **24**(4), 234–244 (1994)
8. C.E. Perkins, E.M. Royer, Ad hoc on demand distance vector routing, mobile computing systems and applications, in *Proceedings of the WMCSA '99. Second IEEE Workshop* (1999), pp. 90–100

Wireless Sensor Networks

13

Abstract

A wireless sensor network (WSN) consists of small sensor nodes equipped with wireless communication facilities that collect data and transfer it to a central and better equipped node called the *sink* or the *base station* for further processing through a wireless channel. Clustering in a WSN is needed to effectively manage activities in a small group of WSN nodes. Localization is the process of determining the coordinates of a sensor node. Effective routing of messages in a WSN is needed for energy efficient communications as the battery of a WSN has limited lifetime. In this chapter, we review clustering, localization, routing and time synchronization in WSN networks by providing algorithms for these processes and implementing them in Python using *mpi4py*.

13.1 Introduction

A wireless sensor network (WSN) consists of small sensor nodes equipped with wireless communication facilities that collect data and transfer it to a central and better equipped node called the *sink* or the *base station* for further processing through a wireless channel as shown in Fig. 13.1. A WSN node has limited resources of power, range, bandwidth and memory. Out of these resources, battery power needs to be taken into account most in all sensor based functions such as data transfer and routing since a WSN node is commonly battery-powered and replacing a battery is not feasible in many applications due to hostility of the environment where the sensor nodes are deployed.

A WSN node may be equipped to sense temperature, light, humidity, acceleration making it possible to use WSNs for a variety of applications such as rescue operations, fire detection and border surveillance. Smart cities are developed using WSNs and

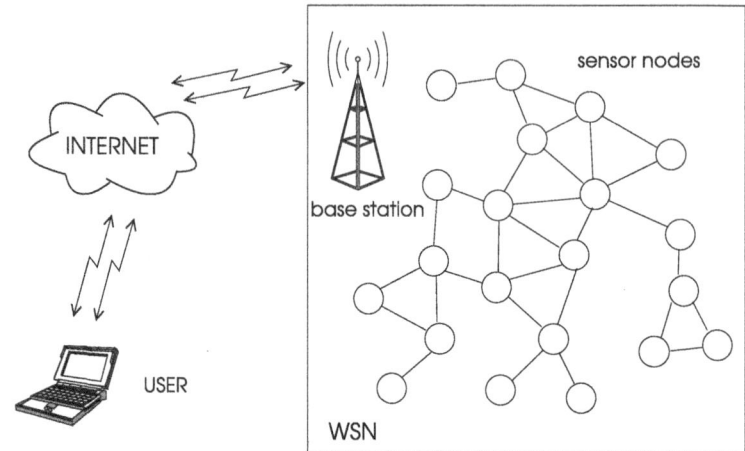

Fig. 13.1 A wireless sensor network structure

e-health applications make use of WSNs when patients and medical help are in distant locations. A WSN operates mainly in two basic modes: event-driven or time-driven. In event-driven node, a WSN node senses and propagates data when there is data that needs to be transferred such as in a border surveillance system when an intruder is detected. Time driven systems are characterized by sensor nodes monitoring the environment and sending data periodically to the sink node.

A WSN is essentially a wireless distributed system with autonomous nodes, however, it is different than an ad hoc wireless network like MANET in certain respects: the number of nodes in a WSN is commonly a magnitude or more larger than the number of nodes in a MANET. Sensor nodes failure rate is much higher due to the environments they are placed and their batteries are usually not replaceable. In this chapter, we review some of the main problems in WSNs such as routing, localization and time synchronization with focus on distributed algorithms and protocols to perform these functions.

13.2 Architecture

The hardware diagram of a sensor node is depicted in Fig. 13.2. The sensing system of a node obtains environmental data and produces signals representing this data typically as electric signals in the range of millivolts. The signal conditioning component amplifies this signal, applies filtering to eliminate noise etc. and the analogue to digital converter simply converts the signal to digital form to be processed by the processor of the sensor node. The job of the processor varies depending on the application. Typically, it performs some preprocessing such as checking whether the

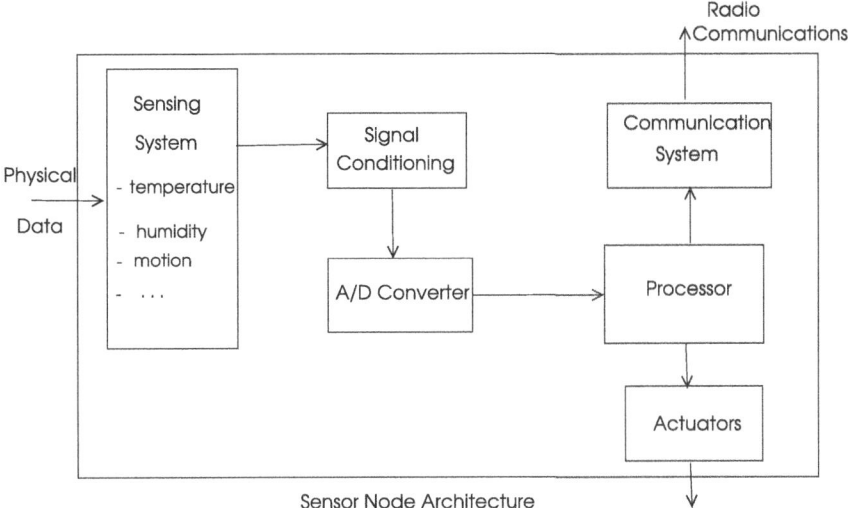

Fig. 13.2 A sensor node architecture

obtained data causes some alarming condition and then applies network protocols and forwards the data packet to the communication systems to be broadcast using radio frequencies. Depending on the application, the processor may also enable local actuators which are electronic devices activating some physical devices to operate.

13.3 Clustering

Clustering in a WSN aims to form groups of nodes that are close to each other as in a MANET. Various duties of a cluster such as routing of messages within a cluster are managed by a special node called the clusterhead (CH). The number of clusters, the size of a cluster and the selection of a CH are the main problems encountered when forming a cluster. Different than a MANET, selection of a CH of a cluster in a WSN should take energy levels of the nodes since conservation of energy is the most important issue to be dealt with in a WSN. A CH is commonly selected based on its residual energy and its distance to the sink. Since a CH basically coordinates data transfer between the cluster member nodes and the sink, it may drain its battery power faster than member nodes; thus, rotation of CH periodically is commonly employed by various clustering algorithms. Yet another issue to consider is whether to have clusters of the same size as in *equal clustering* or with varying sizes as in *unequal clustering*. The main logic in the latter is to have smaller size clusters near the sink as these will be relaying significant network traffic to the sink and thus a CH in such a cluster should have smaller number of nodes to coordinate.

Fig. 13.3 WSN structure of LEACH

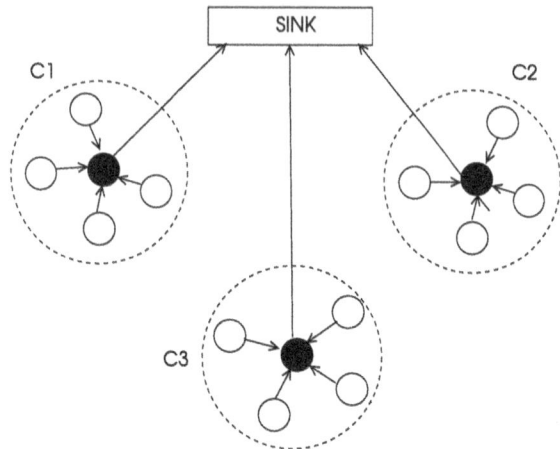

13.3.1 Low-Energy Adaptive Clustering Hierarchy (LEACH) Protocol

The LEACH protocol proposed by Heinzelma et al. [3] is a self-organizing, adaptive protocol that provides rotational selection of CHs where each node randomly becomes a CH in a round based on its energy. A CH is responsible for collecting and compressing data from the member nodes and sending it to the sink. The structure of WSN implementing the LEACH protocol is depicted in Fig. 13.3 with three clusters C_1, C_2 and C_3. There are a number of LEACH-based protocols as reviewed in the next sections.

13.3.2 Threshold Sensitive Energy Efficient Sensor Network (TEEN) Protocol

TEEN is a cluster-based protocol that operates in a hierarchical structure. Two levels of clusters are formed in TEEN: the second level clusters are close to the sink node and the first level clusters are around the second level clusters. Nodes transmit only to their CHs, saving energy; and energy is also saved by CHs as they the only nodes performing additional computation on data. CHs at high levels need to send data to larger distances resulting in fast energy dissipation. For these clusters, rotation of CHs is provided to balance energy usage.

The Adaptive Threshold-sensitive Energy Efficient Sensor Network Protocol (APTEEN) [5] extends the TEEN protocol by providing periodic monitoring of data. The CHs are selected randomly in a circular way by each node generating a random number between 0 and 1 and if the number generated by a node is greater than a predefined threshold, it becomes a CH.

13.3.3 Spanning Tree-Based Clustering

Erciyes et al. proposed a spanning tree based clustering algorithm which provides a spanning tree and clusters at the same time [6]. The spanning tree part of the algorithm is similar to the algorithm of Sect. 9.2 with some modifications. The sink node starts to build the spanning tree by issuing a *probe* message as in that algorithm, however, each message contains a field called *hop_count*. Any node u receiving the probe message tests the *hop_count* value to see whether it can be contained in the current cluster to be formed. If this value is less than a specified threshold, node u increments it, inserts it in the message and broadcasts the message. A boarder node of a cluster will reset this value before transmission. The clusters and the spanning tree formed using this algorithm with maximum *hop_count* 2 are shown in Fig. 13.4 where the CHs are shown in grey.

We will design this algorithm using an FSM with the states shown in Fig. 13.5. The description of node states in this algorithm are as follows:

- CHEAD: This node is the CH of the cluster.
- CINTERM: An intermediate node joining two nodes of a spanning tree or a node to the CH.
- CLEAF: A node in this state is the leaf of a cluster but not the leaf of the spanning tree.
- CHLEAF: Such a node is a CH with no member nodes.
- LEAF: A node in this state is the leaf of the spanning tree formed regardless of being the leaf of a cluster.

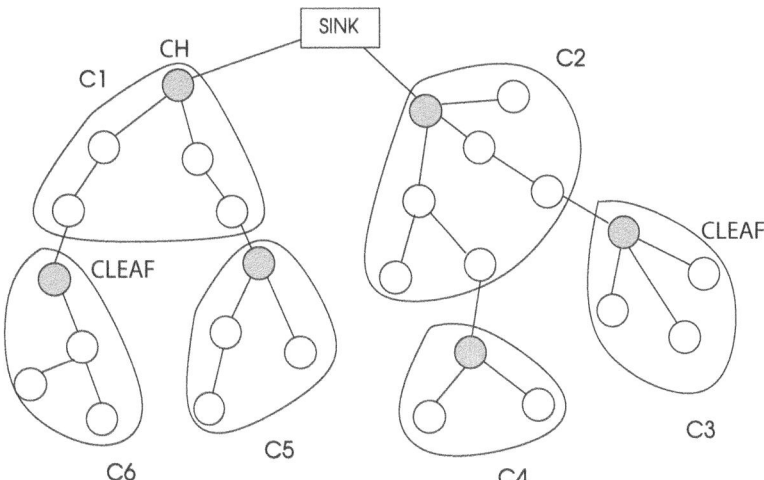

Fig. 13.4 WSN tree and clusters formed by the *ST_Cluster* algorithm

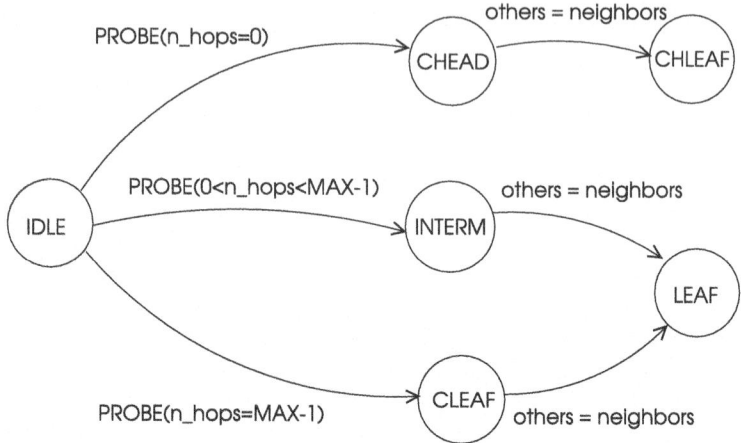

Fig. 13.5 States of a node when running *ST_Cluster* algorithm

Python Implementation

Python implementation of *ST_Clustering* algorithm is based on the above FSM algorithm specifications. The types of messages are PROBE, ACK and REJ for probe message, acknowledgement of a probe message and rejection of a probe message respectively. A node receiving the probe message for the first time sets the sender as its parent, sends ACK to the sender and applies the clustering procedure by testing the *hop_count* as shown in Listing 13.1.

Listing 13.1 Spanning Tree-Based Clustering Algorithm

```
from mpi4py import MPI
import numpy as np

comm = MPI.COMM_WORLD
rank = comm.Get_rank()
size = comm.Get_size()

#states
CHEAD, CINTERMED, CLEAF, LEAF, CHLEAF, SINK = 0, 1, 2, 3, 4, 5

# message types
PROBE, ACK, REJ     = 0, 1, 2

# msg = sender, type, chead, n_hops
msg     = np.array([-1,-1, -1, -1])
neighs, childs, others, members = set(), set(), set(), set()
parent = -1
n_hops = 0
MAX_HOP = 2
state = -1
states=['CHEAD', 'CINTERMED', 'CLEAF', 'LEAF', 'CHLEAF', 'SINK']

A    = np.array([[0,1,1,1,1,1,0,0,0,0,0,0,0,0,0,0,0,0,0,0],
                 [1,0,1,0,0,0,1,1,0,0,0,0,0,0,0,0,0,0,0,0],
                 [1,1,0,1,0,0,1,1,1,0,0,0,0,0,0,0,0,0,0,0],
                 [1,0,1,0,1,0,0,1,1,1,0,0,0,0,0,0,0,0,0,0],
```

13.3 Clustering

```
                    [1,0,0,1,0,1,0,0,1,1,1,0,0,0,0,0,0,0,0,0,0],
                    [1,0,0,0,1,0,0,0,0,1,1,0,0,0,0,0,0,0,0,0,0],
                    [0,1,1,0,0,0,0,1,0,0,0,1,1,0,0,0,0,0,0,0,0],
                    [0,1,1,1,0,0,1,0,1,0,0,1,1,1,0,0,0,0,0,0,0],
                    [0,0,1,1,1,0,0,1,0,1,0,0,1,1,1,0,0,0,0,0,0],
                    [0,0,0,1,1,1,0,0,1,0,1,0,0,1,1,1,0,0,0,0,0],
                    [0,0,0,0,1,1,0,0,0,1,0,0,0,0,1,1,0,0,0,0,0],
                    [0,0,0,0,0,0,1,1,0,0,0,0,1,0,0,0,1,1,0,0,0],
                    [0,0,0,0,0,0,1,1,1,0,0,1,0,1,0,0,1,1,1,0,0],
                    [0,0,0,0,0,0,0,1,1,1,0,0,1,0,1,0,0,1,1,1,0],
                    [0,0,0,0,0,0,0,0,1,1,1,0,0,1,0,1,0,0,1,1,1],
                    [0,0,0,0,0,0,0,0,0,1,1,0,0,0,1,0,0,0,0,1,1],
                    [0,0,0,0,0,0,0,0,0,0,0,1,1,0,0,0,0,1,0,0,0],
                    [0,0,0,0,0,0,0,0,0,0,0,1,1,1,0,0,1,0,1,0,0],
                    [0,0,0,0,0,0,0,0,0,0,0,0,1,1,1,0,0,1,0,1,0],
    [0,0,0,0,0,0,0,0,0,0,0,0,0,1,1,0,0,0,1,0,0]],dtype=int)

for j in range(0,size): # set neighbors
    if A[rank,j] == 1:
        neighs.add(j)

if rank == 0: # root starts ST
    parent = 0
    msg[0], msg[1], msg[2], msg[3]  = rank, PROBE, rank, n_hops
    for node in neighs:
            comm.send(msg, dest=node, tag=PROBE)
    state = SINK

while childs.union(others) != neighs:
    msg = comm.recv(source=MPI.ANY_SOURCE, tag=MPI.ANY_TAG)
    sender, typ, chead, n_hops = msg[0], msg[1], msg[2], msg[3]
    msg[0] = rank
    if typ == PROBE:
        if parent == -1: # if visited first
            parent = sender
            neighs.remove(sender)
            msg[0], msg[1] = rank, ACK
            comm.send(msg, dest=sender, tag=ACK)
            if n_hops == 0:
                state = CHEAD
                chead = rank
            elif n_hops == MAX_HOP-1:
                state = CLEAF
            else:
                state = CINTERMED
            n_hops = (n_hops + 1) % MAX_HOP
            msg[1], msg[2], msg[3] = PROBE, chead, n_hops
            for node in neighs:
                comm.send(msg,dest=node,tag=PROBE)
        else:
           msg[1] = REJ
           comm.send(msg, dest=sender, tag=REJ)

    elif typ == ACK:
           childs.add(sender)

    else:
        others.add(sender)

if state == CHEAD: # determine final state
    members = childs
if others == neighs:
```

```
90      if state == CHEAD:
91          state = CHLEAF
92      else:
93          state = LEAF
94
95 print("Rank: {}, P: {}, C: {}, S: {}, CH: {}, M: {}"
96 .format(rank,parent,childs,states[state],chead,memb
97 ers,others))
```

Listing 13.2 Output of Spanning Tree-Based Clustering Algorithm

```
Rank: 1, P: 0, C: {6, 7}, S: CHEAD, CH:1, M:{6, 7}
Rank: 6, P: 1, C: {11, 12}, S: CLEAF, CH: 1, M: set()
Rank: 3, P: 0, C: set(), S: CHLEAF, CH: 3, M: set()
Rank: 2, P: 0, C:set(), S: CHLEAF, CH: 2, M:set()
Rank: 11, P: 6, C: {16, 17}, S: CHEAD, CH: 11, M:{16, 17}
Rank: 16, P: 11, C: set(), S: LEAF, CH: 11, M: set()
Rank: 15, P: 10, C: {19, 20}, S: CHEAD, CH: 15, M: {19, 20}
Rank: 0, P: 0,C: {1, 2, 3, 4, 5}, S: SINK, CH: 0, M: set()
Rank: 20, P: 15, C: set(), S: LEAF, CH: 15, M: set()
Rank: 7, P: 1, C: set(),S: LEAF,CH: 1, M:set()
Rank: 19, P: 15, C: set(), S: LEAF, CH: 15, M:set()
Rank: 12, P: 6, C: {18}, S: CHEAD, CH: 12, M: {18}
Rank: 8, P: 4, C: set(), S: LEAF, CH: 4, M: set()
Rank: 14,P: 10, C: set(), S: CHLEAF, CH: 14, M: set()
Rank: 17,P: 11, C: set(), S: LEAF, CH: 11, M: set()
Rank: 18, P: 12, C: set(), S: LEAF, CH: 12, M: set()
Rank: 13, P: 9, C: set(), S: CHLEAF, CH: 13, M: set()
Rank: 4, P: 0, C: {8, 9, 10}, S: CHEAD, CH: 4, M: {8, 9, 10}
Rank: 9, P: 4, C: {13}, S: CLEAF, CH: 4, M: set()
Rank: 10, P: 4, C: {14, 15}, S: CLEAF, CH: 4, M: set()
Rank: 5, P: 0, C: set(), S: CHLEAF, CH: 5, M: set()
```

Running of this algorithm in the WSN nodes placed in a mesh shown in Fig. 13.6 results in the clusters shown in bold dashed regions with the spanning tree in bold lines as displayed in Listing 13.2. Nodes 2, 3, 5 and 13 are both CHs and leaves of the spanning tree formed, thus, their final states are CHLEAF as output. Note that a node such as 6 is a CLEAF with children in other clusters.

13.4 Data Aggregation

Data aggregation is a procedure to combine and compress data collected in a WSN to transfer it to the sink node. Two main ways of data aggregation are the following:

- Tree-Based Methods: These methods assume the existence of a spanning tree constructed beforehand. Data aggregation can then be performed by the convergecast of data from the leaves of the tree towards the sink node.
- Cluster-Based Methods: One of the main tasks to be performed by clusters is data aggregation. In this case, data collected by the member nodes in a cluster are transferred to CH for further processing and sending to the sink node.

13.4 Data Aggregation

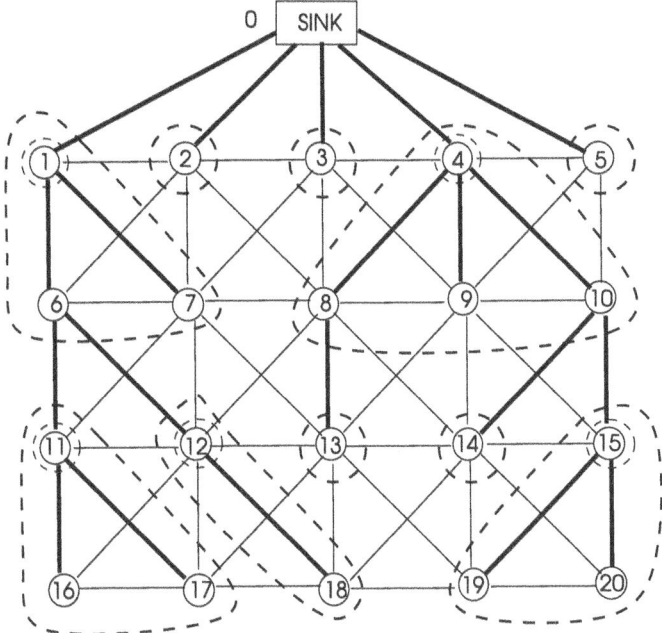

Fig. 13.6 A sample WSN to run *ST_Cluster* algorithm

The spanning tree based clustering algorithm of the previous section provides both a spanning tree and clusters in a WSN as was noted. We will now describe data aggregation using the spanning tree constructed using this algorithm in Python.

Python Implementation

We will run the *ST_Clust* algorithm to first build a spanning tree based clusters in a WSN and then use these clusters for data aggregation. We assume that each sensor detects the temperature value in its vicinity and sends this value to its CH along with its identifier, simulated by drawing a random number between 20 and 40. A CH collects all these values in its cluster and calculates the average temperature value in its cluster to upload to its parent on the way to the sink node. We need to consider the following when designing this algorithm:

- The leaf nodes of the spanning tree and the isolated CHs start the convergecast process. An isolated CH (CHLEAF) has no members and thus can send its data immediately to its parent.
- Two types of messages used are the *node data* (ND_DATA) and *CH data* (CH_DATA) sent by member nodes or CHs respectively.
- A member node that receives a (CH_DATA) message sends it directly to its CH. Note that a member node may only receive this type of message since we have 1-cluster with each member directly connected to its CH.

- The CH of a cluster collects data messages from all of its members along with any convergecast messages brought to it by members, compresses them and sends the processed message to its parent which is transferred to the sink along the spanning tree.

Note that using both a spanning tree and clusters eliminates the need for connecting CHs directly to the sink node. We assume that the spanning tree and clusters formed are the same as was found by the *ST_Clust* algorithm of the previous section and thus initialize each node with the states, parents, children and the CHs with member nodes as was output when that algorithm was executed. The sink node collects all convergecast data and displays CH and average temperature values in each cluster as shown in Listing 13.3 and the output for the graph of Fig. 13.6 is displayed in Listing 13.4.

Listing 13.3 Data Aggregation Algorithm

```
from mpi4py import MPI
import numpy as np
import random

comm = MPI.COMM_WORLD
rank = comm.Get_rank()
size = comm.Get_size()

#states
CHEAD, CINTERMED, CLEAF, LEAF, CHLEAF, SINK = 0, 1, 2, 3, 4, 5

# message types
ND_DATA, CL_DATA, DATA = 0, 1, 2

# msg = sender, type, temp, ch data
msg      = [-1,-1, -1, set()]
parents  = [0,0,0,0,0,0,1,1,4,4,4,6,6,8,10,10,11,11,12,15,15]
children = [[1,2,3,4,5],[6,7],[],[],[8,9,10],[],[11,12],[],[13],
            [],[14,15],[16,17],[18],[],[],[19,20],[],[],[],[],[]]
members_all = [[1,2,3,4,5],[6,7],[],[],[8,9,10],[],[],[],[13],[],
            [],[16,17],[18],[],[],[19,20],[],[],[],[],[]]
recvd, nd_vals, cl_vals  = set(), set(), set()
states = [SINK,CHEAD,CHLEAF,CHLEAF,CHEAD,CHLEAF,
          CLEAF, LEAF, CLEAF, LEAF, CLEAF,
          CHEAD, CHEAD, CHLEAF, CHLEAF, CHEAD,
          LEAF, LEAF, LEAF, LEAF, LEAF]

parent = parents[rank]
state = states[rank]
childs = set(children[rank])
members = set(members_all[rank])

if state != SINK:
    temperature = random.randint(20,40)
    if state == CHLEAF or state == LEAF: # start convergecast
        msg[0] = rank
        if state == LEAF:
            msg[1] = ND_DATA
            msg[2] = temperature
        else:
            msg[1] = CL_DATA
            msg[3] = {(rank,temperature)}
```

13.5 Localization

```
43         comm.send(msg, dest=parent, tag=DATA)
44
45     else: # state = CHEAD or CLEAF
46         nd_vals.add(temperature)
47         if state == CHEAD:
48             senders = members
49         else:
50             senders = childs
51         while recvd != senders: # do convergecast
52             msg = comm.recv(source=MPI.ANY_SOURCE, tag=DATA)
53             sender, typ, temp = msg[0], msg[1], msg[2]
54             if typ == ND_DATA: # node data to CHEAD
55                 nd_vals.add(temp)
56             ch_data = msg[3]
57             cl_vals = cl_vals.union(ch_data) # cluster data
58             recvd.add(sender)
59
60         if state == CHEAD: # calculate average value
61             ave_ctemp = round(sum(nd_vals)/len(nd_vals),2)
62             msg[1] = CL_DATA
63             vals = (rank,ave_ctemp)
64             cl_vals.add(vals)
65         else:
66             msg[1], msg[2] = ND_DATA, temperature
67         msg[0], msg[3] = rank, cl_vals
68         comm.send(msg, dest=parent, tag=DATA) # send to parent
69
70 else: # SINK
71     while recvd != childs: # receive cluster values
72         msg = comm.recv(source=MPI.ANY_SOURCE, tag=DATA)
73         sender = msg[0]
74         ch_data = msg[3]
75         cl_vals = cl_vals.union(ch_data)
76         recvd.add(sender)
77     print("cluster average vals:",cl_vals)
```

Listing 13.4 Output of Data Aggregation Algorithm

```
cluster average vals: {(4, 26.0), (3, 27), (15, 30.5), (5, 38),
(14, 25), (1, 31.33), (12, 25.5), (13, 37), (11, 31.67), (2, 34)}
```

13.5 Localization

The coordinates of an event that is monitored by a WSN is needed in various applications. For example, the location of a wildfire sensed by sensor nodes is crucial in initiating an extinguishing operation and also coordinates are needed for tracking objects and events. Localization is the process of determining the physical coordinates of a sensor node based on its neighbors with known coordinates and sometimes its position relative to its neighbors.

The global positioning system (GPS) provides location of an object that is equipped with it, however, it is not practical for small sensors also resulting in increased cost and fast draining of batteries. A localization method typically consists of two steps: estimation of the distance between the nodes and estimating the locality of the node.

13.5.1 Estimating the Distance

The first step of a localization method is performed by estimating the distance of a node to its neighbors with known coordinates after which various algorithms may be used to determine the coordinates of the node. The main methods to estimate the distance are the *time of arrival, time difference of arrival, angle of arrival* and *received signal strength* procedures.

13.5.1.1 Time of Arrival
Time of Arrival (ToA) method measures the time for a signal to travel between a sender node and a receiver node [8]. The sender node timestamps the message and the receiver records the time it receives the message as in Fig. 13.7a. The time difference provides the distance between the sender node i and the receiver node j using the following equation:

$$d_{ij} = v \times (t_2 - t_1)$$

However, this *one-way* method of determining distance relies on the correct synchronization of the clocks of nodes u and v. A method called *two-way* TOA that is less dependent on the accuracy of node clocks works as depicted in Fig. 13.7b where the sender node i sends a message timestamped t_1 to node j which timestamps the message with the reception time t_2 and sends it to node i at time t_3. Upon receiving the message at time t_4, node i performs the following calculation to find its distance to node u.

$$d_{ij} = v \times \frac{(t_4 - t_1) - (t_2 - t_1)}{2}$$

13.5.1.2 Time Difference of Arrival (TDoA)
The TDoA method [10] uses a different approach where the sender node i sends two signals with different velocities v_1 and v_2, one after the other to node j as depicted

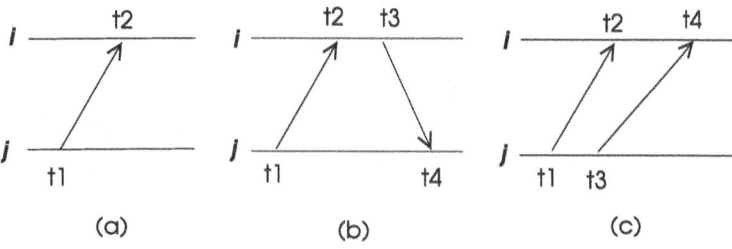

Fig. 13.7 ToA and TDoA methods for localization

13.5 Localization

in Fig. 13.7c. The node i records the reception times t_1 and t_2 and implements the following to find its distance to the node i.

$$d_{uv} = (v_1 - v_2) \times (t_2 - t_1) \qquad (13.1)$$

Commonly, the transmitter sends a radio wave, waits for a specific interval and then sends a sound wave. The receivers record the times of reception of both signals and can determine their distances to the transmitter using Eq. 13.1.

13.5.1.3 Angle of Arrival (AoA)

Directional antennas may be used for the *Angle of Arrival* (AOA) method in which the received angle of signals may be used to estimate the distance to anchor nodes. The receivers are equipped with a number of microphones that are physically apart and the phase and time difference of received signals at microphones may be used to determine the angle of arrival of the signal. This method is expensive and impractical for small sensors due to installment of microphones.

13.5.1.4 Received Signal Strength (RSS)

The signal in the form of an electromagnetic wave fades away in proportion to the distance it travels. Received Signal Strength (RSS) based methods use this fact in determining the distance between two WSN nodes i and j. The power loss due to distance between two modes discarding assuming noise-free medium is given by,

$$\frac{P_t}{P_r} = \frac{(4\pi d)^2}{\lambda^2}$$

where P_t and P_r are signal powers as emitted from the transmitter and received by the receiver respectively, d is the distance between them and λ is the wavelength of the carrier of the signal. Thus, the RSS value of the received signal provides indication of the distance between the nodes. However, reflections, distractions, scattering of the signal is not considered in this model.

13.5.2 Trilateration

This method assumes that distances to three anchor nodes are known and then applies Pythagoras theorem to find the coordinates. Let us assume (x_i, y_i), $i = 1, 2, 3$ are the anchor coordinates and the searched node coordinate is (x_u, y_u). The following equations can be stated,

$$(x_1 - x_u)^2 + (y_1 - y_u)^2 = d_1^2 \quad (1)$$
$$(x_2 - x_u)^2 + (y_2 - y_u)^2 = d_2^2 \quad (2)$$
$$(x_3 - x_u)^2 + (y_3 - y_u)^2 = d_3^2 \quad (3)$$

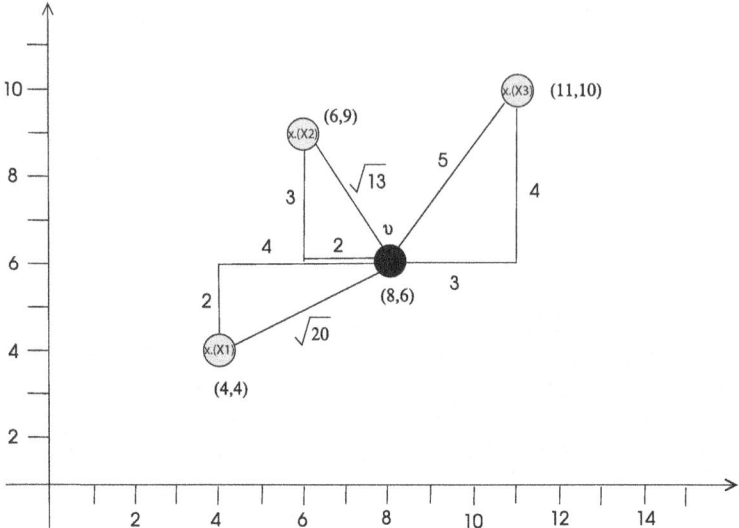

Fig. 13.8 Trilateration example

Subtracting (3) from (1) and (2) and re-organizing yields:

$$2\begin{bmatrix} x_3 - x_1 & y_3 - y_1 \\ x_3 - x_2 & y_3 - y_2 \end{bmatrix}\begin{bmatrix} x_u \\ y_u \end{bmatrix} = \begin{bmatrix} (d_1^2 - d_3^2) - (x_1^2 - x_3^2) - (y_1^2 - y_3^2) \\ (d_2^2 - d_3^2) - (x_2^2 - x_3^2) - (y_2^2 - y_3^2) \end{bmatrix} \quad (13.2)$$

For example, given $(x_1, y_1) = (4, 4)$, $(x_2, y_2) = (6, 9)$, $(x_3, y_3) = (11, 10)$ with distances $d_1 = \sqrt{12}$, $d_2 = \sqrt{13}$, $d_3 = 5$ to a node u as shown in Fig. 13.8, the coordinates of u can be calculated by substituting these values in Eq. 13.2 to result in the the following:

$$2\begin{bmatrix} 7 & 6 \\ 5 & 1 \end{bmatrix}\begin{bmatrix} x_u \\ y_u \end{bmatrix} = \begin{bmatrix} 184 \\ 92 \end{bmatrix}$$

Solving this equation results in $(x_u, y_u) = (8, 6)$ which are the exact coordinates of the node u in the figure.

13.6 Routing

Routing is the process of efficiently relaying a message from a source node to a destination in a computer network as we have reviewed for wired networks and MANETs. Routing in a WSN is radically different than a wired computer network, an infrastructured wireless network and even a MANET for reasons due to specific properties of WSNs.

13.6.1 Challenges

Efficient routing protocols are needed to convey data from sensor nodes to the sink in a WSN. Multihop communication is the basic method of routing in an ad hoc wireless network as noted. The main task of a routing protocol in a WSN is to select a set of nodes to form an energy efficient path between a source node and a destination node.

There are a number of challenges in routing of a message from a source to a destination in a WSN. First, it is difficult to assign unique identifiers to a large number of sensor nodes making identity based routing almost impossible. Secondly, the flow of data is typically from a sensor node to an assigned sink node with much more enhanced capabilities than an ordinary sensor node. Thirdly, data generated by nodes is large and may be redundant in a region; for example, temperature values sensed in a small region will be similar. Data aggregation is commonly used to filter and compress data in such cases. Last but not least, a routing protocol should consider the energy of a node as a WSN node has restricted energy being battery powered. Based on these challenges, we can conclude that a WSN routing protocol should be energy efficient, scalable and failure prone.

Although the basic routing methods such as proactive, reactive and hybrid techniques in a general ad hoc wireless network are still applicable in a WSN, other routing methods described in the next sections exploit basic properties of a WSN.

13.6.2 Data Centric Protocols

A data centric routing protocol is characterized by the sink node making a query to a specific region of a WSN to collect data with some attribute. This type of protocols are common as assigning unique identifiers to sensor nodes is not feasible in many WSN applications with a large number of nodes. The WSN is considered as a virtual database where queries are broadcast over the network. A node that receives the query sends response which contains the required tuples towards the originator of the query. Data aggregation may be performed by the intermediate nodes as described in Sect. 13.4. Various protocols for data centric routing in WSNs exist, we will review Sensor Protocols for Information via Negotiation (SPIN) which is commonly used. SPIN has three types of messages:

- ADV: Advertise data
- REQ: Request data
- DATA: Message containing data

An example SPIN operation to obtain data is depicted in Fig. 13.9. The SPIN2 protocol uses the messages described with nodes involved in energy management by stopping sending and receiving data messages if their energy falls below a threshold.

Hierarchical protocols for routing are commonly based on building clusters and employing intra cluster routing within the clusters and inter cluster routing outside

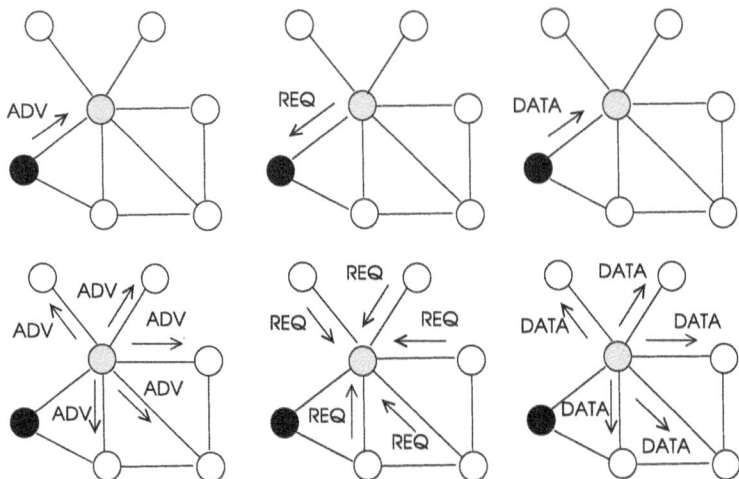

Fig. 13.9 A sample WSN to run *ST_Cluster* algorithm

the clusters. LEACH and TEEN protocols reviewed in Sect. 13.3 are cluster-based routing protocols.

13.6.3 Location-Based Protocols

These protocols make use of the geographical information about the nodes in a WSN to make routing decisions. The Geographic Adaptive Fidelity (GAF) protocol [7] uses the physical location of nodes for routing. A virtual grid is formed in the network where nodes falling in the same grid cell are assumed to be equal. Only one node in each cell can be active while others sleep, providing energy conservation. Three possible states of a node in the grid are *sleeping*, *discovery* and *active*. A node typically starts in *discovery* state and changes to *active* state after exchanging status messages with its neighbors. A node may enter *sleeping* state if another node in *active* state in the same cell is found.

Geographic and Energy Aware Routing (GEAR) [11] is another location-based routing protocol used in WSNs. A node in GEAR stores the estimated cost of reaching a destination node which is a function of its residual energy and its distance to that node. It also stores learned cost which is a refinement of the estimated cost to perform routing as follows.

- *Inter-region packet forwarding*: A received packet is forwarded to a neighbor that is closer to the destination, or to a neighbor node based on its estimated cost.

- *Intra-region packet forwarding*: A packet arriving at a region may be distributed to the nodes of the region by flooding. When the region consists of densely deployed sensors, recursive geographic flooding which divides the region into four subregions and sends the packet to all subregions recursively is employed.

13.7 Time Synchronization

Time synchronization in a WSN is needed for a number of reasons such as in medium access control (MAC) protocols to synchronize scheduling of channel access and in recording of external events. Network Time Protocol (NTP) described in Chap. 4 is widely used in Internet for time synchronization, however, the uncertainty in the message delivery time in MAC protocols of WSN systems makes the use of NTP in WSNs difficult, except in systems that do not require high precision. Moreover, limited processor capabilities, the energy constraints of sensor nodes, the harsh environment they are placed pose additional challenges. Time synchronization using the Global Positioning System (GPS) receivers is not feasible as these are very difficult to install in small sensor nodes due to size and cost factors. Various time synchronization methods in WSNs use sender to receiver synchronization where the sender timestamps the message with its time and the receiver corrects its time with respect to the sender time considering network delay.

13.7.1 Sender-Receiver Synchronization

In the simplest method that employs one-way message exchange, the sender i timestamps the message with its local time t_1 and sends it to the receiver. The receiver j records the reception time t_2 as shown in Fig. 13.10a and calculates its offset time δ from the sender by,

$$\delta = t_2 - t_1 - nd$$

where nd is the network delay.

The receiver of the message sends it back to the sender at time t_3 with a message containing times t_1, t_2 and t_3 in the two-way message exchange based time synchronization as shown in Fig. 13.10b. The sender can now determine the network delay and the offset as below:

$$nd = \frac{((t_2 - t_1) + (t_4 - t_3))}{2}, \qquad \delta = \frac{((t_2 - t_1) - (t_4 - t_3))}{2}$$

A third message is needed if node j should send its offset value to node i. The Lightweight Tree-based Synchronization (LTS) [9] is a network-wide synchronization protocol that assumes a breadth-first tree is built in the WSN and uses the above described pairwise synchronization method to synchronize the parent and children nodes starting from the sink node. Thus, the sink node has the reference clock and three messages are needed for pairwise synchronization resulting in a message complexity of $O(n)$ since a spanning tree with n nodes has $n - 1$ edges. The depth of the spanning tree should be kept as minimum as possible to minimize node delays which is the reason for employing a breadth-first-search tree.

Timing-Synch Protocol (TPSN) [2] also uses pairwise time synchronization to achieve network-wide synchronization. A cluster-based approach to implement TPSN is described in [4]. This protocol consists of the following two phases:

- *Level Discovery Phase*: The sink node starts this phase by issuing a *level discovery* message. A receiver of this message decides its level by incrementing the level in the message and then re-broadcasts it to its neighbors. A hierarchical structure is obtained at the end of this phase.
- *Synchronization Phase*: The sink node starts this phase by sending the *time_synch* packet. Each node at level k synchronizes with neighbor nodes at level $k + 1$ using a similar approach to LTS protocol.

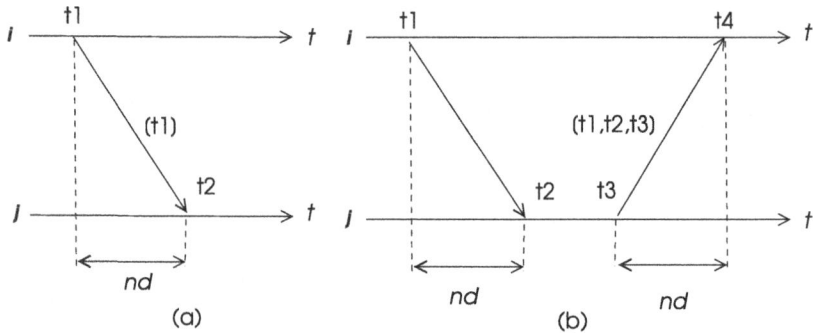

Fig. 13.10 a One-way message exchange b two-way message exchange in sender-receiver time synchronization

Fig. 13.11 RBS message transfers

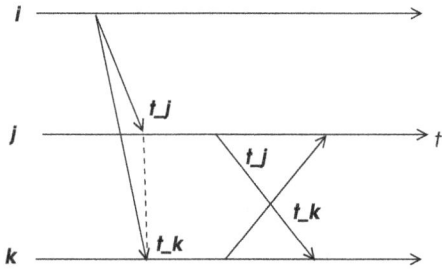

13.7.2 Receiver-Receiver Synchronization

Receiver-receiver time synchronization removes the sender from consideration, the role of the sender is simply sending a beacon message to the receivers. Assuming that reception of a broadcast message will be at approximately the same time in all receivers, receivers exchange messages time-stamped with the reception times with each other and correct their clocks accordingly. The Reference Broadcast Synchronization (RBS) [1] protocol is receiver-receiver synchronization based timing protocol that can work with multiple receivers. Let us consider the case with one sender and two receivers. The message sent by the sender i does not contain a timestamp and the receivers j and k record the times t_j and t_k they receive the message of the respectively and then send these values to each other as shown in Fig. 13.11 after which necessary corrections can be made.

Python Implementation

A Python program can be designed to implement the RBS protocol just to display the clock values of the receivers so that further corrections can be made. We will consider three nodes 0, 1 and 2 with node 2 as the sender and nodes 0 and 1 as the receivers. Node 2 broadcasts a beacon message and the nodes 0 and 1 exchange their time values as shown in Listing 13.5. The outputs of these processes are displayed in Listing 13.6.

Listing 13.5 Reference Broadcast Synchronization with 2 Receivers

```
from mpi4py import MPI
import numpy as np
import time

comm = MPI.COMM_WORLD
rank = comm.Get_rank()
size = comm.Get_size()

# message types
DATA = 0

# msg = sender, type, time
msg     = [-1,-1, -1]
empty = 0
comm.bcast(empty, root=2)
T1 = round(time.time()*1000,6)

if rank != 2:
    msg[0], msg[1], msg[2] = rank, DATA, T1
    comm.send(msg, dest= 1-rank, tag=DATA)
    msg = comm.recv(source=1-rank, tag=DATA)
    T2 = msg[2]
    print("rank: {}, my time: {}, time of {}: {}".format(rank,
T1, 1-rank,T2))
```

Listing 13.6 Output of Reference Broadcast Synchronization Algorithm

```
rank:1, my time:1644993890248.7654, time of 0: 1644993890217.541
rank:0, my time:1644993890217.541, time of 1: 1644993890248.7654
```

13.8 Chapter Notes

A WSN consists of autonomous sensing nodes which collect data in the environment they are placed, and send it to a central node called sink with improved capabilities for further processing. We reviewed main problems in a WSN which are clustering, routing, data aggregation, localization and time management, all from distributed algorithm point of view. Clustering in a WSN is commonly used for routing as we described routing algorithms based on clustering. Localization is the process of determining the position of a sensor node in a WSN using the anchor nodes with GPS capability, and time synchronization in a WSN is needed as in any distributed system. We described main time synchronization protocols in a WSN in the last part of the chapter. A clustering algorithm, a data aggregation and a time synchronization algorithm are coded in Python and the implementation of these algorithms in small sample graphs are shown.

Programming Exercises

1. Implement LTS protocol in Python using $mpi4py$ by first forming a spanning tree using any of the spanning tree algorithms of Chap. 9 on the graph of Fig. 13.6.
2. Improve the RBS protocol Python code using $mpi4py$ to three receivers and obtain the clock values for the nodes.
3. Write a Python program that finds the coordinates of the node u shown in Fig. 13.12 using trilateration. This node asks the coordinates of the anchors first, calculates its coordinates and outputs them.

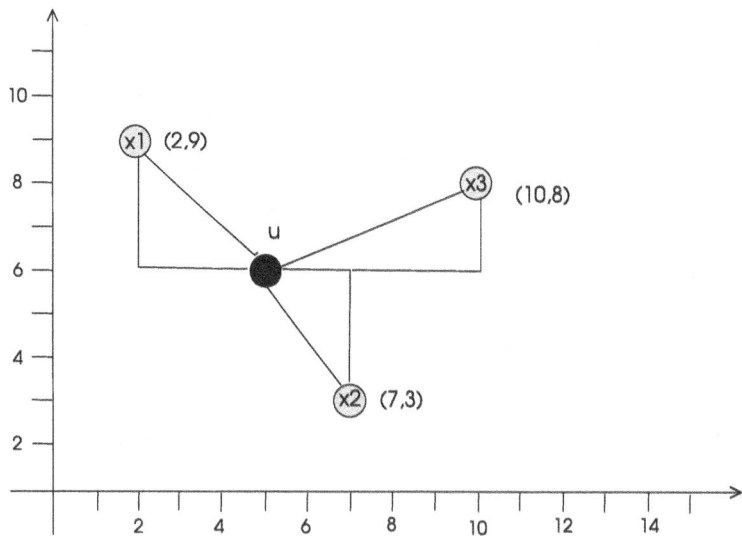

Fig. 13.12 Trilateration example for Exercise 3

4. A heat monitoring system is to be realized by a WSN network with a spanning tree. Every three seconds, the root broadcasts a *probe* message to the nodes. Upon reception of this message, each node exchange temperature data with its neighbors, calculates the average value with its neighbors and sends this value as a *data* message to its parent. The data is in the form $\{id, value\}$ and all of the convergecast values are displayed by the root process. Write this algorithm in Python using $mpi4py$ using the graph of Fig. 13.6 as input and building an arbitrary spanning tree on this graph.

References

1. J. Elson, L. Girod, D. Estrin, Fine-grained network time synchronization using reference broadcasts, in *Proceedings of the 5th Symposium on Operating System Design and Implementation*, Dec 2002 (2002), pp. 147–163
2. S. Ganeriwal, R. Kumar, M.B. Srivastava, Timing-sync protocol for sensor networks, in *Proceedings of the SenSys 03*, Nov 2003, Los Angeles, CA (2003), pp. 138–149
3. W. Heinzelman, A. Chandrakasan, H. Balakrishnan, Energy-efficient communication protocol for wireless microsensor networks, in *Proceedings of the 33rd Hawaii International Conference on System Sciences* (2000)
4. A.B. Kulakli, K. Erciyes, Time synchronization algorithms based on timing-sync protocol in wireless sensor networks, in *2008 23rd International Symposium on Computer and Information Sciences*, Istanbul, Turkey (2008), pp. 1–5
5. A. Manjeshwar, D.P. Agrawal, APTEEN: a hybrid protocol for efficient routing and comprehensive information retrieval in wireless sensor networks, in *Proceedings of the 2nd International Workshop on Parallel and Distributed Computing, Issues in Wireless Networks and Mobile Computing* (2002)
6. K. Erciyes, D. Ozsoyeller, and O. Dagdeviren, Distributed algorithms to form cluster based spanning trees in wireless sensor networks, in *Proceedings of ICCS 2008*, (Springer Verlag LNCS, 2008)
7. S. Roychowdhury, C. Patra, Geographic adaptive fidelity and geographic energy aware routing in ad hoc routing. Int. J. Comput. Commun. Technol. **1**(2, 3, 4), 309–313 (Special issue) (2010)
8. H. Shen, Z. Ding, S. Dasgupta, C. Zhao, Multiple source localization in wireless sensor networks based on time of arrival measurement. IEEE Trans. Signal Process. **62**, 1938–1949 (2014)
9. J. Van Greunen, J. Rabaey, Lightweight time synchronization for sensor networks, in *Proceedings of the 2nd ACM International Conference on Wireless Sensor Networks and Applications (WSNA)*, San Diego, CA (2003), pp. 11–19
10. H. Xiong, Z. Chen, B. Yang, R. Ni, TDOA localization algorithm with compensation of clock offset for wireless sensor networks. China Commun. **12**, 193–201 (2015)
11. Y. Yu, D. Estrin, R. Govindan, *Geographical and Energy-Aware Routing: A Recursive Data Dissemination Protocol for Wireless Sensor Networks*. Technical report, UCLA-CSD TR-01-0023 (UCLA Computer Science Department, 2001)

Index

Symbols
N-version programming, 142
α synchronizer, 134
β synchronizer, 135
γ synchronizer, 135
k-nearest neighbor graph, 250

A
Ad hoc routing, 265
  proactive routing, 265
  reactive routing, 265
Analysis, 17
Angle of arrival, 285
Asynchronous mode, 45
Atomic multicast, 146

B
Basic multicast, 146
Bellman-Ford algorithm, 205
Berkeley algorithm, 56
Breadth first search, 174
  asynchronous, 174
  synchronous, 178
Bully algorithm, 118
Byzantine failures, 141

C
Casual delivery, 151
Chandy-Lamport Algorithm, 98
Chandy-Misra algorithm, 209
Chandy-Misra-Haas algorithm, 111
Chang-Roberts algorithm, 126
Check pointing, 142
Closed process groups, 144
Clustering, 256, 275
Computer architecture, 11

Computer networks, 10
  network layer, 11
  physical layer, 10
  transport layer, 11
Consensus, 158
  Byzantine agreement, 159
  oral messaging algorithm, 160
Convergecast, 172
Crash failures, 141
Cristian's algorithm, 55

D
Data aggregation, 280
Data centric protocols, 287
Deadlock detection, 108, 110
  Chandy-Misra-Haas algorithm, 111
Depth first search, 185
Distributed algorithms, 17
  analysis, 17
  complexity, 21
  loop invariants, 20
Distributed mutual exclusion, 71
  central server algorithm, 74
  Lamport's algorithm, 76
  Maekawa's algorithm, 90
  Raymond's algorithm, 85
  Ricart-Agrawala algorithm, 77
  Suzuki-Kasami algorithm, 81
  token-based algorithms, 81
Distributed Prim algorithm, 193
Distributed snapshot, 98
  Chandy-Lamport Algorithm, 98
  Lai-Yang Algorithm, 99
Distributed synchronous Bellman-Ford algorithm, 205
Distributed systems, 9

Dominating set, 240, 266
  connected, 266

E
Error checking, 142

F
Fail-stop, 141
Failure models, 141
  Byzantine failures, 141
  crash failures, 141
  fail-stop, 141
  temporal failures, 141
Faults, 140
Fault tolerance, 139, 142
  redundancy, 142
  replication, 143
Finite state machines, 15
  hierarchical, 17
FLP result, 158

G
Gabriel graph, 251
GHS algorithm, 197
Global state, 95
  distributed snapshot, 98
Graceful degradation, 142
Group communication, 144
  atomic multicast, 146
  basic multicast, 146
  protocols, 145
    atomic multicast, 146
    causal delivery, 151
    single source FIFO, 148
    total order multicast, 154
  reliable multicast, 147
  unreliable multicast, 148
Group membership, 145

H
Hardware redundancy, 142
Hierarchical process groups, 144
Hirschberg-Sinclair algorithm, 129
Hoepman's algorithm, 212
Huang's algorithm, 105

I
Information redundancy, 143

L
Lai-Yang Algorithm, 99

LEACH, 276
Leader election, 118
  bully algorithm, 118
  Chang-Roberts algorithm, 126
  Hirschberg-Sinclair Algorithm, 129
  in a graph, 129
  in a tree, 132
  LeLann algorithm, 123
LeLann algorithm, 123
Localization, 283
  angle of arrival, 285
  received signal strength, 285
  time difference of arrival, 284
  time of arrival, 284
Location-based protocols, 288
Logical clocks, 60
Loop invariants, 20

M
Matching, 209
  unweighted, 209
  weighted, 211
    Hoepman's algorithm, 212
    Preis' algorithm, 212
Matrix clocks, 65
Maximal independent set, 232
  distributed, 233
Message passing, 13
  blocking/non-blocking, 13
  ordering, 14
Minimum spanning tree, 192
  distributed Prim algorithm, 193
  GHS algorithm, 197
    asynchronous, 203
    synchronous, 202
Mobile networks
  ad hoc routing, 265
  mobility models, 248
  topology control, 249
Mobility models, 248
Models, 14
  fsm, 15
Mpi4py, 26

N
Network layer, 11
Network Time Protocol, 58

O
Omission failures, 141
Open process groups, 144

Oral messaging algorithm, 160

P
Peer process groups, 144
Physical layer, 10
Preis' algorithm, 212
Proactive routing, 265
Process groups, 144

R
Reactive routing, 265
Received signal strength, 285
Redundancy, 142
Relative neighborhood graph, 254
Reliable multicast, 147
Replication, 143
  active replication, 143
  passive replication, 144
Roll back, 142
Routing, 204, 286
  Bellman-Ford algorithm, 205
    distributed synchronous, 205
  Chandy-Misra algorithm, 209
  data centric protocols, 287
  location-based protocols, 288
  wireless sensor network, 286
    data centric protocols, 287
    location-based protocols, 288

S
Single source FIFO, 148
Software redundancy, 142
Spanning trees, 166
  broadcast, 169
  clustering, 277
  convergecast, 172
Stop and Wait ARQ, 28
Synchronizers, 134
  α synchronizer, 134
  β synchronizer, 135
  γ synchronizer, 135
Synchronous single initiator mode, 34
  determined rounds, 34
  undetermined rounds, 41

T
TEEN, 276
Temporal failures, 141
Termination detection, 100
  Huang's algorithm, 105
  ring algorithm, 100
  spanning tree algorithm, 102
Time difference of arrival, 284
Time of arrival, 284
Time redundancy, 143
Time synchronization, 53, 289
  Berkeley algorithm, 56
  Cristian's algorithm, 55
  logical clocks, 60
  matrix clocks, 65
  Network Time Protocol, 58
  physical clocks, 54
  vector clocks, 63
  wireless sensor network, 289
Timing diagrams, 15
Topology control, 249
  clustering, 256
  Gabriel graph, 251
  k-nearest neighbor graph, 250
  relative neighborhood graph, 254
  Yao graph, 255
Total order multicast, 154
Transport layer, 11
Trees, 165
  breadth first search, 174
  depth first search, 185
  spanning trees, 166
    broadcast, 169
    convergecast, 172
Trilateration, 285

U
Unreliable multicast, 148
Unweighted matching, 209

V
Vector clocks, 63
Vertex coloring, 219
  distributed, 220
Vertex cover, 223
  distributed, 224

W
Wait-for-graph, 108
Weighted graphs, 191
Weighted matching, 211
Wireless sensor network, 273
  clustering, 275
    LEACH, 276
    spanning tree, 277
    TEEN, 276
  data aggregation, 280

localization, 283
  angle of arrival, 285
  received signal strength, 285
  time difference of arrival, 284
  time of arrival, 284
  trilateration, 285
routing, 286
  data centric protocols, 287
  location-based protocols, 288
  time synchronization, 289

Y

Yao graph, 255

The manufacturer's authorised representative in the EU is Springer Nature Customer Service Centre GmbH, Europaplatz 3, 69115 Heidelberg, Germany. If you have any concerns regarding our products, please contact ProductSafety@springernature.com

Printed and bound by CPI Group (UK) Ltd, Croydon, CR0 4YY

28/03/2026

02080275-0001